MIGRANTS AND URBAN CHANGE:
NEWCOMERS TO ANTWERP, 1760–1860

Perspectives in Economic and Social History

Series Editors: *Andreas Gestrich*
Steven King
Robert E. Wright

Forthcoming Titles

Female Entrepreneurs in Nineteenth-Century Russia
Galina Ulianova

Barriers to Competition: The Evolution of the Debate
Ana Rosado Cubero

MIGRANTS AND URBAN CHANGE: NEWCOMERS TO ANTWERP, 1760–1860

BY

Anne Winter

Routledge
Taylor & Francis Group

LONDON AND NEW YORK

First published 2009 by Pickering & Chatto (Publishers) Limited

Published 2016 by Routledge
2 Park Square, Milton Park, Abingdon, Oxfordshire OX14 4RN
711 Third Avenue, New York, NY 10017, USA

First issued in paperback 2015

Routledge is an imprint of the Taylor & Francis Group, an informa business

© Taylor & Francis 2009
© Anne Winter 2009

BRITISH LIBRARY CATALOGUING IN PUBLICATION DATA
Winter, Anne.
Migrants and urban change: newcomers to Antwerp, 1760–1860. – (Perspectives in economic and social history)
1. Rural–urban migration – Belgium – Antwerp – History – 18th century. 2. Rural–urban migration – Belgium – Antwerp – History – 19th century. 3. Antwerp (Belgium) – Emigration and immigration – History – 18th century. 4. Antwerp (Belgium) – Emigration and immigration – History – 19th century. 5. Antwerp (Belgium) – Emigration and immigration – Social aspects. 6. Antwerp (Belgium) – Social conditions – 18th century. 7. Antwerp (Belgium) – Social conditions – 19th century. 8. Antwerp (Belgium) – Economic conditions – 18th century. 9. Antwerp (Belgium) – Economic conditions – 19th century.
I. Title II. Series
304.8'493222'009033-dc22

ISBN-13: 978-1-138-66513-2 (pbk)
ISBN-13: 978-1-8519-6646-2 (hbk)

Typeset by Pickering & Chatto (Publishers) Limited

CONTENTS

Acknowledgements   vii
List of Figures   ix

Introduction   1
1 Explaining Migration   9
2 Migration in the Urban Transition   35
3 Migration to a Regional Textile Centre, 1760–1800   69
4 Migration to a Port in the Making, 1800–1860   101
5 Circuits, Networks and Trajectories   147
Conclusions   189

Appendix I: Source Materials, Samples and Classifications   197
Appendix II: Additional Tables pertaining to Chapters 3–5   217

Notes   225
Works Cited   289
Index   313

To Mohammed Casquette

ACKNOWLEDGEMENTS

This book is based on my doctoral dissertation 'Patterns of Migration and Adaptation in the Urban Transition: Newcomers to Antwerp, c. 1760–1860', written under supervision of Hugo Soly, funded by a PhD fellowship of the Research Foundation Flanders (FWO), finalized when working as a research and teaching assistant at the history department of the Vrije Universiteit Brussel (VUB), and defended at the same university on 27 March 2007. Reworking the manuscript into this book was possible in the context of a postdoctoral fellowship of the FWO at the VUB, part of which was spent as an academic visitor to Somerville College (Oxford). I am grateful to the FWO, the VUB, Somerville College and the University of Oxford for their financial and logistic support during research and writing.

This work could never have been realized without the enthusiasm and support of Hugo Soly and Catharina Lis – inspired scholars, caring mentors and sharp critics. I remain greatly indebted to them for their insights, discussions and encouragement over the past years. Many thanks also go to my friends and colleagues from the research team on Historical Research into Urban Transformation Processes (HOST) and the history department at the VUB, who provided an inspirational and amiable work sphere. Special thanks go to Margo De Koster, who shared with me her office, her passion for social history and her friendship. Thijs Lambrecht, Ilja Van Damme, Toon Vrints, Bart Willems and Koen Wouters were inspiring and cordial companions along the way, who have on different occasions given useful tips and comments. Teaching VUB history students has challenged me to straighten my thoughts and strengthen my arguments, for which I am grateful.

Many persons have assisted me on my way in different archival institutions and have helped me to collect the source materials needed to conduct this research. I am particularly grateful for the assistance of the personnel of the Antwerp City Archives and of the State Archives in Antwerp and Brussels, and that of Paul de Commer from the Openbaar Centrum voor Maatschappelijk Welzijn (OCMW) Archives in Antwerp. Torsten Wiedemann from the HIS-GIS project has helped me along by providing a dataset of the Belgian borough population figures as collected by Sven Vrielinck, and Erik Beekink from the Netherlands Interdisciplinary Demographic Institute (NIDI) supplied me with an electronic version of the Hofstee database of Dutch population figures. I am greatly obliged to Jos De Belder, Juul Hannes and Catharina Lis, who generously allowed me access to the original manuscripts of their PhD research.

Different gatherings, seminars and discussions staged by the N. W. Post-humus Institute, ESTER School, International Institute of Social History, European Social Science History Association and Centrum voor de Geschiedenis van Migranten have helped me in structuring my research and arguments. Marco Belfanti, Bruno Blondé, Bert De Munck, Regina Grafe, Hilde Greefs, Pim Kooij, Leo Lucassen, Koen Matthijs, Leslie Moch, Marlou Schrover and Annemarie Steidl provided valuable remarks in different phases of research. I am greatly indebted to my PhD examiners Machteld De Metsenaere, Sylvia Hahn, Jan Lucassen and Keith Snell, whose insightful comments and continued encouragement were of great help in revising the manuscript. Steve King helped me to conceptualize and realize the transformation from dissertation to book. Frank Winter has been an attentive reader throughout, whose corrections and suggestions prevented many mistakes, provided new insights and polished my laborious writing. Julie Wilson's inquisitive editing alerted me to loose ends, unclearness and inconsistencies. Many thanks to all of them. Any flaws or errors that remain are of course my own.

Friends and family were an invaluable source of social support during research and writing, for which I am endlessly grateful. The completion of this book is also their achievement. Special thanks go to my father, who has been a dedicated and scrupulous reader in difficult circumstances. My last word of thanks goes to Nick, for being my fellow traveller, challenging my thoughts, and for bearing with me.

LIST OF FIGURES

Table 2.1: Components of Population Growth during Inter-Census
Periods, 1755–1900 (Annual Averages)   59
Table 2.2: Immigration Yields during Inter-Census Periods, 1806–90
(Annual Averages)   60
Map 3.1: Migration Intensity per Municipality of Birth, 1796 (%)   73
Table 3.1: Occupational Distribution of Immigrants and Non-
Immigrants, 1796 (%)   80
Table 3.2: Wealth Distribution of the Immigrant and Non-Immigrant
Population, 1796 (%)   87
Graph 4.1: Tonnage Entering the Antwerp Harbour, 1800–1860   103
Graph 4.2: Origin Pyramid, C1796I (%)   108
Graph 4.3: Origin Pyramid, CS1812–13 (%)   108
Graph 4.4: Origin Pyramid, CS1815–20 (%)   108
Graph 4.5: Origin Pyramid, CS1829 (%)   109
Graph 4.6: Origin Pyramid, HA1829 (%)   109
Graph 4.7: Origin Pyramid, HA1855 (%)   109
Map 4.1: Immigrants' Regions of Birth, C1796I (%)   114
Map 4.2: Immigrants' Regions of Birth, CS1808–13 (%)   114
Map 4.3: Immigrants' Regions of Birth, CS1815–20 (%)   114
Map 4.4: Immigrants' Regions of Birth, CS1829 (%)   115
Map 4.5: Immigrants' Regions of Birth, IN1850 (%)   115
Map 4.6: Immigrants' Regions of Birth, HA1855 (%)   115
Map 4.7: Migration Intensities per Municipality of Birth, CS1808–13 (‰)   120
Map 4.8: Migration Intensities per Municipality of Birth, CS1815–20 (‰)   120
Map 4.9: Migration Intensities per Municipality of Birth, CS1829 (‰)   121
Map 4.10: Migration Intensities per Municipality of Birth, CS1808–13
(‰)   121
Table 4.1: Employment and Immigrant Participation in 1796 and 1830
(%)   123
Table 5.1: Origin of Long-Distance Foreign Newcomers, 1796–1850 (N)   161
Table AI.1: Available Figures on Antwerp's Population Size, 1755–1866   197

Table AI.2: Origin of the Antwerp Population in Different Censuses,
    1796–1866   198
Graph AI.1: Recorded Numbers of Births, Deaths, Immigrants and
    Emigrants per Year, 1780–1866   198
Table AI.3: Overview of HISGIS/NIDI Base Figures used for
    Calculations   209
Table AI.4: Overview of Migrants' Regions of Birth, 1796–1855 (%)   210
Table AI.5: Overview of Occupational-Category Levels 1–3   214
Table AII.1: Occupations of Immigrant Women in Relation to Age and
    Length of Stay, C1796I (%)   217
Table AII.2: Occupations of Immigrant Men in Relation to Age and
    Length of Stay, C1796I (%)   217
Table AII.3: Average Birthplace Distance of Male Immigrants,
    1796–1829   218
Table AII.4: Length of Stay of Newcomers, 1808–29 (%)   218
Table AII.5: Occupational Distribution of Male Newcomers and
    Immigrant Residents, 1829–30 (%)   218
Table AII.6: Relation between Place of Birth and Last Place of Residence,
    1829–55 (%)   219
Table AII.7: Length of Stay of Non-Native Emigrants, 1829 and
    1855 (%)   220
Table AII.8: Relation between Place of Birth and Destination upon
    Leaving Antwerp, 1829 and 1855 (%)   220
Table AII.9: Importance and Sex Ratio of the Four Major Recruitment
    Circuits, 1796–1855   221
Table AII.10: Mean Age at Arrival for the Four Main Recruitment
    Circuits, 1796–1855   221
Table AII.11: Occupational Profile of the Four Major Recruitment
    Circuits, 1796–1855   222
Table AII.12: Immigration and Emigration Trajectories of the Four
    Recruitment Circuits, 1829–55 (%)   223
Table AII.13: Turnover in the Four Major Recruitment Circuits,
    1808–55 (%)   223
Table AII.14: Relationship between Hosts and Newcomers, CS1829 (%)   224

INTRODUCTION

Migration has long been considered a modern phenomenon that grew to significant importance only in the long nineteenth century, during which Europe was transformed from a largely rural and agricultural society into a highly urbanized and industrialized region. Between 1750 and 1914 the number of people living in European towns of more than 5,000 inhabitants increased sixfold, while their proportion in relation to total population more than tripled from 12 to 42 per cent. In addition, the number of cities of more than 100,000 inhabitants expanded from 28 to 195, raising their proportion of total population from 3 to 13 per cent.[1] Rural–urban migration has often been considered a major factor in achieving this spectacular growth in urban population. Older historiography and sociology regarded urban migration as both a salient symptom and the main vehicle of the ongoing modernization process, which was pushing people out of dwindling rural activities, and pulling them into more productive urban manufacturing. While large-scale migration was considered an essentially new and city-oriented phenomenon driving urban growth, migrants were in turn seen mainly as the desperate victims of rural uprooting. The increasing marginalization of rural income activities left them no other choice but to try their luck in cities, where they became the prime victims of the overcrowding and degeneration, which the unprecedented and unregulated growth of urban populations entailed.[2]

Over the past decades, research in different domains has led to significant revisions of this powerful image of a one-off rural–urban population transfer in the course of the long nineteenth century. One fundamental revision is that migration was not such a new or modern phenomenon as implied in earlier visions. Several studies have by now amply demonstrated that also in the sixteenth, seventeenth and eighteenth centuries many Europeans moved, in search of work, a career, a spouse or simply a better life, sometimes over long distances and often several times in a lifetime.[3] Others have shown that migration patterns in the nineteenth century were much more varied than allowed for in the vision of a simple population transfer from the countryside to cities, and have argued that they did not differ substantially from migration patterns in preceding periods: as before, migration remained mostly short-distance, took place within well-defined regions, occurred as much from small to larger settlements as the other way round, and was primarily inspired by considerations related to work and family.[4] Detailed studies at city-level have confirmed that the nineteenth-century city was a terminus for only a relatively small number of immigrants. Most urban migration was temporary, and rural–urban flows were to a large extent matched by (re)migration streams from the city to the countryside, thus significantly reducing the net contribution of immigration to urban growth.[5] Demographers have in turn argued that natural increase played a far greater role in promoting urban growth than originally thought. Although the precise evolutions of fertility and mortality in the long nineteenth century remain heavily debated, several scholars have indicated that natural increase rather than rural–urban migration became the dominant growth factor in many towns from at least the middle of the nineteenth century.[6] A final major revision is that urban immigrants should not necessarily be regarded as desperate and passive victims of societal uprooting. Research on the socio-economic positions and social mobility of urban immigrants has demonstrated that migrants did not necessarily belong to the most marginal groups of nineteenth-century cities. On the contrary, some could rely on important financial or social resources, while others made use of different individual and collective strategies – such as carving out an employment niche – to establish their position or to climb the social ladder.[7] From a different perspective, econometric research has indicated that urban migration remained a selective affair throughout Britain's long nineteenth century, positively selecting those who stood most to gain from moving to higher-wage cities.[8] These revisions on the relative success of migration in turn link up with a more general shift away from structural explanations of migration as a passive response to push and pull forces at a macro level, in favour of a growing adherence to views stressing the importance of individual and collective agency in migration behaviour.[9]

These revisions of the erstwhile dominant image of long-nineteenth-century urban migration have led to an intriguing paradox. How can the emergent view of urban migration as a relatively undisruptive and successful phenomenon eventually be reconciled with the disruptive processes of economic transformation and population redistribution that were taking place during this period, and with the available evidence on rising levels of gross mobility and urban pauperization? Do the arguments of scholars maintaining an essential continuity in migration patterns imply that there was really nothing intrinsically new about mobility during Europe's transition from pre-industrial to industrial society? An exploration of these questions involves identifying what exactly constitutes continuity, and what embodies change. Although their observations have greatly improved insight in the historical importance of migration by breaking down the artificial boundaries between 'pre-modern' and 'modern' mobility, recent revisions have sometimes ended up eclipsing those structural changes that did take place during the transition from pre-industrial to industrial society. In the same way, the increased attention devoted to individuals, families and social networks in decision-making has substantially enhanced historians' and social scientists' understanding of migration dynamics in the past and present, but it has tended to undervalue the role played by structural societal conditions in determining the stakes, limits and possibilities of these decisions, and therefore to obscure the impact of structural historical change on migration behaviour. Striking a new balance between continuity and change and between structure and agency in the debate on migration and urbanization, then, requires a reappraisal of the actual dynamics of migratory change during the transition from pre-industrial to industrial society, which is the point of this book. Its main purpose is to analyse closely the components of migratory change over a century-long period of profound social transformation by means of an instructive case study. By doing so, it aims to contribute to a renewed conceptualization of migratory change in the urban transition that can eventually transcend the paradox of continuity versus change, and can provide further insight in the distribution of costs and gains of societal transformation.

At the heart of the research questions underlying this book lies the conceptualization of migration as an adaptive strategy, bound up with material conditions, social relations and individual aspirations. The embedded nature of migration implies that it takes place in the form of identifiable patterns, channelling certain groups of migrants to particular destinations. These migration patterns can be regarded as social systems, which are mediated via social networks, information channels, customs and preferences, but are ultimately based on underlying social and economic conditions that will determine whether the decision to move is viable or worthwhile. Its systemic nature makes migration a selective affair and endows existing patterns with strong positive feedback links, predisposing them towards continuity. At the same time, however, migration patterns are vulnerable to structural social change. While infringements on existing livelihoods are likely to make more people turn to migration as an adaptive strategy, the transformation of social and economic conditions may at the same time undermine the usefulness of existing migration patterns. In this sense, structural social change is likely to subject existing migration patterns to processes of both intensification and adaptation, in which new patterns emerge while others are invalidated and eventually disappear from view. Both the establishment of new patterns and the transformation or obsolescence of existing ones are anything but straightforward affairs, and require a new balance to be struck between an unstable array of societal, social and individual factors, whose outcome is by no means guaranteed.

It is exactly at this intersection of continuity and change, between adjustment and readjustment, that a renewed exploration of urban migration in Europe's long nineteenth century can yield important insights. I propose to regard migration patterns in this period as being at the heart of a societal transformation that was both increasing people's likelihood of moving and invalidating the conditions upon which most pre-existing migration patterns had been based. While patterns of long-nineteenth-century urban migration drew upon a lengthy history, growing rural pressure and shifting economic conditions produced mounting challenges of adaptation. Whilst the increasing marginalization of small-scale farming and the demise of rural industry led to the disintegration of many rural livelihoods, income opportunities in cities underwent both a precarious expansion and a qualitative transformation, that was fraught with new rhythms of seasonal and cyclical slumps. The uneven development of labour supply and demand undermined the population exchange patterns that had been characteristic of rural–urban migration in the early modern period, without providing a ready alternative for growing household constraints. Given that we now know that migration was no novelty of the 'modern' age but instead evolved along paths beaten by earlier generations, questions of continuity and change in this period can be recast in a new mould, whereby the focus is shifted to exploring the ways in which different groups of migrants succeeded or not in adapting their migratory behaviour to the shifting constraints and opportunities. Adequately exploring the dynamics of migratory change, therefore, means evaluating the success or otherwise of ongoing adaptive strategies from a long-term perspective and for different groups. This differential perspective is important, as it can be assumed that different groups had to cope with the transformatory challenges of the long nineteenth century in different ways. The direction of social change was such as to make some groups better suited to reap the benefits of newly emerging opportunities, while other groups were disproportionately affected by the negative aspects of rising constraints. All patterns of migration were likely to experience attempts at adaptation, but the speed and success of adaptation was likely to differ for different migrant groups. This study therefore proposes to focus upon these different *speeds of change* to transcend the apparent paradoxes between continuity and change, and between structure and agency, and to re-explore the limits and possibilities of migration as an adaptive strategy during Europe's transition from pre-industrial to industrial society.

The setting of the case study is the city of Antwerp in present-day Belgium between 1760 and 1860. In this period, the city went through a profound economic and social conversion, while its main hinterland regions were confronted with fundamental economic and demographic changes which increased pressure on rural livelihoods. From an earlier medium-sized regional textile centre of around 50,000 inhabitants, Antwerp developed into a major international port of more than 110,000 inhabitants by the middle of the nineteenth century, which entailed a radical transformation of its labour market structure, and which was accompanied by changing patterns of migration. This economic and demographic conversion was not a gradual affair, but a jerky process at different speeds. Several regime changes played an important role in repeatedly restructuring the economic-geographical conditions of urban development, and transforming Antwerp from a relatively peripheral regional centre in the Austrian Netherlands, via a prime naval base of the French Empire, to a major colonial port under Dutch rule, and eventually a prime distribution centre of the precociously industrializing and liberal Kingdom of Belgium and a key node in the integration of the developing Atlantic economy. Meanwhile, the period between the mid-eighteenth and mid-nineteenth centuries witnessed a doubling of the population in Antwerp's main hinterland regions, dominated mainly by smallholding agriculture, which gave rise to a growing proportion of villagers with little or no land. An analysis of the relationship between the changing economic, social and political conditions at origin and destination on the one hand, and the evolution of patterns of migration on the other hand, is the central preoccupation of this piece of empirical research.

The sources that can be used to reconstruct changes in the patterns of urban migration over time are exceptionally rich in the Antwerp case. Its status as a prime naval base under French rule meant that Napoleonic endeavours in the domain of population registration were pursued with particular vigour in Antwerp, resulting in a long series of 'immigration registers' kept during the first decades of the nineteenth century. In addition, a number of important censuses – in 1796, 1815 and 1830 – and a relatively continuous series of population registers yield important complementary evidence on the background of immigrant households and their relationship to wider urban society in terms of occupational or spatial clustering. From 1846 onwards, national legislation ensured a continuation of Antwerp's already well-developed population registration system, underpinned by ten-yearly censuses, dynamic population registers and a separate registry for foreigners. Sources from relief institutions, such as hospital admission lists and settlement examinations, yield important complementary and qualitative information on certain groups of newcomers. A series of representative samples from these different sources resulted in the collection of individual data on a total of 23,000 newcomers entering town between 1760 and 1860, ranging from basic evidence on the age, sex, origin and occupation of immigrants, to more detailed information on the life trajectories of themselves and their parents, which were then processed and analysed by means of database (Access) and statistical (SPSS) software. As both Antwerp's transformation from a regional textile centre to a port town and the materialization of rural pressure into push forces were realized only at the turn of the century, the chronological scope of the collected materials is long enough to reconstruct patterns of migration in the relatively stable context of a middle-sized pre-industrial textile town on the one hand, and to examine the short-term and long-term influence of the rural and urban transformations of the nineteenth century on the other hand.

The main aim of the research is to uncover changes in overall patterns of migration and to relate these to the changing opportunity structure at origin and destination and to the evolution of migration information channels that mediated these changes. The focus therefore lies with exploring changes in the direction and composition of migration flows rather than with examining patterns of settlement. Although the implications of these changes for the prospects of immigrants after arrival will receive due attention, the approach differs from so-called settlement studies in that all forms of movement, not only the presence of those who stayed long term, here hold centre stage, and in that the focus lies not with relations between migrants and non-migrants within the city, but rather on the shifting migratory connections between the city and migrants' places of origin. Research efforts have been concentrated on retracing and explaining changes in the numbers, origin, social composition, length of stay and re-migration destinations of different migration circuits over time, rather than on the affective relationships between newcomers and the receiving society. By analysing the evolution of all types of migration, short and long, in and out, foreign and internal, to a rapidly changing urban economy during the first half of the long nineteenth century, this study aims to provide insight into the differential role of migration as an adaptive strategy in Europe's urban and industrial transitions. While some patterns of migration to nineteenth-century Antwerp were radically new and targeted at newly created port-related opportunities, the degree of long-term continuity in some other migration patterns was remarkable given the profound changes wrought both in the home area and at destination. Examining the nature and causes of these different speeds of change, it is argued, helps to yield a better insight into the influence of a changing local opportunity structure on the composition of immigrant flows, and on the dynamics of migration change in general.

Examining these central research questions in ways which allow the conclusions to transcend the time and place specificity of an empirical case study requires a conceptual and historiographical framework, which is the subject of the first two chapters. Chapter 1 presents the central explanatory framework on the how and why of migration which was employed throughout our research, and elaborates on the research questions which structure this study. Chapter 2 in turn applies these questions to the main debates which surround the issue of urban migration in Europe's industrial and urban transitions, discusses the dynamics of urbanization in the Southern Netherlands, and introduces the Antwerp case study to arrive at the focus of the empirical research. Chapters 3 and 4 explore the diachronic shifts in migration patterns during the city's transformation from a regional textile centre to an international port. Chapter 3 uses the 1796 census and the eighteenth-century burgher books to reconstruct the main features of migration patterns to Antwerp in the second half of the eighteenth century, when the city was a regional textile centre of around 50,000 inhabitants. Chapter 4 draws upon a range of nineteenth-century source materials to map and analyse the changes in migration flows that took place during Antwerp's conversion to a port town in the first half of the nineteenth century. The fifth and final chapter deals with the socially differentiated dynamics that underlay the aggregate shifts identified in Chapters 3 and 4. It explores the dynamics of change separately for different groups of migrants, and tries to explain the different degrees of resilience or adaptability in relation to differences in migrant manoeuvrability.

1 EXPLAINING MIGRATION

Exploring the dynamics of migratory change first of all requires examining the how and why of migration. This chapter first discusses the main explanatory frameworks that have shaped migration research over the past century, from economic disparities and complementarities, over social networks and migration information, to household and individual characteristics. It subsequently builds upon recent attempts to integrate these different approaches in a three-level explanatory framework that allows us to separate the influence of structural historical change on the evolution of migration behaviour from the part played by individual variations. A third section finally explores the implications of the proposed framework for the dynamics of migratory change to arrive at the central heuristic devices that structure this book: selectivity, resilience and the speeds of change.

Explanatory Frameworks in Migration Research

One apparent problem of overall generalizations on the causes of migration is that those that stand the test turn out to be as trivial as they are true: that is, that people move with an eye to better opportunities than they had or expected to have where they were. These propositions in turn have the greatest difficulty in explaining why only some of those in comparable conditions move, and why those who do move go to specific places and not to others where overall prospects might be even better.[1] To explain why people move in the numbers and directions and for the lengths of time they do, migration research generally employs one or more of three main explanatory frameworks: economic disparities, social networks and household and individual characteristics. This book will adopt a theoretical perspective which builds on recent attempts to incorporate various migration research traditions in one theoretical framework by integrating macro (structural social and economic conditions), meso (social networks and information channels) and micro (household and individual characteristics) levels of explanation. To clarify the direction and nature of the different causal mechanisms eventually integrated in the three-level approach, I will discuss each of the three levels and their associated explanatory frameworks separately, before discussing their mutual interactions.

The idea that structural economic and social conditions form migration's driving force is evident in some of the earliest analytical conceptions of the phenomenon in the form of a push-pull model. This conception sees migrants as being *pushed* from their place of origin, by a lack or shortage of income opportunities, and being *pulled* by improved employment or betterment prospects in their place of destination. Other things being equal, migrants therefore tend to move primarily from economically backward regions to thriving regions where they have more and better chances of making a living.[2] The prime mover thus lies with economic disparities between the place of origin and the destination. Although the push-pull model in principle applies to any kind of livelihood – e.g. to the quality of farming land – it is most often used in the context of wage-dependent labour. Neoclassical economic orthodoxy, for instance, reformulated the push-pull model with wage gaps as the prime *explanans* of migration, wage gaps which are in turn considered a reflection of economic disparities. In this model, migrants are expected to flow from regions with low capital-to-labour ratios, where wages are low, to regions with higher capital-to-labour ratios, where labour is more productive and wages therefore higher, thus contributing to a narrowing of the wage gap and to a smoothing out of spatial imbalances in relative factor distributions.[3] The wage-gap model represents only a stylized and reductive version of the push-pull model, as it only allows for *relative* differences – people are driven away only because they have better opportunities elsewhere – but not for *absolute* push or pull forces. As push and pull are seen as existing only in relation to each other, this conception does not allow for qualitative or quantitative discrepancies between the two.

Other reformulations of the push-pull model have instead focused on *disentangling* autonomous push from pull forces, and on questioning the assumed 'match' between the two. In his study of migrants to sixteenth-century Kentish towns, Peter Clark identified as 'subsistence' migrants those whose movements were primarily driven by push forces, while he considered as 'betterment' migrants their counterparts who were mostly attracted by pull forces.[4] By classifying migrants according to a ratio of repulsion to attraction, Clark highlighted the potential mismatch between the two. In periods of severe societal disruption, more or different people may be thrown on the road than can be absorbed by employment opportunities within their reach. This does not imply that push-driven migrants followed a different rationality from a situation in which pull and push are more balanced. As Beier has shown, the migration trajectories of Elizabethan vagrants – Clark's subsistence migrants *par excellence* – corresponded to the logic of labour-market dynamics, in that they moved from poor regions to the cities where wages were higher and opportunities greater.

Their main problem, however, was that these opportunities were too few and too unstable to provide a sufficient living, resulting in continuing mobility.[5] The example illustrates how the balance between the nature and extent of income opportunities foregone (push) and that of opportunities existing or created elsewhere (pull) affects the potential success of migration, while the actual logic of movement – from backward to advanced regions – stays the same.

A similar attention to the potentially problematical relation between push and pull is found in the distinction between 'passive proletarianization' and 'active proletarianization' in Lis and Soly's discussion of increasing wage-dependency in early modern Europe. While the first concept is used to describe the passive event of *being* or *becoming* dependent on wage-labour for a living, the second concept is used to describe the actual integration in the labour market by means of employment. While overall wage-dependency increased considerably throughout the early modern period, Lis and Soly question the extent to which this 'passive proletarianization' went hand in hand with 'active proletarianization'. They highlight the existence of several structural discrepancies in the speed, nature and intensity of the evolution of labour supply and demand, either *in situ* or within migration reach, which hindered a fluent transformation from passive proletarians to active wage-earners, and led to increasing vulnerability of wage-dependent groups and, ultimately, to an exacerbation of 'social problems'.[6] Other than in neoclassical theory, studies such as those of Clark or Beier and concepts such as those of Lis and Soly highlight the extent to which push and pull can be considered absolute and independent factors, and emphasize the importance of a *match* between decreasing income opportunities in the place of origin (push) and existing or developing opportunities in the place of destination (pull) for migration to be successful. This match is important not only in quantitative terms (the number or scope of opportunities) but also in qualitative terms, i.e. in terms of the capacities, skills and characteristics required for the new jobs in relation to those needed for prior income activities. Indeed, in times of societal conversion, those groups hardest hit by unemployment in declining sectors might not be the ones best placed to take advantage of expanding opportunities in thriving sectors, as they may not possess the necessary skills or abilities.

In addition, wages and access to employment opportunities are not only shaped by skill and labour productivity, but also by social custom and norms on the one hand and by formal and informal preferences (exclusion mechanisms) on the other. As conceptions of suitable and valuable work may differ considerably in relation to age and gender, for instance, men and women have mostly operated in very different labour markets. Similarly, formal or informal preferences can strongly limit one's access to specific income opportunities. In many early modern towns, for example, the obligation to pay for rights of citizenship created an extra barrier to independent artisan activity by newcomers.[7] Informal recruitment mechanisms could further hamper the individual's possibility of finding a job. An organization of drapers in Holland complained in 1657 that many cloth-shearers from their province had difficulty finding jobs in Amsterdam workshops, as German masters preferred to hire compatriots.[8] Conversely, Ad Knotter argued that newcomers to nineteenth-century Amsterdam frequently operated in the periphery of a differentiated labour market, while established groups retained more stable and secure positions in the core segment.[9] Existing patterns of formal and informal labour market segmentation at the point of destination thus limit the employment opportunities available to potential migrants. In turn, these may further hamper a 'match' between push and pull, between income opportunities lost at home and those available elsewhere.

Moreover, for much of recent history and still in many parts of the world, a different kind of match between push and pull was and is essential in making certain migration options more favourable than others, i.e. the match between the nature of employment opportunities available (pull) and the other sources of income that an individual or household relies on. Indeed, most wage-dependent families in recent European history, as in much of the contemporary developing world, combine several sources of income – some wage-dependent, others not – in a varied pattern of income-pooling. The potential income gained by the migration of one member of the family is then valued not only in terms of wages, but even more importantly to the extent that the absence does not jeopardize other income sources.[10] In this sense, temporary wage labour could act as a buffer against total wage-dependency, and be pursued in order to safeguard independent sources of income. Such was the case, for example, with the temporary outmovement of male Auvergnats from the French Massif Central – who spent several months per year for up to several years earning cash in Spain or the French lowlands – which was mostly undertaken in order to preserve or acquire independent farming land in the home region.[11] It is essential, then, that migration opportunities should fit into the wider income-pooling structure of an individual or household in the short and the longer runs. Migration opportunities in a lean season were therefore worth much more in terms of opportunity cost than those which fell in a period when much work was required on one's own land or plenty of employment was available in one's own region.[12] In addition to economic disparities between regions, then, the *complementarity* of income opportunities in both regions was an essential factor in promoting migration.

Jan Lucassen used the concept of 'labour cycle' to explain why yearly migration to the Dutch Republic was attractive to the *Hollandgänger* from smallholdings in rural Westphalia, who sometimes travelled up to 300 km to perform labouring tasks on large coastal farms. Certainly, wages compared favourably, but at least as important was the fact that this yearly outmovement could be adequately fitted into a household labour cycle which did not jeopardize migrants' own farming activities. As an ex-official from the area testified in 1811: 'All people from my canton who go to Holland own only a small amount of land which does not yield enough to meet rents and duties. They must therefore choose this secondary work whose advantages ... are more considerable than any other alternative. Nor is their absence a drawback in the least. Those who have travelled out are back by St Jacob's [25 July] and departure for Holland only takes place after the sowing season. This way workers miss only the hay-making which can be carried out by the female family members who remain at home.'[13] In turn, the quasi absence of outmovement to the Dutch coasts from the nearby Bielefeld area could be explained by widespread local linen-weaving, which presented an alternative auxiliary income strategy to complement small farmers' yearly labour cycles.[14]

In sum, whether or not the terms push and pull are adopted, most researchers would agree that economic conditions are an important factor in migration dynamics by influencing, if not determining, the attractiveness and viability of specific migration options in relation to the wider income-pooling strategies of households and individuals. Whether this implies that economic disparities and complementarities in fact *explain* actual geographical mobility, however, is another matter. Explanatory frameworks identifying the cause of migration *only* with push and pull forces at a general macro level have the greatest difficulty in explaining why only some of those in comparable conditions move, and why those who do move go to certain specific places and not to others where overall prospects might be even better. Indeed, one other general observation on migration is that it tends to be selective. At all times and places, some people are more likely to move than others. In addition, those who move do so in ways that are patterned, in the sense that migrants from a certain background often go to a particular destination, while others travel elsewhere.[15] To account for the overall selectivity and patterned nature observed in migration dynamics, researchers have invoked two other main explanatory frameworks, namely those of social networks, and of individual and household characteristics. I shall discuss them in that order.

Migration researchers have frequently observed that in practice people often move to a particular destination because they have relatives or friends living there, who can help them find a job and a place to live. Such a pattern of *chain migration* serves two evident functions, one of which is to inform potential migrants of employment opportunities, while the other is to lower the psychological and material cost of migration by providing supportive institutions upon arrival.[16] Sometimes such patterns of settlement could build on a previous history of temporary migration, which helped to acquaint migrants with their later home and to establish access to certain employment niches.[17] Moreover, it has been observed that original 'pioneers' were somewhat better off than compatriots who followed. Nineteenth-century emigrants from German Hesse-Cassel to the United States who left to join family members, for example, were generally older and carried less cash with them than compatriots who did not move along paths paved by kin. By lowering the cost of migrating, then, the establishment of a chain network allowed people with relatively fewer resources to participate in emigration.[18] One result of these different dynamics is that, once established, existing patterns of migration tend to evoke further migration which in turn helps to strengthen the pattern, by conveying information about employment opportunities in letters and via returning migrants, or by providing material support in the form of pre-paid travel tickets and lodgings.[19] Such feedback mechanisms in turn strengthen patterns linking certain villages or regions of origin with specific destinations.[20] To the extent that migrants from a particular background are predominantly active in certain economic branches, chain migration networks can result in occupational concentration or even niche formation among certain immigrant groups.[21] Furthermore, once established, these migration patterns also help to install a 'culture of migration', in which emigration is more readily considered an option than in villages where no such migration history exists.[22] The same observations apply, by the way, for patterns in which migration is mostly or exclusively temporary. Although supportive networks at arrival do not necessarily depend on already settled compatriots in this case, the regular revisiting of the same destination promotes acquaintance with employment and housing opportunities, and helps to establish auxiliary institutions, which in turn strengthen specific spatial patterns and links.[23] Thus Westphalian *Hollandgänger* from a given village might work for the same Dutch employer year after year.[24] Attention to the role of migration networks not only helps in understanding the existence of different migration destinations and patterns, but it also helps in looking at differences in the actual *incidence* of migration in comparable situations. The absence or presence of a village migration tradition is believed to be a crucial factor in explaining why one of two close and comparably poor villages in the French Massif Central should be actively involved in temporary emigration patterns, while migration intensity was very low in the other.[25]

To fully appreciate the role played by auxiliary institutions in the analysis of migration patterns, however, one needs to go beyond the relatively narrow concepts of chain migration and tangible social networks. In a recent article under the appropriate heading 'Is There Life Outside the Migrant Network?', Clé Lesger et al. warn against too much reliance on the stereotype of compatriot-assisted migration. They observe among other things that only 37 per cent of German immigrants to Rotterdam between 1870 and 1890 moved in with a household whose head was German, and that only one in four of those went to live with a compatriot whose place of birth was less than 25 km from their own. Incidences of origin-linked occupational specialization were limited. To accommodate the

existing variety in migration 'modes', Lesger et al. argue for a three-pronged classification: 1) personal network migration, 'whereby people move because they
are informed (and often helped) by people they know or know of'; 2) organizational or non-personal network migration, whereby people move along paths
set or organized by occupational organizations or large firms, such as artisans
in tramping systems, clerics or twentieth-century multinational workers being
transferred from one branch to another; 3) non-network or solitary migration,
where migrants 'have only a general knowledge of the opportunity structure in
a certain destination, upon which they make their decision to move, without
having personal contacts at destination'. Only the first mode produces the salient 'transplanted networks' which link specific places to specific destinations,
and which often produce origin-related patterns of occupational and settlement
concentration at destination. The other modes of migration operate in more diffuse ways or on larger scales.[26]

More than having tangible relatives, contact persons or acquaintances in the
place of destination, Lesger elaborates in a later article, the diffusion channels
of *migration information* form a crucial factor in promoting specific migration
patterns and trajectories.[27] Migration information, a term also used by Leslie
Page Moch, refers at its most general level to (any kind of) information telling a
potential migrant of promising destinations and possibly also of income opportunities.[28] Even if migrants could not expect ready support structures upon
arrival, they rarely travelled into the completely unknown. Rather, they travelled
to a place with which they were somehow acquainted or had in some way heard
or read about. This prior information might have ranged from vague hearsay
arousing an adventurous spirit to very detailed information on newly emerging
trade opportunities. The crucial factor here, however, is that *some* information on
the eventual destination was available – either before or after departure – which
channelled migrants to certain places, that they had at least *some* idea of what
to expect, however incomplete or wrong this information might have been in
point of fact. The channels through which this information travelled might have
been very diverse, but they were all in some way related to the different spatial
interactions linking one place with another. As migration information was transferred from person to person, in some instances via print, it travelled via the same
routes taken by commuters, market-goers, court attendants, coachmen, estate
agents, officials, sailors and – of course – migrants, and spread most easily where
this spatial movement was densest and most intense. In this sense, migration
information channels were embedded in the spatial dimensions of the different
economic, social, commercial, political, cultural and judicial interactions linking
origin with destination. Actual migration networks and patterns of chain migration can be considered a specific and elaborate form of migration information
channels – the latter ranging along a continuum with vague rumour at one pole

and professional placement agencies and family networks at the other. The more social, cultural, political and economic interaction there existed between different places, the more chance there was for migration information to spread, and for migration to occur. The intensity and patterns of migration were therefore always a reflection of broader spatial interactions at different levels.

The importance of information channels can to a great extent be considered responsible for the distance-decay effect generally observed in migration patterns, namely that relatively fewer people tend to come from relatively greater distances. The recruitment area of migrants to any given early modern city, for instance, generally reflected the broader economic, cultural, political and social interactions between that city, its hinterland and other regions. The recruitment to port cities, for instance, stretched relatively far along river banks and coastal areas, whereas inland recruitment patterns on the whole had a shorter action radius, which is primarily a reflection of differential commercial interactions.[29] Of course, it is difficult in these instances to separate the effect of available migration information from the relative cost of travelling, as these factors were of course interrelated, and all spatial interactions were to a certain extent subjected to distance decay. Migrants born along the banks of the Garonne might have come to Bordeaux from greater distances than their inland counterparts because migration information spread further and easier among the inns, markets and warehouses frequented by boatmen and merchants sailing up and down, and/or because transport over water was relatively faster – and therefore cheaper – than over land.[30] Either way, migration probability was inversely related to what could be called *social* distance – the familiarity with a destination via different spatial interactions – rather than actual distance. This social distance was in turn shaped foremost by the density and direction of political, social, economic and cultural spatial interactions via which migration information was transmitted, which in turn strengthened these interactions.

The importance of spatial interactions as vehicles for migration helps to explain why migration often occurred in different stages. Scandinavian research has, for instance, demonstrated that many nineteenth-century rural-born emigrants moved initially from their village to a large city, before emigrating abroad. While the first move took place within an 'urban migration field' connecting a city with its rural hinterland, the second move took place in wider inter-urban interactions which connected their new place of residence with other cities abroad.[31] This way, regional capitals and major cities could act as gateways connecting rural–urban migration circuits with inter-urban networks.[32] In sum, migration information diffusion channels in general and social networks in particular, and the feedback mechanisms they imply, constitute an essential consideration when trying to explain substantial differences in migration practices in comparable economic circumstances. However, as a means to explaining fully, let alone predicting, actual movements, they are inadequate. Researchers have therefore moved down to the micro level of household and individual characteristics.

Individual and household characteristics have a strong influence on a person's propensity to migrate. It is, for instance, generally observed that single individuals are more likely to move than married couples or households with children, young adults more likely than older persons, orphans more likely than persons with living parents, and proletarians more likely than artisans or farmers, while men on the whole tend to migrate further than women, and elites and skilled workers further than unskilled labour. Although most of these differential propensities to move have grounds in objective conditions determining the opportunity cost of migration, they are mediated via social custom and institutions and coupled with non-material considerations to produce a relatively large and to a certain extent unpredictable variety in individual migration patterns. In order to clarify the issues at stake, I will first discuss the objective material conditions by which household and individual characteristics can influence the propensity to move, before turning to the ways in which these objective conditions are mediated in practice and coupled to other non-material considerations.

Existing literature suggests four major ways in which household and individual characteristics objectively affect the likelihood of moving, namely the ways in which an individual's and household's resource structure – including human capital – determines 1) the exposure to external shocks, 2) the transferability of resources, 3) the possibility of investing in migration, and 4) an individual's access to certain social networks and other migration information channels. The income and resource structure of households and individuals evidently determines their exposure to market developments, lifecycle shifts and other external shocks. Rising food prices, for instance, would benefit a large farmer but threaten a wage-dependent farm labourer, resulting in differential push forces for both groups in a similar situation. In addition, the nature of a household resource structure also determines the ease with which it might be transferred. Fully proletarian households with no, or at best small, cash resources face fewer barriers to moving than farmers whose income activities are bound to their land. Legal obligations and tenancy arrangements might play an important role in this respect too. In nineteenth-century Westphalia, for instance, sharecroppers were much less likely to emigrate than smallholders, as debt and labour obligations bound them tightly to their landlords.[33]

Differences in the transferability of resources and in overall vulnerability help to explain why proletarian families are often more likely to migrate than farmers. In the Groningen clay areas, for example, labourers were almost twice as likely to leave their village than farmers in the wake of the agricultural crisis of the 1870s.[34] On the other hand, even fully proletarian families in rural Utrecht were reluctant to move in this period because certain assets remained tied to their place of residence, such as rights to poor relief, a personal contact network which was necessary in order to find work, and the possibility for all family members of finding work. While migration might have been a beneficial option for the father, it was likely to have a negative impact on the income of the family as a whole. In this respect, household size might form an important variable with regard to the transferability of resources and income-structures: the larger the family, the greater the difficulty in establishing a full labour cycle elsewhere.[35] Even fully proletarian households, then, may hold certain assets which are difficult or impossible to transfer. Rather than the nature of the household's resource structure in itself, the actual sustainability of its income cycle elsewhere appears to have formed a more crucial variable in stimulating or discouraging migration.

Resource structures not only determine the propensity or need to leave, but also the possibility and attractiveness of moving. For one thing, migration demands a certain investment, if only in terms of travel and opportunity costs. Individual and family resources determine the extent of the investment which *can* be made. This resource threshold explains why it is generally not the poorest who leave, but rather those who have some – be it modest – financial backing.[36] Second, it is not only the possibility of making the investment that matters, but also the expected return. To the extent that these returns are in the form of wages, they are determined primarily by gender, age, dependency ratio and skill, with men on the whole earning more than women, young single adults having more chance of finding an adequate income than dependency-burdened families, and skilled labour remunerated more highly than unskilled labour. Of course, the wage structure determining these returns is shaped not only by labour productivity, but also by bargaining positions, social conventions and customs underlying the labour market structure in the places of origin and destination, and by the transferability of skill.[37] On the whole, persons best placed to reap relatively higher returns on migration investments are often among those most likely to move; in most times and places, most migrants are young adults, who have relatively more to gain and relatively less to lose than families.[38] Although their actual trajectories are shaped by the intermediate level of social networks, custom and information channels, differences in earning capacities often help to explain why some groups travel more and further than others. Nineteenth-century white-collar workers, for instance, were often among the most mobile and wide-ranging groups, as they were typically engaged in an upwardly-mobile career along paths set by 'organizational migration' modes.[39] The variable that matters most here is not the absolute nominal or even real wages which could be earned elsewhere, but the opportunity cost. The large involvement of Groningen's poor farm labourers in costly transatlantic migration rather than in cheaper travel to closer destinations is explained by the fact that they had *relatively* more to gain from travelling far, as the penalty for lack of skills was substantially lower in the United States than in the Netherlands.[40]

It is evident how objective differences in earning capacities between different family members can create intra-household conflicts of interests, especially as regards outmigration of the most 'productive' members. Young proto-industrial workers in the Zürich-region of the seventeenth and eighteenth centuries, for example, used the threat of leaving their parents' household in order to minimize the contribution they had to make to the family income.[41] In this sense, too strong a focus on households as the unit of analysis might have led historians to assume too easily that the behaviour of individual members responded solely to the interests of the whole family.[42] In a recent article, Wendy Gordon criticizes the tendency in European historiography to analyse single women's migration solely in terms of broader family interests. Rather than remitting all their wages to the home family, Gordon demonstrates that single female textile workers in nineteenth-century Britain pursued and often gained financial independence from their family, without having to break emotional and supportive ties.[43] Similarly, domestic servants in Dutch Zeeland between 1850 and 1950 have been shown to follow not only family interests, but also individual strategies and aspirations in terms of emancipation, personal consumption and the broadening of horizons in their decision to move out.[44] When considering costs and benefits of migration options, then, not only those affecting the whole family, but also those affecting individual members should be taken into consideration. Whether one or the other took the upper hand depended not only on the respective opportunity costs and benefits, but also on social norms and on emotional, affective and psychological ties. One more objective factor of influence here involves inheritance practices, as these further influence the opportunity cost of staying. In landholding families practising primogeniture, for instance, the eldest son has an evident interest in staying and in obeying parental authority, while his siblings might be more inclined to leave than in a situation where each child inherits equally.[45]

A fourth manner in which the resource structure of individuals and households has a direct objective impact on the propensity to migrate is by the ways in which it determines access to certain networks and migration channels. As migration information is generally spread via personal contacts, the nature and variety of one's personal network and contacts determine the kind of information to which one has access. Relatives are particularly important channels of migration information, and help to mould migration traditions and networks in specific families.[46] In addition, the ability to read conditions a person's access to migration information in printed form. Personal networks, contacts and literacy are in turn a matter of human capital and social status, which are directly related to resource and income structures. Members of the administrative or commercial elites, for instance, can be expected to have access to relatively reliable, accurate and elaborate information channels on relevant career opportunities. Skilled artisans could rely on professional organizations to provide detailed information on, and access to, employment opportunities in different places, which sometimes also provided institutions to support frequent moves.[47] In this sense, the social distance between two given places, which we have identified above as a crucial factor in shaping migration patterns, differed according to the social status of the potential migrant concerned. In other words, Antwerp is assumed to have been less 'distant' to an eighteenth-century Ostend insurance broker than to a shrimp fisherman from the same town. That he was more likely to move to Antwerp than his shrimp-fishing neighbour was not only a result of larger resources and greater potential benefits, but also of status-dependent access to specific social networks which linked the commercial circles of the two ports.[48]

So far, I have discussed the objective ways in which household and individual resource structures influenced the likelihood of moving. Their effect on migration, however, was not direct or straightforward, but mediated via social custom and institutions such as marriage patterns and migration traditions. In addition, non-material considerations like emotional attachments and sexual vulnerability and honour also played an essential role in migration decisions. Apparent or true safeguards against sexual exposure, in the form of guarded living quarters or control by other family or village members, for instance, can be a prime consideration in the migration of – especially single – women. Conversely, illegitimate pregnancy can be a reason for departure.[49] Bad relationships with other household members, for their part, can form a powerful motive for leaving, in particular between step-parents and children of a previous marriage.[50] More positively, emotional ties can also be a prime reason for staying, or for coming back. Muriel Neven has, for instance, shown that a crucial variable determining whether or not nineteenth-century emigrants from the Belgian Pays de Herve returned to their home villages, either temporarily or definitively, was the presence of living siblings, a variable which was even more important than the distance travelled or the occupation involved.[51] On the one hand, this apparent attachment to family members might have had objective material grounds, in that family relations can provide important supportive networks in times of need, but on the other hand it is clear that emotional ties played their part too.

In general, the impact of household and individual characteristics and considerations on migration behaviour generally takes the form of an intricate mix of objective, emotional and normative factors. Such an intricate mix is, for instance, manifest in the general observation that much migration is related to specific life-cycle phases, and that movement often coincides with certain life-course transitions, such as leaving home, marriage, the birth of a child or the death of a household member. That the loss of a parent might lead to a break-up of the household unit, for instance, can be related not only to defective household income-pooling, but also to a loosening of emotional bonds. Patterns in the timing and direction of leaving home are evidently related to emotional ties as well as earning capacities, while social conventions on, for instance, the timing of marriage are also an obvious factor.[52] In any decision to migrate upon marriage, it is evident that prevalent norms on neo-locality played an important role.[53] That families with children are on the whole less mobile than married couples, who are in turn less mobile than single adults, can on the one hand be related to differential earning capacities and the importance of local support networks in the vulnerable family cycle of child-rearing, but on the other hand also to the extent of emotional ties involving different family members after a certain length of stay.[54]

As with regional economic disparities or social networks, then, objective household and individual conditions cannot fully explain migration in terms of a necessary or inevitable outcome, as both social mediations and immaterial considerations interfere to produce outcomes which are impossible to predict at an individual level. However, these three explanatory levels do help to narrow down the likelihood of certain outcomes by limiting the possibilities of variation. As such, they provide sufficient heuristic value to construct an integrative explanatory framework to evaluate and explain shifts and evolutions in *patterns* of migration over a period of structural change, which is the ultimate purpose of the present study.

An Integrative Approach

The above discussion of the three main explanatory frameworks in migration research has illustrated how economic disparities and complementarities, social networks and migration information, and individual and household characteristics all influenced the likelihood and nature of movement. In practice, however, these frameworks have supported very different strands of migration research, employing very different questions, sources and methodology. Much contemporary research in the field is situated either at an abstract level of econometric modelling, using large sets of quantified serial data and aimed at explaining the timing, intensity and direction of large flows of people, or in the cultural realm of ethnicity studies, focusing mainly on community relations, social networks and migration *experiences*, and employing mainly qualitative data such as in-depth interviews. Although less marked, methodological cleavages between different explanatory frameworks have nurtured very different approaches, questions and answers in historical research too. The main cleavage here is a variation on the structure–agency debate, with one – generally older – strand of research stressing structural material conditions in the places of origin and destination to explain the existence or evolution of certain migration patterns, and another – generally more recent – strand of research rejecting such so-called economic determinism and stressing the importance of social networks, norms and cultural factors as autonomous and even principal factors shaping migration practices.[55] However, I tend to agree with historical demographer Michel Oris that 'the opposition between these approaches is at least partly illusory ... In fact, we do not really face competing hypotheses, but a new level of complexity, the challenge of integrating more possible explanations and interactions.'[56] Rather than to disregard one for the other, this work builds upon recent attempts to integrate the three main explanatory frameworks discussed above as three different explanatory *levels* – a macro, meso and micro level – of a single integrative framework.[57] The approach rests on two basic ideas. First, it concedes that migration behaviour is influenced by a conglomeration of factors, from economic disparities and complementarities, over social networks and migration information channels, to individual and household characteristics, whose outcome is impossible to predict at an individual level. At the same time, it maintains that these different factors are subjected to a causal hierarchy, whereby the room for manoeuvre of collective and individual agency at a meso and micro level is fundamentally shaped by structural conditions of labour supply and demand at a macro level.

The proposed causal hierarchy works its way down from the macro to the micro level. At the most fundamental level, the prime determinant of the intensity and direction of overall movement lies with material conditions at the macro level, such as the scale and organization of wealth production and the spatial and social distribution of resources and income opportunities. These conditions do not so much form the direct cause of migrations in practice as set out the limits of possible variations. In shaping actual migration patterns, the meso level is considered decisive. In practice, migrants move along paths beaten by previous migrants, family members, merchants, peddlers, officials and travellers, carrying with them detailed and less detailed, correct and less correct, information on possible destinations. The establishment and maintenance of these migration information channels, however, takes place within the limits set at macro level. Although not all movement is necessarily motivated by livelihood-related reasons, behaviour which results in the complete loss of one's resources is simply not sustainable. Hence, even movements primarily inspired by non-material motives cannot defy the limits set by material conditions.[58] Put differently, migrants who find insufficient or unsuitable means for a living at a particular destination are not likely to stay or to serve as an example. Objective constraints and opportunities therefore delimit the possible variety in migration patterns which can emerge and persist. Moreover, even within the boundaries of this structural room for manoeuvre, certain patterns are likelier than others. To the extent that migration information travels faster along pathways created and maintained by intense spatial interactions, the likelihood of certain patterns emerging is also influenced by specific political, logistic, commercial and legal connections between one place and another. Finally, at the micro level, household and individual characteristics further circumscribe the actual options considered by potential migrants, as they shape the eventual access that one has to migration information, one's susceptibility to the attractions of leaving, and the suitability of income or career opportunities available at a given destination. Migration is thus conceptualized as an adaptive strategy whose aims and success have to be related to their proper context, i.e. within whatever narrow limits – incomplete information, limited resources, social conditions and traditions, household strategies, political constraints and psychological factors – decisions on migration take place. In order to cope with changing constraints and opportunities at a household and individual level, people can mobilize an array of possible strategies, one of which consists of the temporary or definitive migration of one or more members of a household.[59] While the choice of one or other adaptive strategy is shaped by familiarity and example, and by individual or family resources, these decisions take place as a reaction to material constraints and opportunities which are essentially determined by economic conditions at the macro level.

Let me clarify my methodological stance with reference to an interesting discussion which has recently received some attention in Dutch historiography, and which is to be seen against the context of seventeenth-century Amsterdam. When Knotter and van Zanden compared the birthplaces and occupations of brides- and grooms-to-be in this booming metropolis on the basis of so-called *ondertrouwakten* (formal engagements), they observed not only that immigrants had a very dissimilar occupational profile from those born locally, but also that different regional groups of immigrants clustered in specific occupations. They found, for instance, that migrants from the coastal provinces of the Republic, Germany and Scandinavia were predominantly active in port-related occupations, while those from the inland Dutch and German regions worked mainly in local servicing trades, as bakers, smiths, tailors and shoemakers. After having established that these peculiarities were not attributable to formal exclusion mechanisms nor a marginalized position, Knotter and van Zanden attributed these differences in occupational orientation to the economic structure of the region of origin. In their opinion, a strong concentration of certain immigrant groups in specific jobs was primarily a reflection of the higher incidence of these occupations in their regions of origin.[60] This explanation was recently rejected by Erika Kuijpers, who contended that previous job experience or *a priori* qualities could not have mattered much in immigrants' quests for jobs in seventeenth-century Amsterdam, as most of their jobs were low-skilled and because there existed several institutions for vocational training after arrival. What *was* crucial, however, were circuits of chain migration and informal recruitment preferences, through which migrants from similar backgrounds were channelled to similar occupational activities – and which were to a large extent 'coincidental' factors unrelated to characteristics of the point of origin.[61] Lesger in turn went beyond the concept of chain migration by extending her argument and attributing the observed patterns of occupational clustering to the existence of specific channels of migration information in different regions.[62] In my opinion, the apparent opposition between the two strands of explanation is more a matter of different explanation *levels* than truly contrasting arguments. On the one hand, Kuijpers and Lesger have a point in questioning any automatic relationship between characteristics of a region of origin and migrants' occupational activity at their destination – especially in the case of relatively unspecialized occupational activities like baking or tailoring. On the other hand, however, too large an insistence on the meso level of social networks in turn obscures the underlying importance of economic conditions at origin and destination. Although social networks and informal recruitment chains shaped specific patterns of occupational clustering in the last instance, they could only operate within the limits set by structural material conditions and labour market characteristics in the regions of origin and at destination.

Take the observed shift from the Dutch coastal provinces to Scandinavia as the prime recruitment region of Amsterdam sailors in the course of the seventeenth century. At a fundamental level, this shift can be understood only with reference to macro-evolutions concerning labour supply and demand in both regions. While the demand for seafarers increased considerably in the wake of Amsterdam's seventeenth-century commercial expansion, the supply from the erstwhile prime recruitment region declined owing to a number of fundamental changes in population and landholding structures. Most maritime occupations had traditionally been undertaken as part of a diverse income-pooling by smallholding households in the provinces of Holland and Friesland, but in the course of the sixteenth and seventeenth centuries these pluri-active peasant households disappeared from the stage in the wake of the increasing scale and commercialization of coastal agriculture. Instead came a population slowdown and more specialized village communities, with little interest in temporary sailing jobs, leading to a strong reduction of the maritime labour supply available from these regions.[63] That the increasing shortage of Dutch-born sailors was then compensated by an intensified recruitment from Scandinavia rather than from elsewhere has evident roots in region-specific characteristics rather than being solely explicable by the operation of autonomous social networks. First, this specific migration pattern complied with the underlying structural condition that in Scandinavia suitable labour was available and willing to travel to Amsterdam, which was, for instance, no longer the case in the Dutch/Frisian hinterland.[64] Second, several characteristics of the Scandinavian region made it a more likely supplier of sailors on Dutch shipping than other probable alternatives. Although work on board was not necessarily skilled, and many young Scandinavian sailors were farmers' sons,[65] the existence of a seafaring tradition along the Scandinavian coasts had helped to establish labour and life cycles with which (temporary) seafaring was compatible, and had made sailing a familiar and therefore more readily considered income strategy than in a region where no such tradition existed.[66] Moreover, the existence of maritime activity at home ensured that the experience gained aboard Dutch ships formed a valuable asset upon return.[67] Finally, the expanding Baltic trade provided a channel between Scandinavia and Holland by which to establish and maintain supportive migration networks in this specific occupational branch.[68] In this sense, information streams, social networks and chain migration might have constituted a crucial variable in shaping Scandinavian occupational specialization to the Amsterdam labour market, but only in the last instance, in the sense that they operated within the limits set by structural conditions at a macro level, and were supported by several auxiliary factors at the macro and meso levels. If these structural conditions ceased to exist, so would the associated patterns of migration – whatever intermediary social networks existed.[69] It was not inevitable that so many seventeenth-century sailors marrying in Amsterdam had been born in Scandinavia, but the economic structure of the region and the nature of its commercial interactions made it a more likely supplier of Dutch seafarers than other alternatives. To be sure, circumstantial support for certain occupation-specific patterns was not always as strong as in the Scandinavian case, and in all instances supportive social networks undoubtedly played an important role. Even in the case of well-established immigrant niches, as with straw-hat makers from the Geer valley near Liège,[70] brick makers from Lippe,[71] pot vendors from the German Westerwald,[72] or tinkers from the Auvergne,[73] the exact boundary between the role of expertise and that of social networks is impossible to draw. However, the point is that these networks never stand on their own, but are subject to material constraints and opportunities at both origin and destination, and are to a greater or lesser extent 'embedded' in the spatial interactions connecting one place with the other. Although people in practice move primarily because certain networks and migration traditions exist, the mere existence of these meso structures is itself dependent on broader material conditions at a general macro level.

These comments are in line with some of the conclusions reached by Nancy Green in her comparative study of immigrant workers in the twentieth-century garment trades in Paris and New York, one of the most unstable, unregulated, labour-intensive and unenviable industries in the urban headquarters of twentieth-century capitalism. The specificities of the sector, with relatively low – or easily learnt – skill requirements and little regulation, made access relatively easy to newly arrived immigrants in need of a job, while the low-wage and flexible exigencies of production exerted a demand for cheap and docile labour: 'The industry has needed the labor; the newcomers have needed the jobs, capital and labor barriers to entry are low'. The sweatshops of Paris and New York employed mostly women, and mostly immigrants, whose ethnic composition varied according to the successive arrival of new immigrant waves. Social networks and circuits, supported by ethnic entrepreneurship, were of great importance in shaping specific migration patterns and occupational specializations. However, these networks were superposed on conditions of push and pull at a more structural level. When new opportunities opened up, or political and economic conditions in the homelands became less pressing, existing networks were replaced by new ones. In this sense, their influence remained subject to broader push and pull forces at origin and destination.[74]

Migration is thus seen as the result of an intricate decision-making process, whose the structural room for manoeuvre is set by push and pull forces at a macro level, but whose eventual choices and practices are mediated by social institutions and information channels, and by individual and household conditions. However intermingled the factors which underlie migration patterns may be in practice, their impact is subject to a hierarchy whereby macro structures of labour supply and demand predetermine the possible impact of factors at other levels. When related to the dynamics of migratory change, this perspective leads to three main and to a certain extent paradoxical implications, which in turn serve as heuristic devices in the formulation of the main research questions in this book. One is that migration tends to be selective; the other is that migration patterns are simultaneously resilient and vulnerable to societal change; the third is that migration is a differentiated and heterogeneous process. I will discuss them in this order.

The argument that existing patterns of migration are always subject to material constraints and opportunities at origin and destination implies that migration patterns to any given place are always to a certain extent attuned to what is termed the local opportunity structure, which is primarily determined by local labour demands.[75] This is not so much because migration is *necessarily* targeted at specific employment opportunities, but rather because migration which is not at all compatible with existing opportunities is simply not sustainable. In this sense, migration can be considered a selective process, in that existing migration patterns always bear *some* relationship to the local opportunity structure, and that the profile of migrants recruited via these circuits is always to a certain extent moulded by local labour demands. That migration is a selective process has been well attested empirically. One obvious illustration is, for instance, that the overall profile of immigrants to any given town in early modern and industrializing Europe tended to differ according to the town's economic (or in some cases cultural or political) function, and thus tended to be attuned to a greater or lesser extent to the actual economic (or other) opportunities available, as for instance with the gender bias (i.e. male domination) of immigration to expanding heavy industrial centres.[76] Part of this observed selectivity might take place via retroactive mechanisms of selection, through the departure of excess or unsuitable migrants ('failure'). However, most selection occurred – and still does – in a more proactive manner, via existing patterns of migration, often with regard to specific employment niches, which have become embedded in traditions and customs, as was for instance the case with young girls entering towns as domestic servants from the nearby countryside, or with many early modern seasonal labour flows covering sometimes great distances.[77]

This observed selectivity of migration implies a supply of immigrant labour which is more or less suitable to the local demand structure. To be sure, neither supply characteristics nor the local demand structure are wholly objective external conditions of the economic macro-setting. On the one hand, the local opportunity structure is moulded not only by objective labour demands, but also by social and cultural labour market segmentation and recruitment preferences. Immigrants' opportunities therefore depend not only on the economic structure of the place of destination, but also on the nature and strength of potential exclusion mechanisms. On the other hand, some room exists for collective and individual agency by immigrants themselves to try actively to adapt to an existing local opportunity structure, for instance by establishing new activities, carving out specific niches, or by (re)training after arrival. The temporary migration of male Auvergnats to nineteenth-century Spain was, for instance, made possible by an active restructuring of labour and family relations at home which allowed other household members to take over the men's agricultural tasks in their absence.[78] Likewise, small-scale ethnic entrepreneurship can form a successful way to establish a new living, as for instance with twentieth-century Italian pizzeria owners.[79] However, even such an active involvement in the shaping of income possibilities can only take place within the structural limits set by the material conditions of the host and sending societies: Italian restaurateurs would not have made much of a living in eighteenth-century Ghent – or at least not in the same number – nor would their compatriots occupied in the grape harvest in nineteenth-century Languedoc have been able to make such an investment.

Ewa Morawska's study of East European Jewish immigrants to small-sized Johnstown in Pennsylvania during the first half of the twentieth century provides an evocative illustration of this tension between structure and agency. On the one hand, she demonstrates how the Jewish community of Johnstown successfully mobilized collective strategies and old-country resources to establish an ethnic entrepreneurial niche – mostly petty trade – in a highly constrained environment. On the other hand, their specific occupational orientation was also circumscribed by the limits inherent in their predominantly rural background, in

which they differed significantly from the majority of their fellow East European
Jewish immigrants of the period. While most East European Jewish immigrants
to the United States in the period were skilled workers from urban backgrounds
who were easily absorbed by the expanding industrial opportunities in America's
big cities, the Jews of middle-sized Johnstown had mainly been rural traders and
artisans before their move across the Atlantic. Compared to their Johnstown compatriots, Jewish communities in big cities were far larger, more socially mobile and
more rapidly assimilated. On the one hand, the specific occupational structure of
Johnstown's immigrant Jews was partly a result of the – highly constrained – local
opportunity structure, but on the other hand the specificity of this opportunity
structure also had an influence on the kind and number of immigrants attracted
to Johnstown in the first place. While allowing for the importance of collective
strategies in eking out a new existence in the place of destination, then, Morawska's study demonstrates how the overall direction, composition and settlement
process of migration flows are fundamentally structured by economic constraints
and opportunities at both origin and destination.[80]

By and large, then, migration processes are characterized by a certain 'match'
between the characteristics of immigrant supply and the local opportunity structure. While this match depends on the existence of information channels able
to convey implicit or explicit information on opportunities at destination, it is
structurally dependent on the availability of a labour supply which is suitable and
willing to migrate, but not pressed too hard. The configuration of constraints
and opportunities at origin must be such as to make migration attractive and
worthwhile. As Jan Lucassen's concept of the labour cycle indicates, the complementarity of the migration option with other income activities can in this
sense sometimes be more important as a factor promoting migration than simple
differences in income. If migration is largely temporary, this requires that its relation to income strategies at home allows the establishment of sustainable labour
or life cycles. To the extent that sufficient income opportunities exist in the place
of origin, the pull of opportunities elsewhere will result in a positive selection of
those likely to gain most from moving. Rising constraints in the place of origin,
however, will lower the opportunity cost of moving and limit overall room for
manoeuvre, resulting in a higher level of migration, less selectivity in terms of
earning capacities, and far bleaker further prospects for newcomers after arrival,
as the increased inflow is bound to exert a downward pressure on local wages.
To the extent that earning capacities are largely a matter of gender, age, skill and
dependency ratio, a dominant pull will primarily recruit young, single adults,
while a high-push scenario is likely to put more families on the road.[81] The overall balance between structural push and pull forces at a macro level, then, has
a crucial impact on the scale of migration, the sort of people moving and the
overall prospects migrants face at their destination.

In this respect, it has been well attested that an increase in the importance of push over pull forces can upset migration's selective balance, as for instance with towns being overrun from time to time by rural people seeking shelter in times of agrarian (or other) crisis, a familiar image in early modern historiography. Hence the distinction proposed in migration studies of this period between 'subsistence' and 'betterment' migrants, i.e., in short, those disproportionately driven by push factors, as against those moving more with an eye to actual economic opportunities open to them.[82] I have argued elsewhere that such a distinction sheds little light at the individual level, as it suggests that migration motives were qualitatively different in the two situations, which I do not think was the case. The problem lies in part with the translation of objectified push and pull factors at the individual level, whereas people themselves probably only consider relative options open to them. However bleak their prospects, people do consciously try to make the best of them: constraints do not preclude aspirations (probably on the contrary).[83] What does vary is the structural room for manoeuvre that people have in realizing their aspirations or aims, which is ultimately determined by constraints and opportunities at both origin and destination. In this sense, I argue that evaluating the balance between objective push and pull forces provides essential insight into the causes and consequences, limits and possibilities of movement, as long as the implications of this balance are analysed at an aggregate level of objective room for manoeuvre rather than at an individual level of subjective motivation. To employ a distinction between pull-driven and push-driven migrants obscures the observation that even primarily push-driven migration remains a selective affair. Even in times of dire crisis, not all people move, let alone to the same destinations. The relevant question then is not whether or not migration is selective, but *to what extent* it is selective. The degree of overall selectivity, in other words, provides a measure of the underlying relationship between push and pull forces at a structural macro level, and for the objective space and prospects for agency, adaptation and betterment at the meso and micro levels. Of course, this degree of selectivity is almost impossible to quantify or make use of in any absolute way.[84] However, as an *indicative* measure of shifting push and pull forces at a structural level, it can prove of important heuristic value in comparing and evaluating the implications of changing recruitment patterns over time.

The socially and culturally 'embedded' nature of migration patterns in turn provides existing patterns with a degree of resilience of their own. Migration does not take place as some automatic response to abstract push and pull forces at a macro level. Rather, within the structural conditions shaping constraints and opportunities at origin and destination, migration is *mediated* via social networks, customs, norms and migration traditions. This meso level of migration channels provides the man-made connections between constraints in one place and opportunities in another. The corollary is that once a particular pattern of migration is established, it is self-reinforcing. Via the establishment of social networks and supportive institutions, the further diffusion of migration information, and the nestling of certain migration traditions in the realm of social norm and custom, patterns of migration are path-dependent and strengthened by powerful links of positive feedback. The result is that an established migration pattern can be conceptualized as a *system*, by which practices are brought into line with various conditions at different levels, and which is fortified by the strong glue of positive feedback in the social, cultural and demographic realms.[85] The more a pattern is embedded in diverse spatial interactions, social networks, customs and traditions, the less it is directly reliant upon material conditions for its persistence, at least in the short run. As such, this embeddedness allows existing patterns to overcome temporary shocks in the distribution of constraints and opportunities – such as the temporary 'flooding' of early modern cities in times of crisis – and to establish a degree of continuity which yields the familiarity necessary to trickle through to the realm of customs and norms. Nevertheless, *some* correspondence to the objective material conditions making migration worthwhile remains necessary for any migration patterns to persist in the medium and long runs, otherwise they are simply not sustainable.[86] In this respect, while migration patterns have a tendency to reproduce themselves, they are by definition vulnerable to structural societal change.

Although resilient and shock-resistant to an important degree, migration patterns can be structurally undermined by a fundamental shift in economic and societal structures in so far as they impair the labour and life cycles underpinning existing patterns of migration. Structural societal change, in other words, confronts existing circuits with fundamental challenges of adaptation, which conflicts with the tendency of migration patterns to reproduce themselves. The inherent inertia of migration practices can be appreciated by considering an established pattern of migration as a sunk investment built on social and cultural capital – among other things information, social networks and local traditions. Both the establishment of new patterns and the transformation of existing ones is a costly and anything but straightforward affair, as it demands the establishment of a new precarious balance between an intricate array of changing factors at the macro, meso and micro levels, whose outcome is by no means guaranteed. In this sense, all types of migration patterns possess a certain resilience and a certain capacity for adaptation, but can at some point run into structural contradictions which make it impossible for them to continue. In times of structural societal change, then, we can expect existing migration patterns to display various signs of adaptation and reorganization and to see new patterns emerging, while other patterns become wholly invalidated and disappear from view. This unavoidable but costly process of adaptation can moreover be expected to take place at different speeds and with varying degrees of success depending on the different migrant groups involved. This is so because of a third major characteristic of the general dynamics of migration processes, namely that they are very differentiated and heterogeneous.

That migration is a very differentiated process involving very heterogeneous groups is already implicit throughout the above discussions of migration selectivity and resilience. This inherent heterogeneity is generated and reinforced by factors at all three levels enumerated above as governing migration processes. Given that income structures both at origin and destination are heavily determined by gender, age, skill and resources, the translation of overall push and pull forces to constraints and opportunities at individual and household levels differs greatly between men and women, single persons and families, young adults and older people, farmers and artisans, skilled and unskilled workers, rich and poor people. Income opportunities both at origin and destination are not situated in one homogeneous and fully integrated labour market, but in several relatively separate labour market segments. Access to these different labour market segments is governed not only by age, gender and skill, but also by social custom and informal or formal recruitment patterns. Migration channels too are generally segmented and differentiated, with different kinds of migrants making use of different channels, among others according to social status and resources.[87] To the extent that certain migration channels are oriented towards specific labour market segments, they strengthen existing patterns of labour market segmentation and informal recruitment preferences. At the same time, they limit the overall scope of individual and household adaptability, as their migration options ultimately depend on the kind of migration channels to which they have access.

The end result of these different mechanisms of segmentation and exclusion is that migration takes place via different circuits, as was the case, for example, with region-specific patterns of occupational specialization in seventeenth-century Amsterdam. I use the term 'circuit' to designate a certain correspondence between the migration channels used and the labour market segments on which migrants are active. To speak of circuits, it is necessary that certain migrant groups share essential similarities in terms of general characteristics, origin, the channels used for migration and the labour market segments in which they are active at destination, which they do not share to the same extent with other groups. These circuits can be distinguished at a very broad level, for instance between rural-born and urban-born migrants, or at a very detailed level, when separating different circuits from two nearby villages. At a detailed level, they can overlap with actual networks, while at a broad level they may correspond to differentiated flows of migration information without constituting actual social networks. The point is that both at a very general level and at a very detailed level, different groups of migrants move in different directions with different

aims and are attracted by different pull forces, according to individual characteristics on the one hand (age, gender, skill) and their socially mediated access to
migration channels and labour market segments on the other.

This observed heterogeneity of migration processes implies that migration's
overall selectivity, resilience and adaptability differs among different groups. For
one thing, the relative scarcity of individual skills and capacities determines the
overall scope of migration options, and the objective feasibility of reacting to
declining opportunities in one place by moving to another place where prospects
are better. Similarly, the precise extent to which migration channels counter
migration's selective tendency – by providing supportive structures outside the
labour market – might vary considerably according to the precise nature and
specific embedding of these channels. On the whole, career migrants moving
via non-personal network migration modes – to borrow from Lesger's terminology – targeted on very specific employment opportunities, such as government
officials, clergymen or skilled artisans, can be expected to be much more reactive
to the evolution of actual opportunities than, for instance, less specialist workers
who have to rely more on diffuse and highly 'embedded' migration information
channels and personal networks.[88] However, even the first type of migration
channels may sooner or later be confronted with objective limits to its adaptability, for instance when the occupational qualities in question become completely
obsolete due to technological change. The essential observation here is that in
times of structural social change all patterns of migration are likely to experience
change and attempts at adaptation, but that the speed and success of adaptation
– ultimately determined by collective *room for manoeuvre* – differs for different migrant groups. The interesting question then becomes not to determine
whether continuity or discontinuity has the upper hand at an aggregate level,
but rather to evaluate the *speeds of change* at which different groups try to adapt
to changing push and pull forces.

The Speeds of Change

In sum, migration can be conceived as an adaptive strategy whose likelihood
and form are shaped by individual and household characteristics such as gender,
age, skill and resource structure, by meso-level institutions such as information
channels, migration traditions and social networks, and by macro-level developments determining the spatial and social distribution of resources and income
opportunities. Although the eventual outcome of the interplay of macro, meso
and micro factors is difficult to predict on an individual level, overall migration
patterns bear a causal – and thus identifiable – relationship to considerations at
these three levels. The focus of the forthcoming chapters lies not so much with
analysing the outcome of individual migration decisions, as with investigating the

shifting room for manoeuvre – shaped by macro conditions and meso options – within which they took place. The general macro setting, itself a manifestation of historical change, thus predetermines the considerations at play in migration decisions, and the various patterns which evolve in reality can be interpreted as variations within these limits, shaped by the variety in mediating meso structures and micro circumstances. The causal hierarchy of the integrative approach allows us to disentangle the role of structural historical change from the existing variation in migration patterns in practice. Although migration is *in the last instance* structured by meso factors and micro considerations, a diachronic analysis of the evolution of migration practices in relation to changing push and pull developments at a relatively abstract macro level remains not only useful in itself but also a necessary step to evaluating societies', households' and individuals' adaptability in a proper context of material constraints and opportunities.

The integrative nature of migration processes in practice implies the fulfilment of different conditions at different levels. At an essential structural level, sustainable migration patterns demand a certain match between push forces at origin and pull forces at destination, whereby migration strategies fit into the wider labour and life cycles of individuals and families, and whereby the immigrant labour supply is to a certain extent attuned to the local opportunity structure. In addition, migration flows require the existence of information channels connecting origin with destination. These channels are essentially man-made, and provide existing patterns with a certain resilience of their own. These conditions in turn lead to a number of implications which are to a certain extent contradictory, namely that migration is at once a selective and resilient process, which is vulnerable to societal change. In times of relative stability these contradictions can be resolved via the establishment of selective patterns of recruitment which are well fitted to existing labour and life cycles, well connected via channels of migration information, and well established in the realms of social custom. In times of accelerated and structural social change, however, the essential material conditions underlying established patterns become undermined, and the social and cultural institutions which have previously supported them become invalidated, thus posing the challenge of adaptation at different levels. In this inevitable but costly process of societal adaptation, the tension between selectivity, resilience and adaptability will result in different speeds of change for different migrant groups, with different degrees of success. The extent to which different migration patterns succeed in retaining a certain selectivity and resilience in eras of structural change proves an important heuristic device by which to analyse the capacity and success of adaptation by different groups. In turn, these indications convey essential insight into the social costs and human dimensions of societal change. The main questions then become to assess the capacity and incapacity of change of different migrant groups, to explain the speed and success of migratory change in relation to changing factors at the macro, meso and micro levels, and to evaluate the impact of different speeds of adaptation for the migrants involved and for society more generally at origin and destination. This is why the evolution of urban migration patterns in the long nineteenth century forms such an interesting research subject to study, as it sheds light on the ability and inability of social adaptation in an era of structural societal change, during which increasing pressure on existing patterns of migration produced greater obstacles to change and adaptation for different groups, and restructured the relationships between winners and losers.

2 MIGRATION IN THE URBAN TRANSITION

In the course of the long nineteenth century, roughly between 1750 and World War I, Europe's population was confronted with profound economic, demographic, social and political transformations that in retrospect wrought its transition from a pre-industrial to an industrial society. Although few of the developments contributing to this transition were in themselves novel, the acceleration in processes of proletarianization, demographic growth and agricultural and industrial reorganization cumulated in a process of structural and irreversible societal change which eventually resulted in the highly urbanized and industrialized society of twentieth-century Europe. This transition was not an automatic, self-evident or straightforward affair, but an uneven process at different speeds characterized by regional, temporal and structural discrepancies in the development of labour supply and demand. Structural changes at macro level resulted in changing constraints and opportunities at household level, and implied considerable challenges of adjustment. Migration constituted an important strategy in trying to adapt to the changes in households' material conditions. At the same time, existing patterns of migration had to accommodate themselves to shifts in the structural conditions which had underlain most early modern migration practices. The uneven development of push and pull forces and the 'embedded' nature of many migration channels meant that migration patterns underwent a costly process of adaptation at different speeds, whereby costs and gains were distributed unequally.

Cities were certainly not the only possible destination for migrants. However, to the extent that cities formed the focal point of many of the economic, political and social transformations of the long nineteenth century, the evolution of urban migration patterns is of particular interest in assessing continuity and change in people's adaptive strategies. While urban migration was no new phenomenon, its scope and function were significantly altered as both cities and their hinterlands underwent structural transformations which remoulded the spatial distribution of income opportunities. To what extent did established patterns of urban migration succeed in adapting to the structural change in constraints and opportunities at points of origin and destination? To what extent did these changing constraints and opportunities result in a remoulding of the migratory flows between a town, its hinterland and more distant regions and places? And how can the evident challenge of adaptation and restructuring be reconciled with conclusions of recent studies stressing an essential continuity of nineteenth-century spatial mobility compared to the preceding period?

This chapter juxtaposes the explanatory framework and concepts established in the previous chapter with the historiography of urban migration in the early modern and early industrial periods to arrive at the central research questions dealt with in this book. The chapter starts with an exploration of the existing literature on the characteristics of urban migration in the early modern period, and then moves on to discuss recent and less recent findings on the evolution of migration and mobility during the transition to industrial society. The chapter ends by sketching the regional and local background to Antwerp's socio-economic and demographic evolution in the eighteenth and nineteenth centuries, thus setting the stage for the empirical case study.

Labour Exchange Patterns in the Early Modern Period

Contrary to earlier views, research over the past decades has amply demonstrated that migration was a pervasive characteristic of Western European society in the early modern period. Many people moved, over various distances, to different destinations, for different reasons and for different periods of time. Most patterns of migration took place within local and regional land, labour or marriage markets, and were integrated in well-established labour or life cycles.[1] Only a fraction of all mobility was directed towards towns, but these migrations were greatly important for urban economic and demographic development in the early modern period. Because early modern cities as a rule recorded more deaths than births, most cities relied on a permanent influx of newcomers in order to maintain their population size, let alone grow.[2] In a fast growing town, the majority of the population was likely to have been born outside the city limits, while the proportion of immigrants could easily amount to more than 30 per cent in a more or less stable population.[3] As most migration was temporary, the total volume of urban immigration and emigration was much higher than the number of urban immigrants at any given moment might suggest, and the total proportion of persons engaged in urban migration patterns at some point of their lives was substantial throughout the early modern period.[4] While the precise demographic contribution of urban migrants remains subject to debate, even critics of the model of urban natural decrease do not question the magnitude of urban migration in the early modern period, nor its importance as 'the linchpin of the urban economy'.[5] The constant flow back and forth of labourers, domestic servants, tradesmen and artisans played a key role in the development of early modern labour and commodity markets and in the diffusion of technology, and was essential to the working of the urban economy.[6]

Migration to early modern towns often followed different circuits, whereby the direct hinterland was the main supplier of apprentices, domestic servants and relatively unspecialized labour, while specialized artisans and white-collar workers generally moved between different cities and over greater distances.[7] While the structural reasons for this dual recruitment pattern lay with the relative scarcity of certain qualifications – goldsmiths were less easily found in the countryside than in cities – the direct reason can be related to differences in the nature of, and access to, the respective migration channels used. Whereas skilled artisans and other upmarket migrants had better access to extensive and far-reaching inter-urban networks, the scope of information channels used by people situated lower on the social ladder was more limited, more diffuse and more embedded in – and thus dependent upon – broader spatial interactions, such as those between town and hinterland. With the majority of urban newcomers drawn from the surrounding countryside, 'city walls [were] not ... barriers but rather ... semi-permeable membranes through which nearby populations flowed'.[8] Migration relations with the surrounding countryside tended to be of a privileged nature, in the sense that urban migration from these villages was exclusively directed towards the town in question, providing a demographic reservoir for the town's population. Jean-Pierre Poussou has proposed the concept of *demographic basin* to designate this area of privileged recruitment: 'a collection of municipalities which somehow constitute a city's *domaine réserve*: from this zone, it constantly attracts more immigrants than any other city'. He observed for eighteenth-century France that these were to a large extent mutually exclusive, in the sense that the country was virtually subdivided into separate demographic basins, each grouped around a major city.[9] The migration flows between these demographic basins and the towns in question formed part of a set of broader social, economic and political relationships and interactions linking a city to its hinterland – including market relations, land ownership, communication networks and jurisdiction, which in effect functioned as the main channels of migration information for most country dwellers.[10] Although they tended to expand and contract somewhat according to the rhythms of urban economic development, the essential long-term continuity observed in the contours of demographic basins further attests to the strong social and geographical 'embeddedness' of migration channels between a town and its hinterland.[11]

Migrants who were recruited from beyond the demographic basin generally followed very different types of migration channels from those of their hinterland counterparts. Long-distance migrants were more likely to have come from urban backgrounds, and to move along the inter-urban networks of trade and administration connecting different cities. Generally higher skilled and/or socially superior to their rural counterparts, they were engaged in more exclusive social networks, providing them with migration information of a more selective and efficient nature and a wider spatial scope, such as artisans' associations, merchant networks or state bureaucracies.[12] Not bound to a specific destination and oriented towards specialist income opportunities, long-distance migration patterns were also less stable than those over short distances. Thus the development of new employment opportunities in specialist branches was often accompanied by the emergence of medium- and long-distance recruitment channels of skilled workers. When local opportunities dwindled, these patterns disappeared rapidly, as the workers moved on to places where they could make better use of their scarce skills.[13]

Schematically, then, migration to early modern cities can be pictured as a pyramid, with a broad base of migrants from the nearby countryside possessing few specialist skills and moving predominantly within embedded and resilient hinterland circuits, and a more volatile top of specialist and upmarket migrants who moved over longer distances, via more exclusive migration channels, and who were more sensitive to specific opportunities in specialist branches of the urban opportunity structure. That rural hinterland circuits were generally the most important in quantitative terms was a reflection of the large demand for unskilled and semi-skilled labour inherent in almost all urban production processes in the early modern period.[14] Further differentiation than simply that between rural-born and urban-born migrants was often evident, as for instance with the region-specific occupational profiles observed among immigrants to seventeenth-century Amsterdam.[15] Different circuits of recruitment were thus bound up with differences in skill and information channels on the one hand, and with patterns of urban labour market segmentation on the other hand. The dimensions of base and top, the pyramid's further differentiation and the spatial reach of overall recruitment patterns were a reflection of the city's opportunity structure and its spatial interactions. Depending on the size of a town and the nature of its rural and inter-urban relations, therefore, an urban migration field could be limited to the immediate surroundings or might stretch out over different regions or even countries, as in the case of metropolises like Amsterdam or London.[16] Although the degree of resilience differed according to recruitment circuits and the stability of a town's opportunity structure, most urban migration proceeded via well-established and relatively resilient channels or networks which were to a large extent embodied in the cultural, political, commercial and legal links connecting regions with cities, and different cities with each other.

Although not all urban immigrants came from the countryside, early modern urban economies were crucially dependent on a permanent supply of labour – both temporary and permanent – that had been raised and nurtured in the countryside. According to Jan de Vries's estimates of rural–urban net migration in the early modern period, an increase of one unit in the northern European urban population required at least two rurally born permanent immigrants. Expanding the calculation to cover the risk of early death, the increase in urban population revealed in the early modern period required a net inflow of between 18 and 63 per cent of the rural birth surplus at different points of time.[17] The constant influx of young single adults provided early modern cities with a favourable age structure and a sizeable input of human capital which compensated for cities' poor reproductive record as a result of infant and child mortality. As urban labour demands were to a large extent seasonal, cyclical and unstable, patterns of labour recruitment depended crucially on the existence of life and labour cycles which were compatible with a temporary urban residence. This was possible because of the varied and heterogeneous nature of the different sources of income combined in the income-pooling of most early modern households. Temporary wage labour – in cities or elsewhere – figured only as one source of income alongside a variety of other sources of livelihood, such as small-scale agriculture, rural industry, relief provisions and various other income strategies based on communal and forestry activities, such as gleaning, poaching and cattle-grazing.[18] While many rural migrants came to work in the city for several months or several years, they rarely depended completely or for the whole of their lives on urban wage labour as their only source of income. Rather, the incidence of urban wage labour often corresponded to a specific phase in the labour or life cycle which was substituted for or complemented by other sources of income in a later part of the year or stage of one's life. In turn, these temporary patterns of *seasonal migration* (for part of a year) and *labour migration* (for several years) were generally embedded in social custom, migration traditions and social networks, as for instance with young adults moving to the city for several years, or seasonal labourers coming to town every year to cover peak periods in urban economic activity. To be sure, some migrants remained in towns and became permanent immigrants, but they formed a small minority at most.[19] The continuation of these different migration patterns throughout the early modern period implies that temporary urban residence yielded tangible benefits to the migrants involved – in terms of wages, savings or training – which where compatible with, and useful in, their labour or life cycles as a whole. Both life and labour cycle-specific patterns and even permanent forms of urban migration, then, depended structurally on the existence of a rural economy where labour could be maintained and reproduced before, and often also after, periods of urban residence.

This characteristic constellation whereby cities were continuously provided with temporary and permanent labour inputs from the countryside was identified by Jan Luiten van Zanden as one of the unequal exchange mechanisms that characterized early modern capitalism. According to van Zanden, the urban centres of 'merchant capitalism' formed 'an open labour market, in which use is made of a continuous stream of workers from outside the system'. The continuous influx of permanent and temporary migrants made wages possible that were below the reproductive cost of labour, thus shifting this cost largely to the pre-capitalist sphere. In addition, these migrant workers often 'acted as a buffer for the labour market in merchant capitalism: fluctuations in economic activities were met by "attracting" and "repelling" seasonal migrant workers'.[20] Whatever the appreciation of van Zanden's thesis in regard to the much-debated historical development of capitalism,[21] it helps to focus our attention on the ways in which early modern rural–urban labour recruitment could separate spatially the reproductive cost and the productive use of labour, most obviously by attracting and repelling migrants in line with labour demand.[22] The efficacy of such a separation depends on the existence of a labour reservoir outside the 'system' (whatever its spatial dimensions) with some autonomous means of (re)production, which is responsive to labour demands within the system. In other words, early modern patterns of urban labour recruitment were dependent on the existence of relatively resilient rural income structures that could free mature labour for urban activities when needed.

These patterns of urban labour recruitment did not always operate smoothly, as the selectivity and flexibility of recruitment was hampered by several inelasticities and inefficiencies related to the strongly embedded nature of migration channels. Moreover, the incidence of rural crises evidently upset existing balances of labour exchange patterns, as when cities were temporarily 'flooded' by rural refugees in times of war or shortage.[23] On the other hand, such crises and the associated patterns of push-driven migration were always of a temporary nature. The rapidity with which patterns were restored after periods of crisis attests to the structural functionality and resilience of existing rural–urban labour exchange modes. At the same time, they were not immutable. The apparent ease with which new circuits of recruitment emerged when new urban activities were established, as for instance with serge and cloth workers in seventeenth-century Leiden, attests to an important degree of flexibility in recruiting groups of migrants as a result of changes in the local opportunity structure.[24] Nonetheless, at a structural level the selectivity and sustainability of early modern urban recruitment patterns remained critically dependent on the existence of various alternative – primarily rural – sources of income to which potential or previous migrants could turn when urban opportunities were inadequate. At the same time, the overall long-term developments of labour supply and demand throughout the early modern era implied a gradual but structural undermining of the premises on which existing patterns of urban migration were largely based. In particular, the rising scale of proletarianization and the marginalization of many rural livelihoods increased the pressure on existing patterns of migration while at the same time weakening migrants' fallback position. The acceleration of these developments in the course of the long nineteenth century, coupled with important changes in the urban employment structure, implied a radical restructuring of urban patterns of labour recruitment and of existing patterns of urban migration.

Migration in the Urban Transition

Because of the extreme exigencies of urban growth in terms of food, fuel, raw materials and people in relation to the level and organization of wealth production and transfer mechanisms of the age, early modern urbanization had been subjected to some sort of ceiling, or upper limit. The densely populated, favourably located and economically advanced seventeenth-century Dutch Republic probably most approximated this early modern urban limit, with one out of every three people living in cities of more than 10,000 inhabitants.[25] In most other early modern European regions, the proportion living in cities was much lower, and the combined figures for the whole of Europe amounted to 10 per cent at most during the closing decades of the *ancien régime*.[26] In the course of the long nineteenth century, however, this urban ceiling was demolished by an unprecedented increase in both the size of cities and the proportion of the population living in cities, in a process which had an irreversible impact on the geographical, economic, social, political and cultural structures of contemporary society. Between 1750 and 1914 the total European population living in cities of more than 5,000 inhabitants increased more than sixfold, and their proportion of the whole population tripled to more than 42 per cent. During this process, the number of cities of more than 100,000 inhabitants increased from 28 to 195, and their share of the total population rose from 3 to 13 per cent. The process was earliest in England, where the urban part of the population had risen to 45 per cent as early as 1850, and rose to no less than 75 per cent in 1910, and it was most rapid – although later – in Germany, where the respective proportions grew from 15 to 49 per cent during the same period.[27] At a fundamental level, the structural causes of the process can be identified with a general economic-geographical reorganization of production which made for an increasing spatial concentration of capital and labour in cities.[28] Although what came after was fundamentally different from what came before, the actual mechanisms by which both the economic conversion and the spatial redistribution of population were carried out have recently been newly questioned and explored. While revisions of the nature of the Industrial Revolution have tended to downscale the revolutionary character of change in the period,[29] earlier perceptions of migration as an essentially modern and by definition discontinuous process have likewise been substituted for views which emphasize essential continuities in the patterns, directions and purposes of movement between the early modern period and the long nineteenth century.

In earlier visions of the urban transition, the image of a one-off rural–urban population transfer loomed large. The spectacular growth in urban population was linked by many contemporaries to the observable process of rural–urban migration, which was in turn viewed predominantly in terms of uprooting: because of the increasing marginalization of rural income activities, ever more people were pushed out of the countryside and forced to try their luck in cities. This 'desperate' move from countryside to town by uprooted and impoverished peasants was seen as the root cause for the swelling of Europe's cities, and the prime cause of increasing urban congestion and the exacerbation of social problems in the cities. Especially in Germany, but also elsewhere, social observers juxtaposed the social cohesion of countryside life in pre-industrial times with the social anomie and alienation which ruled the industrial city. Bereft of the supportive social structures of village life, urban immigrants were left prey to the dissolution of moral and social order in the inner cities, where crime, poverty, individualism and lawlessness ruled.[30] Neither the reality of rural impoverishment nor that of urban squalor are in themselves contested in recent revisions of the dynamics of the urban transition. What they do question, however, are the direction, definitiveness, novelty, scale and impact of urban migration implied in the image of a one-off rural–urban population transfer, since renewed attention to the demographic dynamics in the period has led to a number of important, and sometimes somewhat contradictory, revisions of the erstwhile dominant image.

A first important revision in this respect is that natural increase on the whole appears to have played a far greater role in the urban growth of the long nineteenth century than was originally imagined, owing to a considerable decline in urban mortality – the causes of which remain subject to intense debate.[31] The precise balance between natural increase and net migration as a source of urban growth varied greatly through time and space, but the first component generally acquired predominance in most European cities somewhere in the course of the second half of the nineteenth century.[32] In England, the switch from migration-driven to natural-increase-driven urban growth is likely to have occurred earliest, somewhere in the 1810s and 1820s. According to Williamson, net immigration accounted for 60 per cent of city growth in England and Wales between 1776 and 1811, but for only 40 per cent between 1846 and 1871.[33] Jan de Vries has suggested that the nineteenth-century urban transition is best regarded as the intertwining of two processes, namely a 'typical migration-led growth phase that led to urban–rural differences in vital rates based on favourable urban age–sex distributions' – which had also been familiar in early modern times – that was 'carried forward by the historically unique consequences of the demographic transition'. In other words, the first phase of growth which was primarily migration-driven – and thus by definition not self-sustaining – would have run up against the same 'ceiling' as before, had it not been coupled to a process of mortality decline that generated rising rates of urban natural increase, and in turn diminished the relative importance of rural–urban migration as a source of urban growth.[34] These observations suggest, then, that, although the end result – unprecedented urbanization – was radically new, the prime contribution of migration dynamics to the urban transition did not necessarily differ much from phases of considerable urban expansion in the past, i.e. a net contribution of migrants and a derived effect on fertility and mortality rates.

A second major revision of the idea of a one-off rural–urban transfer is that gross rates of urban migration were far greater than the net numbers derived from population figures suggest. Where direct sources on immigration and emigration are available, they show that most urban migration was highly transient, and that the eventual 'yield' of overall mobility, i.e. the share of net migration gain in relation to the total number of inward and outward moves, was very small. Thus the increase of 96,000 inhabitants which the city of Duisburg in the German Ruhr valley recorded between 1845 and 1914 was the net result of a total of 724,400 recorded moves in and out of the city over the same period.[35] Likewise, the migration gain of 103,000 residents which Rotterdam recorded between 1851 and 1899 was the result of a total of 799,000 recorded inward and outward moves, implying a net yield on total mobility of only 13 per cent.[36] At only 10 per cent this return was even smaller in late nineteenth-century Amsterdam, when a net increase of 110,250 immigrants between 1870 and 1900 was all the Dutch capital gained from more than one million recorded moves in and out of the city during this thirty-year period.[37] The implication of these low rates of return on overall urban mobility is that much of urban migration was highly temporary, and that rural–urban flows were to a large extent matched by (re)migration streams from the city to the countryside. Of Duisburg's newcomers in 1890, 42 per cent stayed in town for less than one year, while 40 per cent of those leaving the city moved to a rural destination with fewer than 10,000 inhabitants.[38] Through the analysis of autobiographical data on more than 16,000 Britons born between 1750 and 1930, Colin Pooley and Jean Turnbull demonstrated that moves from a small to a larger settlement were by no means dominant in the nineteenth century, and were generally matched by an equal importance of moves from large to smaller settlements.[39] Contrary to the definitive and pervasive character of rural–urban migration envisaged in earlier accounts of the urban transition, then, the city was a terminus for only a relatively small number of immigrants, and most people moved along various paths of mobility, in various directions, at different points in their lives.

A third major revision, which is to a certain extent the corollary of the former, is that migration patterns on the whole displayed far greater continuities with those of the early modern period than had been previously imagined. In their longitudinal analysis of British migration behaviour, Pooley and Turnbull observed strong continuity in the patterns, directions, distances and motives of movement from the second half of the eighteenth century to the early twentieth century. Throughout, migration remained mostly short-distance, took place within well-defined regions, occurred as much from small to larger settlements as the other way round, and was primarily inspired by considerations related to work and family.[40] Similar continuities in urban migration patterns have been exposed for other regions too, for instance by Steve Hochstadt and James Jackson for nineteenth-century Germany.[41] Given that early modern society was far more mobile than previously thought, nineteenth-century migration patterns appear to have been far less novel or 'modern' than had been proposed in earlier accounts.

Fourth, a number of studies have discredited the essentially marginal and desperate image of the nineteenth-century urban immigrant presented in earlier surveys. In his study of British urbanization, Williamson stresses how even in periods with very high rates of net migration, migrants remained very circumscribed in terms of age and gender. Although rural push-factors were undoubtedly at work too, these did not impede migration from 'positively' selecting those with most to gain from urban life.[42] A recent econometric survey of English rural–urban migration between 1851 and 1881 reached similar conclusions, and confirmed that this positive selection was generally matched by a positive effect on social mobility after the move.[43] Most migrants to nineteenth-century Marseille likewise demonstrated better indications of social mobility than local-born residents.[44] In addition, the studies on both Duisburg and Marseille found that even in the most rapid phases of urban expansion, migrants were not isolated when they arrived, but were able to rely on friends, family, village networks or other supportive institutions to cushion the shock of urban life.[45]

Recent revisions have therefore demonstrated that the contribution to the urban transition from net rural–urban migration was much smaller than envisaged in early accounts of the process, that the position of the urban immigrant was less marginal and alienated, and that overall patterns and directions of movement displayed important continuities with those established for the early modern period. Does this mean that there was really nothing intrinsically new about mobility during the urban transition? It depends on what we look at. From the perspective of the outward characteristics of all possible moves made by all people during their lifetimes, it is not wholly surprising that the end impression is one of essential continuity: most people for most of their lives moved along paths which had already been familiar to earlier generations.[46] However, although the single individual moves by which the eventual redistribution of population took place were in themselves not particularly new or revolutionary, at an aggregate level they did amount to a greater orientation of migration flows towards urban centres.[47] More people came to the cities than ever before, and left their mark on the changing urban structures. Moreover, as labour markets connecting town and country underwent ongoing transformations, the underlying conditions and actual constraints and opportunities which got migrants on the move were increasingly new. At a fundamental level, the rural and urban conditions underlying the exchange mechanisms of the early modern period became structurally undermined by the uneven development of push and pull forces at different speeds. On the one hand, the increasing marginalization of small-scale landholding and the decline of rural industry led to a disintegration of rural livelihoods and a substantial increase in rural push forces. On the other hand, labour demands in many cities underwent not only a quantitative expansion, but also a qualitative transformation, which did not allow for easy adjustments.

In the course of the long nineteenth century, several socio-economic macrodevelopments led to the erosion and eventual disintegration of rural livelihoods throughout different European regions. In regions characterized by large-scale and capital-intensive farming activities, the increasing commercialization of agriculture and the spread of certain technological innovations acted together to reduce year-round income opportunities in agricultural wage labour. Keith Snell has demonstrated how the increasing commercialization and specialization of grain-growing in the English south-east in the eighteenth and early nineteenth centuries led to a decline in female employment opportunities and an increase in the seasonal nature of male (harvest) employment, thus jeopardizing year-round family labour cycles and stimulating out-movement.[48] In regions characterized by small-scale peasant landholding, the extensive increase in population growth which set in by the second half of the eighteenth century increased demographic pressure on remaining resources, and led to increasing rents and a further subdivision and marginalization of smallholders' plots.[49] Where rural industry was widespread, income-pools were further upset by the eventual replacement of cottage industries by mechanized production, which deprived millions of rural homeworkers of a major source of livelihood.[50] Rural labour cycles were further violated by various infringements of communal rights. As further enclosures obstructed forestry and grazing activities by the poorer members of village communities, several communal rights such as gleaning were increasingly restricted.[51] In addition, these different structural dynamics of rural crisis were exacerbated in many regions by crop failures, food shortages and famines, the most famous of which was the potato blight of the 1840s.[52]

Of course, none of the cited developments engendering the erosion and eventual disintegration of rural livelihoods was in itself new. While pressure had been building up over the previous centuries, the long nineteenth century was the scene of a strong and fundamental acceleration in these different processes of macro-economic change which led not to a destabilization but to a fundamental invalidation of the income strategies on which the livelihood of most pluri-active households in the early modern countryside had been based. Most fundamental in this process was a general upsurge in overall wage-dependency. In his by now classic and frequently cited study, Charles Tilly estimated the proportion of the European population dependent on wage labour for (part of) their livelihood to have risen from roughly 24 per cent in 1550 to 58 per cent in 1750 and to 71 per cent by the middle of the nineteenth century, while the degree to which households became dependent on wage-labour also increased.[53] These different dynamics of proletarianization and rural marginalization developed at different speeds in different places. While some developments were gradual, others were abrupt. Rather than a steady transition from one societal structure to another, the long nineteenth century was the scene of a fundamental and disruptive transformation engendering change at different speeds, whose net result was a substantial increase in rural push forces and a breakdown of rural labour and life cycles which had formed the necessary complement to early modern patterns of urban migration.[54]

While rural conditions were being structurally altered, labour demands in many cities were undergoing profound transformations. The eventual demise of corporative institutions, the increasing commodification of labour, and the new exigencies of large-scale factory production changed both the nature and scale of the urban employment structure. These changes, too, were anything but straightforward. Economic conversion generally took place at different speeds, resulting in highly mixed urban economic structures, in which small-scale labour-intensive production continued to exist alongside factory-based production. Thus in many economic sectors of nineteenth-century Amsterdam, such as printing, metallurgy, baking and cigar making, small-scale artisanal workshops survived alongside large industrialized units well into the twentieth century. In this dual economic structure, the 'traditional' sector functioned as a buffer in the labour-provisioning of the modern sector, providing young people with training and education and supplying a ready pool of specialized labour.[55] Many other dynamics typically identified with 'pre-modern' structures, such as domestic industrial activities, actually experienced (sometimes prolonged) Indian summers before finally disappearing from view, and in this they were indeed part and parcel of the industrial transition, rather than remnants of a bygone age.[56] While the expansion of large-scale urban-based production exerted new demands for labour, these demands remained highly volatile and vulnerable to seasonal, cyclical and conjunctural shifts on increasingly international markets. Possibilities of establishing relatively stable year-round labour cycles, let alone life cycles, were scarce in nineteenth-century cities. Finding income opportunities in the transforming urban economies was no easy task in the face of the often highly segmented nature of urban labour markets, and of the precariousness and casual nature of many of the employment opportunities in expanding sectors, especially in those greatly dependent on international trade dynamics.[57] The viability of such opportunities was thus often critically dependent on the 'recourse resources' at hand to cover casual or cyclical unemployment.[58] It is precisely at this point that any discrepancies between new and old income opportunities, both at macro and micro levels, were likely to pose the greatest problems for those trying to establish a new and relatively reliable labour cycle: not necessarily in the absence of income opportunities per se, but in the absence of those allowing sufficient income-pooling throughout the year – or lifetime – with enough resiliency to cope with the vulnerability of wage-dependency. While rural labour cycles became structurally undermined, then, urban opportunities did not provide a ready substitute.

The uneven evolution of labour supply and demand in the course of the long nineteenth century posed evident problems of adaptation to existing patterns of urban migration: to labour in finding new sustainable labour cycles, and to employers in setting up new types of labour recruitment. Migrants' adaptability to changing constraints and opportunities was hampered not only by the inherent discrepancies in labour supply and demand, but also by the embedded and resilient nature of migration patterns. At the same time, the significant improvement and expansion of means of communication and transport as well as the changing political and commercial context of the long nineteenth century, led to the development of new spatial units and interactions, and created new flows of information about migration, in particular across the Atlantic.[59] Together with discrepancies in labour supply and demand and the inherent resilience of migration patterns, differential access to new information flows and opportunities not only precluded any smooth adaptation of overall migration patterns, but also led to the shifting costs of adaptation being unevenly distributed among different social groups. If Williamson is right in stating that migration remained highly selective even in the most turbulent periods of the urban transition, this was nothing short of an impressive achievement of societal adaptation to rapidly evolving push and pull forces. However, as his study takes into consideration only the net result of urban migration dynamics, Williamson's statements unavoidably pertain almost solely to 'stayers' – which we know formed only a fraction of all urban immigrants. The same is – inevitably – true for studies of immigrants' trajectories of social mobility, which therefore provide only a very selective view of costs and benefits.[60] It is only by expanding the perspective to incorporate *all* forms of urban migration that the immense scope of social adaptation, adjustment and readjustment can be appreciated.

Because gross migration figures for early modern cities are lacking, it is difficult to evaluate the overall scale of nineteenth-century urban mobility in relation to earlier periods. One of the only points of comparison available consists of the yearly immigration and emigration figures which Jean-Claude Perrot was able to reconstruct for the city of Caen in Normandy in the second half of the eighteenth century, which then had between 30,000 and 40,000 inhabitants. Between 1753 and 1774, immigration and emigration attained average annual rates of 1.2 and 0.2 per cent respectively, and between 1775 and 1790 the respective figures were 1.6 and 1.9 per cent.[61] Although late-eighteenth-century Caen can arguably be considered a typical example of early modern urban migration, its rates of movement in and out in any case remained far below those recorded for most nineteenth-century growth poles. Although consistent comparisons are lacking and the *net* impact remained relatively small, gross mobility rates in most nineteenth-century cities probably underwent a substantial increase in the course of the urban transition. In Duisburg, yearly rates of immigration and emigration increased from around 3 per cent in the early 1820s to 21 and 19 per cent respectively when industrialization was well on its way at the end of the century, while the total number of persons involved grew from around 400 per year in the 1820s to no less than 15,000 in the 1890s.[62] Not only did absolute volumes of migration increase considerably in the long nineteenth century, then, but so did gross rates of mobility in many cities, and probably also migration rates of the rural population. More people were on the move and more people migrated to cities than ever before, both in absolute and relative terms.[63] That their eventual contribution to urban growth formed only a fraction of urban mobility rates is a powerful indication of the complications that the increased numbers of urban migrants experienced in establishing new and sustainable income cycles.[64] That these 'shock troops and buffers of an erratic and ill-organized labour market'[65] of early industrialization continued to move back and forth between town and country along paths which had been familiar to earlier generations is in itself no indication of the absence of structural change. Although the routes migrants took might have been familiar, their sheer volume, their economic role and their further perspectives became radically altered in the course of the urban transition.

The end result of the reshaping of the economic-geographical structure of town and country in the course of the long nineteenth century has been interpreted by Jan Luiten van Zanden as the establishment of a new economic system, termed 'industrial capitalism'. It differed crucially from the system preceding it in that labour power was now reproduced within the system itself: according to van Zanden, the nineteenth century witnessed a fundamental transition from an 'open' to a 'closed' labour market, in which wages came to cover the cost of the reproduction of labour.[66] Although van Zanden does not elaborate on the implications for the patterns of urban migration that had been one of the recruitment channels of merchant capitalism,[67] the concepts of an open and closed labour market underline the structural transformation which urban recruitment patterns underwent in the course of the urban transition. Somewhere in this process, urban labour recruitment lost its *exchange* nature that was so characteristic of the early modern period, and became less dependent on rural labour reservoirs and more self-sufficient. Van Zanden does not really elaborate on the causes of the observed transition from an open to a closed labour market. As preconditions, he mentions primarily factors enhancing labour productivity on the one hand, such as technological and managerial innovations and the intensification of labour, and factors reducing the reproductive cost of labour on the other, such as improvements in urban sanitary conditions and the increasing dietary importance of potatoes.[68] However, the mere *possibility* of rewarding labour to the value of its reproductive cost does not in itself make this happen.[69] Rather, I would argue that the undermining of previous systems of labour recruitment played a more crucial role in bringing change about.[70] The actual mechanisms by which this transition took place cannot at all be taken as evident, but should be placed in a context of structural and uneven societal transformation at different speeds, during which the earlier balance became not only upset, but structurally invalidated, and whose outcome was by no means clear at the time.

Given the resilience of established migration patterns, it is not surprising that coping strategies would develop along lines which were familiar to earlier generations too. The point is that much of the evolution in migration patterns depended not only on the ways in which, but also on the extent to which established labour cycles were upset. To the extent that migration patterns can be seen as a sunk investment, initial infringements on income opportunities were likely to be countered by an even greater participation in established migration patterns. Thus many seasonal patterns of migration established during the early modern period actually experienced further intensification in the nineteenth century, and new seasonal patterns took shape, before they finally disappeared by the early twentieth century. Only when they became untenable, owing to the economic transformation of both town and country, would these existing patterns be completely abandoned.[71] Conversely, labour shortages in certain seasonal sectors, owing to the undermining of previous temporary labour reservoirs, were often initially met by recruiting more distant seasonal labourers, who in turn often became definitive migrants, as with, for instance, the Irish in England.[72] Both push and pull developments evolved at different speeds, and the rate of change at which existing patterns and strategies could or could not be remoulded to cope with the changing constraints and opportunities depended not only on the extent to which older income cycles were undermined and on the availability of alternative opportunities and spatial connections, but also on the different groups involved. Rural and urban developments alike affected different groups in different ways according to, for instance, income sources, gender, age, schooling and region. While some groups might have abandoned rural–urban exchange patterns for more definitive or at least inter-urban forms of migration at an early stage in the transition, the reflection of this change might well have been eclipsed at the aggregate level by an increase in the participation of other groups in older exchange patterns. The point is, then, that we are not dealing with a gradual transition from one dominant pattern to the other, but with a punctuated transformational development at different speeds. Europe's transition from pre-industrial to industrial society, in other words, was not the result of any linear, gradual or inevitable transition from one system to another, but of a fundamental process of societal transformation engendering destruction and reconstruction, during which old conditions were undermined before new ones were shaped, and whose outcome was by no means self-evident at the time. This context of change at different speeds of course renders any intelligible analysis of changes in patterns of migration an intricate matter, for which a differentiated approach is indispensable. On the other hand, it does make it an extremely interesting field as well, for a thorough insight into migration behaviour in this transformational context enhances the appreciation of human capacity for adaptation in the face of destabilizing macro developments (i.e. the place of agency in transforming structures), and insight into the human dimension of societal change in general.

In sum, then, although recent revisions as regards the novelty of patterns of urban migration during the transition from pre-industrial to industrial society have the merit of highlighting the links with patterns familiar to earlier generations, they have overstated continuity in form as compared to discontinuities in content. The evolution of urban pull and especially rural push forces over the period was such as to undermine structurally the viability of most early modern patterns of labour recruitment, and to call for a fundamental adaptation of existing patterns of urban migration. This adaptation was a costly and difficult affair, in which there were winners and losers, and stayers and leavers. Given that we now know that these patterns of urban migration were no novelty of the 'modern' age but instead built upon existing pathways marked out by earlier generations, questions of continuity and change, of resistance and adaptability, can be recast in a new mould, whereby the actual degree of continuity at an aggregate level does not appear to be the most appropriate or interesting question, but rather the *speeds of change* with which different migrant groups succeeded or not with respect to the changing constraints and opportunities at origin and destination. This book will address these questions from the perspective of one particular case study, that of the city of Antwerp between 1760 and 1860. Both the profundity of social and economic change in this period and the wealth of available source materials make the study of Antwerp's migration flows a particularly instructive way to explore the dynamics of migratory change in the transition from pre-industrial to industrial society. The following two sections will sketch the background of the case study by first outlining the main dynamics of the urban and industrial transitions in the Southern Low Countries, and then briefly introducing the social, economic and demographic evolutions in eighteenth- and nineteenth-century Antwerp.

The Urban and Industrial Transitions in the Southern Low Countries

By the end of the *ancien régime*, the Southern Netherlands could already count on a strong urban tradition. From the late Middle Ages onwards, the region had been characterized by a high degree of urbanization and by the presence of several important urban centres. As early as the end of the fifteenth century, 28 per cent of the population within the boundaries of present-day Belgium lived in cities of more than 5,000 inhabitants, making it one of the most urbanized European regions of the time. At the end of the eighteenth century, this proportion stood at 26 per cent, and with an average of 80 people per square km, the region was among the most densely populated in the area.[73] This apparent continuity in general urban experience, however, masks several important spatial and temporal shifts and differences. Throughout the early modern period, the County of Flanders and the Duchy of Brabant – corresponding more or less to the present-day provinces of East and West Flanders and those of Antwerp and Brabant respectively – had by far the highest levels of urbanization, while today's provinces of Luxemburg, Namur and Limburg remained largely rural, together including less than 5 per cent of all urban dwellers in 1800 yet representing more than a third of the territory of present-day Belgium. With an urban percentage of 30 per cent, today's province of Liège had come to near parity with the County of Flanders and the Duchy of Brabant by 1800, while that of Hainaut occupied the middle ground.[74]

In addition to these spatial differences, several temporal shifts marked the urban tradition of the Southern Low Countries. Whereas late medieval dynamics of urban growth had manifested themselves most strongly in the Flemish towns of Bruges, Ghent and Ypres, by the later fifteenth century the centre of gravity shifted to Brabant, with Antwerp developing as a commercial and industrial epicentre of international trade. At the height of Antwerp's 'golden age' around 1560, its population exceeded 100,000, while 23 per cent of the population of the Southern Low Countries by that time lived in cities of more than 10,000 inhabitants. Yet the turmoil of the Dutch revolt and the Spanish reconquest of the later decades of the sixteenth century brought the urban percentage down to 19 per cent by 1600. With the blockade of the Scheldt by the Dutch

Republic, Antwerp lost its key role in international maritime activity to Amsterdam, and its first rank in the Southern Netherlands to Brussels. While the first half of the seventeenth century signalled an important urban revival, restoring the proportion of large-city dwellers to levels of 21–4 per cent, by the early eighteenth century the Southern Low Countries entered a phase of absolute and relative urban decline. While rural industries proliferated, most urban luxury industries – with the exception of low-paid lace production – dwindled in the face of declining domestic demand, heightened protectionism in neighbouring countries and increased imports, bringing the urban percentage down to 20 per cent by 1750. In the second half of the eighteenth century cities regained in numbers, but this recovery benefited primarily small and medium-sized cities, and was offset by the extensive demographic expansion of the rural population, which further decreased the proportion of large-city inhabitants to 19 per cent in 1800.[75]

While the structural causes of urban expansion and contraction in the Southern Low Countries throughout the early modern period lay with an intricate array of factors influencing relative prices, investment strategies and demand structures, the proximate reasons mainly involved migratory movements. With few cities in the region able to rely on natural increase, the prime factor determining urban growth and decline was the volume and direction of population movement between cities and the countryside.[76] Following the same propositions as de Vries in his calculations on rural–urban migration in pre-industrial Europe, Morsa calculated that the different phases of urban growth in the early-modern Southern Low Countries took up around 10 per cent of all rural births, or between 40 and 113 per cent of the rural birth surplus.[77] Conversely, phases of urban decline were generally associated with sizeable outward flows.[78] By the end of the eighteenth century, when the first census to distinguish immigrants from those born locally was held, the proportion of inhabitants born outside their place of residence was between 25 and 35 per cent for most cities within the Southern Netherlands.[79] It is obvious, however, that this proportion had been substantially higher during earlier and more rapid phases of demographic expansion, such as that of Antwerp in the first half of the sixteenth century.

In the first half of the nineteenth century, the urban population of the Southern Low Countries again grew considerably. The proportion of total population living in cities of more than 5,000 inhabitants increased from around 26 per cent in 1800 to 33 per cent in 1846, making the new Kingdom of Belgium one of the most urbanized countries of mid-nineteenth-century Europe. An important part of this increase, however, reflected the expansion of small towns, while the proportion of people living in cities of more than 10,000 inhabitants – 21 per cent in 1846 – remained comparable to that of earlier phases of urban expansion.[80] A further breakthrough in absolute and relative urbanization was realized in the second half of the century, when the proportion of urban dwellers increased to 52 per cent in 1900, 38 per cent of whom lived in towns of more than 10,000 inhabitants. On the eve of World War I, one in four Belgians lived in one of the five major cities or their mushrooming suburbs.[81] Although urbanization was relatively precocious in nineteenth-century Belgium in comparison to other European countries, it did not radically overturn the structure of urban hierarchies and networks as it did, for instance, in certain regions of England and Germany. Most of the urban growth was accommodated within the already highly urbanized city structure of the early modern period. Those new clusters that did develop, as in the Hainaut region, rather took the shape of conurbations of modest industrial centres than of new industrial growth poles like Manchester, Duisburg or Bochum. Most of the growth of the urban population, then, took place in cities that had already occupied the top of the urban hierarchies during the *ancien régime*. Brussels, Antwerp, Ghent and Liège, which at least from the seventeenth century onwards were the most populous cities in the region, remained highest in the urban classification.[82] This does not imply that no important changes took place in the relationships between cities or between town and country, and in the functions taken up by the respective urban growth poles. It does suggest, however, that these relationships had already had a long history, and that the changes taking place were intertwined with existing traditions.

Notwithstanding important continuities in urban structure and hierarchy, the growth of Belgian urban centres in the long nineteenth century was founded on a new economic basis which was accompanied by a process of urban specialization. Belgium was the first country on the Continent to adapt the new technologies of mechanized production developed in the United Kingdom. In this precocious process of industrialization, the Southern Low Countries were able to build on an important industrial tradition in town and country alike. Mechanization of textile production in Ghent was initiated by Lieven Bauwens's foundation in 1801 of a cotton spinning mill based on English design, and expanded rapidly though not evenly. In the Liège-Verviers region the mechanization of wool production and the development of a diversified heavy iron and steel industry were instigated at the end of the eighteenth century by the entrepreneurial activities of the British engineer William Cockerill and his son. The Borinage in Hainaut had been an important coal-mining region from the seventeenth century onwards, and its annual coal production developed spectacularly after the introduction of modern machinery, especially after the 1840s – when the adjacent region of the Centre also became involved in coal production. In the surroundings of Charleroi, the traditional metal industry became one of the most modernized industries by adopting the production techniques developed in the valley of the Meuse. In the wake of these revolutionary develop-

ments in the production techniques of the secondary sector, Brussels emerged
as the administrative and financial centre of the developing national economy
– although it also retained an important manufacturing sector. Specialization
was much more pronounced in Antwerp, which developed from a regional textile centre into an international gateway for the transportation and distribution
of raw materials, goods and people in the industrializing European and Atlantic
economies.[83]

The sweeping impact of different innovations on the productivity and organization of industrial activity notwithstanding, their overall effect on a national
basis remained relatively limited in the first half of the nineteenth century. By
1846, the year of Belgium's first national population and industrial census,
the 'new industries' of Ghent, Verviers, Liège, Borinage, Centre and Charleroi
together employed at most 100,000 people, or only 2 per cent of the total Belgian population, and 10 per cent of the total industrial workforce.[84] Likewise,
urban growth had been evident, but not spectacular. Between 1800 and 1846,
the four most important urban growth poles, Brussels, Antwerp, Ghent and
Liège, had grown at an average annual rate of between 1.0 and 1.4 per cent.[85] The
majority of the population remained engaged in the same agricultural, proto-
industrial or artisanal activities as their parents and grandparents, and eked out
their living in rural and urban settings which were more or less similar to those of
the eighteenth century.[86] On the other hand, all Belgian regions were confronted
with dynamics of demographic expansion, land concentration (i.e. subdivision)
and increasing proletarianization, which were intensifying pressure on rural
livelihoods. The process was particularly pronounced in the County of Flanders, where population density had increased from around 120 inhabitants per
square km in 1700 to 180 in 1800 and to more than 240 by 1840. This process
of strong rural demographic expansion went hand in hand with a proliferation
of micro-holdings and an increasing reliance on a rural textile (linen) industry as
a complementary or even main source of income for many peasant households,
particularly in the inland regions. Although the eighteenth-century spread of
the potato relieved pressure on rural livelihoods, this proved only a temporary
respite from a structural process of economic transformation.[87]

In the second half of the nineteenth century, the impact of the economic and
industrial change underway would penetrate deeply into rural and urban settings
alike. An important catalyst of change was the crisis of the 1840s, when a collapse
of the cottage linen industry coincided with a series of crop failures in 1844–6 to
undermine dramatically the basis of many rural livelihoods. The rural districts of
East and West Flanders, which in 1840 had still included at least 222,000 spinners and 57,000 weavers in the linen industry, were hardest hit, but other regions
also bore part of the burden. Undernourishment and starvation produced high
levels of surplus mortality in the years during the crisis and its aftermath, and its

long-term impact resulted in a drawn-out process of economic peripheralization of the erstwhile County of Flanders, and of marked rural impoverishment.[88] The dominant contention in Belgian historiography is that the impact of the crisis on patterns of rural–urban migration was relatively limited. With most country dwellers tied to their small plots of land, misery largely remained indoors, and was countered primarily by increasing self-exploitation.[89] Between 1845 and 1850 the recorded migration deficit from the provinces of East and West Flanders, which were hardest hit, was only some 14,000 people out of a total of 1.4 million.[90] Permanent relocation to the expanding cities was moreover not the only migration option open to the impoverished smallholders. A considerable number decided rather to try their luck in the New World, sometimes actively supported by government initiative. Nevertheless, the scale of Belgian Atlantic migration remained modest compared to that from other European countries.[91] Much more popular was the intensification of seasonal patterns of agricultural migration to Hainaut and the bordering regions of northern France, where the urban textile centres also absorbed important numbers of Belgian immigrants – some permanently, but many temporarily.[92] Finally, others commuted to work in the industrializing regions of Wallonia or elsewhere without moving house – an option made possible by the early development of Belgium's dense railway network from 1835 onwards, and which would expand enormously after the creation of a system of government-subsidized rail passes in 1870.[93]

Although it is clear that the crisis of the 1840s did not entail a large-scale rural exodus, however, another strand of research has tended to stress its role as a watershed in the Belgian process of urbanization, and its coincidence with an overall increase in rates of mobility.[94] Likewise, local research has demonstrated that although the proportion of rural dwellers migrating to cities might have been *relatively* modest compared to the total population of Belgium's densely populated countryside, their rising volume in the late 1840s and 1850s did have a profound effect on local demographic and economic structures. While the relative proportions might be considered comparatively modest, an important number of rural residents did end up swelling the expanding cities, and in particular their mushrooming suburbs, in nineteenth-century Belgium.[95] While the combined population of Belgium's four largest cities expanded from 316,000 in 1830 to 772,000 in 1900, the number of people living in municipalities adjacent to these cities leapt from 97,000 to 728,000 over the same period, amounting to an average annual growth rate of 1.3 and 2.9 per cent respectively, implying fundamental transformations in the organization of urban space and a geographic restructuring of economic activity.[96]

Hitherto, no comprehensive study has been made of the demographic dynamics of the Belgian urban transition. Several studies have attempted to address the issues at town level, with the industrial growth poles in the south of the country attracting most attention.[97] Most of these demographic case studies present an image which is on the whole compatible with Jan de Vries's representation of the urban transition as the intertwining of a familiar migration-led growth phase that was carried forward by the demographic transition, aided by immigrants' high birth rates.[98] The varying migration experiences of larger and long-established urban centres have attracted considerably less historical attention, especially as regards the north of the country.[99] Migration to Brussels has been addressed in two important doctoral studies, neither of which, however, was primarily concerned with the relationship between migration and urban economic development: one focused on the impact of migration on social and linguistic relationships within the capital, the other was oriented exclusively towards foreign immigration.[100] Notwithstanding the increasing attention paid to such topics in the international literature, no direct research has been undertaken on the role of urban mobility in the northern regions of Flanders and Brabant during the country's precocious industrial transition. Several studies have dealt with it incidentally, and provide important leads for research,[101] but the overall view of the inter-relationship between migration and the transformation of labour markets in town and country in this geographical area remains obscure.

Although the overall mechanisms of population redistribution still await comprehensive research, it is evident that migration dynamics remained important and often predominant sources of urban growth in Belgium's urban transition in the long nineteenth century. At the same time, it is clear that these migrants' movements cannot be explained solely in relation to increasing push forces, as this cannot explain why so many more stayed put. Rather, the disintegration of rural livelihoods at most increased the likelihood of migration, which materialized in actual migration only in specific instances, in which the developing pull forces at destination must have played an important role too. However tangible the impact of changing push and pull forces, selectivity determined who left and who stayed, and where their migration paths took them when they left. In turn, the economic evolution of Belgium's cities in this period was heavily determined by the number and types of migrants who entered their gates. In these respects, the comparatively modest but nevertheless tangible role of migrations in the process of Belgian urbanization in the first half of the long nineteenth century represents an interesting case by which to analyse the balance between push and pull in migration dynamics, the role of mediating factors at the meso and micro levels, and the balance between continuity and change in a period of uneven societal transformation.

Presenting the Case Study: Migration to Antwerp, 1760–1860

The particular relevance of the Antwerp case in relation to questions of migratory change lies with the profundity of the economic, political, social and demographic transformations which the city and its recruitment regions underwent in the first decades of the nineteenth century, which in turn laid the foundations for the city's further expansion in the second half of the nineteenth century. Between 1760 and 1860 Antwerp was confronted with several important regime changes that continuously reshaped the political and economic space in which the city operated. While the blockade of the Scheldt and the trade policies of the Habsburgs had peripheralized Antwerp's commercial functions by the eighteenth century, the naval ambitions of Napoleon revived the city's maritime potential while it was under French rule (1796–1814). This potential became fully realized under the favourable conditions of Dutch rule (1815–30), and became a matter of prime concern for the liberal-oriented Kingdom of Belgium after 1830. These different regime changes underpinned Antwerp's acute transformation from a middle-sized regional textile centre at the end of the eighteenth century to a booming international port town of more than 100,000 inhabitants by the middle of the nineteenth century. This conversion had profound repercussions on the structure of the urban labour market. Between the censuses of 1796 and 1830, the proportion of the active population involved in the production of consumer durables fell from more than 50 per cent to only 26 per cent, while the proportion involved in trade and services expanded from 33 to 53 per cent to become the main employment of the urban population. The decline in industrial activity was attributable exclusively to the collapse of textile industries: the proportion of textile producers fell from 18 to 4 per cent, while lace work and embroidery fell from 18 to 7 per cent, decimating the absolute number of textile and lace workers from 9,400 in 1796 to just 3,300 in 1830. The fastest growers, on the other hand, were to be found in sectors that were directly or indirectly related to port and service activities, such as construction work, trade and transport, casual labour, office work, retail activities and domestic service.[102]

The consequences of this labour market transformation for the lives of Antwerp's labouring poor have been elaborately and vividly explored by Catharina Lis, whose final conclusions were anything but rosy. Income opportunities for women, children and the elderly were most affected. These lost their main source of employment in the collapse of textile production, while the newly developing port activities held few opportunities other than an unrewarding informal sector of petty trade, services and prostitution. Men fared better at first sight, as the number of male workers in maritime sectors expanded markedly. Most of the new jobs at the docks, shipyards or commercial offices, however, suited only young and able-bodied and/or specialist male workers, which did not necessarily correspond to the profile of erstwhile weavers, silk winders or dyers. Even those who did find work, moreover, were confronted with an increasing irregularity of most employment, making the stability of the family income one of the greatest casualties of Antwerp's conversion to a port town. As almost all expanding sectors were directly or indirectly dependent on trade and shipping, the urban labour market was increasingly governed by the seasonal and cyclical fluctuations in port activity, resulting in a growing irregularity and vulnerability of most jobs in the course of the nineteenth century.[103] Over the same period, the smallholding regions in its immediate hinterland were facing a growing population and increasing proletarianization, resulting in an overall increase of rural push forces. Together with Antwerp's political and economic conversion, these changes would come to alter radically the local opportunity structure for potential migrants.

Antwerp's economic conversion went hand in hand with an uneven demographic expansion. While population remained relatively stagnant at 50,000 inhabitants in the second half of the eighteenth century, a growth spurt set in under French rule, when Antwerp's population reached 60,000 at the time of the 1806 census. A considerable loss of population in the wake of the political turmoil of 1814 brought population figures back to around 50,000 in 1815, which steadily recovered to 55,000 in 1820. The 1820s witnessed the strongest average annual growth rate recorded between any two censuses in the nineteenth century, swelling the city's population to 72,000 by the time of the 1830 census. The unrest of Belgian independence, when the Antwerp port was temporarily blockaded and under siege, again inaugurated a phase of population loss followed by moderate growth, raising numbers to 83,000 inhabitants in the census of 1846. After that, growth picked up at a higher speed, expanding the city's population to 101,000 in 1856, and 117,000 in 1866. Only after 1867 would growth rates again approximate those of the 1820s, in a renewed spurt that would bring the city's total population to more than 250,000 at the turn of the century. The city's 'legal population', as it was recorded in these official census figures, was in turn supplemented by an amalgamate of 'factual' residents who for various reasons were excluded from the population registers, like soldiers, seamen, lodging-house guests or children at boarding schools, who together provided an extra 5,000 residents or so at the time of the different censuses.[104]

Antwerp's uneven process of demographic expansion was occasioned more by changes in net migration figures than by substantial variations in birth and death rates, as can be seen from an analysis of its growth components (Table 2.1). Although the quality of the figures varies, the available year-to-year figures of births and deaths indicate the existence of three different 'natural regimes' during the period under consideration. In the later decades of the eighteenth century, the numbers of deaths more or less outweighed those of births, leaving natural increase alone unable to produce substantial demographic growth – an observation which is in line with general early modern urban demography.[105] During the French regime, mortality surged, yielding a considerable natural deficit. The high numbers of deaths were due to the war conditions and were greatly influenced by the surplus mortality occasioned by the considerable number of wounded soldiers brought to the Antwerp hospitals for treatment.[106] From 1815 onwards, the city embarked on a new natural regime, in which a positive rate of natural increase was occasioned by a decline in mortality in combination with relatively constant birth rates – a development observable in many European regions and cities in that period, but whose causes, timing and scale are still subject to considerable debate.[107] In general, crude birth rates and, in particular, death rates were higher in Antwerp than in Belgium as a whole.[108] Mortality suffered in particular from the ravaging effect of temporary epidemics – the overexposure to which was a distinctive characteristic of many port cities.[109] While the balance between births and death tended to produce a natural surplus of some 500 to 1,000 inhabitants per 'normal' year, this was sometimes reversed dramatically by momentary mortality crises such as the general crisis of 1817, and the cholera epidemics of 1832, 1848/49, 1859 and 1866.

Table 2.1: Components of Population Growth during Inter-Census Periods, 1755–1900 (Annual Averages).[110]

Inter-census period	PC		Births		Deaths		NI		Residual		
	N	Rate (‰)	N	Rate (‰)	N	Rate (‰)	N	Rate (‰)	N	Rate (‰)	% of PC
1755–84	167	3.4	1,707	34.5	1,669	33.8	38	0.8	129	2.6	77
1785–95	-118	-2.3	1,715	33.4	1,695	33.0	20	0.4	-138	-2.7	117
1796–1805	936	17.0	1,904	34.5	2,093	37.9	-189	-3.4	1,124	20.4	120
1806–15	-800	-14.3	2,323	41.5	3,046	54.5	-723	-12.9	-77	-1.4	10
1816–20	723	13.4	2,174	40.4	1,896	35.2	278	5.2	445	8.3	62
1821–9	1,797	28.4	2,389	37.8	1,888	29.8	501	7.9	1,296	20.5	72
1830–9	690	9.2	2,389	31.8	2,164	28.8	224	3.0	466	6.2	68
1840–6	590	7.3	2,617	32.4	1,969	24.4	648	8.0	-58	-0.7	-10
1847–56	1,398	14.7	3,185	33.4	2,524	26.5	661	6.9	737	7.7	53
1857–66	2,081	18.5	3,910	34.7	3,334	29.6	577	5.1	1,505	13.4	72
1867–80	3,627	24.7	5,530	37.7	3,979	27.1	1,551	10.6	2,076	14.1	57
1881–90	5,113	25.8	7,502	37.8	4,797	24.2	2,705	13.6	2,408	12.1	47
1891–1900	4,961	19.9	7,907	31.7	5,064	20.3	2,843	11.4	2,118	8.5	43

Abbreviations: PC: Population change; NI: Natural increase. The last column measures the contribution of the 'residual' to the observed change in population size.

Although natural increase rates did rise in the first half of the nineteenth century, they came nowhere near explaining the observed rate of Antwerp's growth during most of the period. The available demographic figures indicate that the 'residual' – i.e. that part of net growth which is not explained by natural increase, and is hence attributable to net migration – proved a more important contribution to growth than did natural increase. Even when we allow for a flexible interpretation of the unavoidably imprecise figures, it is clear that the importance of net migration – which amounted up to 2 per cent per annum – was far greater than the rate of natural increase, which at best fluctuated around 0.5 per cent. The contribution of net migration was particularly important in times of rapid population expansion, such as the French regime and during the demographic spurt of the 1820s. Periods of demographic contraction, such as the transition from French to Dutch rule, were in turn characterized by negative residual figures, hinting at the importance of net *emigration* in certain phases. Only after 1880, when natural increase rates reached levels of over 1 per cent per annum, would this component become predominant in Antwerp's renewed growth phase. Between 1760 and 1860, however, shifts in net migration were the prime determinant of the ups and downs in the evolution of the Antwerp population size.

Net migration figures tell only a very small part of the migration story. To investigate shifts in migration regime over time, it is necessary to take into account the gross figures of immigration and emigration, of which net migration figures are only the residual. Unfortunately, data on immigration and emigration are generally less readily available and reliable than on births and deaths, because migration registration was much less a tradition than the recording of life events, and because migration data entailed more ambiguities in interpretation. The specific context of the Antwerp sources has, however, provided us with a relatively continuous series of yearly immigration figures from 1806 onwards. These can be compared with the calculated figures of net migration to provide an estimate of emigration volumes (immigration minus net migration), gross mobility figures (the sum of immigration and emigration), persistence ratios (net migration as a proportion of immigration) and migration yields (net migration as a proportion of gross mobility) (Table 2.2). Although the exactness of the calculations is complicated by changes in registration zeal and method of the city authorities, the main trends are manifest enough to indicate important shifts in migration regime during the period under consideration.

Table 2.2: Immigration Yields during Inter-Census Periods, 1806–90 (Annual Averages).[111]

Inter-census period	Immigration		Net migration		Gross mobility		Persistence	Yield
	N	Rate (‰)	N	Rate (‰)	N	Rate (‰)	%	%
1806–15	2,160	38.6	-77	-1.4	4,397	78.6	-4	-2
1816–20	1,614	30.0	445	8.3	2,783	51.7	28	16
1821–9	2,285	36.1	1,296	20.5	3,274	51.8	57	40
1830–46	1,830	23.7	254	3.3	3,406	44.2	14	7
1847–56	4,445	48.6	737	7.7	8,153	85.5	17	9
1857–66	6,300	57.9	1,505	13.4	11,096	98.5	24	14
1866–80	8,480	60.2	2,076	14.1	14,885	101.4	24	14
1880–90	12,841	66.0	2,408	12.1	23,273	117.4	19	10

The evolution of gross immigration figures was characterized by five main phases. Although precise figures are absent for the earlier period, available data suggest that the yearly inflow did not in any case exceed the figure of 1,500 during the later decades of the eighteenth century, i.e. the equivalent of 3 per cent of total population at the very most. Second, in the later Napoleonic era, recorded (civilian) immigration reached high levels of around 2,500 per year, even peaking to 3,300 in the top year of 1811, while combined with military newcomers the real volume of immigration probably reached levels of up to 4,000 or even 5,000 in peak years. After a steep drop in the early Dutch period, numbers rose again to reach figures of over 2,500 in the 1820s, or the equivalent of around 4 per cent of the urban population. A fourth phase, from 1830 to the middle of the 1840s, was marked by a sharp drop in immigration in the dramatic years immediately following independence, and an only moderate recovery to an average of around 2,000 per year by the early 1840s. Finally, immigration experienced a dramatic upsurge in the later 1840s, reaching yearly recorded levels of over 5,000 per year for most of the 1850s – or up to 5 per cent of the urban population – up to 6,500 or 6 per cent in the early 1860s, and higher still in subsequent decades.

High levels of immigration, however, did not necessarily imply high levels of net migration. Net migration figures were, for instance, significantly greater in the 1820s than in the later 1840s, 1850s and 1860s, although total immigration figures were substantially smaller. These differences indicate that the level of *emigration* mattered at least as much as the level of immigration in determining the eventual contribution of migration to Antwerp's demographic growth. Although the identities of Antwerp's emigrants are largely unknown, the majority were undoubtedly former immigrants.[112] High emigration rates and low persistence rates, like in the 1850s or 1860s, therefore indicate a large degree of turnover among newcomers and relatively shorter lengths of stay, while high persistence rates, as in the 1820s, point towards longer lengths of stay. Migrants' length of stay rather than the mere number coming in, therefore, appears to have been the prime determinant of the evolution of net migration levels: after having shot up from 22 per cent in 1796 to 33 per cent in 1830, the proportion of migrants within the Antwerp population remained at that level right through to the 1866 census, and this notwithstanding the explosion of gross migration rates in the latter decades.[113]

When abstraction is made of the exceptional war context of the French regime and the temporary fallback after independence, the general tendency over the period under consideration was clearly towards increasing levels of mobility, which would set the stage for decades to come. Where the number of yearly moves in and out of the city equalled only around 5 per cent of total population size before mid-century, it increased to the equivalent of no less than 10 per cent of Antwerp's population by the period 1857–66, and would further increase to levels of more than 12 per cent in later decades. Migration yields went down over the same period, from up to 40 per cent in the 1820s to only 10 per cent by mid-century, at which level it would remain throughout the nineteenth century. By mid-century, gross mobility and net migration rates in Antwerp had risen to levels which were comparable with those of Amsterdam and Rotterdam in the last quarter of the nineteenth century, when these cities likewise went through a phase of economic transformation, demographic expansion and rising gross mobility rates.[114] On the other hand, they remained significantly below the record mobility rates recorded in rapidly urbanizing and industrializing centres such as Duisburg at the end of the century, where gross mobility attained levels of more than 40 per cent – confirming the fundamental difference in growth patterns between long-established cities and mushrooming industrial centres in the long nineteenth century. Although nineteenth-century Antwerp could evidently build on a long history as a sizeable urban centre with an important migration tradition, the overall trend was a considerable increase in mobility and turnover, which must have had important effects on urban society and the experience of migration alike. The observed shifts concerning the quantitative and demographic aspects of migration behaviour indicate that important qualitative changes in migration patterns and experiences were taking place over this period. To analyse these dynamics of migratory change adequately, a long-term perspective was deemed essential. The chronological focus of research therefore starts early enough to bring into view patterns of migration in the second half of the eighteenth century when Antwerp was still a regional textile centre. At the other end, the time focus is extended until the 1860s, so as to explore the influence not only of Antwerp's conversion to a nineteenth-century port town, but also of the acceleration of societal change wrought by the crisis of the 1840s.

This proposed long-term perspective is only feasible because of an exceptionally rich array of sources that provide us with oblique and sometimes more direct views of patterns of migration to Antwerp from the mid-eighteenth to the mid-nineteenth centuries. Two contexts in particular have provided useful sources for the present study: general population registration and records from institutions related to poor relief. For Antwerp as for many places in the region, the later eighteenth and early nineteenth centuries constitute the earliest period in which more or less systematic records of population registration are available.[115] Moves towards an increasing mapping and registering of society were evident in earlier periods and regimes, but they gained momentum in the closing decades of the *ancien régime*,[116] when they became incorporated and consolidated in an extensive 'registration offensive' in the wake of the French Revolution, which benefited from the strong ambitions and efforts of the developing state bureaucracy.[117] The crux of post-revolutionary French registration policy was that any person in the state should be identified and associated with a local *commune* (country or city municipality). This was to be accomplished by the compulsory registration of the resident population by the local authorities, the obligation to carry various proofs of identity and residence when leaving home, and the compulsory declaration of temporary guests or new residents to the local authorities.[118]

Antwerp's status as a prime naval base meant that French endeavours in the domain of population registration were pursued with particular vigour, establishing administrative practices that would be maintained and further improved under the Dutch and Belgian regimes. Early nineteenth-century source materials attest to the carrying out of different censuses in 1796, 1800, 1806, 1815 and 1830, of which those of 1800, 1815 and 1830 were used as a basis for dynamic population registers.[119] The registers of *l'état civil* were set up from 1796 onwards as successors to the earlier parish registers, recording the births, marriages and deaths occurring in each municipality.[120] Fragmentary registers of passports, several hotel and visa registers, and a summary emigration roll attest to the diligence with which new instructions on the registration of mobility were implemented in the Antwerp case, yet these unfortunately contain relatively little information about the migrant or the motives for travelling.[121] Of far greater importance, however, was the establishment of a continual and voluminous series of 'registers of residence cards', which originally went from at least 1803 to 1846, but complete registers of which have been conserved only for the periods 1803–20 and 1828–30.[122] By keeping a record of the basic characteristics of all newcomers who received a residence card from the urban authorities, including name, age, place of birth, occupation, address and sometimes also last place of residence and date and destination of re-departure, these registers offer a privileged and exceptional view of the dynamics of *gross* urban immigration at an early date. They were not prescribed by any recorded national legislation, and I have found no reference to similar sources of a comparative scope conserved elsewhere.[123]

The origin of these 'residence card registers' appears traceable to the practice of providing the Antwerp population with *cartes de sûreté* ('security cards') in the late eighteenth century, which originally functioned as local identity documents to facilitate greater police control.[124] When the obligation to carry security cards was abolished for the population as a whole, the system appears to have been maintained for immigrants only.[125] We can think of many advantages that a selective continuation of local identity documents had from the perspective of the town administration. Obliging all newcomers upon arrival to apply for a *carte de sûreté*, later more appropriately called *permis de séjour* ('residence permit'), satisfied in one policy instrument many of the requirements imposed by different strands of legislation regarding the *police des étrangers*, such as the registration of overnight guests and the special monitoring of non-nationals in

port cities. At the same time, it avoided difficult and rather arbitrary classifications between temporary and definitive immigrants, and absolved the urban
administration from recording, following and deleting some of the most volatile
and transient groups in the unwieldy population books. In practice, the registers
of *cartes de sûreté / permis de séjour* (from here on referred to as 'residence cards')
therefore functioned as an intermediary annex to the population registers with
a *de facto* very broad conception of immigration.[126] Only after spending some
time in the city were holders of a temporary card 'transferred to the population
registers'. Alternatively, they were provided with a new passport if they left town
again.[127] From practice it is clear, however, that somewhere along the way a second administrative route was established for newcomers, by which they could
be enrolled directly in the population registers without first passing through
the residence card registers.[128] Unfortunately, the criteria on the basis of which
a choice was made between the two possible administrative procedures for newcomer registration are not at all clear.[129] The result is that the residence card
registers of the 1820s were less comprehensive as an 'immigration register' than
their earlier counterparts had been, both in theory and in practice, and recorded
only between two thirds and three quarters of all immigrants who presented
themselves to the local authorities.[130] Although most later registers have been
lost, residence cards appear to have remained in use until 1846,[131] when comprehensive Belgian legislation on the organization of ten-yearly censuses and the
maintenance of population registers made them obsolete.[132] Symptomatic of the
growing importance of national over local definitions of belonging, the function
of the earlier residence card registers was partially taken over by the *Bulletins
des étrangers*, which only covered non-national newcomers.[133] In Antwerp, these
'information sheets' on newly arriving non-nationals who wished to stay in town
for a while form a continual and voluminous series of aliens' records from 1840
onwards.[134] Although their definition of newcomer is more limited, the information recorded is more elaborate than in the residence card registers, and provides
useful insight into the backgrounds of foreign newcomers.

Apart from changes in normative scope, the eventual usefulness of the different sources produced in the context of increasing population registration,
from censuses and population registers over residence card registers and aliens'
records, ultimately depends on the extent to which people felt compelled to
observe identification requirements and to inform the relevant authorities of
their whereabouts. Although the establishment of the French secular registration regime met with initial resistance in the Southern Netherlands,[135] broad
segments of the Antwerp population appear to have become accustomed to
the new administrative practices from an early date – aided by a relatively well-
endowed administrative and repressive apparatus,[136] and by the fact that several
entitlements, such as access to poor relief or suffrage, became conditional on a

well-attested (i.e. registered) stay.[137] The relatively broad and early compliance with the Antwerp registration regime is further attested by the high numbers that passed through its administration – with for instance more than 30,000 newcomers recorded in the residence card registers between 1803 and 1819 alone. Does this mean that the resulting registers and sources are exhaustive? That they are a 'mirror of reality'? Of course not – they are not even today.[138] However comprehensive in relative terms, registration in Antwerp suffered from flaws, incompleteness and biases – some identifiable, others not. Women in particular were often treated with ambiguity in registration legislation, and in some cases were explicitly exempt, as were domestic servants.[139] Likewise, soldiers, prisoners, and sailors temporarily at anchor in the Antwerp port were generally excluded from civilian registration procedures, and often remain hidden from the sources it produced.[140] Emigration registration also suffered from marked under-reporting compared to that of arrival, an imbalance continued even in recent history.[141] Although demonstrably incomplete, however, population registration – and in particular immigration registration – provided a remarkably broad coverage in Antwerp from a relatively early date, and was complete, broad and continuous enough for its sources to offer at least an indicative view of continuities and changes in population composition and turnover for an extended period of time, with some caveats where necessary.

A second area of source production that was particularly relevant for research was that of poor relief and settlement. In the Southern Low Countries as in other European regions, poor relief was essentially organized on a local basis, and a sundry body of formal and less formal rules determined which parish or municipality counted as a person's 'settlement' and was responsible for relief in case of need.[142] In the course of the first half of the nineteenth century, the conditions for acquiring a new settlement became more standardized and more stringent, from one year's residence under the French regime, to four consecutive years in 1818, and eight years in 1845, when non-nationals became barred altogether from establishing settlement.[143] This legislative evolution produced many interesting sources, of which settlement examinations were the most relevant in the context of this research. Taken from non-settled poor upon their application for relief, these examinations recorded all the information deemed necessary to establish one's place of settlement, including the residential history of the sojourner in question, and of his or her parents, spouse and children. Three volumes recording such settlement information on non-settled poor and dating from before 1860 were retrieved, two of which pertained to non-national (1844–58) and Belgian (1854–9) applicants for outdoor relief respectively, the other one to non-national patients of the city hospital of St Elisabeth (1850–5).[144] Inevitably, the life stories contained in these sources are selective, among other things owing to the stringent criteria for relief operated by the Antwerp

Charity Office,[145] and therefore biased towards a relatively permanent and vulnerable subsection of immigrants, often in a medium or advanced phase of family formation. As such, these settlement examinations provide a privileged if biased view of migration trajectories and integration patterns in the longer run. The settlement examinations with regard to patients of the St Elisabeth hospital display less of the administrative predispositions towards long-resident families, as intake to the city hospital was in principle open to all the indisposed except children, and illness was frequent in the unhealthy and unsanitary conditions of most people's lives.[146] Although biased towards the proletarian and lower middle-class sections of the population, the patients of the St Elisabeth hospital were relatively representative of the city's labouring population as a whole. Hence, the hospital admission lists, a continual series from 1804 onwards mentioning patients' place of birth alongside name, age, address and details of treatment, and containing several thousand entries each year, likewise form a useful source by which to map changes in the geographical origin of Antwerp's growing population. Moreover, these lists bring into view certain 'coincidental' passers-by, who would never have turned up in census results or even in migration statistics, such as ship's passengers and crew members struck by illness before or while mooring in Antwerp.[147]

In all, local, provincial and national archives have produced a variety of sources in which it is possible to look for migrants during the period on which this study concentrates. At the same time, the existing doctoral studies by Jos De Belder, Juul Hannes and Catharina Lis provided essential and invaluable contextual and cross-sectional information on, among other things, the censuses of 1796 and 1830, allowing me to concentrate my archival research on more dynamic sources on migration.[148] Because my research questions concentrated on uncovering (changes in) migration flows, sources concentrating on the arrival (and, to a lesser extent, departure) of various types of migrants were favoured over those yielding a more selective view of long-term stayers. Even so, the sheer volume of available materials necessitated further selections and samples. Taken together, I have retrieved detailed and less detailed information on a total of 23,000 migrants between 1760 and 1860, clustered around three periods.[149] A first cluster of data on around 5,500 immigrants was compiled from the 1796 census sheets to uncover patterns of migration when Antwerp was still a regional textile centre. A second set of data on 8,500 newcomers was collected from the immigration registers from 1808–19 and 1828–30, from the population registers of the same period, and from the emigration registers and hospital admission lists of 1829, in order to explore patterns of migratory change during the acute transformations that Antwerp underwent during the first three decades of the nineteenth century. Finally, a variety of source materials dating from the early 1850s, from aliens' records to hospital admission lists, population registers, settlement examinations and emigration registers, was explored with an eye to evaluating the long-term impact of Antwerp's conversion as well as the consequences of the crisis of the 1840s, which resulted in another 9,000 nominal entries on migrants in this period. Various published reports in addition provided useful aggregate background information on, for instance, the composition of the census population or the yearly number of recorded immigrants and emigrants.[150] Of course, the combination of very different types of source materials in different periods poses important problems of comparison and interpretation, while each of the sources used entails specific historical-critical problems of its own. Given adequate attention to the possible distortions and interpretation problems, however, the empirical diversity of the materials used also forms an important asset in mapping the diversity and heterogeneity of migration flows and experiences over the period under consideration.

There are many questions which a town-centred case study cannot answer, such as the precise role of household situations at origin in influencing the decision to migrate, or the interrelationship between urban and alternative migration destinations. There are other questions, however, for which the chosen perspective is particularly appropriate and relevant. First and foremost, the Antwerp case provides an excellent opportunity to explore the balance between adjustment and resilience in nineteenth-century patterns of urban migration, i.e. to gauge the extent to which the evolution and adjustment of migration patterns was shaped by the limits of their previous history. The long-term perspective in the Antwerp case allows us to examine to what extent, why and for how long pre-existing migration connections influenced urban migration flows in the radically altered economic context of the nineteenth century. As such, the case provides an important insight into the relationship between changing labour supply and demand factors on the one hand (macro level), and social networks, migration information channels and social custom on the other hand (meso level), in shaping the reality and adaptability of migration patterns. At the same time, it sheds light on the contribution of migrants to urban paths of demographic growth and economic transformation in the long nineteenth century, on the balance between push and pull forces associated with migrants' moves, and on the role of immigrant heterogeneity in producing different patterns of adaptation. The city's conversion from a regional textile centre to an international port entailed very different costs and benefits for older women than for young men, for trained weavers than for skilled shipbuilders, and for farmer's daughters than for educated clerks. Analysing the internal heterogeneity of immigrant groups is therefore vital to contextualizing push and pull forces, and to understanding the dynamics of change. By assessing their different speeds of change in an analytical framework which brings together the three determining factors – macro conditions, meso channels and micro characteristics – the

Antwerp case study can shed further light on the relationship between structure and agency, between the past and the future, and between the costs and gains of societal transformation.

3 MIGRATION TO A REGIONAL TEXTILE
CENTRE, 1760–1800

By the middle of the eighteenth century, Antwerp had lost virtually all of its sixteenth-century splendour as a mercantile centre in the developing world economy. The closure of the Scheldt by the Dutch had thwarted international commercial activities, and the passage from Spanish to Austrian rule had further closed off privileged participation in the Spanish colonial trade. The urban luxury industries that had flourished in the seventeenth century under impulse of the counter-reformation had dwindled in the early eighteenth century in the face of declining domestic demand, greater protectionism in neighbouring countries and increased imports. Those merchant families who had remained in Antwerp had undergone a process of gentrification and almost completely retreated from active commercial activities. Their extensive family fortunes were invested in public loans, company shares and foreign undertakings rather than in direct commercial or industrial investments. In the second half of the eighteenth century, a few such families engaged in setting up capital-intensive industries in Antwerp, such as sugar-refining and cotton-printing, but they remained the exception. The dominant trend was an expansion of low-wage, labour-intensive textile industries on a putting-out basis, producing relatively cheap goods for a mainly domestic market. The most successful branches, such as lace manufacture and the production of mixed fabrics, were those that could most directly exploit the reservoir of cheap child and female labour which the impoverished Antwerp workers provided in ample quantity.[1] The expansion of low-wage textile production further increased the social polarization characterized by a small but extremely wealthy upper class and a very large poor population. By 1796 only 14 per cent of the city's population could be considered wealthy, while only another 21 per cent could rely on some form of independent resources alongside income from labour. In turn, no less than two-thirds of the population consisted of poor and propertyless labourers and servants.[2]

Existing census figures indicate that Antwerp's population remained relatively stable throughout the second half of the eighteenth century at a level of around 50,000 inhabitants. This stagnation deviated from the overall popula-

tion increase with which most towns and cities in the Austrian Netherlands
recovered from the urban crisis of the first half of the century – a population
increase that was particularly marked in small market towns. The underlying
basis of this re-urbanization process of the second half of the eighteenth century
has been identified with an increased demand for non-agricultural goods and
services by urban and rural elites, driven by an agrarian upswing and the proliferation of commercial networks. That Antwerp profited comparatively little
from the process has been attributed primarily to its industrial base and its relative geographical isolation. The preponderance of low-wage textile employment
implied that local demand was depressed by rising food prices, while Antwerp's
Campine hinterland, the most isolated and underdeveloped agricultural region
in the Duchy of Brabant, remained relatively unaffected by the general rise in
agricultural prices and rents. Austrian transit trade policies, moreover, favoured
the development of ports in the County of Flanders and of paved transport
routes passing through the south of the Duchy of Brabant, so that Antwerp was
situated at the periphery of the modest commercial revival of the late eighteenth
century.[3]

Within the existing demographic context, urban decline and recovery took
place primarily through changes in the scale and direction of migration flows.
While net flows from the countryside to towns had come to a virtual standstill
and were even reversed during Brabant's urban crisis of the first half of the century, after 1750 growing numbers of rural inhabitants again started to migrate to
towns and cities.[4] The limited extent of Antwerp's demographic recovery implies
that the city exerted only a modest appeal to migrants compared with most
other urban centres in the area. Exploring the reasons for this comparatively
weak appeal presupposes two separate questions: one is why comparatively few
migrants came to Antwerp (or in other words, why many did not), the other is
what motivated those few who did come. This chapter addresses both questions
by exploring the backgrounds and trajectories of Antwerp's late-eighteenth-century migrants in relation to the urban opportunity structure.

Paths to the City

Before the census of 1796, no historical sources exist to tell us about the volume
and character of migration to Antwerp in its totality. The only partial indications
available on the evolution of migration patterns to Antwerp are the 'burgher
books', in which newly granted citizenships were recorded, and which are conserved in a more or less continual series from 1533 to 1795. Unless a newcomer
married an Antwerp burgher, he (or she) had to pay a certain sum to become a
fully-fledged *poorter*, a status of privileged resident which bestowed certain legal
and fiscal liberties and required them, for instance, to become a guild master or

independent trader. Evidently, only a specific selection of immigrants was able and willing to pay the necessary fee. As an indication of year-to-year fluctuations in migration patterns, the 'burgher books' are highly inadequate, not only because of their selective nature, but also because the time of status acquisition did not necessarily correspond to the time of arrival, and yearly fluctuations were strongly influenced by changes in the conditions of acquisition and by political circumstances.[5] Overall trends in the volume and origin of new *poorters* from the sixteenth to the eighteenth centuries, as outlined by Verbeemen's research, do however provide valuable pointers to the evolution of Antwerp's migration field in the long run. His analysis shows a steady decline in the number of new citizenships, from an average of three hundred per year at the height of Antwerp's 'golden' sixteenth century, to an all-time low of around forty by the first quarter of the eighteenth century. Thereafter, a modest revival set in, which raised the average number of new burghers to eighty-four per year in the second half of the eighteenth century. The recruitment area of new burghers shrank considerably and consistently between 1585 and 1795. Whereas in the sixteenth and early seventeenth centuries the majority of new burghers had come from distant regions *beyond* the borders of the Duchy of Brabant, by the eighteenth century this tendency had been reversed. By 1750 almost four in five new citizens came from no further afield than the erstwhile Duchy of Brabant, i.e. today's provinces of Antwerp, Brabant and North Brabant, and more than half came from within the province of Antwerp itself.[6] The reduced range of new burghers' recruitment in the second half of the eighteenth century is confirmed by more recent analyses of the burgher books for this period, which describe an overwhelmingly regional recruitment from east of the city.[7]

While the register of new citizens provides broad indications of the evolution of Antwerp's migration field between the sixteenth and eighteenth centuries, the census of 1796 is the first comprehensive source to dig deeper into the how and why of Antwerp's comparatively weak appeal. As this was the first census ever to record both birthplace and year of immigration, next to name, address, age and marital status, it allows us to reconstruct the urban migration field, to examine patterns of labour market segmentation, and explore a dynamic view of the life and labour cycles of the migrants involved.[8] The census data on migrants' birthplaces confirm the protracted nature of Antwerp's migration field as indicated by the burgher books. Almost one in two immigrants (48 per cent) from the census sample was born within the boundaries of today's province of Antwerp, and another quarter (26 per cent) came from today's provinces of Brabant (13 per cent) and North Brabant (12 per cent), yielding a total of almost three in four (73 per cent) immigrants originating from within the erstwhile boundaries of the Duchy of Brabant.[9] Today's provinces of Dutch and Belgian Limburg each provided 4.5 per cent, and East Flanders another 4 per cent. Migrants from further regions were limited in number and typically came from specific centres, such as Liège, Namur, Rotterdam and Amsterdam. In all, only 17 per cent came from centres classified as large cities, most of them from within the Brabantine region.[10] In turn, rural-born immigrants supplied the lion's share (65 per cent) of Antwerp's immigrants in 1796. Setting the number of migrants from one particular *commune* against the total number of inhabitants in that municipality provides a measure of the *intensity* of Antwerp-bound migration – i.e. the average probability that residents of a particular place would move to Antwerp – which in turn provides an oblique view of the city's demographic basin.[11] The result of the exercise is to accentuate the eastern position, with regard to the city, of Antwerp's prime recruitment area (Map 3.1). Immigration from regions west of the River Scheldt was very limited, while the city's appeal to the south was weak beyond the River Rupel. That the Scheldt proved a true barrier to Antwerp's attraction depended more on political and economic structures than on plain geography. The century-long continued role of the Scheldt as the physical boundary between the two most important political entities in the region – the County of Flanders and the Duchy of Brabant – is a prime factor in explaining the limited exchange of people (and goods) which took place across the river in the late eighteenth century. Economic and political interaction between the two entities was very limited, creating a far greater social distance between the east and west banks of the Scheldt than that produced by mere geography. Moreover, the Waasland region immediately opposite Antwerp on the west bank was one of relatively productive agriculture combined with an important industrial activity, both in the countryside and in the region's main centre, Sint-Niklaas. This availability of diverse income-sources tempered overall mobility in the region, much as in Flanders as a whole, where – especially in the inland areas – rural linen production was strongly developed and rural mobility rates were below average.[12] Likewise, the marked dilution of Antwerp's southern recruitment area beyond the Rupel was undoubtedly due to the competing influence of Brussels and the minor competition from Mechelen, but possibly also because of lower levels of out-migration from these areas, where agriculture was relatively productive and diverse.[13]

Antwerp's main recruitment area thus lay to the east of the city, and stretched into the south-eastern and western parts of the Dutch province of North Brabant to the north, and to the Dijle River in the south. The upper part of this recruitment area corresponded to a geographic region of sandy infertile soils located between the vale of the Scheldt, the Demer, the river-clay areas in the northwest of North Brabant, and the valley of the Meuse. This Campine/Peel region was a relatively outstretched but thinly populated area covered by heathlands and moors, and characterized by small-scale subsistence agriculture. Cities were sparse and situated towards the boundaries. The only urban centre of impor-

Map 3.1: Migration Intensity per Municipality of Birth, 1796 (%).[14]

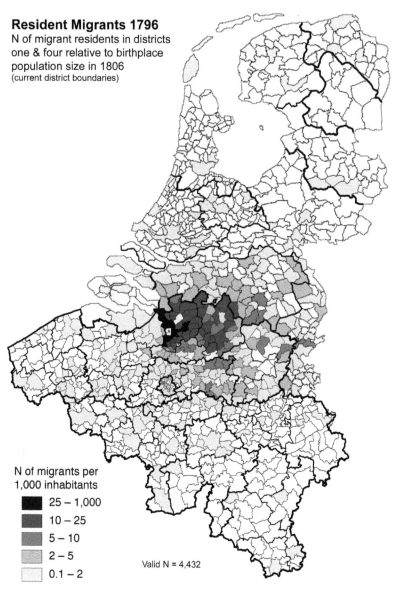

Resident Migrants 1796
N of migrant residents in districts
one & four relative to birthplace
population size in 1806
(current district boundaries)

N of migrants per
1,000 inhabitants

- 25 – 1,000
- 10 – 25
- 5 – 10
- 2 – 5
- 0.1 – 2

Valid N = 4,432

tance within the area was the regional centre of Turnhout with around 10,000
inhabitants in 1800, which might have functioned as a gateway for some of the
Campine migrants to Antwerp, especially from the north and east.[15] Many parts
of the Campine region were still wasteland in 1834, and the average land rent
in 1846 in the district of Turnhout amounted to less than half that for the more

fertile soils in the southern Brabant district of Nivelles.[16] Manufacturing activity was limited, domestic and mostly intended for local use. Only in the north-east of today's Antwerp province were a handful of proto-industrial villages engaged in export-oriented textile production, in particular of linen and woollen goods,[17] while proto-industry was somewhat more widespread in the *Meierij* (bailiwick) of Den Bosch in North Brabant, with the development of wool spinning and weaving near Tilburg, and the production of mixed linen-cotton fabrics in the area of Eindhoven.[18] The relative backwardness of the area was reinforced by its peripheral and cross-border location within the political structures of the Austrian Netherlands and the Dutch Republic, and the limited transport links available.[19] To the south of this Campine/Peel region another recruitment area stretched east of the Dijle River and was crossed by the Gete River, covering the eastern part of lower Brabant – known as Hageland – and an adjacent area in the south of Limburg. This Dijle-Demer-Gete region formed a link between the infertile sandy soils in the Campine region, and the fertile loess areas in the northern Walloon areas. Although land here was generally of a somewhat better quality than in the Campine area, most soils remained relatively infertile, especially in the northern part of the belt.[20] Even more markedly than in the Campine areas, rural industrial activities were virtually non-existent here. The rural areas concentrated on agriculture and were dominated by small-scale peasant families who often combined the cultivation of a small plot of land with limited cattle breeding, fruit tree cultivation and the picking of pine cones to fill out their pluri-active labour cycles. In many respects, the income activities of peasants from the Dijle-Demer-Gete region showed strong resemblances to the marginal labour cycles of their Campine counterparts.[21]

Transport links clearly played an important part in structuring Antwerp's migration field, both as routes for travelling and as transmission channels for migration information. Established land and water links were particularly important as catalysts for recruitment from more distant regions. The Dijle-Demer-Gete region, for instance, was connected to Antwerp not only via the Gete and Demer rivers, but also via the paved main road which connected Antwerp with Liège and which passed through Sint-Truiden, Tienen, Leuven and Mechelen. Because of the specificities of transport links, most Hageland centres were in fact better connected in a northern direction than east to west.[22] For Flemish recruitment from beyond the adjacent Waasland, the triad of Leie, Schelde and Dender rivers formed important migration channels, while the paved main road to Ghent via Sint-Niklaas also appears to have stimulated movement towards Antwerp. In the south of Brabant, the River Senne and the Willebroek canal connecting Brussels with the Scheldt provided routes for a number of Antwerp's immigrants. Further to the north-east, the Meuse River also facilitated Antwerp-directed migration, possibly via an intermediary stop in Maastricht or Liège. While transport connections to the east were under-developed – only in 1819 were Antwerp and Turnhout connected by a paved road – migrants from the city's immediate surroundings could make use of a multidirectional yet short-ranging network of paved roads connecting Antwerp with its direct hinterland.[23] Antwerp's main recruitment area, then, consisted of the sparsely populated, infertile and underdeveloped regions east of the city, complemented by a more distant range of regional and national centres such as Maastricht, Roermond, Ghent, Liège and Amsterdam, which were connected to Antwerp via inter-urban transport routes. Connected to Antwerp by distinct circuits, different regions supplied different types of migrants: short-distance migrants were mainly rural-born, with a preponderance of females, while more distant circuits recruited more townspeople and more men (see below, Graph 4.2). The larger the proportion of townspeople among a given regional contingent, moreover, the more likely it was that their country-born counterparts had not come to Antwerp directly, but via another city or town closer to home.[24]

The restricted size of Antwerp's migration field in the second half of the eighteenth century compares poorly with the international allure it had had in previous centuries or with the recruitment range of cities of comparable size in other countries, such as eighteenth-century Bordeaux.[25] In the context of eighteenth-century Brabant, however, neither the rural nor the regional characteristics of the city's migration field were exceptional. Even the capital city of Brussels recruited the majority of its new burghers from within a range of 20 km in the second half of the eighteenth century, and in Leuven the median birthplace distance of new burghers was only 15 km; figures against which a median birthplace distance of 41 km among Antwerp's immigrant residents compares relatively favourably.[26] That Antwerp's spatial pull was larger than for other Brabantine centres can be attributed to the economic-geographical specificities of the city's location at the western boundary of a relatively outstretched and 'empty' region at the periphery of the Northern and Southern Netherlands, where urban competition was low. That most of its immigrant residents were born in hinterland villages was a characteristic shared with other Brabantine centres, and which confirms that the main source of the re-urbanization process of the second half of the eighteenth century was an increased inflow of migrants from nearby rural regions.[27] Likewise, the fact that most of Antwerp's immigrants were female was a characteristic which the city shared with most other towns in the Austrian Netherlands, as with many early modern regional centres in general, and which is generally related to the importance of female employment in the service sectors, in particular in domestic service.[28]

Although Antwerp's migration field was comparatively large, the net supply of immigrants remained substantially below that of other cities in the Duchy of Brabant, where immigrants made up 34–41 per cent of the population older than 12 recorded in the 1796 census.[29] At 27 per cent, even if somewhat under-recorded, Antwerp's proportion of immigrants was comparable to that of the Flemish city of Ghent and close to that of Sint-Niklaas.[30] The latter two cities, however, were situated in the middle of one of the most sedentary regions of the Southern Netherlands, whose immobile character was reflected in low rural migration rates, and was attributable to the prevalence of rural linen indus-tries.[31] A similar stay-at-home outlook in the surrounding countryside cannot be invoked as an explanation for Antwerp's low immigrant percentage. On the contrary, the mobility rates *within* Antwerp's rural hinterland regions were substantially higher than in East Flanders, and proto-industrial activity was underdeveloped (the remote district of North Turnhout excepted).[32] That rela-tively few migrants found their way to Antwerp can therefore not be attributed to an inherently immobile hinterland. Rather, the explanation needs to be sought in the city's limited appeal as compared to alternative – rural or urban – destina-tions. How to explain Antwerp's weak appeal to potential migrants? On the one hand, the relatively isolated and badly accessible nature of its eastern hinterland undoubtedly played a part in hindering the intensity of recruitment. On the other hand, assigning too much explanatory value to the underdevelopment of hinterland interactions and transport networks constitutes a largely tautologi-cal argument. At a fundamental level, the causes of Antwerp's modest attraction must have lain with push and pull factors on the local and regional scales. While rural pressure was already building up in the Brabantine countryside, its effect as a migration-stimulating push force would only truly materialize in the course of the nineteenth century.[33] Antwerp's comparatively limited pull, then, needs to be attributed primarily to the specificities of its opportunity structure. With most other cities in the Duchy of Brabant experiencing a demographic recovery and intensified commercial interaction in the second half of the eighteenth cen-tury, Antwerp's attraction as an increasingly specialized regional textile centre was modest. How did the specificities of this industry-dominated economic base interact with the local opportunity structure to produce only a limited appeal to potential migrants? And how did existing patterns of recruitment relate to a local opportunity structure that appears to have been comparatively restricted?

Immigrant Employment and the Local Opportunity Structure

Several studies have shown how immigrants in early modern towns generally worked in other sectors than did locally-born residents. Differences in overall occupational profile have also been observed for different immigrant groups, in relation to gender, region of origin and size of birthplace – such as in the case of seventeenth-century Amsterdam.[34] The existence and nature of these origin-specific patterns of occupational orientation are generally attributed to one or two main factors: origin-specific skills, and informal and formal preferences on the urban labour market. Explanations invoking the role of origin-specific skills are best known and accepted in the case of often highly recognizable and tightly knit groups of migrants who possessed an expertise that was particularly widespread and renowned in their home town or villages. Their clustering in specific occupations is then seen as the consequence of a comparative advantage in terms of skill and expertise, such as in the case of serge workers from Hond-schoote in seventeenth-century Leiden,[35] or glass workers from Murano.[36] The impact of origin-specific expertise had a more negative side too, in the sense that by determining the variety of occupational skills which newcomers *could* have acquired, geographical background at the same time limited migrants' options upon arrival. If an adult migrant came from a region where there was no metal-working tradition, his chances of ending up as, say, a gunsmith were very meagre. For understandable reasons, the potential range of occupational expertise was much smaller for a rural-born migrant than for an urban-born migrant, as the degree of occupational diversification was much larger in cities than in the countryside.[37] Hence origin-specific skills or, more broadly, the range of occupational diversification and specialization in the place of origin could not only constitute a comparative advantage for certain specialist groups, but also necessarily constrained immigrants' options on the urban labour market, especially in the case of rural-born newcomers.

A second main factor in explaining origin-specific occupational clustering is that of formal and informal preferences on the urban labour market, which could be to the advantage or disadvantage of newcomers. They could have a negative effect when locally established groups excluded or hampered immigrants' access to certain economic activities by means of formal or informal entry barriers. As many urban economic activities were regulated by guilds, these could provide an important vehicle for such exclusion strategies, for instance by demanding differential entry or master fees from immigrants and non-immigrants. Even in the absence of discriminatory guild regulations, established groups could resort to informal recruitment preferences so as to maintain strongholds and exclude immigrants from certain activities.[38] On the other hand, immigrant groups could sometimes themselves mobilize informal and formal preferences to their own advantage, by establishing region-specific recruitment carousels to acquire or maintain regional strongholds, as in the case of the Amsterdam-based Hamburg clothiers who refused to hire Dutch cloth-shearers, but preferred to hire compatriots instead.[39] As the example of Italian silk-weavers or chimney-sweeps in early eighteenth-century Vienna well illustrates, a strong immigrant position in certain guilds did not necessarily imply openness. Rather, it could reflect the mobilization of successful exclusion strategies to establish a secure niche on the part of the immigrants themselves.[40]

Both factors, origin-specific skill and formal and informal preferences, generally worked together to establish or reinforce patterns of urban labour market segmentation, which makes their respective impact sometimes impossible to disentangle. Even strongholds apparently based on skill advantages, such as the Flemish serge workers mentioned above, depended heavily on recruitment preferences and chain migration for their maintenance.[41] Once a migrant stronghold was established, be it on the basis of expertise, exclusion or force, it tended to be reinforced via the positive feedback of chain-migration and information exchange with the home area.[42] Like social networks, the role of preferences and skills takes place within the conditions posed by labour demand and supply at origin and destination. Labour supply conditions were shaped among other things by the range of occupational diversification and specialization in migrants' places of origin, which determined the potential range of occupational activity which migrants from that area *could* develop.

To explore the ways in which preferences and skills shaped immigrants' occupational profile in eighteenth-century Antwerp, then, it is first of all necessary to establish their occupational *baggage*, i.e. the experience they brought with them at the time of entry. As most migrants came to Antwerp in their late teens or early twenties (see below), most of their training period was already behind them when they entered the city. This implies that they relied primarily on skills and abilities acquired elsewhere. As most migrants came from villages in regions with little specialization outside agriculture and with few medium-sized centres which could have functioned as intermediary gateways, most entered Antwerp from a primarily rural background. The basic occupational range of most Brabantine villages – variations notwithstanding – did not encompass much more than an innkeeper and/or local brewer, a miller, a blacksmith, shoemaker, clog-maker, tailor and some woodworkers, and the occasional village weaver and baker, while the more isolated villages in the Campine areas in addition also benefited from the presence of a village shop, various woodworking artisans, such as a carpenter, a cooper and a wheel- or cartwright, and the ubiquitous presence of village bakers.[43] Even so, the diversity in the occupational experience of most rural migrants necessarily remained limited. Even if they had moved to a larger centre in the region before coming to Antwerp, it is unlikely this would have substantially widened their occupational range. Most centres in the Campine region, the Dijle-Demer-Gete region or North Brabant had barely more than 5,000 inhabitants, and functioned primarily as marketplaces for their hinterlands. The most important sectors in these centres, in other words, were those that were also present in a basic form at village level, like the production and transport of beer.[44] Unless migrants had received their training in a centre considerably larger than their place of birth – and these were not plentiful in the 'empty' Antwerp hinterland – their options on the urban labour market were limited to activities which were either familiar in the context of a village or small town, or which did not involve specialist skills.

Having identified immigrants' occupational background, let us now turn to their occupational activities on Antwerp's labour market (Table 3.1). The most striking difference between immigrants and non-immigrants is that Antwerp-born workers were predominantly active in the production of durable consumer goods (65 per cent), in particular of textiles and lace (50 per cent), and to a much lesser extent in the service sectors (26 per cent), while the situation was completely the reverse among migrant workers, of whom only 29 per cent worked in the production of consumer durables (of which only 18 per cent in textiles and lace), yet 60 per cent in the service sectors. In structuring the specificities of immigrants' occupational profile, both origin-specific skills (or lack thereof) and informal preferences appear to have played a role. The fact that so few migrants were involved in the production of textiles and lace can be related to the limitations of their rural background on the one hand, and the unenviable working conditions in most branches on the other. Although the manufacture of textile fabrics and lace was a prime source of employment for the urban population, working conditions in most branches were very unattractive. The numerically most important activities, such as lace making, the spinning of cotton and wool, and the winding of silk, were also the worst paid, undertaken primarily by women, children and the elderly, who were paid pittances for long working hours, often in very unhealthy conditions. The wages they received functioned as a necessary but minor addition to the family income, and were plainly insufficient as a livelihood. Working in these branches was only viable as part of a broader family income-pooling, and often involved an input from all household members.[45] This observation helps to understand the substantial gender differences in migrants' involvement with textile production: while immigrant men were markedly under-represented when compared to local-born residents (11 versus 32 per cent), the participation rate of female migrants and non-migrants was more or less comparable (16 and 15 per cent). Most female immigrants working in this sector were married or widowed, had lived in town for a relatively long period, and participated in a wider family income-pooling. In turn, a high proportion of the large number of locally-born male textile workers were actually young boys, who likewise operated in the context of broader income-pooling, and received only a pittance for wages.[46] Due to the age-specific characteristics of immigration, most male migrants were single or head-of-household adults, for whom involvement in such activities was manifestly inadequate for their survival.

Table 3.1: Occupational Distribution of Immigrants and Non-Immigrants, 1796 (%).[47]

	Men			Women		
	A (%)	I (%)	% I	A (%)	I (%)	% I
Primary sector	2	3	38	–	1	57
Domestic service	1	7	70	5	40	74
White-collar workers, clergy & proprietors	8	11	33	2	5	52
Shipping	3	1	8	–	–	–
Transport workers & casual labour	3	8	45	–	–	–
Trade, retail & local services	12	18	34	14	19	35
Food industries	2	8	65	–	–	–
Tools & construction	12	15	30	–	–	–
Textiles	32	11	10	15	16	28
Lacework	–	–	–	55	8	6
Clothing & leather	14	8	16	7	10	35
Luxury goods & other consumer durables	8	5	16	–	–	–
Other & miscellaneous	3	5	35	–	–	–
Total	100	100	26	100	100	28
Active population (N)	5,635	1,930	26	5,266	2,019	28
No occupation (N)	714	111	13	2,920	1,053	26
Grand total (N)	6,349	2,041	24	8,186	3,072	27

Abbreviations: A: Antwerp-born; I: Immigrants; % I: percentage of immigrants in sector totals.

In addition to low wages, skill played a part too in gender-specific and immigrant-specific participation in the production of textiles and lace. While immigrant women were engaged in textile production to an extent comparable to that of those born locally, lack of skill helps to explain why they were virtually absent from lace production (8 per cent), which employed the majority of Antwerp-born women (55 per cent). Although severely underpaid and as unenviable as most textile work, lace work was a highly skilled activity that demanded considerable training, which was passed from mother to daughter or provided in several urban 'lace schools', and was an almost exclusively urban undertaking in Brabant. It is therefore no surprise that trained lace workers would have been few and far between among the predominantly rural immigrants.[48] Spinning, in contrast, the most common female job in textile manufacture, demanded relatively little skill, and was widely practised in town and country alike – hence more accessible to rural-born women.[49] Coming from rural regions with little tradition of proto-industrial textile activity, most male immigrants likewise lacked the necessary skills to gain access to the more specialized positions in textile production for which remuneration was higher.[50] A predisposition towards unspecialized or unskilled activities likewise forms the backdrop to immigrants' general under-representation in virtually all other specialized industrial branches. They were virtually absent from highly skilled sectors such as printing or the production of luxury goods, and best represented in those industrial activities that demanded little skill and/or were not unfamiliar in a village context. Immigrant men were therefore not only well represented in tool production and in building activities (15 per cent versus 12 per cent of locally-born men), but they also showed a strong predilection for the least specialized activities within this sector: they were better represented among carpenters and coopers than among cabinet makers, more frequently to be found among blacksmiths than among bell-founders, and more likely to have been active as masons than as glaziers. The only industrial sector in which immigrants outnumbered local-born residents was that of food and drink processing, which employed 8 per cent of immigrant men, but only 2 per cent of their local-born counterparts, producing an immigrant majority (65 per cent) in the baking and brewing workforce – two branches with an obvious rural connection and familiarity. Migrants, then, tended to cluster in those industrial activities that formed part of the occupational profile of most Brabantine villages. One exception is that relatively few migrants worked as tailors or shoemakers, although these activities featured frequently in villages. Fashion-orientation and differentiation in urban clothing production, involving different skills from rural settings, might constitute part of the explanation here. In addition, the marked female presence in the garment trades hints at the importance of sweated labour, which could have made these sectors unattractive to adult men in much the same ways as cotton-spinning or silk-winding.[51]

A counterpart to migrants' limited presence in industrial activity was a strong orientation towards urban service sectors. This was most marked in the sector of domestic service: three in four maids, servants, butlers, waitresses, shop assistants, housekeepers and nursemaids recorded in the census were immigrants. More than 40 per cent of all immigrant women whose occupation was listed worked as domestic servants, as against only 5 per cent of locally-born women. That men took up comparatively less of this labour market – 7 and 1 per cent respectively – simply reflects the female predominance in the urban housework market. Apart from a specialized upmarket segment of butlers and chambermaids, the main conditions for the performance of the menial and domestic tasks involved were obedience, diligence, youth, strength and an unmarried status. The urban demand for living-in maids far exceeded the local supply and was fed mainly by (temporary) recruitment from the nearby hinterland in virtually all western European cities in the early modern period, which in this particular case might have been strengthened by a substitution effect to compensate for Antwerp-born women's and children's extensive involvement in textile production.[52]

With the exception of shipping (1 versus 3 per cent), transport and hauling activities also constituted a favoured terrain for immigrants (3 versus 8 per cent).[53] Here, not only do relatively low skill requirements appear to have played a role, but also the importance of hinterland connections. That migrant men were virtually absent from shipping activities can be explained by the depressed state of the sector, and a lack of significant waterways or any tradition of shipping activities in the eastern quadrant where most immigrants came from.[54] Overland transport, on the other hand, was all the more important in linking Antwerp with its prime hinterland. A close cooperation between coach operators and inn-keepers provided for a regular network of coach services to transport goods and people from Antwerp to major and minor cities in the Austrian Netherlands and abroad.[55] The importance of established contacts and networks in the places of departure and arrival probably helped to establish migrants' predominance among coachmen and drivers, and in other inter-urban transport activities. The handling of goods within the port of Antwerp – used at that time mainly by inland shipping – also offered important opportunities for immigrant employ-ment. Freight-handling on the docks and warehouses was the monopoly of the so-called *naties* ('nations'), each of which was more or less specialized in the loading, unloading and transportation of specific goods and/or at specific quays. They consisted of a fixed number of members, called *natiegasten* ('nation jour-neymen', or gangers), who hired additional casual workers – i.e. non-members – to carry out freight handling jobs at piece rates. Membership of a nation was limited and expensive, and could be acquired only by buying out another *nati-egast*, for prices of sometimes up to more than ten years' wages of an unskilled labourer – evidently, such sums were way out of reach of the large majority of the population.[56] Immigrants appear to have occupied an important to pre-dominant position among both the gangers and the casual workers of Antwerp's dock labour market in the late eighteenth century. Considering the importance of informal social networks both in the acquisition of membership and in the organization of work via subcontracting, this strong immigrant presence appears to have been supported by informal recruitment chains with hinterland, and in particular Campine, villages.[57]

Migrants were also markedly over-represented in the sectors of trade, retailing, catering and local services, both among men (18 versus 12 per cent) and women (19 versus 14 per cent), and this notwithstanding their low occurrence among meat vendors, fishmongers and vegetable vendors – an absence which was a result of spe-cific corporate restrictions.[58] Among the remaining traders and vendors, migrants held an even stronger position, and they even provided the majority of all shop-keepers and grocers. To the extent that traders and retailers increasingly depended on dealings with hinterland markets in the course of the eighteenth-century 'con-sumer revolution', immigrants with well-established commercial networks in the home region would have enjoyed certain comparative advantages in the sector.[59] Retail and trade in general represented a sector *par excellence* in which formal entry barriers to immigrants were low, and where immigrant status could constitute a comparative advantage, via such privileged connections with production centres and markets in the home area.[60] Similarly, in the sector of hotels, lodging houses, inns and taverns, immigrant status could have been of direct help in securing a clientele among fellow immigrants or travellers.[61] Although the occupational terminology used in the census is not without problems of interpretation, the high number of *boutiquiers* and *aubergistes* (shopkeepers and innkeepers) recorded among migrants in any case indicates that they were not relegated to the lowest segments of the commercial sector. Although the actual scale of commercial activity could vary considerably, keeping even a small shop, stall or inn in any case implied a minimal capital outlay, which was out of reach of the poorest sections of the urban population.[62] Finally, the concentration of immigrants in the service sector was further reinforced by their strong presence among white-collar workers and the clergy. While the latter reflected the presence of several religious congregations in Antwerp, most members of which resided in a place other than that of their birth, the former was also stimulated by the recent arrival of representatives of the French authorities.

The differences in occupational activities between migrants and non-migrants in late eighteenth-century Antwerp, then, were very pronounced. Studies of the structure of urban economies often make a basic distinction between economic activities oriented towards export markets, and those oriented towards the local market. The latter includes a variety of retail, service and artisan occupations working mainly for local consumption, such as bakers, shopkeepers, butchers, tailors, shoemakers, cleaners and laundresses, found in every town to a greater or lesser extent of diversification. The export category in principle covers those occupations whose end products are sold outside the city walls, and whose precise nature can vary greatly according to the city's economic orientation.[63] Although the distinction is not always clear-cut,[64] migrants in late eighteenth-century Antwerp seem to have clustered mainly in those basic 'maintenance' activities directed at a local or at best a hinterland market. They were particularly numerous among domestic servants, in the distribution sectors (transport, trade and retail), and in a limited number of basic industries catering for a local market and familiar in a village context, such as baking, brewing, carpentry and masonry. In contrast, they were conspicuously under-represented in the export-oriented sectors of textile and lace production, which were by far the largest employers of the Antwerp-born population.

There are few indications that formal exclusion strategies, for instance via guilds or other corporative organizations, played a significant role in moulding immigrants' occupational orientation as a whole. It is true that the requirement of being a legal 'burgher' – a status conveyed by birth for the locally born, but which had to be paid for by immigrants – when setting up as an independent tradesman in guild-regulated sectors, implied a discriminatory barrier to immigrant participation. However, the price of citizenship was relatively low in late-eighteenth-century Antwerp. In 1785 it was the equivalent of some eighty days' wages of an unskilled labourer, about a third of that required in Brussels. Moreover, in certain years and for certain groups it was even free.[65] In addition to being a burgher, a person wanting to set up as an independent master in guild-related activities had to produce a work proving mastery of the trade and/or pay a master's fee to the guild, while journeymen and labourers also often had to pay a – considerably smaller – fee to become guild members. These fees could sometimes reach very high levels, and the proof of mastery criterion evidently left further room for entry control. The current state of research on Antwerp guilds does not allow any conclusive statements on the matter, but there is lit-tle indication that entry requirements were systematically more stringent for immigrants than for non-immigrants. The only documented exceptions are the butchers' and fishmongers' trades, where existing regulations made them *de facto* hereditary activities throughout the eighteenth century.[66]

No general correlation existed between the strength of corporate organization and the barriers to entry on the one hand, and immigrant participation on the other. Migrants were, for instance, well represented among some of the most 'pro-tected' and exclusive guilds, such as the freight-handling 'nations' whose numbers of ganger-members were fixed, and where membership could only be acquired by buying out another associate for considerable sums of money.[67] In turn, migrants were relatively absent in some of the least regulated 'new industries' situated out-side established corporate structures, such as cotton production.[68] Neither did the comparative costs of guild membership or master status in themselves chan-nel immigrants towards certain occupations: immigrants were well represented among some of the most expensive guilds such as those of the bakers, the carpen-ters and the *natiegasten*, where master's fees were as high as 100, 300 and 2,000 guilders respectively, as well as in some of the cheapest, such as the retail cor-poration of mercers, where becoming a master member cost only 24 guilders.[69] Although corporate admission regulations evidently created (primarily financial) barriers to entry in certain occupational activities, these barriers do not appear to have specifically targeted or handicapped immigrants. While more research is needed to provide conclusive insight into the matter, the only general observation that appears to hold so far is that immigrants were generally under-represented in those trades demanding skills that could be acquired only by urban training, such as diamond processing and printing. This exclusion was in turn a result of their unspecialized rural background rather than of selective institutional barriers *per se*. In so far as corporative preferences played a role in moulding immigrants' occupational profile, then, they probably operated in subtler ways, for instance by discouraging the immigration of better skilled or vocational immigrants, rather than by directly limiting the occupational options of those who did come.

That the overall immigrant occupational profile was essentially a *rural* occu-pational profile, rather than the result of institutional exclusion, is confirmed when immigrant employment is related to birthplace size and distance. Both men and women born in the countryside were far more likely to cluster in the service occupations of domestic service, transport, retail and trade, local services and catering than their counterparts from larger centres, and participation in the production of bread and beer was also inversely related to birthplace size. In turn, migrants born in large cities worked predominantly in industrial branches, and displayed an occupational profile more or less comparable to that of the Antwerp-born population. This is also reflected in immigrants' average birthplace distance per occupational sector: specialized workers, especially in industry, were more frequently recruited from further afield and from non-rural places than their unspecialized counterparts, predominantly employed in the service sector, who generally came from a rural setting and covered shorter distances, which corresponds to the frequently observed divergence in occupational specialization between (longer distance) inter-urban and (shorter distance) rural–urban circuits (see also Table AII.3 in Appendix II).

At a more detailed level, incidences of occupational specialization in relation to a specific places of origin were actually very limited.[70] Even at a regional level, direct indications of the operation of chain migration networks were few. Bakers were recruited from northern Campine centres as much as from certain places in Hageland or from nearby villages around Antwerp – as were brewery workers or coachmen.[71] Rural migrants from the Dijle-Demer-Gete and Campine regions as well as from the Antwerp suburbs displayed a similar occupational profile with strong concentrations in the rurally familiar sectors of retail, transport, food industries and domestic service. In contrast, migrants recruited from more distant and specialized areas did reflect the rural specializations from their home regions: the relatively greater participation of rural migrants from North Brabant and East and West Flanders in textile industries, for instance, was a reflection of proto-industrial textile activity in those regions.[72] However, their overall importance in relation to the predominantly short-distance regional migration patterns was small, and even so the overall deviation from the predominant occupational profile remained limited. The only branch in which regional specialization appears to have played a significant role was that of intra-urban freight handling, where migrants from the Campine region occupied a very strong position in the *naties* network.

These observations on the limited incidences of local and regional occupational specialization do not imply that origin-based networks and connections played no role at all, but they do suggest that these connections operated both at a narrower and at a broader level of social interaction. On the one hand, they were probably most active at micro, individual, household and family levels, in that an assistant or trainee was likely to work for a master from the same village or for one who had established connections with the village or with the family of the migrant.[73] On the other hand, as these connections were to a considerable degree embedded in the wider social connections that existed between Antwerp and its hinterland, many migrants probably also mobilized family and social networks that were not occupation-linked.[74] Unfortunately, the size and scope of these and other social networks remain poorly documented in a static nominal census – only a more systematic confrontation with other archival sources such as the burgher books and guild archives would allow a more revealing analysis of the influence of social networks on occupational orientation.[75]

Although migrants' options on the urban labour market were limited by the constraints inherent to a rural background, this does not imply that immigrants' occupational profile was merely a passive reflection of this background. On the contrary, within the room for manoeuvre set by these origin-derived limits, opportunities appear to have played an important role too in producing specific immigrant clustering. The disproportional absence of male migrants in the low-paid and low-skilled segments of the textile – and to a certain extent also of the garment – trade, for instance, had less to do with an absence of relevant skills than with the unenviable working conditions and low wages in these sectors. In contrast, important strongholds were situated in those branches where an immigrant status might in various ways constitute an asset or convey a comparative advantage. Thus the strong immigrant presence in the sectors of trade and retail was probably supported by the growing importance of hinterland markets, that in the sector of extra-urban transport and lodging by the importance of established connections at origin and arrival, that in the sector of intra-urban transport by the possibility of commanding flexible labour supplies from the home villages, and that in baking and brewing by existing connections to grain supply networks. Does this mean that immigrants' occupational preferences on the labour market were part of a successful strategy? Were they actually better-off than the local-born population? A partial measure of migrants' wealth and success is provided by De Belder, who linked the 1796 census data with four fiscal sources in order to classify all households into differentiated wealth categories.[76] His analysis of the relationship between wealth and occupational activity demonstrates that migrants tended to cluster in better-off activities. Except for domestic servants, migrants were concentrated in those sectors with the smallest number of propertyless practitioners. In turn, a high proportion of poor persons in an occupational category – as in textile production, the poorest branch in the city – typically corresponded with a low proportion of immigrants. In this sense, migrants' occupational preferences appear to have been part of a well-judged strategy.

However, the picture was not all rosy. Although immigrants tended to cluster in better-off branches, *within* each occupational category they supplied relatively more propertyless workers than the population as a whole. This particular constellation was also reflected in the occupational data from the census. Although occupational denominators in the 1796 census are too vague and varied to determine social positions consistently, it is telling that immigrant workers were far more frequently listed in an explicitly subordinate position than locally-born counterparts.[77] In the sector of tools and construction, for instance, no less than 46 per cent of all immigrants were explicitly recorded as journeyman, assistant, helper, worker, apprentice or some other such denomination of a subordinate position, as against only 12 per cent of their locally-born counterparts. In the food industries, the respective figures were 55 versus 17 per cent, while in the production of consumer durables other than textiles, the respective figures were less marked, at 20 versus 15 per cent. Hence, migrants appear to have been considerably worse off than their local-born colleagues. According to De Belder, no less than 66 per cent of immigrants recorded in 1796 had no possessions at all, as against 58 per cent of the locally-born population (Table 3.2). The high proportion of the propertyless among immigrants, however, was strongly affected by the disproportionately high number of (single) persons living-in with other households, who were automatically categorized as propertyless in De Belder's classification scheme.[78] This group predominantly consisted of living-in personnel such as domestic servants (the lion's share), lodgers, and journeymen and apprentices living under their master's roof, in which migrants were over-represented: while this living-in category made up only 5 per cent of the locally-born population, it comprised more than a third (38 per cent) of all immigrants. When this category is omitted from the comparison, which is then limited to persons constituting independent households, immigrants actually included substantially fewer (46 per cent) propertyless people among their ranks than did the local population (56 per cent), and were in contrast better represented among the wealthier groups, in particular among independent artisans, shopkeepers and other patent-holding entrepreneurs of the middling sort.[79]

Table 3.2: Wealth Distribution of the Immigrant and Non-Immigrant Population, 1796 (%).[80]

Wealth class	Local-born residents	Immigrants (all)	Immigrants according to year of arrival		
			1786–96	1766–85	before 1766
Very & moderately wealthy	19	14	7	13	26
Limited independent means	23	19	12	25	20
Propertyless	58	66	81	62	54
Forming independent households	53	29	24	32	31
With living-in arrangements	5	38	57	30	23
Total	100	100	100	100	100
Valid N	26,553	9,936	3,358	4,200	2,378

The overall poorer profile of the immigrant population as a whole, then, was attributable to a substantial group of subordinate workers with living-in arrangements, mostly domestic servants. For most of these persons, however, this was part of a temporary life-cycle phase rather than a permanent situation: 51 per cent of all living-in migrants had arrived in town less than ten years before the census, as against only 23 per cent of those forming independent households. On the whole, wealth and length of stay were strongly positively related: recent arrivals were overwhelmingly poor, while longer-term immigrants were considerably wealthier. Given that many life-cycle migrants left town within ten years of arrival (see below), selective departure was an important factor in occasioning this shift: poorer migrants, and in particular those with living-in arrangements, were far more likely than their wealthier counterparts to stay for only a short time.[81] Social mobility played a part too, transferring migrants to a wealthier category after a certain length of stay, albeit on a more modest scale. Still, even among those who had been in town for more than thirty years, slightly more than half remained propertyless – indicating that a long stay was not always synonymous with social mobility. These observations point in the direction of a general bifurcation between a transient group of wage-dependent migrants on the one hand, mostly living-in servants and personnel, and a more stable group of relatively better-off and economically independent migrants on the other. Some of the incoming servants and journeymen moved up the wealth scale by establishing themselves as independent masters or traders after a certain length of stay (or by marriage), but for many of them residence in Antwerp was only a temporary phase. It is clear, then, that after their arrival immigrants followed different life-cycle trajectories, and that overall career perspectives probably differed between occupations. In order adequately to assess the various opportunities which Antwerp offered to its newcomers, then, it is necessary to introduce a more dynamic view of life cycle and career.

Life Cycles and Careers

With a median age of entry of twenty-four for men and twenty-one for women, most migrants had entered Antwerp in their teens or early twenties. While men were on average older than women, the large majority of both men (60 per cent) and women (62 per cent) had entered the city gates aged between sixteen and thirty, with most of them younger than twenty-five (40 and 47 per cent respectively).[82] The low proportion of immigrants who had arrived as children (16 per cent) or as married couples (12 per cent) confirms the limited scale of family migration. That most migrants were youngsters was a dominant feature of urban migration in the early modern period. Both in town and country, young adulthood formed the life-cycle phase during which mobility rates were highest, falling off considerably in later age groups when persistence became more widespread. Young urban migrants were attracted primarily by the opportunities in terms of employment, training or career advancement which diversified urban economies offered.[83] While some stayed on to become permanent migrants, most came to town only temporarily in often well-established patterns of life-cycle migration, in which the urban stay functioned primarily as a period of training and/or as a means to accumulate some savings, which could be used in a later phase of life when establishing an independent household.[84]

The available data on year of arrival in Antwerp point to a high degree of turnover and a considerable diversity in terms of length of stay, although patterns of seasonal migration unfortunately largely escape the census's view.[85] Extrapolations on the basis of partial figures for the year 1796 suggest a total *gross* inflow of around 1,500 immigrants per year for the whole city, and a re-migration rate of up to 50 per cent in the first year after arrival, yet these figures remain tenuous and indicative at best.[86] More convincingly, the available data in any case indicate that turnover was considerable, and differed, among other things, according to origin and gender. Women, for instance, were over-represented among migrants who had been in town between one and seven years on the one hand, and among those present longer than forty years on the other, while men were comparatively better represented in the intermediary group. While women's predominance among long-term stayers can be attributed to sex-specific mortality rates, the remaining pattern suggests that women were more likely than men to leave town again after a few years. For every 100 female immigrants who had arrived in town less than five years before the census, there were only 74 women who had immigrated in the five years preceding that period. Among men, this ratio was 100:86. Coupled with women's comparatively young age at entry, this indicates a greater involvement in temporary life-cycle patterns of migration associated with young adulthood than for men. Men, for their part, displayed a much stronger tendency towards relatively permanent forms of stay on the one hand, and possibly a more extensive, though largely obscured, involvement in short-term seasonal patterns of migration on the other hand, suggesting that they engaged less in patterns of life-cycle migration than their female counterparts.[87] Patterns of vocational migration, whereby boys came to town for a number of years at an early age for the purpose of training or schooling, do not appear to have been common.[88] At best, male immigrants came to Antwerp only in a final stage of their training, to complement the experience and skills already acquired elsewhere, while they were more likely to settle eventually in town than were their female counterparts. Finally, life-cycle-specific patterns of stay differed also between different circuits of recruitment. While rural-born migrants were more likely to have been young and single at the time of arrival, family migration was relatively more frequent among inter-urban migrants: 40 per cent of rural-born men had arrived between the age of sixteen and twenty-four as against 34 per cent of their large-city counterparts – among women, the respective figures were 48 and 34 per cent. If Antwerp still held some attraction as a vocational centre for young adults, then, it was with regard to its rural hinterland. Even so, the norm for all migrants remained that of entry during young adulthood. While some stayed, others moved on. Exploration of these different trajectories, then, forms a necessary complement to the static observations on labour market segmentation and immigrant success made so far. Although the census does not allow us to reconstruct occupational trajectories at an individual level, the extent to which the occurrence of certain occupational activities correlated with overall length of stay, and the extent to which certain jobs were associated with specific life-cycle phases, provide important indications of the direction and scale of social mobility.

Among women, the influence of life cycle and length of stay on their overall occupational profile was manifest (Table AII.1 in Appendix II). The most important female occupation, that of domestic servant, correlated strongly with a specific phase of young adulthood, and showed conspicuous rates of turnover, in the sense that the majority of domestic servants had been in town less than ten years. In contrast, virtually all other occupational categories increased in relative, and often also in absolute, importance among longer-term residents. The absolute number of housewives and textile workers, for instance, was substantially larger among long-resident cohorts than among more recent arrivals, indicating a net transfer to this sector of women previously working in other occupations. Among providers of local services, mainly laundresses and cleaners, the largest absolute numbers were recorded among immigrants present longer than twenty years, indicating a connection with an even more advanced life cycle. The net gains of occupational mobility in relation to length of stay were greatest in the sectors of retailing, trade and catering: for every two female shopkeepers, vendors or innkeepers who had been in town less than ten years there were five who had arrived in the ten years prior to that. While the incidence of domestic service was inversely related to length of stay, then, employment in the sectors of textile production, trade, catering and local services expanded notably among women with a longer state of residence.

Two dynamics appear to have contributed to this overall shift in female employment. On the one hand, an important number of female domestic servants undoubtedly left town after a few years to return home or settle down elsewhere. This was already indicated by women's larger involvement in migration patterns associated with young adulthood, and corresponded to the temporary life-cycle-specific patterns of migration which characterized the movements of many female servants in early modern Europe.[89] On the other hand, those who did stay in town and eventually married there had to look for other sources of income because their married status often barred them from service. In this sense, the sectors of textile production (spinning), distribution and local services were more or less the only available sources of income to which unspecialized rural-born women could turn in a life-cycle phase which precluded domestic service. Although the actual trajectories cannot be reconstructed, it is therefore likely that many recorded spinners, vendors, innkeepers and laundresses among medium- and long-term stayers were erstwhile maids who had married and settled in town after their initial period of service. As it is unlikely that women working as spinners, laundresses or cleaners belonged to households from the wealthier categories, it is clear that a long stay need not have implied upward social mobility.[90] In sum, the itineraries of female immigrants after arrival broke down into three main trajectories: those entering town as domestic servants and leaving again after a couple of years, those entering town as domestic servants but settling down in the course of time, and those entering town in another occupational and/or marital position, displaying a relatively high persistence. This implies that domestic service was part of the migration experience for a majority of female immigrants: at least two female migrants out of three appear to have entered town as maids. The great part of these migrant servants stayed in town only for a couple of years at most, and by the time ten years had passed, the majority had left. Those who did stay necessarily changed occupational status if they married, in which case they appear predominantly to have reinforced the ranks of housewives 'without occupation' or to have entered the sectors of retailing, local services and textile production.

Among men, the occupational distribution and shifts were more varied (Table AII.2 in Appendix II). The marked presence of white collar workers among recent arrivals was undoubtedly (in part) due to the exceptional circumstances of the establishment of the French regime in the months leading up to the census. Much like their female counterparts, and probably for much the same reasons, male domestic servants were characterized by a rapid turnover: for every hundred male domestic servants present for less than ten years, there were only thirty-nine who had arrived between ten and twenty years before the census. The importance of the distribution sectors, on the other hand, expanded notably in relation to length of stay. This illustrates how the acquisition of independent entrepreneurial positions, such as shopkeeper, *natie* member or master artisan, was generally associated with a certain length of stay, training and experience. In the industrial sectors, the proportion of workers in an explicitly subordinate position was inversely related to length of stay, indicating that these positions were related to an early life-cycle phase – or at least some of them. After working in such a position, immigrants could leave again, change occupation or move up the ranks to establish themselves as independent producers. The greatest room for occupational mobility appears to have been situated in the food industries, where a decrease in the number of auxiliary workers over time went hand in hand with an increase in the number of masters. In this respect, an important difference existed between brewing and baking. Whereas both 'assistants' and 'masters' abounded among immigrant bakers, immigrants supplied *all* of the fifty-seven recorded workers and assistants in brewing, but only three of the sixteen employer brewers. Clearly, immigrants' opportunities for social mobility were considerably less in brewing than in baking, most probably owing to the higher degree of production concentration and the greater capital outlay involved. The only other industrial sector in which the number of independent producers expanded notably over the different cohorts, thus suggesting previous 'assistants' who had climbed the social ladder, was that of carpentry – but to a much lesser extent than the case of baking.[91] At the end of the road, then, it was in the 'auxiliary' positions that male immigrants recorded the greatest decline in relation to length of stay. Many of these positions were related to a specific life cycle of young adulthood, sometimes for purposes of training, but not always. For instance in the building, textile and brewing trades, age and marital status of assistants were comparable with their independent counterparts, indicating that life-cycle-determined social mobility played virtually no role in these labour market segments. In contrast, domestic servants and assistants in baking and woodworking occupations were considerably younger than the male immigrant population as a whole. As with female domestic servants, some of those in younger life-cycle positions were likely to leave town again after working, saving and learning for a few years. However, as men engaged much less frequently in life-cycle patterns of temporary migration than women, and were more likely to stay on for longer periods of time, occupational mobility was probably as important as job-specific patterns of stay in bringing about the observed occupational shifts.

As the number of independent producers and entrepreneurs increased in relation to length of stay, 'ready-made' immigrant entrepreneurs or independent producers were few in number: most became shopkeepers, innkeepers, *natie* members or master artisans only after a certain length of stay.[92] Most probably, they had spent their previous years in town garnering the necessary training and experience, and establishing commercial and social connections, probably in a subordinate position. Next to training and experience, however, setting up as an independent craftsman, shopkeeper or *natiegast* required a considerable capital outlay, which was impossible to mobilize without personal or family resources.[93] Considering the important investments involved in most of these independent entrepreneurial activities, it is unlikely that they were feasible for the poorer immigrant groups. Although they seldom entered town as ready-made shopkeepers, *natiegasten* or master bakers, then, most of these later entrepreneurs were probably earmarked in the sense that they came from families with a tradition in the same branch or at least with some capital resources, and that they had come to town with an eye to training and eventual settlement. An example of such a trajectory is that of fifty-four-year-old Jacques Smeyers from the small Campine village of Retie, who in 1796 was recorded as an established baker with *petite fortune* in the proletarian Boeksteeg.[94] He had entered town in 1766 at the age of 24, most probably as an assistant baker, and is recorded in the burgher books as a baker having acquired citizenship in June 1782, which probably corresponded to the moment of his establishment as an independent baker.[95] By this time he was almost forty, and had lived and worked in Antwerp for sixteen years. Most likely he had spent part of this time with his namesake and probably close relative Peeter Smeyers, a fellow villager and baker, who had entered town one year earlier, and set up as an independent baker in 1771 – and was still active at the age of sixty-four as a well-to-do baker in the Suikerrui.[96] A third namesake from Retie, Joannes Smeyers, was recorded as a shopkeeper acquiring citizenship in 1782 – complementing the apparent family profile in independent retail activities.[97]

Most male immigrants, then, entered town in a 'subordinate' or 'auxiliary' position. Some of the jobs they held in this position were connected to a specific life-cycle phase, others not. The greatest differentiation in subsequent trajectories appears to have been whether or not such newcomers were to move up the social ladder and establish themselves as independent entrepreneurs or artisans after a certain length of stay. Such career opportunities appear to have been greatest in the sectors of retail, transport, catering and baking – sectors in which immigrants often had a comparative advantage by nature of their hinterland connections. In contrast, the sectors of building, brewing, and textile and clothing production revealed rather 'flat' dynamics of occupational mobility at best, offering no substantial opportunities to assistants for establishment as an independent artisan in due course. Forty-four-year-old Jacques Hairbots from the village of Halle (near Tienen), for instance, had lived in Antwerp for more than twenty years and had set up a family, but remained *sans fortune* as a *garçon brasseur*, or brewer's assistant.[98] Likewise, De Munck observed that the building sectors attracted predominantly low-skilled rural immigrants, who would work as unfree journeymen without any intention of becoming independent masters.[99] The remaining 'propertyless' immigrants in the long-resident cohorts noted above probably came mainly from these sectors.

On the whole, then, two main crossroads appear in general terms to have governed the different observed trajectories which male and female immigrants followed after arrival. The first was the decision of whether or not to leave again after a few years; the second was success or failure in moving up the social ladder when one stayed on. The direction taken at these crossroads probably had less to do with individual failure or success than with belonging to different circuits of migration, which were conditioned by different preferences and strategies, and by different family backgrounds. In that sense, most moves were probably

'successful' in relation to their respective goals. Although they ranked low on the
overall wealth ladder, the moves of young, temporary, relatively unskilled working migrants, in particular female domestic servants, were probably successful in
terms of the specific purpose of the move, i.e. the acquisition of savings and/or
training with an eye to setting up an independent household. They catered to
a specific urban demand for manual and menial workers in which youth and
strength were important assets, and most probably received an important wage
premium.[100] Their settled counterparts, in turn, show various signs of upward
social mobility which in themselves were an indication of success. Again, this
social mobility was primarily dependent on *life-cycle* advancement, in the sense
that these positions necessarily demanded not only a certain preparation, experience and maturity, but also a capital investment which was not available to the
poorest immigrant groups. The third group of immigrants, those who stayed on
but who did not experience noteworthy betterment, is most difficult to evaluate.
That they stayed on in town most probably had to do more with individual and
family circumstances – such as the presence of kin or a suitable marriage partner
– than with attractive economic prospects. Most worked in sectors that offered
few career opportunities, so that betterment prospects had probably not been an
issue from the start. That they were generally poor and propertyless was a characteristic they shared with the majority of the locally-born population – and it
remains questionable whether they would have had better prospects elsewhere.
Although their moves cannot be interpreted as having been an unqualified success, then, they most probably did not constitute a failure either – rather, the
move and subsequent settlement were functional in providing a living, which
remained the prime objective for the majority of Antwerp's impoverished population in the late eighteenth century.

Migrants were not only vital to the functioning of Antwerp's local economy,
their presence also had important demographic ramifications. The constant
influx of young and single workers replenished the ranks of young adults in a
city unable to raise its own infants and children. While migrants supplied 21 per
cent of all inhabitants of the first and fourth town districts, they made up 33 per
cent of all those aged between twenty-one and fifty. The predominance of female
over male migrants in turn reinforced the femininity of the urban population:
while locally-born residents counted 82 men for every 100 women, the low sex
ratio of the immigrant population (69:100) lowered the overall urban sex ratio
to 79:100.[101] Although a great proportion of all incoming migrants, especially
women, left town again after a few years, for those who stayed on, marriage and
founding a family marked important transitions, with major repercussions on
the further life cycle. Only 10 per cent of all migrants were recorded as married
to a spouse with whom they had made the move to town, the great majority of
immigrants having entered town single.[102] The fact of whether or not a single

immigrant found a suitable partner and eventually married during his or her stay may well have formed one of the decisive elements in making the original move permanent. At least 41 per cent of Antwerp's resident immigrants had married after moving to town – which in many cases also provided them with a number of (step)children under twelve – and among those present longer than ten years, more than half (51 per cent) had married in the city.[103] Origin-specific preferences clearly played a role in the search for a marriage partner. Immigrants and non-immigrants were more likely to marry someone from the same group: the actual proportion of mixed marriages between immigrants and locally-born people (25 per cent) was twelve percentage points smaller than it would have been in the case of 'neutral' partner choice. Both male and female immigrants were twice as likely to choose an immigrant spouse than if there had been no bias towards immigrant status. Rural-born immigrants, moreover, were less likely to marry an Antwerp-born spouse (49 per cent) than their urban-born counterparts (59 per cent). Such a frequently observed difference in marriage patterns among immigrants from the country and those born in town is usually explained in terms of avoidance: because they were less similar to the local population than migrants from another town, rural migrants were more easily considered 'outsiders' and were shunned by locally-born potential brides and grooms.[104] It is plausible that a similarity in background and experience was indeed a factor in promoting marriages between people born in Antwerp and immigrants born in another town, whose overall profile – for instance in terms of employment – showed more resemblances to the locally-born population than to their rural-born counterparts.[105] At the same time, however, marriage preferences and strategies on the part of rural immigrants *themselves* probably also played a role, as a general preference for marrying a rural immigrant need not have been synonymous with a weak position on the marriage market, but might have helped reinforce the expansion of supportive networks.[106]

Notwithstanding these evident preferences, however, mixed marriages between immigrants and locals did represent a quarter of all concluded marriages, and involved 46 per cent of all immigrant grooms and 54 per cent of immigrant brides – which does not reflect a marked isolation or segregation of immigrants on the marriage market. Moreover, where migrants married fellow immigrants, they seldom came from the same village or even region. Although rural-born migrants displayed a comparatively greater preference for partners born in the same region, the geographical mix in immigrant marriages was wide ranging. Immigrants marrying another immigrant predominantly chose a spouse born outside his or her own region of birth. Marrying a fellow immigrant, in other words, did not necessarily imply a taste for common geographical origins. If unions with Antwerp-born spouses are included, 59 per cent of all marriages involving immigrants were inter-regional marriages, i.e. between partners born in different regions.[107] Even among the rural-born, this proportion was 48 per cent, which was a degree of heterogamy substantially greater than in rural villages.[108] In other words, the likelihood of marrying a partner from a more distant place was significantly increased by the move to Antwerp, which points to the great importance of the city as a locus encouraging the encounter of marriage partners from diverse backgrounds, and to the impact of urban migration on the widening of marriage horizons.

The Weak Appeal of a Regional Textile Centre

In the second half of the eighteenth century, Antwerp's marked orientation towards the production of low-wage, labour-intensive textile goods on a putting-out basis exerted only a modest appeal to potential migrants. The relative size of the immigrant population was substantially lower than in other Brabantine cities, and most were recruited from within the city's main hinterland regions. Labour migration was predominantly oriented towards the more unspecialized segments of the urban labour market, which were familiar in a rural context. The strong clustering of immigrants in the sectors of domestic service, retail, transport, catering, food industries and – to a lesser extent – woodworking was predicated by the limits of their unspecialized background, in that most came from nearby underdeveloped rural areas with little specialization outside agriculture. Their options on the urban labour market were therefore limited *a priori* to those activities which were familiar in a village context or which did not demand specialist skills.

Of course, the geographical dimensions of Antwerp's recruitment area do not by themselves *explain* the position of migrants within the urban labour market at a structural level, as the city's spatial reach was bound up with the local opportunity structure in the first place. The essential question then becomes why there was not more specialized recruitment from more distant regions. As the example of seventeenth-century Leiden amply illustrates, an urban specialization in textile production did not necessarily preclude the existence of specialized long-distance migration patterns.[109] Moreover, until the seventeenth century, Antwerp's textile activities – then mostly cloth finishing and later silk industries – had recruited a considerable number of specialized textile workers from elsewhere.[110] It is clear, however, that the working conditions in Antwerp's low-wage textile industries of the second half of the eighteenth century – by far the poorest occupational branch in the city – were not such as to have a strong attraction for specialized workers. Even unspecialized rural immigrants appear to have shunned those textile activities to which their limited skills did allow access. In turn, the ample availability of cheap and disciplined female and child labour *in situ* – which was further expanded by the Antwerp poor-law reforms of 1779 – reduced employers' interests in recruiting textile and garment workers from elsewhere.[111] Other sectors in which specialized or long-distance recruitment might have played an important role, such as the urban luxury, diamond or printing trades, had suffered major blows in the urban crisis of the first half of the eighteenth century and had dwindled in importance.[112] The only substantial or attractive employment opportunities in Antwerp's opportunity structure, then, were located primarily in the urban maintenance sectors, which were a corollary of a city's market functions, and to which rural immigrants had relatively easy access. Owing to the city's pervasive specialization in low-paid textile production, however, the local servicing and distribution sectors were considerably less developed in eighteenth-century Antwerp than in other Brabantine cities.[113] To the extent that the Brabant re-urbanization process of the second half of the eighteenth century ultimately depended on the transfer of part of the rural population to the cities, the limited employment and career opportunities which textile-oriented Antwerp offered to unspecialized rural migrants, owing to the underdeveloped nature of its tertiary sector, constituted the direct cause of Antwerp's limited and retarded demographic recovery.

Although they were fewer than in other Brabant cities, those migrants who did come to Antwerp nevertheless took up a prominent place in the urban economy. That they primarily clustered in local distribution and service sectors was not only a result of the limits of their predominantly rural and unspecialized background, but was also moulded by positive choices and preferences on the part of the immigrants themselves, aided by certain comparative advantages in the form of various hinterland connections and by family networks. The degree of 'success' of their occupational choices was closely connected with careers and life cycles, the exploration of which points towards different patterns of occupational orientation in relation to length of stay. Most migrants entered town as young adults, and either left again after a number of years or stayed on for a more indefinite length of time. While men on the whole displayed more persistent patterns of stay, women were engaged more frequently in patterns of temporary labour migration, which was related to the great importance of domestic service in the (single) female urban labour market. Socio-economic positions tended to be higher the longer migrants resided in town. Although individual trajectories could not be reconstructed, cohort comparisons suggest that most migrants entered town either as domestic servants or as workers in a subordinate position, while independent masters and entrepreneurs were more frequent among long-term residents, thus attesting both to occupation-specific patterns of stay and dynamics of upward social mobility. Whether one left town again or climbed the social ladder was probably determined less by individual failure or success than by family backing, which helped to provide social and financial resources. Even migrants belonging to lower-status or less persistent segments, however, such as domestic servants or journeymen, may probably be considered to have been relatively successful with respect to the specific – sometimes limited – purpose of their move, such as the acquisition of savings or training, marriage and household formation, or – in some cases – mere survival.

Although the numerical weight of immigrants in Antwerp was relatively smaller than in other Brabant cities, their presence was essential to the functioning of an urban economy that was predicated upon a general division of labour between more specialized urban-based industrial jobs performed by locally-born workers, on the one hand, and service and menial activities in which rural immigrants abounded, on the other. A supply of predominantly temporary young and fit immigrant labour provided Antwerp with the greater share of its domestic servants and more than half of all recorded non-textile industrial 'assistants', providing a free supply of human capital on a permanent basis. The more permanent migrants, for their part, played a key role in providing services and the distribution of goods in the urban space. Moreover, as the census necessarily underrates the permanent labour replenishment maintained by a continuous coming and going of immigrants, the importance of labour migration to the functioning of Antwerp's economy was even greater than this one-off cross-sectional view allows for. Also at the demographic level, migrants' contribution was crucial. The influx of young, single and predominantly female newcomers compensated high levels of child mortality, rejuvenated the city's population, and reinforced the city's skewed sex ratio. Those men and women who eventually settled down played an important part on the urban marriage market, and in turn helped to maintain urban birth rates.

The implication of the relative 'success' of newcomers and the selectivity of recruitment with regard to the local opportunity structure is that those immigrants who did move to Antwerp in the second half of the eighteenth century were more attracted by the city's (comparatively few) employment and career opportunities, than pushed by adverse circumstances at home. In practice, this relationship between push and pull was mediated via participation in migration patterns with a long tradition and of marked familiarity to those involved. The move to Antwerp was unlikely to have been a disruptive occasion, as most migrants moved along paths beaten by their predecessors, had probably visited the town before, and knew family members or co-villagers who lived in town. Some stayed for only a relatively short period of time, others remained in town and founded a family. Most migrants must have come to town with a relatively clear plan, based on the experience of predecessors and acquaintances, and which probably often corresponded to actual opportunities: the garnering of experience or savings, the establishment of a career or the finding of a partner. In turn, migrants were not seen as an alien element in urban society. No systematic signs or strong incidences of exclusion, segregation or discrimination on the basis of immigrant status were found either in the domain of occupational activities, marriage preferences or residential patterns. Migrants appear to have formed a familiar and well-integrated segment of urban society, and to have moved along paths which were unlikely to hold large surprises either for the migrants involved or for the receiving and sending communities. The profound changes which both Antwerp and its recruitment regions underwent in the first decades of the nineteenth century, however, would upset the familiar balance on which most of these eighteenth-century patterns of population exchange were based, and result in major adaptations and transformations of existing patterns of migration.

4 MIGRATION TO A PORT IN THE MAKING, 1800–60

In the first half of the nineteenth century, Antwerp went through a total transition from a middle-sized regional textile centre to a booming international port town of more than 120,000 inhabitants. An easily accessible and well-connected inland port in the densely populated Low Countries, Antwerp was favourably located to act as a major transit centre for the Southern Netherlands, part of the Northern Netherlands, the German Rhineland and the north of France – mostly densely populated and rapidly industrializing regions. The exploitation of these geographical assets became possible only as a result of the conjunction of certain economic and political conditions, and took place at the cost of deteriorating living and working conditions of Antwerp's labouring poor. The smallholding regions in the city's immediate hinterland, meanwhile, were confronted with strong population growth and increasing proletarianization, resulting in an overall increase of rural push forces. Migration patterns in turn displayed several important shifts over the first decades of the nineteenth century. Mapping these changes in space and time and analysing their relationship to the changes in the city's local opportunity structure is the main point of this chapter. The nature of this relationship, in turn, sheds light on the adaptability of migration patterns, and on the contribution of migrants to the observed transformation of Antwerp's economic structures. What was the role of newcomers in the city's rapid conversion to a port town? What implications did the changes in local opportunity structure have for the socio-economic prospects and life-cycle trajectories of newcomers? And how did new patterns of migration relate to those established for the late eighteenth century?

Converting to a Port Town

Antwerp's conversion from a regional textile centre to an international port town was anything but a gradual or linear process. It took place at different speeds in different phases, which were tied up with the different political regimes under which the urban economy operated. The seminal and most radical shifts took place in the years under French rule (1796–1814), which saw the collapse of the textile industry and a precarious revival of maritime activity. Several factors acted together to devastate the city's textile industry on the threshold of the nineteenth century. Warfare, tense international relations and a lack of investment in mechanizing technologies created severe outlet problems, in which the Antwerp textile industries rapidly lost ground to increasing competition from industrializing textile centres in neighbouring (Ghent) and foreign (English) regions.[1] In the absence of mechanization, Antwerp's textile industries were wiped out in only a few years. The relatively new cotton industry, that had expanded rapidly in the last decades of the eighteenth century, was reduced to insignificance in the first ten to fifteen years of the nineteenth century. Linen production, used mainly for the manufacture of mixed fabrics (with cotton), followed in its wake. By 1820, only the lace and embroidery branch survived as a sector of importance, and textile production as a whole had completely lost its previous predominant significance in the urban economic base.[2]

Commercial and transport sectors, on the other hand, received important stimuli under French rule. The proclamation of free navigation on the Scheldt by the treaty of 1795 terminated the Dutch blockade which had closed the Antwerp port off from the North Sea for more than two centuries. Although the treaty came into real effect only after 1800, the swift increase in maritime traffic that followed was a clear indication of Antwerp's natural assets as a maritime gateway (Graph 4.1).[3] However, despite its favourable location, the city was ill-equipped to assume its new function. The existing commercial and port infrastructure was plainly inadequate to accommodate large sea-going vessels or big commercial undertakings.[4] In both domains, however, energetic state activity would provide essential support. Locally, the departmental prefect d'Herbouville, in charge from 1800 to 1805, encouraged the establishment of auxiliary institutions such as a chamber of commerce, a navigation school and preliminary quay improvements to support the expansion of commercial maritime activity.[5] At a higher level of political authority, Napoleon himself took the lead in designing a new infrastructure fit for a major maritime and naval port, which he envisaged as becoming 'a pistol aimed at the heart of England'.[6] During his inspection visit of 1803, he took the first steps to ordering large-scale construction work in the Antwerp port area, which was to include the construction of an arsenal and military wharf on the land of the former abbey of St Michael to the south of the city, and an additional shipyard outside the city walls, two docks with a lock in the north, fortification of the military infrastructure, and the construction of a 1,500 metre-long continuous quayside and a network of locks and bridges connecting both installations. In 1804, preliminary demolition work for the building of the new docks started, and by 1807 an estimated 2,000 workers were engaged in excavating the two docks. The first ('small') dock was finished in 1811, and in

1812 the second ('large') one was ready. The newly built arsenal shipyard was in use by 1805, and would from then on produce between twelve and fifteen ships per year. In 1811 an additional, bigger wharf outside the city walls started operation.[7] In a first phase, the reopening of the Scheldt and the government support initiatives led to a swift revival of commercial shipping from 1800 onwards. The number of seagoing ships entering the Antwerp harbour increased promptly, as did the volume of overseas – mostly colonial – trade, and the influx of foreign commercial agents.[8] Stifled by the consequences of the continental blockade, however, the revival was short-lived. While coastal shipping and smuggling still offered certain – risky – commercial opportunities, maritime shipping came to a virtual standstill around 1808, which was to last until the end of the French regime.[9] Although government initiatives to modernize the Antwerp port infrastructure had partly envisaged the support of commercial shipping, after the resumption of hostilities with England they catered almost exclusively to navy needs. From around 1806 onwards, Antwerp became the single most important naval base of the French empire, both in terms of the number of personnel employed – up to 6,000 at the height of its activity – and the volume of ships and armour produced.[10] When the allied troops captured Antwerp on 5 May 1814, the naval infrastructure and equipment they encountered were considered a major potential threat to the European military balance. The treaty of Paris signed on 30 May 1814 explicitly contained a ban on future naval activities in Antwerp. The frigates that had remained in Antwerp were divided between the winning armies, the military wharves were dismantled and the naval personnel were sent home.[11]

Graph 4.1: Tonnage Entering the Antwerp Harbour, 1800–60.[12]

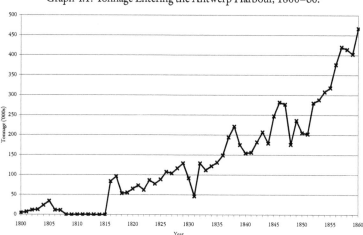

After the defeat of Napoleon, the Southern Netherlands were united with the north under King William I. Both internal and international conditions of the post-Napoleonic era were very favourable to a new launch of Antwerp's commercial port activities. In the United Kingdom of the Netherlands, complete freedom of trade was guaranteed between north and south, including participation in the Dutch colonial trade. In the stable international situation, Antwerp could fully exploit its advantageous location as a prime maritime distribution centre for a wide and densely populated commercial hinterland stretching deeply into the Netherlands, Germany and France. Apart from its favourable location and easy access from the sea, Antwerp possessed several other advantages over Amsterdam and Rotterdam, the other main Dutch maritime ports. It could count not only on a superior French-built port infrastructure, but also on a cheaper and quicker handling of cargoes due to the absence of strict labour regulations. Antwerp also profited greatly from the expansion of economic activity in the industrial growth poles of the later Belgium, for which it came to function as the prime centre for imports and exports. In addition, active government support of national trade and industry, in particular the establishment of the Nederlandse Handel-Maatschappij (Dutch Trading Company – the later Société Générale), also gave an important boost to the further development of the Antwerp commercial and transport activities, including insurance and banking institutions and shipbuilding. Under the management of the city authorities, who had been granted possession of the Antwerp port infrastructure in two steps in 1815 and 1819, further improvements and enlargements of the maritime and other traffic facilities took place.[13]

It took until the 1820s, however, before these different advantages were fully exploitable and Antwerp engaged in a rapid expansion of its port activities. Activity during the first years of Dutch rule was stifled by remaining international tensions and by industrial crisis, harvest failure and an agricultural malaise, all of which severely limited demand and trade volumes.[14] In the 1820s, however, and in particular after 1825, port activity in Antwerp increased rapidly, stimulated among other things by a revival of industrial activity in the Southern Netherlands, in particular of Ghent textile production and the Liège metal industries. Antwerp also progressively increased its share of Dutch colonial imports to as much as 55 per cent in 1829, to the disadvantage of Amsterdam and Rotterdam. By 1829, the annual tonnage entering the Antwerp harbour was more than double that of 1820, and more than 1,000 seagoing vessels came and went every year.[15] Conversely, however, as commercial and transport activities increased their importance in the post-Napoleonic era, industrial activity in Antwerp shrank even further. The loss of protected French markets and the increased competition from mechanized production in the late 1810s dealt the final blow to the textile activities which still remained, with the exception of the new tulle embroidery activities which did well until the late 1820s. Industrial activities that did progress were port-related auxiliary industries, most notably sugar refining, salt production, tobacco processing, rope making and shipbuilding. Employment in these branches was, however, nowhere near the earlier numbers engaged in textile production. On the whole, then, industrial activity was on the retreat. During the Dutch period, the former industrial base of the Antwerp economy was conclusively replaced by a predominant commitment to commercial and transport activities.[16]

This greater dependency on international trade activities, however, implied a very vulnerable economic position, as was amply illustrated by the serious problems that the Belgian revolution of 1830 created for the Antwerp economy. The separatist striving of the Southern Netherlands dealt several blows to the major trade links and supply channels of the Antwerp port. The establishment of an independent Belgium closed off Antwerp's access to the Dutch colonial and internal markets, hindered connections with the German hinterland and more generally troubled international trade because of ongoing hostilities with the Dutch. The city itself was bombarded by Dutch troops in 1830 and remained under constant threat from the continued presence of the Dutch garrison in the Antwerp citadel until this was ousted by French troops in 1832. Although officially sanctioned by the Dutch only with the signing of the Treaty of XXIV Articles in 1838 (in exchange for a hefty toll), navigation on the Scheldt itself was unhindered after 1831. Of longer lasting impact was the obstruction of Antwerp-bound traffic – either by closure or by differential taxation – on the Dutch inland waterways which connected the Scheldt with the Rhine, blocking the major connection from the Antwerp port to the German hinterland.[17] Yet growing imports and exports for Belgium's precocious industries, technological advances in shipping and vast improvements in overland transport would herald a new spurt of maritime expansion from the late 1830s onwards. In 1836, Antwerp was linked to the earliest Belgian railways which ran from the north-west to the south-east, from Ostend to Liège and Verviers, and from north to south from Antwerp to Brussels, with a crossroads at Mechelen.[18] In 1843 the completion of the 'Iron Rhine', a railway link between Antwerp and Cologne, re-established a direct connection with Germany. The speed, regularity and reliability of the railway connection provided many advantages over Rhine shipping, and became a strong argument for Antwerp, rather than Rotterdam, in the competition for German transit traffic. Via Cologne, Antwerp came to function as a prime transit port for a wide inland central-European area, while regular sailings to Rotterdam, London, Hull and Le Havre secured the intensification of contacts with British, French and Dutch markets. At the same time, its intercontinental routes expanded. By the mid-1840s, the Antwerp port had regular connections to Rio de Janeiro, Bahia, Vera Cruz, New York, Valparaiso, Constantinople and

Singapore – at the time still exclusively served by sailing ships. Growing imports encouraged the further development of a limited number of export-processing industries, such as tobacco processing, sugar refining and rice polishing, and the further expansion of local shipbuilding with the establishment of the Cockerill shipyard in 1844.[19] After a difficult start-up phase, the expansion of Atlantic passenger traffic also added the emigrant trade as a key commercial undertaking. Between 1843 and 1859, an average of 10,000 emigrants per year made the Atlantic crossing via Antwerp, most of whom came from German inland areas. These numbers would eventually triple and quadruple in the following decades when the establishment of the Red Star Line in 1873 and a continued expansion of shipping volumes would make Antwerp one of the major Atlantic ports of the second half of the nineteenth century.[20]

Catharina Lis has demonstrated that Antwerp's transformation from a regional textile centre to an international port town went hand in hand with a process of impoverishment of the labouring population, and with a general degradation of urban living conditions in terms of housing, sanitary conditions and food consumption over the first half of the nineteenth century. One major factor in occasioning the increase in working class vulnerability was the decline of stable employment opportunities – especially for women and children – as textile production collapsed, and the growing irregularity of many port-related jobs.[21] Yet if conditions worsened so dramatically, how can we account for the growing levels of immigration observed over this period? Lis herself explained this paradox mainly in terms of push factors. Although she conceded that developing port activity expanded local employment opportunities, she maintained that increasing rural pressure was the predominant cause of Antwerp's growing number of newcomers in the first half of the nineteenth century, and that chronic unemployment prevented migrants from taking root.[22] Yet, uprooting can only be part of the story, and masks a more varied picture of migrants' adaptability and manoeuvrability through space and time. A diachronic and differentiated exploration of the changing patterns of migration over this period can help us to disentangle the interaction between push and pull forces in greater detail, and to bring to the fore the varying room for manoeuvre of different migrant groups.

Changes in the Urban Migration Field

Antwerp's process of economic transformation went hand in hand with a profound restructuring of migration patterns. The demographic figures in Chapter 2 have already exemplified how the volumes of immigration and outmigration recorded several important shifts in the first half of the nineteenth century. These changes in scale were complemented by various alterations in the origin and social background of newcomers. Like the ongoing quantitative changes,

these changes in the composition of migration streams were no gradual or linear affair, but were bound up with different phases in Antwerp's economic and
political history, which repeatedly remoulded the local opportunities and spatial
connections that structured the city's migration field. A quick overview of the
origin pyramids representing the places of birth of Antwerp's immigrants at various points in time between 1796 and 1855 illustrates how the regional pattern
that had been the norm in the second half of the eighteenth century shifted to a
much more diverse but much less stable migration field throughout the first decades of the nineteenth century (Graphs 4.2–7 and Maps 4.1–6, below). While
there was a general tendency for the urban catchment area to enlarge throughout
the period, yielding a gradual increase in the average birthplace distance from 61
km in 1796 to 133 km in 1855, these extensions took place in different directions – recruiting different groups of migrants at different points in time.[23] Thus,
while a large French presence proved characteristic of the late Napoleonic period,
the Dutch period recorded a marked increase in the proportion of German and
other long-distance migrants, while the 1850s were in turn characterized by a
notable increase in both foreign migrants and the number of migrants from the
Flemish provinces beyond the Scheldt.[24] Each of these origin pyramids reflects
different phases of the ongoing process of migratory change, each associated with
different episodes in Antwerp's political and economic development. Exploring
and dating the how and why of the observed shifts in the urban migration field
therefore helps elucidate the extent to which they were bound up with the profound and sometimes sudden changes in the urban opportunity structure over
time. Three main phases can be discerned in this respect, which more or less
overlap with the different political and economic regimes discussed above: the
period under Napoleonic rule (1804–13), the period under Dutch rule (1815–
20) and the early decades of the Belgian Kingdom (1830–60).

The period under Napoleonic rule (1804–13) represented a first important
break away from the migration patterns that had been dominant in the eighteenth century. Immigrants came in far greater number and from more distant
regions than they had in the closing decades of the *ancien régime*: the annual
number of newcomers leapt from 1,500 at most in the late eighteenth century to
an average of almost 3,000 yearly entries in the residence card registers between
1808 and 1813, while the average distance from their places of birth more than
doubled from 61 km to 133 km. As some groups, such as women, military
recruits and forced labourers, remained under-recorded or even unrecorded in
the residence card registers, these 3,000 yearly newcomers represent only a lower
limit of the true volume of immigration in the Napoleonic era, which was probably closer to 4,000 or even 5,000 in certain peak years.[25] Even so, the profile
of newcomers recorded in the residence card registers remains indicative of the
profound enlargement of Antwerp's migration field under Napoleonic rule. The

Graphs 4.2–4.7: Origin Pyramids, 1796–1855 (%).

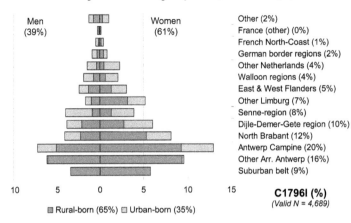

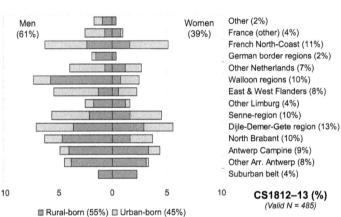

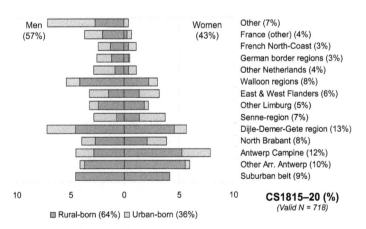

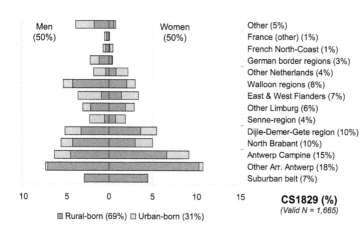

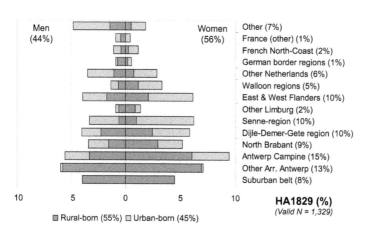

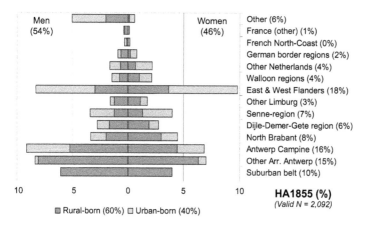

most conspicuous new group of long-distance migrants came from a broad area along the northern coast of France, stretching from Artois to Normandy, raising the share of French-born newcomers from 1 per cent in 1796 to 19 per cent in the Napoleonic period. In addition, a secondary inflow of migrants from a range of villages alongside the Sambre-Meuse axis substantially increased the share of Walloon migrants (from 4 to 13 per cent), while smaller increases were recorded for immigrants born north of the Moerdijk, east of the Meuse-Rhine and west of the Scheldt.[26] With most women continuing to move along regional circuits of migration, the Napoleonic enlargement of Antwerp's migration field remained an almost exclusively male affair.[27] The result was that men outnumbered female newcomers for at least most of the French period, representing another important rupture with the female-dominated recruitment patterns of the later eighteenth century.

The relationship between these migratory changes and Antwerp's new naval activities under Napoleonic rule was manifest. In general, those workers most in demand in the booming shipyards, construction sites and offices, which we know employed up to 6,000 persons at the height of their activities, were those recruited in the highest number and from furthest afield.[28] Carpenters, for instance, came to represent the single most important occupational group of male newcomers in the Napoleonic era (22 per cent), while their average birthplace distance tripled from 60 km in 1796 to 179 km in 1808–13 (Table AII.3 in Appendix II). A paired growth in numbers and recruitment range is also observable for other construction workers, metalworkers and casual labour. Together these different activities employed half of all male newcomers between 1808 and 1813, and were most directly related to the vigorous expansion of Antwerp's function as a prime naval base. In addition, the increase in the recruitment range of administrative personnel, too, was related to the increased demand for public and private clerical workers in the wake of Antwerp's expanding naval, military and commercial undertakings. Immigrants from the more distant regions that had previously remained outside Antwerp's migration field were most markedly oriented towards naval employment. Those from France's northern coast represented the most extreme instance of such regional specialization: while more than half (55 per cent) were caulkers, shipwrights or other woodworkers, the remainder mainly consisted of other construction workers and administrative personnel. Immigration from the Walloon regions, in turn, was primarily oriented towards construction activities (37 per cent), with important numbers of masons, stonecutters, labourers and carpenters, in addition to a large supply of *journaliers* (casual labourers) (28 per cent). Among smaller contingents from beyond the regional hinterland, such as East and West Flanders, the Netherlands and the German border regions, too, the orientation towards naval-related branches was predominant. Interestingly enough, a relatively large proportion of these new and relatively long-distance migrant groups came from a relatively wide range of rural backgrounds – especially in the case of French and Walloon workers – whereas long-distance migration, other things being equal, normally tended to be of an inter-urban nature.

How, then, did these numerous and often rural-born newcomers from distant areas find their way to Antwerp's booming shipyards so swiftly? Evidently, labour demand was an important pull factor. Notwithstanding the rampant unemployment among the local population, there was an objective shortage of workers for Antwerp's naval activities, which is reflected in many sources. As no local tradition of shipbuilding had survived, expertise and trained workers were in short supply.[29] At the same time, those residents who were hardest hit by the collapse of textile production, mainly women, children and the elderly, were badly suited to carry out even the less specialized, but physically demanding, jobs in the shipyards and construction sites.[30] In addition, anecdotal evidence indicates that work on the naval sites was shunned by some local workers because of relatively low wages and irregularities of payment.[31] However, even an objective shortage of local workers does not by itself establish new recruitment patterns, particularly if the wage premium arising from the shortage remained limited. A crucial auxiliary mechanism at meso level in this particular case was the operation of the *inscription maritime* to which certain occupations in the French coastal regions had been subject since the late seventeenth century. Established by Colbert in 1681, maintained after the revolution and extended to the Belgian regions in 1795, it required all men working in occupations deemed useful for the working of the national fleet to have their names and whereabouts recorded in order to be called upon to man navy vessels or shipyards when needed.[32] The only explicit trace of the *inscription maritime* in the Antwerp immigration registers is when certificates from it were produced by newcomers to establish their identity.[33] This was the case with 22 per cent of male immigrants between 1808 and 1811. Although evidently only a lower limit, it is illustrative of important regional differences in this respect: while the great majority of workers from the French north coasts (65 per cent) and from East and West Flanders (55 per cent) produced a naval document to establish their identity, the proportion from other regions doing so was well below 10 per cent, and was often negligible. The channels along which naval-related and construction workers outside the scope of the *inscription maritime* were recruited, such as most of the Walloon labourers and stonecutters, remain obscure. In some instances, this immigration might have been built on the social networks and information channels established by groups already present in the 1796 census.[34] However, since many newcomers came from places of birth which did not figure in the 1796 census,[35] additional channels and media of information, such as newspaper advertisements, word-of-mouth, active recruitment (directly or via subcontracting) and *levées extraordinaires* (conscription) are likely to have played an important role in extending Antwerp's migration field in this period of intense naval construction activity.[36] Although some might have moved via informal social networks, many naval workers were part of a mobile and specialized workforce moving between the different naval bases of imperial France via a long-standing system of state-organized labour allocation. These would have been even more in number if we include the military personnel not recorded in the residence card registers. The scope and complexity of these allocation mechanisms help to explain why these often long-distance workers were recruited so promptly in such large numbers and with a considerable proportion of rural-born in their midst – characteristics generally associated with longer-standing migration patterns of a certain maturity and well-established migration information channels.

To be sure, not all medium- and long-distance migrants entering Antwerp in the Napoleonic period were oriented towards naval or construction activities. Smaller, but nevertheless noticeable, groups of longer-distance migrants were, for instance, made up of mainly French *couturiers* and *couturières*. While some of these might have been engaged in sailmaking, others probably catered to an expanding French-oriented fashion demand as Antwerp became the scene of many lustrous official receptions and festivities, and the city's elite was supplemented by a numbers of commercial, official and military dignitaries.[37] In addition, some of the French women recorded as seamstresses might in fact have been prostitutes, the market for whom expanded considerably with the arrival of the predominantly male naval and military labour force.[38] Finally, an important number of *commis négociants* and traders came to Antwerp from a variety of important and sometimes far-flung commercial centres, such as Amsterdam, Rotterdam, Cologne, Bordeaux, Rouen and Bremen – an indication of the increasing (though precarious) role of Antwerp as an international commercial hub, which was to be reinforced in the following decades.

One more salient characteristic of immigration in this period was the high incidence of temporary and seasonal patterns of migration: approximately 48 per cent of men and 33 per cent of female newcomers in the period 1808–13 left town again within one year after their arrival (Table AII.4 in Appendix II). Long-term stayers constituted only a fraction of the inflow and were also dissimilar in terms of gender: 26 per cent of women stayed longer than five years, as against 11 per cent of men. While birthplace distance was generally negatively correlated with length of stay, it is worth noting that some of the local market occupations which were supplied mainly by hinterland workers, such as assistant bakers or farm boys, also displayed very temporary patterns of stay – which must have been obscured from view in the 1796 census. The highest incidences of seasonal migration were recorded in construction-related occupations, such as stonecutters, bricklayers, metalworkers and day-labourers, while the most persistent groups were found among officials, office workers, clergy and domestic servants, the majority of whom were likely to stay in town longer than one year. Interestingly, only 34 per cent of migrants from the northern coast of France left town again within one year of their arrival, suggesting that the trained workers recruited via the naval registry were kept in place year-round, possibly to secure adequate labour supplies, while the auxiliary construction workers recruited via less formal circuits came only for the busy season and returned home in the winter. As they generally stayed only for two or a maximum of three years, however, most naval workers were also essentially temporary migrants, whose eventual legacy was limited: after Antwerp's naval shipyards were dismantled in the wake of the Restoration's new balance of power, most of them left the town for good.[39]

As the labour demand that had recruited the bulk of extra workers under the French regime evaporated when the Napoleonic shipyards were abandoned, the transition from French to Dutch rule coincided with a steep drop in immigration. This fall was primarily attributable to the implosion of those relatively new and distant recruitment patterns that had been oriented almost exclusively towards the naval construction works of the French period, most notably those from the French north coast and the Walloon areas.[40] Although patterns of regional migration resumed some of their earlier predominance, the Dutch period did not mark a return to the migration regime of the late eighteenth century, owing to a substantial expansion – both in relative and absolute terms – of the number of (very) long-distance migrants. Even if the radical fall in the number of French-born immigrants is left out of the calculations, newcomers from beyond the boundaries of the then Kingdom of the Netherlands increased their share from 3 per cent in 1796, and 4 per cent in the Napoleonic era, to more than 10 per cent in the first years of Dutch rule, representing an average yearly inflow of 120 long-distance newcomers between 1815 and 1820. Most of these were Germans (an average of 80 per year) and Britons (29), in addition to smaller numbers from Eastern and Central Europe, Italy and Switzerland, and Scandinavia. Predominantly active in (wholesale) trade and shipping, these upmarket long-distance migrants were attracted by the opportunities which Antwerp's resumed commercial and shipping activities presented.

This post-Napoleonic influx of foreign businessmen and merchants laid the foundations for some of the most illustrious nineteenth-century Antwerp trading companies, while at the same time establishing new migration circuits with a lasting impact. Several of the commercial agents who immigrated in the early Dutch period to establish or expand an Antwerp-based venture, such as the Frankfurt-born Jacob Fuchs, or William Wood from Mansfield, would remain important players on the commercial scene for decades to come.[41] Once established, these offices in turn exerted a substantial demand for auxiliary clerks, agents and

Maps 4.1–6: Immigrants' Regions of Birth, 1796–1855 (%).[42]

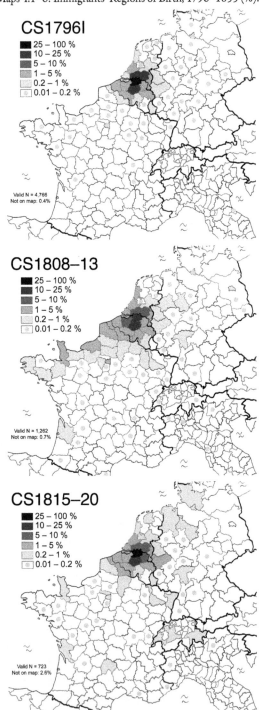

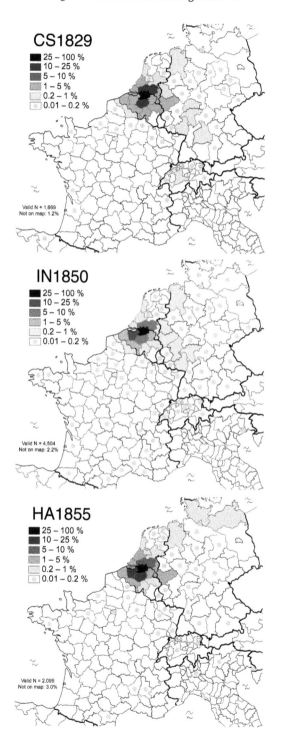

merchants from the home region and other commercial centres – supporting a permanent flow of long-distance migrants by establishing Antwerp as an important node in commercial circuits of international migration, as illustrated by the large number of mainly German office clerks and commercial agents recorded in the 1829 residence card registers.[43] In addition, the expansion of maritime shipping in itself further increased the foreign presence in Antwerp, in the sense that a growing number and diversity of seamen, sailors, passengers and travellers passed through the Antwerp port, who because of their fleeting presence largely escape from the census' or residence card registers' view. The list of admissions to the St Elisabeth hospital in 1829 attests obliquely to this increased 'exotic' presence, recording at least thirteen admissions of persons born in the United States of America (all from East Coast cities such as Boston, New York, Philadelphia and Baltimore), nine patients born in Scandinavia, two born in Indonesia, and one each from India, Riga (Latvia) and Varna (Bulgaria). That almost all foreign migrants but those from the German border regions came from coastal regions or port cities attests to the importance of increasing maritime traffic in (selectively) shaping and extending Antwerp's foreign migration field.

While the first years after independence witnessed a slump in foreign immigration, the catchment area of Antwerp's long-distance newcomers continued to grow wider and more diverse as the city's maritime activities again expanded in the early decades of the Belgian Kingdom.[44] The median birthplace distance of non-Belgian newcomers increased further from 98 km in the 1829 residence card registers to 131 km in the 1850 aliens' records, while the proportion of very-long-distance migrants born more than 240 km away grew markedly from 21 to 38 per cent. While the largest number of 'foreign' immigrants in 1850 continued to come from the cross-border province of North Brabant (30 per cent) and other Dutch regions (21 per cent), important contingents were supplied by a varied range of German places (24 per cent), especially along the Rhine and in Westphalia, and smaller numbers came from France (10 per cent), the British Isles (7 per cent), Switzerland (2 per cent), Scandinavia (1 per cent), and even from as far away as Warsaw, Riga and St Petersburg. Among the most exotic, we find newcomers born in Rio de Janeiro, the East Indies and Algiers. The importance of maritime and commercial connections in supporting the observed extension of Antwerp's recruitment area remained obvious: almost all migrants from beyond a 100 km radius came from coastal regions, main commercial centres, and/or places located along important waterways. As before, long-distance movement continued to be an almost exclusively male and urban affair,[45] oriented towards the upmarket and specialist segments of Antwerp's increasingly metropolitan opportunity structure, such as wholesale trade, shipping, office personnel, the professions and the production of luxury goods.

While the outer range of Antwerp's migration field was repeatedly expanded, reoriented and repositioned over the first decades of the nineteenth century, regional migration remained a significant and relatively stable component of immigration streams during the whole period. Throughout the French and Dutch regimes, migration from those hinterland areas that have already been identified as the main regional recruitment locations in the late eighteenth century, continued to account for a sizeable proportion of the total inflow. While migrants born within the Antwerp province provided between 22 and 44 per cent of newcomers in these years, those from the neighbouring provinces of Brabant and North Brabant continued to supply another 10–19 and 8–10 per cent respectively – attesting to a continued importance of the greater Brabantine area as the city's main regional recruitment area. These regional migrant streams also appeared least affected by the sudden ups and downs associated with regime changes: fluctuations in their relative contribution to overall immigration flows tended to be attributable more to shifts in distant migration streams than to marked oscillations in the absolute number of Brabantine newcomers. If anything, the latter were more or less continually on the rise throughout the first decades of the nineteenth century, and would continue to be so in the early decades of the Belgian Kingdom.[46]

By the 1840s and 1850s, however, when overall migration numbers peaked, the long-standing Brabantine connection would be supplemented, and to a certain extent surpassed, by a notable expansion of Antwerp's regional recruitment area in a western direction (Map 4.10, below). While published census results indicate a disproportionate growth of inter-provincial immigration streams in this period,[47] more detailed nominal sources allow us to establish that most of this growth was attributable to the rising number of migrants from Flanders, in particular from the province of East Flanders. Previously located largely outside Antwerp's recruitment area, by the 1850s the latter province supplied more migrants than the province of Brabant, which had up until the 1830s constituted by far the most important province of origin next to Antwerp itself.[48] By mid-century, recruitment from Flanders displayed many characteristics that have been identified as typical of regional patterns of recruitment: large numbers, a relatively high proportion of women and rural-born migrants, and a relatively diffuse area of recruitment.[49] Important origin clusters were the Waasland region down to Dendermonde and Aalst, and the villages and townships in the Ghent area. Meanwhile, recruitment from other Belgian and Brabantine regions, although still on the rise in absolute terms, declined in relative importance. The end result of these uneven developments was that the wider Brabantine connection – which had formed Antwerp's main recruitment area in the preceding centuries – gave way to a stronger Flemish connection, resulting in a durable restructuring of Antwerp's regional migration field in a western direction that would retain its impact well into the twentieth century.

By far the largest increases in the numbers of migrants throughout the first half of the nineteenth century, however, were recorded for villages in the immediate surroundings of the city and in the Campine region, confirming their position as the mainstay of the city's demographic basin. Defined in terms of emigration intensity in order to approximate the concept of *bassin démographique*, the geographic contours of Antwerp's prime recruitment area indeed remained markedly stable throughout the first half of the nineteenth century – and were restricted mainly to the province of Antwerp. Around 1850, those boroughs sending the highest number of migrants to Antwerp in relation to their population size were more or less the same ones that had constituted the city's demographic basin in the late eighteenth century – albeit that the Flemish connection had constituted a moderate expansion towards the west. While the contours may have remained markedly stable, however, the *intensity* of migration to Antwerp from within its demographic basin increased markedly over time, as the continuous growth in the numbers of immigrants from these boroughs far exceeded their rates of population growth (Maps 4.7–10). While the yearly number of intra-provincial immigrants had amounted to 1.6 per thousand of the population of the Antwerp province (excluding its capital) in the Napoleonic period, in 1815–20 the equivalent figure had risen to 1.8 per thousand, and by 1829 to as high as 2.6 per thousand. The greatest spurt, however, took place during the 1840s: by 1850 no less than 0.7 per cent of the provincial population migrated to Antwerp each year, by which time no less than forty-three municipalities sent more than 0.5 per cent of their total population to Antwerp *each year*, and twenty-five boroughs – most of which were situated in the immediate surroundings of the city – sent more than 1 per cent. Although the imprecision of the population and immigration figures available hampers the exactness of the calculations, the overall tendency towards increasing levels of migration intensity was very marked.[50] In other words: people born in the province of Antwerp became ever more likely to move to its capital city as the century progressed. At the individual village level, this meant that migration to Antwerp was becoming an ever more important and common component of daily life in many places.

The occupational profile of most regional migrants was marked by a strong continuity throughout the whole period under consideration. While the male component became more important as time wore on, and the importance of certain occupations shifted through time, they remained focused mainly upon those relatively unspecialized jobs in the local service, distribution and maintenance sectors that had been their main terrain of action in the late eighteenth century. The fact, too, that these less specialized hinterland recruitment circuits persisted and even intensified in the face of large-scale unemployment of the local population raises more poignant questions about the precise role of migrants in Antwerp's conversion from textile centre to port town.

While each of the major phases of political and economic change was characterized by distinct patterns of recruitment, then, the evolution of Antwerp's migration field in the first half of the nineteenth century displayed two general trends: various expansions of its outer limits on the one hand, and an intensification and partial restructuring of its regional mainstay on the other – which resulted in ever larger and more diverse flows of newcomers. Transport developments evidently played a part in achieving these changes. The growth of maritime trade, railways and road systems provided the city with new and denser connections to both its regional hinterland and far-flung areas, facilitating the flow of goods, information and people. In addition, political conflicts and regime changes also played a role in favouring or weakening certain geographical connections. The examples of French naval workers or German commercial clerks illustrate how newly emerging channels of migration – be they public or private – were likewise important in guiding new streams of migrants. While the precise role of networks and circuits will be addressed in greater detail in the next chapter, the following paragraphs first aim to look closer at the evolution of push and pull forces that underlay the observed changes in aggregate migration patterns. As was argued in the first and second chapters, these push and pull forces at the macro level can be considered as moulding the conditions within which networks, circuits and individual agency were able to operate. Before evaluating the adaptive strategies of different migrant groups, then, the discussion now concentrates on the relationship between the observed changes in aggregate migration flows and the changing structure of constraints and opportunities – and on their implications for the general experience of moving to Antwerp. On the one hand, the rising numbers of both long-distance and short-distance migrants seem to suggest that Antwerp's overall attractive power increased considerably as it changed from a regional textile centre to an international port town. On the other hand, however, the intensified and expanded nature of regional recruitment also hints at the importance of growing rural distress in driving larger numbers of migrants to Antwerp.

A Migrant-Friendly Opportunity Structure?

What were Antwerp's immigrants looking for when they moved to the city in ever larger numbers and from a growing variety of origins during the first half of the nineteenth century? And what did they actually find when they arrived? To what extent did the conversion to a port town create new and sizeable opportunities for newcomers, and how can this be reconciled with the available evidence on rampant unemployment and worsening living conditions among the labour-

Maps 4.7–10: Migration Intensities per Municipality of Birth, 1808–50 (‰).[51]

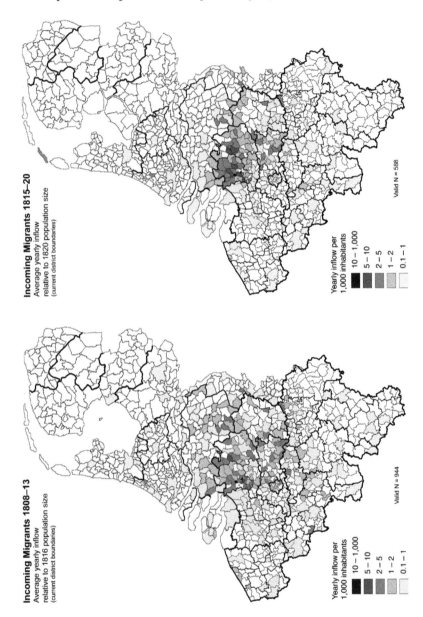

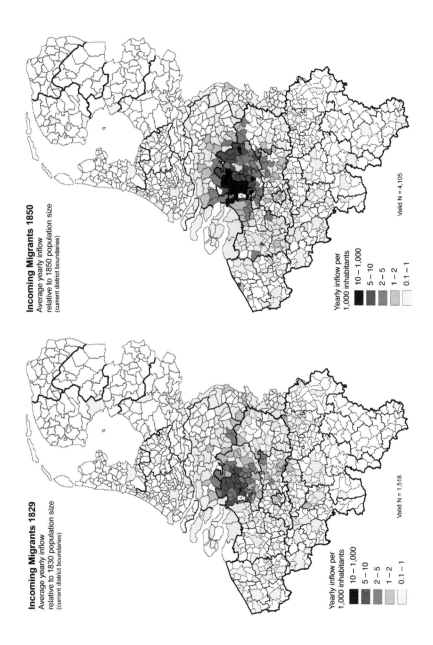

Incoming Migrants 1850
Average yearly inflow
relative to 1850 population size
(current district boundaries)

Yearly inflow per
1,000 inhabitants
10 – 1,000
5 – 10
2 – 5
1 – 2
0.1 – 1

Valid N = 4,105

Incoming Migrants 1829
Average yearly inflow
relative to 1830 population size
(current district boundaries)

Yearly inflow per
1,000 inhabitants
10 – 1,000
5 – 10
2 – 5
1 – 2
0.1 – 1

Valid N = 1,518

ing poor? While the picture already given has hinted at some of the factors at play, a more comprehensive view of the changing positions of migrants within the shifting local opportunity structure can be gained from comparing occupational data from the census of 1830 with those derived from the 1796 census. The thirty-odd years that separated the two censuses were the scene of some of the most radical shifts in Antwerp's political and economic history: still a middle-sized regional textile centre in 1796, by 1830 it was already well underway to becoming a major international port town. This drastic makeover of course had profound effects on the structure of the urban labour market, which reflect the overall thrust of change wrought by the city's economic conversion.

Figures on the occupational distribution of the active population in both censuses bear witness to the dramatic collapse of textile production on the one hand, and the vast expansion of port-related employment on the other. Between 1796 and 1830, the proportion of the urban population active in the production of durable consumer goods fell from more than 50 per cent to only 26 per cent. This decline in industrial activity was attributable exclusively to the collapse of textile and lace industries, whose combined employment shares fell from 36 per cent in 1796 to only 11 per cent in 1830 – representing an even bigger fall in absolute numbers. The fastest growers, on the other hand, were situated in sectors that were directly or indirectly related to port activities. The rise in numbers of workers engaged in tool production and building work (from 7 to 12 per cent) – such as carpenters, stonecutters and metalworkers – attests to the proliferation of shipbuilding and various infrastructure works. The increase in the number of workers explicitly engaged in transport and the outright explosion of those plainly recorded as 'day labourers' (from 3 to 17 per cent) in turn forms one of the most direct indications of the growing importance of irregular and casual labour in the periphery of the burgeoning port labour market. While source-specific problems hamper comparison in exact numbers between the two censuses, it is apparent that wholesale activities and the auxiliary army of clerks and bookkeepers likewise expanded over the period. A more limited growth rate, more or less commensurate with the path of demographic increase, was apparent among domestic servants, shopkeepers, bakers, butchers, barkeepers and other activities oriented mainly towards the local demand structure. Together, these occupational shifts increased the combined share of trade and services from 33 to 53 per cent, so firmly replacing the production of durable consumer goods as the city's main sector of employment.

Further analysis of the census data demonstrates that the costs and benefits of these employment shifts were very unevenly spread. Not only were they heavily gender-biased, with women particularly hard hit by the collapse of textile industries and badly suited for the new employment opportunities at the docks, shipyards or commercial offices, but the shifts can also be shown to have been markedly biased in terms of geographical origin (Table 4.1). Comparing origin-specific occupational census data shows that those sectors that were hardest hit by the collapse of the town's industrial base were generally those in which migrants had been markedly under-represented in the eighteenth century. The expanding sectors, on the other hand, were those in which migrants had already been well represented in the eighteenth century, and in which their participation increased even further over the first decades of the nineteenth century. Not only were migrants relatively unscathed by the collapse of textile production, then, but they also appear to have succeeded in securing most of the new employment opportunities in the expanding port-related sectors.

Table 4.1: Employment and Immigrant Participation in 1796 and 1830 (%).[52]

	Men				Women			
	City Total (%)		% of I in CT		City Total (%)		% of I in CT	
	1796	1830	1796	1830	1796	1830	1796	1830
Domestic service	5	5	70	80	21	32	73	81
White-collar workers	6	8	31	52	1	1	20	48
Trade & retail	9	10	32	56	7	5	33	41
Shipping	2	3	8	62	–	–	–	–
Transport workers & casual labour	4	17	45	47	1	16	32	49
Catering, local services & food industries	6	7	51	68	4	4	35	43
Tools & construction	13	19	30	44	–	–	–	–
Textiles & lace	22	5	10	15	51	19	12	11
Clothing & leather	13	12	16	24	7	14	35	37
Luxuries & other consumer durables	6	5	16	23	–	–	–	–
Primary sector	5	3	38	49	1	–	57	–
Clergy & proprietors	5	4	36	43	5	8	60	49
Other & miscellaneous	3	2	34	42	1	–	26	–
Total	100	100	28	45	100	100	30	50
Valid N	13,671	18,803	3,795	8,550	12,410	11,969	3,709	5,949
No occupation	1,802	4,177	198	873	8,606	16,995	2,234	6,465
Grand total	15,473	22,980	3,993	9,423	21,016	28,964	5,943	12,414

Abbreviations: % of I in CT: % of immigrants in city total.

The dynamics of this migrant bias were most salient in the male labour market, where migrants increased their share of the active population from 27 per cent in 1796 to 45 per cent in 1830. In the early decades of the nineteenth century, male migrants succeeded in enlarging their participation in virtually all sectors that were on the winning side of the employment shift. While the multiplication of shipyards and construction sites drove up the numbers of carpenters, masons, metalworkers and other tools and construction workers from 13 to 19 per cent of the active male population, immigrants increased their share of this particular sector from 30 to 44 per cent. Similarly, immigrants firmly established their predominance among merchants, shopkeepers and vendors by raising their participation in the growing sector of trade and retail from 32 to 56 per cent. The growing numbers of clerks and other white-collar workers employed in the mushrooming commercial and civil offices – from 6 to 8 per cent – were also disproportionately provided by migrants, augmenting their share from 31 to 52 per cent. Immigrants' marked progression in the sector of shipping (from barely 8 to 62 per cent) was associated with a radical switch from inland shipping in 1796 – dominated by Antwerp-born shipmasters and boatmen – to maritime shipping in 1830 – dominated by immigrant sailors. The dramatic expansion of the numbers of freight handlers and casual labourers, from 4 to 17 per cent of the active male population, went hand in hand with a small increase in the already large proportion of immigrants in the sector (from 45 to 47 per cent). While *natie* workers continued to form a stable core of transport workers, most of the men in this group were recorded in the census as labourers or day-labourers, since the greater part worked on a casual basis along the bustling quaysides, warehouses, dockyards and construction sites.[53] Finally, migrants also reinforced their majority position in inns, bars, bakeries and breweries by raising their share in the maintenance sectors of catering, local services and food industries from 51 to 68 per cent. Immigrants were, however, much less numerous in sectors on the losing side of the employment shift. Migrants' relative absence in the production of textiles, clothing, leather goods, luxury goods and other durable consumer goods – constituting only 20 per cent of the total workforce in these sectors – should not be interpreted as a retreat in the face of industrial decline, but was essentially the continuation of an earlier pattern: in 1796, their participation in those sectors – then still the major employers of the urban population – had been even smaller still (13 per cent).

Developments in the female labour market paralleled those in the male labour market, but were more negatively affected by the collapse of textile industries and lace production, which together had employed more than half of the female workforce in the eighteenth century. By 1830, the production of textiles employed barely 1 per cent of the active female population, as against 13 per cent in 1796, while the proportion of lace workers had fallen from 38 per cent to 18 per cent – and would soon collapse completely.[54] This breakdown went hand in hand with an overall retreat of women from regular or formal gainful employment. Even allowing for variations in the scope of registration of the two censuses, the proliferation of the number of women 'without occupation' between 1796 and 1830 (from 8,500 to 17,000) forms a clear indication of how the collapse of their main breadwinning activity posed mounting problems to securing a regular income base. Not all women, however, were equally affected. Much like their male counterparts, female migrants appear to have steered clear of most of these adverse developments. While they had been markedly under-represented in those sectors showing the largest job losses, the growth of alternative opportunities was mainly situated in branches where they had already established a strong presence in the eighteenth century, resulting in a marked increase in the proportion of immigrants in the female labour market, from 30 to 50 per cent. The growth in the number of domestic servants is a case in point. While demand was stimulated by mercantile wealth, the proliferation of inns and shops along the quaysides, and overall demographic growth, both custom and exigencies in terms of marital status continued to reserve this expanding sector largely to single, young immigrants. The impressive growth in the sector of casual labour, from virtually nothing in 1796 to 16 per cent of the female workforce in 1830, was more evenly distributed between locals and immigrants, illustrating women's attempts to compensate employment losses by performing a variety of odd jobs, such as out-house cleaning, laundering, vending, occasional dock work[55] and prostitution.[56] Finally, the growth in the number of seamstresses, partly stimulated by the fashion demands of high-income and middle-income groups, went hand in hand with a strong feminization of the garment trades, which probably paralleled a decline in overall working and earning conditions.[57] Even those sectors recording expansion, however, could not match the growth of employment opportunities in the male labour market nor offset the loss of textile jobs: while the active male population grew from 13,700 to 18,800 between 1796 and 1830, the number of women stating an occupation actually *decreased* slightly from 12,400 to 12,000 over the same period.

Antwerp's conversion from a regional textile centre to a port town, then, had a mixed and somewhat paradoxical effect on the local opportunity structure. On the one hand, there is no doubt that the collapse of textile production occasioned a severe crisis and entailed rampant unemployment for the majority of the local population.[58] On the other hand, the revival of maritime trade and associated activities created a sizeable demand for both specialized and less specialized labour. Migrants on the whole were on the winning side of this equation. While the locally-born population was most heavily hit by the collapse of textile industries, migrants succeeded in securing most of the newly created port-related employment opportunities. In fact, migrants were the main, if not sole, contributors to the growth of the urban workforce. While the number of Antwerp-born men stating an occupation remained constant at a level of 10,000 between 1796 and 1830, their immigrant counterparts more than doubled in number from 3,600 to 8,600 – thus effectively filling virtually all of the 5,000 additional male jobs created over this period. In the female labour market, the influx of migrants even ended up compensating for an absolute loss of Antwerp-born workers over the same period: while the number of Antwerp-born women with a recorded occupation actually fell from around 8,600 to 6,000, that of immigrant women rose from 3,800 to 6,000.[59]

At the same time, it is clear that different migrant groups clustered in different occupational sectors. A closer comparison of immigrants' occupations in 1830 in relation to their geographical origin demonstrates that Antwerp's expansion as a port town provided important – but different – opportunities for short-distance and longer-distance migrants (Table AII.5 in Appendix II). Important occupational sectors for immigrants born in the province of Antwerp were those of domestic service, casual labour, food processing, retailing, plain carpentry and freight handling – in other words, a reinforcement of immigrants' strongholds in the later eighteenth century. Migrants born further away, most of whom were men, in turn had a distinctive edge in wholesale trade, shipping, office personnel and specialized construction work. Among migrants born outside the then United Kingdom of the Netherlands, a general specialization in either trade-related activities or highly skilled industry was even more marked. Migrants from the regional hinterland thus tended to maintain their orientation towards relatively less specialized occupational branches, while the more distant migrants aimed for employment opportunities of a more skilled and specialized nature. Both groups, however, succeeded in enlarging their share of the urban labour market at the cost of local workers.

The uneven distribution of losses and gains of Antwerp's transformation of the early nineteenth century is evocative of the degree of its labour market segmentation. The destruction of one economic sector and the blossoming of another were not accompanied by a simple relocation of the working population from the former to the latter. Instead, labour recruitment evolved along lines and channels shaped largely by pre-existing patterns of segmentation, in turn moulded by an intricate mixture of skills, ability and custom. Gender, for instance, was a powerful barrier. As most of the new port-related jobs were only open to men, they could not compensate for the huge loss in female jobs due to the collapse of the production of textiles and lace. Even within gender-specific labour markets, the intrinsic differences in the nature of employment opportunities foregone and those newly created were such as to impede a smooth reallocation of labour. In some instances, differences in life-cycle and working conditions precluded a move from declining to expanding sectors. Domestic service, for instance, was open only to young, single women, who were expected to live in and were paid largely in kind. Hence, the growth of this sector did not provide a ready alternative to erstwhile spinners and lace makers of an advanced age or with family responsibilities. Skills and ability likewise played a discriminatory role. Some of the new port-related labour demand was directed at specialist workers, like shipwrights, compass makers or bookkeepers. As no maritime tradition was left in the early nineteenth century, few such skills were locally available, and even fewer were suited to the profiles of erstwhile weavers, spinners or dyers. Differences in age and physical strength placed young and healthy country folk in a better position than erstwhile textile producers for the unskilled but physically demanding hauling and carrying jobs that proliferated. Few indications survive of the earnings of casual labourers at the docksides, warehouses and construction sites, but the available evidence indicates that rates were relatively high, providing an important wage premium to rural migrants.[60] However, casual earnings were extremely temporary and irregular, which is why they may not have been a desirable alternative to the lost stable incomes of erstwhile industrial producers. Furthermore, one can only speculate on the precise nature of cultural and social barriers that interacted with skill, strength and wages to compartmentalize the urban labour market. Yet these mattered a great deal. The fact that migrants as early as the eighteenth century had established a strong position in most of the branches that would expand markedly in the wake of Antwerp's conversion put them in a commanding position to take up most of the newly created employment opportunities. To do so, they could not only build on a number of comparative advantages in terms of age, skill and strength, but also mobilize the socially embedded recruitment circuits that had been established in the preceding period, and which formed the key to employment in sectors as irregular and informal as dock labour or construction work. That migrants had already held an important stake in the pre-revolutionary freight-handling *naties*, for instance, undoubtedly helped them maintain a virtual monopoly among transport workers in the 1820s. After having been abolished in the early years of French rule, the Antwerp *naties* had continued to function on an informal basis until they were restored in a corporate form to act as the main organizers of dock work in the early nineteenth century – a position they would maintain throughout the nineteenth and twentieth centuries. Hence, *natie*-linked recruitment patterns and social networks remained of prime importance in the organization of nineteenth-century dock work.[61]

As a nineteenth-century port town, then, Antwerp presented considerably more opportunities for both highly skilled and unspecialized immigrants than it had done as a regional textile centre in the eighteenth century. The analysis of the eighteenth-century labour market in the previous chapter has demonstrated how jobs in trade, services, construction and transport were considerably more accessible to Antwerp's mainly rural newcomers than the production of durable consumer goods. Transformation into a port town therefore had the effect of encouraging the expansion of jobs that in the eighteenth century had already constituted the favoured terrain of newcomers. Although such speculation is fraught with difficulty, it is unlikely that migrants would have found so many employment opportunities if Antwerp had remained a textile centre that had mechanized its production. The majority of the industrial workforce would in that case probably have been supplied by locally-born textile workers – as was, for instance, the case in contemporary Ghent – while opportunities for rural immigrants would have remained limited or in any case underdeveloped, much as in the eighteenth century.[62] In 'consumer' cities where small-scale (upmarket) handicraft production occupied an important position, like Brussels or Vienna, opportunities for newcomers were considerably greater, but were concentrated in semi-skilled or skilled segments that were less accessible to unspecialized rural migrants.[63] By developing into a port town, then, Antwerp created significantly more opportunities accessible to unspecialized rural migrants than nineteenth-century cities that concentrated on mechanized or industrial production. This comparatively large demand for unspecialized labour, in turn, is likely to have been a prime factor in stimulating immigration, and in eventually making Antwerp the fastest growing city in nineteenth-century Belgium.

The migrant-friendly nature of Antwerp's conversion corresponds with some of the general characteristics of many nineteenth-century port towns, much as the observed high mortality and fertility rates, the constrained female employment opportunities and the prevalence of cyclical unemployment. Similarly, a large demand for unspecialized labour is often encountered as an important pull factor, and a large number of immigrant residents – often operating on a distinctive and extremely casual secondary dock labour market – is considered a socio-demographic characteristic of many nineteenth-century port towns.[64] Although temporary migrants abounded, and turnover would rise markedly in the course of the nineteenth century, Antwerp appears to have been exceptional in that newcomers succeeded in gaining predominance in both the core and the periphery of its developing port labour market: migrants abounded both among the gangers and regular workforce of the *naties*, and the more peripheral segment of temporary day-labourers. In contrast, most other port towns of similar or larger size, like Amsterdam, Rotterdam or London, saw the core positions in the port labour markets generally taken up by local workers, while migrants were mainly relegated to the peripheral segments.[65] That this was not the case in Antwerp can be attributed to the fact that port activity was an essentially new sector, with few vested interests on the part of local groups. It was helped, moreover, by the contingency of a strong immigrant presence in the eighteenth-century *naties*, which resurfaced in a modified form to coordinate much of Antwerp's swelling port activity from the Dutch period onwards.

Both for specialized and less specialized migrants, then, the expansion of Antwerp's port-related employment opportunities seems to have constituted a major pull factor in increasing the number of newcomers throughout the first three decades of the nineteenth century. This was the case both during the Napoleonic period, when large-scale naval projects necessitated large inflows of skilled and unskilled workers, and during the period under Dutch rule, when the expansion of commercial maritime shipping continued to enlarge the demand for different types of construction, transport, trade and service workers. On the other side of the balance, moreover, adverse developments in Antwerp's hinterland simultaneously acted as important push forces for many regional migrants. The processes of demographic expansion and proletarianization that had been accelerating in the Duchy of Brabant since 1750 were leading to growing distress by the first decades of the nineteenth century. Real wages in the Antwerp countryside were declining, falling to levels well below their urban equivalents.[66] The proportion of those in regular receipt of poor relief in turn increased markedly as the century progressed – while eligibility criteria if anything were tightened over the period.[67] The gradual deterioration of rural livelihoods increased people's vulnerability to subsistence shocks like the 1817 crisis, when a series of harvest failures led to high grain prices and severe food crises in what John Post has called the last European pre-industrial famine.[68] Barely recovered from the political and military upheavals of Napoleon's downfall, the region of Antwerp was hit hard by the agricultural crisis, with average grain prices rising to more than double their normal level, and the subsequent sharp and prolonged fall in prices in turn complicating matters for agricultural producers.[69]

Evidence from the immigration registers suggests that the 1817 crisis did not so much occasion a large increase in the numbers of newcomers – the dearth years actually witnessed a reduction of the numbers of immigrants, while the following years recorded relatively modest growth – but rather a shift in their life-cycle profile and their patterns of stay.[70] With the proportion of older-age and family migration significantly on the rise as food prices peaked, the waning selectivity of newcomers in the late 1810s forms a strong indication of the increased importance of push over pull forces in governing their moves. However, as the earlier preponderance of young, single migrants was restored in the 1820s, the distortion in terms of life-cycle selectivity was short-lived.[71] Although growing agricultural distress undoubtedly encouraged the intensification of regional recruitment, then, its impact was not so overriding as to flood the city with indiscriminate streams of destitute country dwellers, or to affect permanently the selectivity of migrants. Yet rural misery also contributed to another more lasting shift in migrant behaviour, namely a general trend towards significantly longer periods of stay (Table AII.4 in Appendix II). While the demographic calculations in Chapter 2 have already indicated that persistence rates increased considerably in the 1820s, the collected data on migrant cohorts confirm that their overall length of stay was more or less continually on the rise from the late Napoleonic period on, in particular among rural-born and regional migrants. With almost one in two newcomers likely to stay longer than five or even ten years by the 1820s, persistence attained levels that were unprecedented in Antwerp's recent history.[72] That more men and women stayed in town longer was no doubt partly because there was less to go back to. That they were able to stay, however, was only possible because of real and expanding income opportunities. That pull factors were at least as important as push factors in driving the migration patterns of the 1820s is confirmed by the sudden drop in immigration levels when Belgian independence disrupted Antwerp's port economy in the early 1830s.[73] Another indication is the increasing masculinization of the immigrant population over this period, from 69 men for every 100 women in the 1796 census to a sex ratio of 77:100 in the census of 1830, which signals a selective adaptation to the growth of employment opportunities in the male labour market. To the extent migrants were partially driven by rural push forces in the Dutch period, then, they were also positively selected in terms of age, sex and skill. Hence, push forces were balanced in a more positive manner by the expanding employment opportunities in the city's commercial and maritime facilities, which were sizeable and suitable enough to absorb the intensified inflow from the regional hinterland.

An impression of the absorptive capacities of the 1820s port labour market with regard to longer-term stayers can be gained from comparing the 1830 census data with the 1829 residence card registers (Table AII.5 in Appendix II). Much in the same way as the 1796 census data on the timing of arrival were used to provide a more dynamic view of job-specific mobility, contrasting the occupational structure of recent arrivals in 1829 with that of all immigrant residents in 1830 can give an idea of the direction of trajectories after arrival. On the one hand, the comparison demonstrates the continued importance of certain patterns of temporary migration – mainly in domestic and farm service, construction work and food industries – and of the time-conditioned upward trajectories of small entrepreneurs like shopkeepers, *natiebazen*, innkeepers, bakers and independent artisans that were similar to those established for the late eighteenth century.[74] On the other hand, the comparison demonstrates how the growth in unspecialized wage-dependent jobs not only expanded income opportunities for recent arrivals, but also for long-term stayers. The single most important difference in occupational trajectories in the 1820s as compared to those of the second half of the eighteenth century was the greater number of unspecialized labourers among long-term residents. Because jobs in the casual port labour market did not require any capital outlay or specialist training – unlike setting up an independent shop or business – and were not life-cycle specific – unlike positions such as domestic servant, farmhand or journeyman baker – the expansion of employment opportunities in these branches can be identified as a crucial factor in enabling the long-term settlement of unskilled and less affluent newcomers, and as a major contributor to the observed increase in persistence during the Dutch period. Although work as a casual labourer was hardly an upwardly mobile or enviable career, the favourable and continuous port development of the 1820s helped to establish it as a viable way of getting a foot in urban society. This is confirmed when following the occupational trajectories of the 1817 and 1819 cohorts through the population registers: most of those who were still present at the time of the 1830 census had either entered town in a wage-dependent job in the port-related or service sectors, or had since shifted employment to these branches.[75] The argument is, however, less applicable to female newcomers, whose most common trajectory continued to be that from domestic servant to housewife, while a large number remained in domestic service, suggesting a shift from life cycle to lifetime service.[76] Both trajectories are nevertheless indicative of how maritime expansion also increased women's opportunities for long-term settlement, albeit indirectly: the greater possibilities for young male migrants to settle down also raised women's chances of marriage in town, while the expansion of Antwerp's middle and upper classes increased the demand for experienced domestic servants – providing lifetime career options to those who did not marry.

Most migrants, then, continued to enter town as young, single and unspecialized adults, much as they had in the late eighteenth century. What was new, however, was the great expansion of jobs (or marriage opportunities) accessible in terms of skill and capital requirements which they could perform on a long-term basis – which radically changed the life-cycle context within which migration took place. For an increasing number of newcomers, the move to Antwerp no longer coincided with the *belle saison* or a life-cycle phase of young adulthood, but rather inaugurated a quasi-permanent urban residence. This shift in patterns of stay amplified the medium-term and long-term effects of migration on urban demography and society. During their longer stay, migrants developed more diverse and intense relationships with urban society, including the rites of passage of marriage, childbirth and death. While the likelihood of contracting marriage in town was stronger among men than women, an important number of whom remained in domestic service, the majority of long-term stayers married in Antwerp within ten years of their arrival.[77] Once married, their likelihood of leaving town again decreased significantly, which confirms the contribution of marriage opportunity dynamics to the general lengthening of stay.[78] Hannes' analysis of the 457 marriages contracted in 1830 shows that origin-specific spouse preferences decreased somewhat as compared to the late eighteenth century, leading to a growing number of 'mixed' marriages (32 per cent) between Antwerp-born and migrants.[79] Not only did more newcomers stay in town, settle down and marry there, but they also regularly ended up marrying someone from a different place or region of origin, thus contributing to the integration of Antwerp's enlarged and varied group of newcomers into the urban fabric. In some – possibly rare – cases, domestic servants ended up marrying a member of the household in which they served. Cornelie Wouters from Turnhout, for instance, arrived in Antwerp in December 1819 at the age of nineteen to work as a domestic servant in the household of Cornelius Janssens, a wood trader from Willebroek. She was still there when Janssens' wife died in 1821 leaving two children, and ended up marrying her widowed master four years later, giving birth to a third child herself only six months after marriage. The vacant maid's position was filled by a namesake from the same place of birth, possibly a younger sister or cousin.[80] Most migrants, however, probably met their future spouses elsewhere, on the streets and markets, or via friends and family.

Although there are no aggregate figures available on the origin of parents of newborn children, the combination of migrants' favourable age structure and their growing tendency to settle down and marry in town was no doubt an important contributor to the observed increase in urban birth rates of this period. Francisca Van Hemelrijck from Brussels, for instance, who came to Antwerp as a domestic servant in 1819, gave birth to no less than ten children after marrying a locally-born coppersmith's mate in 1823. Five of these, however, died at an early age – a reflection of Antwerp's high infant mortality and the ravaging effects of the cholera epidemic of 1832, when she lost three of her children.[81] Female migrants also appeared particularly prone to unmarried motherhood, contributing to the comparatively large number of 'illegitimate' births in Antwerp.[82] While some of these births took place within the context of non-marital unions,[83] most immigrant single mothers remained on their own, possibly because they lacked the social clout to persuade the fathers of their child into marriage.[84] With single motherhood representing a particularly vulnerable position in Antwerp's male-dominated labour market, some illegitimate children soon disappeared from the population books, while their mothers (re)turned to domestic service or prostitution.[85] Other migrant unmarried mothers, however, appear to have got by with sewing, casual labour or petty retailing, and with the help of relief provisions or family networks. Finally, the lengthening of migrants' stay meant that they were also to constitute a larger proportion of the number of urban deaths. With no less than 47 per cent of adult mortalities in 1830 relating to persons born outside the city, death too became part of the experience of a growing number of migrants.[86] In all, 5–10 per cent of newcomers from the late 1810s who settled in town died before the 1830 census.[87] While exploration of the precise contribution and rates of migrant-specific mortality requires a demographic analysis of age-specific risks,[88] the data at hand in any case indicate that migration became irreversibly permanent for quite a substantial number of newcomers. The overall increase in migrants' length of stay also implied that the incidence of circular and return migration decreased. Not only did re-migration become less likely the longer migrants stayed in town, but if long-term migrants did leave again, they were less likely than their short-term counterparts to return to their place of birth or previous place of residence.[89] While immigrants' prospects became more firmly situated within the horizons of city life, then, the ties with their home villages – at least in terms of physical return – became increasingly weakened.

Antwerp's conversion to a port town in the course of the first three decades of the nineteenth century therefore greatly expanded local income opportunities for both specialized and unspecialized migrants. By reason of age, skill, and/or pre-existing recruitment circuits and informal preferences, migrants enjoyed better access to expanding port-related employment than local-born residents, who were disproportionately hard hit by the collapse of textile production. While growing rural distress became an important push factor, it did not lead to a permanent distortion of overall migrant selectivity, or to an indiscriminate rise in the number of regional migrants. The intensified flow of hinterland migrants was to a large extent absorbed by the expansion of long-term income opportunities for non-specialized migrants, which allowed newcomers to stay in town for far longer periods of time than in earlier decades. This in turn entailed important modifications of the life-cycle context in which migration took place. Rather than being engaged in temporary or life-cycle patterns of migration, increasing numbers of newcomers by the 1820s settled in town, married, had children and eventually died there, enlarging the impact they had on varied aspects of urban life. In this sense, Antwerp's transformation to a port town clearly appears to have resulted in a migrant-friendly opportunity structure. However, the balance sheet between push and pull forces would become radically redrawn in the wake of the further transformation of town and country in the early decades of the Belgian Kingdom.

The Limits of Urban Absorption

While the first decades of the nineteenth century had already set the stage for a gradual disintegration of rural livelihoods, the first decades of Belgian independence were to experience dramatic and structural breakdowns in the viability of country life. The combination of structural mass unemployment and food crises was the final straw for a rural society that had for many years been under increasing pressure and which suddenly gave way to a stark undermining of living conditions during the crisis of the 1840s. The consequences of the harvest failures of 1845/6 were exacerbated by the dramatic collapse of rural linen industries in the early 1840s, which resulted in mass unemployment for great numbers of the rural population. Although the impact of the crisis of the 1840s was felt hardest in the densely populated Flemish regions, where reliance on rural textile production had been strongest, other regions were also strongly affected by the agricultural failure. I have explained earlier how the influence of the rural crisis of the 1840s on patterns of mobility has a somewhat mixed record in Belgian historiography. The dominant opinion is that the impact was relatively limited, but some studies have provided indications that local migration patterns could be greatly affected. Exploring the further evolution of Antwerp's migration patterns in the wake of the crisis will show how it represented a turning point in urban migration patterns. The effects of increased rural pressure on the one hand, and of the uneven development of the local opportunity structure on the other, would come to lay bare the absorptive limits of the urban labour market.

Although the turmoil of Belgian independence delivered a hard blow to Antwerp's maritime expansion, by the 1840s the city was back on track in its development towards a prime international node of transport and trade, aided by the establishment of the Iron Rhine, the precocious industrialization of Belgium and its border regions, and supportive measures by the liberal-oriented authorities of the new constitutional kingdom. The renewed growth of maritime traffic led to a further increase in the demand for both specialized and less specialized labour, along the same immigrant-friendly lines as in previous decades. The proliferation of various commercial agencies, insurance firms and banking companies further increased opportunities for white-collar workers and commercial specialists, and contributed to a derived demand in the upmarket service sectors and to the city's growing cultural allure.[90] The growth in the volume of transported goods also further increased the demand for dock labour, while the expansion of transit activities supported construction and maintenance works on warehouses, ships, trains and carts. Growing imports also stimulated the further development of a limited number of processing industries, such as tobacco processing, sugar refining and rice polishing, and of local shipbuilding, while the rising number of Atlantic emigrants and passing ships supported a growing emigrants' and sailors' sector of lodging houses, shops and inns.[91]

Together with Antwerp's growing reliance on global trade, however, came an ever greater seasonal character in the rhythms of employment and a growing vulnerability to fluctuations in the unstable world market. While total incoming tonnage in the 1840s and 1850s would reach levels that were on average two to three times as high as in the 1820s, the year-to-year fluctuations at the same time became much more pronounced. While the accumulated falls in incoming tonnage in one year compared to the previous year amounted to 26 per cent of average yearly traffic in the 1820s, in the 1840s this would rise to 74 per cent. The 1850s would witness a more stable rate of expansion, but would entail an even more marked seasonality of labour demand. As a result, labour demand – especially at the bottom end of the labour market – became increasingly more volatile than it had been during the take-off phase of relatively continuous expansion that had characterized the later 1820s. The end result of the increasing volatility of the urban labour market, however, was not so much a simple decline in local opportunities. The heavy fluctuations in port activity actually increased the demand for labour at certain times of the year. As demonstrated by Lis's research, however, the growing irregularity of employment went hand in hand with increasing vulnerability. In 1860 the administration of the Charity Bureau observed: 'Antwerp is no longer an industrial town. Nearly all of the needy are

jacks-of-all trades without permanent occupations ... The overwhelming majority are described as "casual labourers" ... and that is generally correct."[92]

This overall restructuring of limits and opportunities held very different implications for different migrant groups. While these differences will be looked at in
more detail in the next chapter, it suffices here to indicate the continued relevance
of a broad distinction between long-distance migrants, who tended to be relatively well-off and/or specialized, and migrants from closer areas, who clustered
in less specialized segments of the labour market. While Antwerp's international
migration field widened further in the wake of its maritime expansion of the
1840s and 1850s and came to display a certain degree of 'national' specialization,
foreign migrants maintained their orientation towards the more upmarket or
specialized income (or schooling) opportunities which the city's growing metropolitan allure provided, mainly in commerce, high-end retail, intellectual and
artistic activities, and luxury crafts.[93] Their socio-economic profile shows many
resemblances with the foreign immigrants who migrated to Brussels in more or
less the same period, and who were the subject of the doctoral study by Sophie
De Schaepdrijver. Among these 'elites for the capital', predominantly recruited
from France, the Netherlands, Germany and the British Isles, she noted a strong
over-representation of businesspeople, professionals, scientists and artists, while
those engaged in commodity production were mainly specialized and qualified
artisans. In addition, quite a number of foreigners worked in catering services as
cooks and waiters, thus enhancing the cosmopolitan appeal of the developing
café and restaurant culture in the capital. The further away migrants came from,
the stronger this overall orientation was apparent towards specialist and upmarket social strata. In Brussels, as in Antwerp, women constituted only a small
minority of all foreign newcomers, worked predominantly as domestic servants, and were recruited mostly from relatively nearby areas, like the province of
North Brabant – described by De Schaepdrijver as 'regional foreign migration'.[94]
Most long-distance migrants to Brussels were young and single, and attracted
by the expanding opportunities in upmarket commercial, service and artisanal
sectors which the development of the capital as the political, administrative and
financial headquarters of an industrializing nation entailed. The majority had
been born in big cities, and many of the recorded leavers stayed in town for only
a few months or up to a few years at most. Most were engaged in a cosmopolitan
career trajectory along an international network of large cities and many chose
Paris or Antwerp as their next destination, and were likely to return to Brussels
at some later point in time.[95]

Like their counterparts in Brussels – with whom they partly overlapped
– and their predecessors in earlier decades, most of Antwerp's foreign newcomers were engaged in inter-urban migration trajectories, recorded relatively
short periods of stay, operated in upmarket segments of the local opportunity

structure, and can indeed be considered as moving along mainly pull-dominated circuits – as De Schaepdrijver argued in the Brussels case. However, this group of long-distance migrants represented only one specific and very selective segment of newcomers in the 1840s and 1850s. Internal migrants from more neighbouring areas, who were considerably more important in numerical terms, remained oriented primarily towards less specialized segments of the urban labour market. As the employment opportunities in these branches became less stable and less secure, the predominance of pull-factors was less straightforward in the case of internal and short-distance migrants than in that of long-distance newcomers.

While the growing number and diversification of foreign migrants was a salient aspect of migratory change, it was the far greater expansion in the number of Belgian migrants that pushed total volumes of migration to record levels. While recorded immigration levels increased from less than 2,000 in the early 1840s to more than 4,000 by 1850, half of the increase was attributable to a rise in intra-provincial migrants, and another third to the growth of inter-provincial immigration.[96] The unprecedented rise in the volume and intensity of internal migration in turn forms a first indication of the growing importance of rural distress as a migration factor, in particular in combination with the greater presence of migrants from the erstwhile County of Flanders. Previously located outside Antwerp's regional migration field, several boroughs situated west of the Scheldt River would by the 1850s record intensity levels that were comparable to those in Antwerp's long-standing 'demographic basin'. Given that the hungry forties delivered their hardest blows to the Flemish countryside, there is no doubt that the westward expansion of Antwerp's migration field in this period was aided by the shock of famine and mass unemployment that hit Flanders disproportionately hard. Like other regions and cities, Antwerp received its share of the increasing number of migrants fleeing the proverbial poverty of Flanders.[97] That push forces played an important role in Flemish migration is reflected in the life-cycle profile. Compared to migrants moving along long-standing regional circuits, those from Flanders were generally older and more often arrived as families.[98] With their level of occupational specialization no higher than that of Brabantine migrants, the fact of constituting a relatively 'new' migrant group must have hindered their access to social recruitment or supportive networks, while their high dependency ratio made it particularly difficult to make ends meet in an increasingly unstable and male-oriented labour market. A further testimony to the bleak prospects that awaited many of them is that Flemish households were markedly over-represented in relief-related sources. While they made up 18 per cent of Belgian emigrants by mid-century, they accounted for 24 per cent of hospital admissions, and for 28 per cent of sojourners' relief applications.[99]

Although the Flemish displayed the most salient signs of the increasing pressure of rural push forces, analogous symptoms were observable for other migrants as well. While the overall intensity of Antwerp-directed migration increased, so did the importance of older-age or family migration. By 1855, 35 per cent of male emigrants had been aged thirty or more when entering Antwerp, as against only 24 per cent in 1829.[100] The growing proportion of newcomers from North Brabant who were accompanied by a spouse and/or children, from 4 per cent in 1829 to 14 per cent in 1850, likewise attests to the increased importance of family migration among Brabantine migrants.[101] Another indication of the growing role of push forces, or in any case of increasing income instability, was that fewer migrants came to Antwerp directly from their place of birth. Figures for re-migration from Antwerp shed more light on these trajectories: while in 1829, 59 per cent of non-native emigrants had moved to Antwerp directly from their place of birth, in 1855 this had fallen to 41 per cent (Table AII.6 in Appendix II). At the same time, the scope and complexity of their prior migration trajectories increased markedly. The proportion of newcomers whose last place of residence had been in a region other than that of their birth, increased from 19 per cent in 1829 to 32 per cent in 1855, while the proportion who had moved to a large city of more than 20,000 inhabitants before coming to Antwerp shot up from 9 to 24 per cent. Even among intra-provincial newcomers, the proportion of direct migrants fell from 58 to 49 per cent, and the proportion of rural-born migrants who had travelled via one or more regional centres of more than 5,000 inhabitants increased from 5 to 24 per cent. Clearly, the move to Antwerp was seldom conceived as a one-off solution to decreasing opportunities at home, but rather formed one of many attempts to adapt to changing constraints and opportunities on an increasingly complex migration trajectory.

The sources at hand thus indicate growing volumes of internal immigration, and an overall increase of family, older-age and indirect migration, which form telling signs of rural distress. In itself, the growing importance of push forces need not necessarily have affected newcomers' chances of finding an income, a job or a career in town – the more so as the majority of newcomers continued to be young, single and increasingly male adults, and their occupational profile remained orientated towards service, construction and transport sectors. However, by mid-century the absorptive capacities that had allowed a growing number of partly push-driven newcomers to settle down during the steady expansion of the 1820s became eroded by the increasing irregularity of port employment and rising immigration levels. The decline in long-term income opportunities made it increasingly difficult for newcomers to gain a foothold in the urban economy. Coupled with the marked increase in the number of newcomers, this encouraged the development of exclusionist and protective strategies on the part of established groups.[102] In the 1840s and 1850s, then, there was less opportunity to settle down more or less permanently than there had been in the 1820s, which resulted in a tendency towards shorter and more complex patterns of stay. With regard to Antwerp's demographic evolution, it was noted in Chapter 2 that the late 1840s and 1850s witnessed a momentous increase in the levels not only of immigration but also of emigration, together with a concomitant drop in persistence levels. This increasing level of turnover was accompanied by an overall shortening of migrants' length of stay (Table AII.7 in Appendix II). The median length of stay of non-native emigrants decreased substantially from 686 days in 1829 to 403 days in 1855.[103] The prime shift was a substantial decrease in patterns involving more than three years of stay (from 37 to 24 per cent) in favour of a substantial increase in the proportion of those who stayed in town less than a year (from 32 to 47 per cent). While the latter increase in short-term stayers was marked for male newcomers (from 34 to 49 per cent), it was even more momentous among women (from 29 to 45 per cent), signalling a sharp shift away from patterns of life-cycle or labour migration involving at least a few years of stay, and towards a growing incidence of transitory and seasonal forms of migration.

While a growing number of newcomers had already made one or more moves before coming to Antwerp, their destinations on leaving again were equally symptomatic of a general rise in the level and scope of geographical mobility. First of all, the proportion of return migration, already on a downward trend in the 1820s, declined even further: while in 1829, 42 per cent of recorded emigrants returned to their place of birth when they left Antwerp; in 1855 this was only 29 per cent (Table AII.8 in Appendix II).[104] Instead, an increasing number of emigrants was heading for another town or city: in 1829, 33 per cent of non-native emigrants had aimed for another city of more than 20,000 inhabitants on leaving Antwerp, but by 1855 this had increased to 41 per cent. In addition, another one in five non-native emigrants headed for one of the villages in the immediate vicinity of the city, which may be considered a form of intra-urban mobility.[105] Overall, the distance between birthplace and destination increased significantly, indicating an increase in the action radius of individual migrants: in 1855, 43 per cent of non-native emigrants left for a destination which was not located in their region of birth, as against 38 per cent in 1829. Brussels emerged as the primary pole of attraction: no less than 22 per cent of all emigrants – immigrants and those born locally – moved on to the nation's capital, as against only 14 per cent in 1829. Other important urban destinations in 1855 were – in order of decreasing importance – Mechelen, Ghent, Paris, Leuven and Rotterdam, illustrating the increasing involvement of Antwerp in inter-urban networks and migration channels.

While all migrant groups displayed certain of these aggregate shifts to a larger or lesser degree, it is noteworthy that each of the three hallmarks of migratory change – growing indirect migration, shortening of stay and decreasing return migration – left their strongest marks on the migratory behaviour of women and those born in the countryside. In fact, the growth in the proportion of urban destinations for those leaving Antwerp was entirely made up of a growing number of rural-born migrants who moved on to another city instead of returning to their birthplace: by 1855 almost a third of all rural-born newcomers moved on to a city of more than 20,000 inhabitants when leaving again, as against only one in five in 1829. Women in turn became more intensely engaged in these rural–urban trajectories than men: although the number of female urban-born migrants was comparatively small, women emigrated to cities to an extent comparable to that of men, and even more so when they worked as a domestic servant, hinting at the development of an increasingly integrated inter-urban market for domestic servants.[106] The overall action radius of migrants, however, remained heavily dependent on the distance between Antwerp and their place of birth. In 1855 as in 1829, the majority of regional migrants continued to move along rural circuits, i.e. they were born in a village of less than 5,000 inhabitants, and they went to live in one again when they left Antwerp – albeit frequently in the immediate surroundings of the city. Although most regional migrants did not overstep the long-standing boundaries of population exchange between town and hinterland, a growing proportion did move on to other large cities, often situated in a region other than that of their birth. In these trajectories, Antwerp increasingly came to fulfil a gateway function between regional recruitment patterns on the one hand, and longer-distance patterns of inter-urban migration on the other.

The increasing volume of migration and turnover had important implications for the social fabric and morphology of the city. While migrants' age profile continued to reinforce the ranks of young and single residents, male migrants came to outnumber their female counterparts from at least 1846 onwards, contributing to a further levelling of the city's male to female ratio, from 92:100 in the 1830 census to 99:100 in 1866.[107] Yet the demographic impact of migrants over these decades was restrained by their high levels of turnover, causing the proportion of migrants in the urban population to stagnate around 33 per cent throughout the same period, notwithstanding ever increasing volumes of gross migration. As turnover rates increased, a growing proportion of the urban population consisted of transient migrants, who would stay in town for only a relatively short space of time and then move on to other destinations – which would remain the case throughout the nineteenth century. Moreover, they came from a wider array of origins than before, not all of which were equally familiar to the urban population. According to the census of 1846, 14 per cent of Antwerp's recorded migrants were born outside the boundaries of Belgium and the Netherlands, as against only 5 per cent in 1796. By 1856, 39 per cent of immigrants was born in a Belgian province other than Antwerp, as against only 27 per cent in 1796.

Added to the coming and going of sailors, passengers and Atlantic emigrants, the growing number of largely temporary migrant residents contributed to a transformation of the waterfront areas, where most lodging houses and bars were situated, and to the development of a flourishing red-light district around the Haringvliet and adjacent streets. By stimulating the proliferation of cheap and squalid lodging houses, and increasing the level of overcrowding in the most central and poorest town districts, the growing level of turnover also contributed to the decline in living conditions which affected Antwerp's housing situation throughout the nineteenth century. Between 1797 and 1845, the average built-up surface per head of the population within the city walls fell by no less than one-third, from 36 to 24 square metres, while the average number of inhabitants per house increased from 4.9 to 6.8, or even 7.8 if empty dwellings are left out of consideration.[108] Meanwhile, the precocious growth of the fifth district, located outside the city walls and in 1796 still largely rural, was largely bereft of supportive infrastructure: its roads remained unpaved, water mains absent and most of its dwellings were primitive wooden constructions.[109] These patterns of growing congestion and squalor led to the increasing concentration of poverty in smaller or larger slum areas – where many migrant families ended up.[110] Intervention in the living conditions in these slum areas was virtually nonexistent before the second half of the nineteenth century, and singular reports attest to the squalid sanitary and living conditions, which were only exacerbated as the numbers of residents increased.[111]

The aggregate changes in migration flows also had profound effects on the individual experience of migration. One of the most salient effects was to increase the complexity of individual migration experience. While the move to Antwerp became only a momentary phase for a growing proportion of its newcomers, it also became a junction in increasingly complex itineraries, in which inter-urban patterns of migration were becoming more important. The result was that the move to Antwerp came to occupy a very different position in individual life courses than in earlier decades. Both in the last decades of the eighteenth and the early decades of the nineteenth centuries, the experience of moving to town, especially in the case of regional migrants, had typically overlapped with a life-cycle phase of young adulthood, whereby young men and women spent a few years working in town for the purposes of training and/or saving, after which they returned home or – especially in the 1820s – settled in town. In either case, the period spent in town as a life-cycle migrant often amounted to several years, and had an important influence on the further life course, among other things on careers and the choice of marriage partner. Others had engaged in highly temporary patterns of seasonal migration in earlier decades too, yet the high incidence of return migration had framed their moves firmly within well-established patterns of population exchange between town and hinterland. Most moves in the late eighteenth and early nineteenth centuries, both of life-cycle and seasonal migrants, then, had taken place along patterns and functions which had been familiar for many generations. Their presence in town corresponded to a recognizable common identity of life-cycle migrants, and they could prepare and compare their own migratory moves with those of family members and fellow villagers. As most of their moves took place between the town and its hinterland, newcomers were generally familiar with their destination, and were likely to have acquaintances or family members living in town. In the course of the 1840s and 1850s, however, this association between life-cycle phase, migration and hinterland relations weakened. For one thing, more people entered town in a more advanced life-cycle phase than before, and although most newcomers were still young adults, they were unlikely to stay in town throughout the phase of young adulthood. Rather, they moved on to multiple destinations, and spent time in several different places, downscaling the role and influence of the move to Antwerp in the wider life-course context. As their migration experience became more varied and more complex, the move to Antwerp would come to take up a less prominent position in their personal life experience and memories. At the same time, the migration trajectories of newcomers prior to entry were more varied than in earlier periods, and more often comprised periods of residence in regions other than the city's hinterland. As these trajectories were increasingly new, the migrants involved could rely less on the migration experience of older generations, and would on the whole have been less familiar with their destination than in earlier periods. It is interesting to note in this context that James Jackson actually interpreted the high re-migration levels which he observed for late nineteenth-century Duisburg as a sign of continuing social cohesion between the city, its migrants and the wider region, and as an argument against viewing the urban newcomer as a solitary, uprooted and unattached individual left to his or her fate in a hostile urban environment.[112] Although I think the revision of this image was valuable and justified in several respects, I would hesitate to treat high levels of re-migration – which did not necessarily or even predominantly cover return moves – as an argument *against* uprootedness or as an indication of social cohesion.[113] In particular in the Antwerp case, where a longer-term perspective could be applied and return migration could be defined more narrowly, the observed increase in the level of re-migration reflected primarily a decrease in the absorptive qualities of the urban labour market, and resulted in a weakening of migration as a binding force between town and hinterland – as it was coupled with an actual decrease in the proportion of return migration. Rather, if anything, it helped to forge new patterns and spatial connections on a wider scale, but these necessarily involved a considerable social cost of adaptation.

To be sure, the increasing complexity of newcomers' trajectories was partly a consequence of Antwerp's expanding spatial interactions, but long-standing patterns of migration were also affected markedly by these growing levels of mobility and turnover. In this respect, growing migration intensity and complexity was a sign of the time: Antwerp's newcomers of the 1840s and 1850s were part of an increasingly mobile and unstable generation. That their migration trajectories reached further than those of the preceding generation is illustrated by contrasting the whereabouts of sojourners examined in 1849 and 1855 with those of their parents.[114] While only 14 per cent of all married male sojourners had married a spouse from the same place of birth, the equivalent proportion among their fathers had been 48 per cent – indicative of far lower earlier levels of pre-marital mobility.[115] Even more pronounced results are obtained by comparing their parents' current or final (when dead) place of residence with that of their birth: no less than 54 per cent of sojourners' fathers and 59 per cent of their mothers turned out to be still living or to have died in the place where they had been born, and only 25 and 21 per cent had moved on to a different region from that of their birth. While the reliability of parental information is somewhat variable,[116] and the observations do not rule out the incidence of circular migration trajectories among earlier generations, the differences in pre-marital and lifetime mobility between parents and offspring is sufficiently large to indicate a fundamentally different migration experience.

While the growing volume of newcomers and the increasing irregularity of employment increasingly acted together to limit migrants' room for manoeuvre on the urban labour market, in particular with regard to those without specialist skills, this did not imply that newcomers caught up in these adverse macro developments were necessarily pitiable or miserable, nor did it preclude the pursuance of successful adaptive strategies on the part of the migrants themselves. The observed shortening of overall patterns of stay, for instance, although indicative of the declining absorptive capacities of the urban labour market, at the same time also bears witness to migrants' adaptation to an increasingly seasonal local opportunity structure. Similarly, the increasingly transient migration trajectories of domestic servants can be read as a reflection of their problems in finding stable employment, but at the same time they attest to a widening of their geographical horizons which may have enabled them to pursue more options.[117] Take the example of Paulina De Backer, a twenty-six-year-old unmarried labourer from Vlierzele in East Flanders, who was examined in May 1855 on her prior whereabouts after applying for medical assistance. She declared that at the age of twenty she had left her native village to work in Brussels as a domestic servant. There she had served three different employers, for six months, one month and five months respectively, before returning to her birthplace for seven months. Then she spent around three years in Antwerp as a domestic servant, where she switched employers three times: with the first she stayed for eight months, with the second for more than a year, with the third half a year, after which she returned to the second one for another eight months. She then returned to Brussels to her first employer for a whole year. Next, she returned to Antwerp, and served four different employers – one of which she had earlier served twice – for terms of respectively one, six, six and one months, before she started to live independently as a casual labourer – possibly because she had health problems or was pregnant.[118] Paulina's transition from a rural–urban migration trajectory – from Vlierzele to Brussels – to an inter-urban circuit – between Antwerp and Brussels – was not necessarily or solely an indication of uprooting, but equally well indicates an expansion of her geographical action radius. While the crisis of the 1840s diminished her possibilities of returning to her Flemish home village, this did not keep her from pursuing different employment opportunities. With the expansion of transport and communication facilities in the course of the nineteenth century, it became easier to switch towns while switching employers – whereas this type of job mobility had previously been limited to within the city walls. To the extent that the expansion in action radius also entailed an increase in employment options, Paulina's increasing mobility might have actually signalled an expansion of her room for agency.

The fact that greater flexibility and transience was not a choice but a necessity, then, did not necessarily prevent migrants from trying to make the best of growing constraints. In this respect, it is worth noting that it was not those who eventually stayed in Antwerp who were best off. On the contrary, most migrants recorded in the emigration registers had a relatively favourable age and life-cycle profile, while family migrants with a high dependency ratio were most likely to stay, and swelled the distribution lists of the Charity Office. In this respect, the greater re-migration rates of young and single migrants can be interpreted as the result of a comparatively larger array of options, and therefore as a (relatively) positive sign. On the other hand, however, as age was by definition a transitory asset, the medium-term and long-term perspectives of Antwerp's newcomers are likely to have been worse than those of their predecessors. As family formation, childbearing and old age all formed life-cycle phases that increased the vulnerability of the working poor, the decrease in relatively stable income opportunities in the medium and long run, coupled with the loss of return options, would considerably jeopardize the options of most migrants in a later phase of their lives.[119] In this respect, the gloomy position of most families recorded in the settlement examinations probably represented not just those unlucky enough to belong to less well-off migrant groups, but was more generally a precursor of the future life course of many of those still young, single, fit and relatively well off at the time they were recorded in the migration registers.

While migrants largely maintained their privileged access to most port-related employment, then, by mid-century certain urban and rural developments would come to upset the conditions which had made for a relatively inclusive reception of newcomers in the earlier phase of port expansion. While the increasing dependency on unstable global trade movements and seasonal port traffic eroded the long-term absorptive capacities of the labour market, the developing rural crisis at the same time put ever greater numbers of people on the road in search of a better living. While specialized long-distance migrants continued to be attracted primarily by the income opportunities which the further expansion of commercial and port activity provided, migrants moving within regional patterns of recruitment showed several signs of growing distress, such as rising migration intensities, an ageing of the inflow and a heightened incidence of indirect migration. Whether Antwerp's increased number of newcomers were initially pushed or pulled, it is any case clear that the mounting flow could no longer be adequately absorbed into the urban fabric, which resulted in an overall shortening of stay and increasing migration turnover. Indicative of the problems in the countryside are declining rates of return migration, which led to the proliferation of increasingly complex inter-urban trajectories, and growing problems of urban congestion and degeneration. In many respects, the crisis of the 1840s appears to have formed a turning point in patterns of urban mobility. While it unleashed unprecedented levels of urban migration, these would only increase further in the following decades, without any concomitant rise in persistence. Likewise, the growing levels of inter-provincial and inter-urban mobility which followed in the wake of the crisis appear indicative of the loosening of regional ties between a town and its hinterland, and the growing integration of larger spatial units under the auspices of the developing Belgian state.

Migration to a Port Town in the Making

As a nineteenth-century port town, Antwerp held considerably more opportunities for both highly skilled and unspecialized immigrants than it had done as a regional textile centre in the eighteenth century. While the local population bore most of the cost of the collapse of textile production, migrants secured most of the expanding employment in the sectors of trade, services, retail, construction and transport. The uneven distribution of costs and gains of Antwerp's conversion attests to the strength of pre-existing patterns of labour market segmentation, reinforced by differences in skill, ability and custom. The change into a port town expanded the range of unspecialized jobs that had in the eighteenth century already constituted the favoured domain of newcomers, while it also stimulated an array of new and specialist activities that were out of reach of erstwhile textile workers. Therefore, migrants found themselves well placed to take up most of the newly created employment in both skilled and unskilled segments of the port labour market. While the presence of a large immigrant labour force was a common characteristic of other nineteenth-century port towns too, Antwerp appears to have been relatively exceptional in that migrants took up a central position in both the core and periphery of its port labour market. This was probably helped by the fact that port activity was a relatively new and previously marginal undertaking, with few vested interests on the part of the established population.

Much as Antwerp's conversion was favourable to newcomers, migrants played a fundamental role in making the city's economic transformation possible. Their presence proved essential to the fulfilment of the new demand for port-related labour, which could only (very) partially be met by the local labour supply so dramatically affected by the collapse of textile industries. The recruitment of suitable migrant labour was a necessary condition to overcoming the potential bottlenecks of a rapidly changing urban labour market, and to achieve the town's dramatic economic conversion. While this was initially carried out with the help of elaborate state-organized allocation systems, from the 1820s onwards a constant inflow of specialized and less specialized migrant workers was assured mainly by the operation of informal migration and information channels, which steadily enlarged Antwerp's migration field in various directions. While most of the locally-born population remained unwilling or unable to make the move from the production of textiles to the building of port infrastructure and the handling of cargo, then, migrant dockers and builders in effect were the shock troops of maritime expansion and the facilitators of economic change.

Although Antwerp's port economy greatly expanded the employment opportunities for newcomers, rural pressure increased throughout the first half of the nineteenth century to eventually overcome the town's absorptive capacities. While the initial expansion of port activity had been accompanied by an increase in both the numbers of newcomers and their length of stay, the growing rural crisis combined with unstable port expansion to make migration to Antwerp an increasingly transient experience by the middle of the nineteenth century. While the average length of stay decreased, the proportion of return migration equally declined, leading to a growing rate of inter-urban mobility, and structurally transforming the experience of urban migration. The subsistence crisis of the 1840s represented an important turning point in the dynamics of urban migration. The upsurge in the number of newcomers, the decline of return possibilities and the irregular nature of urban employment would exceed the absorptive capacities of the expanding cities in the new Kingdom of Belgium, stimulating transient patterns of stay, the weakening of hinterland ties, the growth of inter-urban mobility and mounting problems of urban poverty and congestion. However, even though the evolution of push and pull forces constrained the room for manoeuvre of Antwerp's newcomers in the course of the 1840s and 1850s, urban migration remained a remarkably selective affair throughout the whole period under consideration. While most of the newcomers continued to be young and single migrants, who were best suited for the demands of Antwerp's irregular labour market, several dynamics, such as the growth in seasonal migration patterns, bear witness to migrants' adaptations to the changing local opportunity structure. Yet, it is also clear that the room for agency differed from one migrant to another: different migrant groups were subject to the changing constraints and opportunities in different ways. In order to explore the variations in migrant adaptability in greater detail, the final chapter will look at the role of migration circuits.

5 CIRCUITS, NETWORKS AND TRAJECTORIES

The previous chapters have demonstrated how the transformation of the Antwerp economy between the late eighteenth and the middle of the nineteenth centuries went hand in hand with a constant restructuring of migration patterns. Although migrants secured the better half of the employment shift's mixed blessings, rising rural pressure and growing employment instability would by mid-century increasingly limit their room for manoeuvre on the urban labour market. The above discussion has indicated, however, that *within* the group of migrants there existed considerable differences in the extent to which they succeeded in adapting to the manifold changes in the local opportunity structure. This room for manoeuvre appears to have been strongly dependent on migrants' geographical backgrounds and personal characteristics such as sex, age and skill, which together determined their susceptibility to push dynamics and responsiveness to specific opportunities. Geographical background and personal characteristics, moreover, appear to have borne a meaningful relationship to one another, in the sense that migrants from specific backgrounds also tended to display certain characteristics, although the extent to which this was the case differed according to the distinct migrant groups. Such a correspondence between migrant origins and profile has in the first chapter been loosely defined as a *circuit*, a term which has also in the previous chapters been used to highlight newcomers' heterogeneity. After sketching out the overall diachronic shifts in migration patterns in the preceding chapters, it is now time to take a closer look at the meaning and characteristics of these circuits, which eventually shaped the adaptability of different migrant groups, and which determined the speeds of change with which certain transformations took place.

Four Major Migration Circuits

The preceding chapters have several times referred to the existence of different circuits. The associated distinctions were often cast in relatively general terms, such as urban-born versus rural-born, short distance versus long distance, intra-regional versus inter-regional or foreign migrants. To discuss the characteristics of these different circuits in more exact terms, it is necessary to subject the observed complexity of reality to some categorization, which is always arbitrary to a certain extent, and which unavoidably creates grey areas of certain 'border' groups which share characteristics of different categories. I have strived to minimize both the number of categories and the grey areas as much as possible by distinguishing four main circuits:

1) *Intra-provincial rural migration*: Migrants born within the boundaries of today's province of Antwerp, in a place which had less than 10,000 inhabitants in 1800 and 1850.

2) *Internal inter-urban migration*: Migrants born in cities with more than 10,000 inhabitants in 1800 or 1850, and located within the boundaries of today's Belgium and the cross-border provinces of Limburg, North Brabant and Zeeland.

3) *Long-distance foreign migration*: Migrants born beyond the borders of today's Belgium and the cross-border provinces of Limburg, North Brabant and Zeeland.

4) *Other rural migrants*: All other migrants, i.e. those born within the boundaries of today's Belgium and the cross-border provinces of Limburg, North Brabant and Zeeland, in places with less than 10,000 inhabitants in 1800 and 1850.

Of course, the benchmarks used for this categorization are debatable. Their purpose was to capture sufficiently the main distinctions between rural-born and urban-born migrants, and between short-distance and long-distance migration, which were observed to have been of prime importance in guiding different migration behaviours. At the same time, the categories were to remain sufficiently large to allow for meaningful diachronic analysis and further refinements within each category.[1] The relevance of the proposed distinction can be underpinned by a brief overview of the intrinsic differences between the four categories in terms of immigrant profiles and trajectories, such as sex, age, occupation and patterns of stay (Tables AII.9–13 in Appendix II). This also demonstrates that all four circuits were affected by the same diachronic trends, albeit to varying degrees. While men were more numerous among long-distance and urban migrants, for instance, all circuits became more masculine over time, which is indicative of a gradual adaptation to the growing male bias in the local opportunity structure. Similarly, while rural-born and short-distance migrants were generally younger than urban-born and long-distance newcomers, all circuits underwent a certain ageing of the inflow over time – although the large majority within each category remained made up of young, single adults. At the same time, there was an overall continuity in the nature of occupational differentiation between the four different circuits, with rural migrants oriented mainly towards unspecialized service and distribution activities, urban migrants displaying an edge in the production of durable consumer goods, white-collar jobs and the professions, and foreign migrants well represented among white collar workers, trade and shipping, and the production of luxury goods. The different circuits also confirm the differences in migration trajectories observed in the preceding chapters. Foreign-born migrants had the lowest proportion of direct migration, internal inter-urban migrants were most likely to have come to Antwerp directly from their place of birth, and rural-born migrants from beyond the provincial boundaries were more likely to have come via an intermediate city than their intra-provincial counterparts, yet all circuits displayed a similar tendency towards growing rates of indirect migration over time. Notwithstanding a common trend towards increasing (until the 1820s) and then decreasing lengths of stay, long-distance and urban-born migrants also continually displayed the highest rates of turnover, while rural-born and intra-provincial migrants were more likely to stay on for a longer period of time. Throughout the whole period, long-distance foreign migrants were also the least likely to return to their birthplace when they left Antwerp again. While the three other circuits initially recorded significantly higher rates of return migration, these decreased considerably in the 1850s in favour of urban and suburban destinations. At the same time, the spatial scope of distinct recruitment circuits remained remarkably constant over time. In 1829 as in 1855, intra-provincial rural-born migrants rarely crossed the boundaries of their province of birth, while inter-urban and foreign migrants did so frequently. The most marked widening of geographical scope was recorded among 'other rural migrants', which was an indication of the growing incidence of inter-provincial mobility. Although diachronic change was observed for each of the four main circuits, then, intra-provincial rural-born migrants tended to display the strongest degree of continuity in their migration patterns, while the second and fourth circuits were most strongly affected by the overall trend towards increasing turnover and mobility. Foreign migrants, already the most transient and mobile circuit in the early decades of the nineteenth century, further reinforced this overall trend.

Before embarking on a more qualitative exploration of these different speeds of change, a last general consideration involves the question of arrival modalities or, more broadly, residential patterns. Did migrants cluster in specific neighbourhoods? The only more or less systematic indications in this respect derive from the available data on migrants' addresses on arrival. Tracing their distribution over Antwerp's five town districts indicates that migrants tended to cluster in specific areas in certain periods. Newcomers' distinctive preference for the fourth district in the Napoleonic period (34 per cent), for instance, had everything to do with the location of the naval shipyards and warehouses in this area. In most other periods, migrants' residential distribution was more evenly

spread over the different town districts, yet all circuits shared a preference for
the first district that was continually higher than among the locally-born population (between 20 and 26 per cent). Situated in the city centre, bordering the
docks, and including a large number of shops and warehouses, the first district
was the commercial centre of Antwerp's port activity and an obvious rallying
point for transport workers, retailers and small businessmen alike.[2] The growing
proportion of newcomers flocking to the fifth district (from 2 per cent in 1796
to 17 per cent in 1855) as the century progressed mirrored the urbanization of
this previously rural area outside the city walls, yet it mainly attracted rural-born
migrants from within the Antwerp Province, paralleling their preference for
suburban destinations already noticeable in the emigration registers. Long-distance migrants, in contrast, confirmed their upmarket profile by their preference
for the bourgeois third district, where most of the city's administrators, *rentiers*,
professionals, merchants and bankers could be found. That the poor and proletarian fourth district, which housed most of the city's (erstwhile) textile workers,
attracted comparatively few newcomers bears out the latter's strong orientation
towards commercial and service activities. Yet, the relatively larger proportion
of fourth-district-dwellers among non-native emigrants and sojourners suggests
that some migrants appear to have moved to the poorer ghettos at a later point
of their urban stay, after spending some time in the city centre.[3]

While these district distributions corroborate some of the social and economic characteristics of different migrant groups, exploring the role of residential
clustering in sustaining supportive institutions like chain migration requires a
spatial analysis at street level, which unfortunately fell beyond the scope of this
study.[4] However, some further clues on the operation of inter-personal arrival
networks could be gathered by collecting further details on the persons with
whom newcomers were staying: for one in two entries in the 1829 residence card
registers I have looked up place of birth and occupation of those persons mentioned as hosts, in order to establish whether newcomers were likely to be taken
in by fellow migrants from the same area of origin (Table AII.14 in Appendix
II).[5] This exercise demonstrates that Antwerp-born hosts were markedly under-
represented: only 29 per cent of newcomers stayed with a locally-born host,
whereas at that time 58 per cent of the adult population was born in Antwerp.
The fact that newcomers were more likely to move in with a fellow immigrant,
however, did not imply that hosts and newcomers shared the same geographic
background: only 18 per cent moved in with a person who was born in the same
area of origin. Even long-distance migrants stayed with compatriots only in a
very small minority of cases (14 per cent).[6] In contrast, rural-born intra-provincial migrants recorded the highest proportion of Antwerp-born hosts (34 per
cent), and were the most likely to move in with someone from the same district
of birth (22 per cent). Both observations attest to the social interconnectedness

between the town and its direct hinterland: grouped together, up to 55 per cent of intra-provincial newcomers shared some geographical familiarity with their hosts, and were likely to have been acquainted prior to arrival, whereas the equivalent figure for other circuits was only 20 per cent at most.

Evidence on the role of occupational ties is on the whole stronger than on that of origin-based relationships. More than one in two male newcomers, and virtually all female newcomers, moved in with a person who on the basis of his or her occupation could be identified as an employer (in most cases) or colleague (less likely).[7] Origin-based relationships were of minor importance in forging the link between living-in workers/servants and their employers, as very few newcomers in this situation came from the same area as their hosts. What does emerge is that intra-provincial rural-born servants were most likely to move in with an Antwerp-born employer, again confirming the stronger development of social connections between the city and its direct hinterland. The proportions of newcomers moving in with employers/colleagues upon arrival were highest for the rural-born migrants from circuits one (61 per cent of men and 96 per cent of women) and four (54 and 89 per cent), and lowest for the mostly urban migrants from circuits three (43 and 62 per cent) and two (33 and 76 per cent), who more often stayed with persons identified in the population books as professional lodging keepers (24 and 21 per cent of men respectively).[8] Although some of these lodging keepers might actually have been employers,[9] the higher proportion of urban-born migrants staying with *hoteliers*, *cabaretiers* and *logeurs* attests to the existence of more formal – and probably also more upmarket – migration infrastructures in these circuits. Another third of male newcomers and 10 per cent of women in turn stayed with a host who – as far as could be gathered from the population books – was neither a colleague or employer nor a professional lodging keeper. Most likely, these patterns figured with informal lodging arrangements, with newcomers renting a room or a bed with households where lodging activities provided a minor addition to the family income.[10] Even in these instances, origin-based networks were unimportant. Only 20 per cent of hosts who were not employers, colleagues or lodging keepers came from the same area as the newcomer they accommodated. In addition, there is no indication that family-based networks played an important role with regard to lodging arrangements: only 2 per cent of newcomers stayed with a host who on the basis of patronymic or other indications could be identified as family.

Although the selectivity of the 1829 residence card registers hampers the generalization of the findings in all their aspects, these data on the backgrounds of newcomers' hosts indicate that chain migration networks played a negligible role as far as the provision of lodging facilities upon arrival was concerned: the large majority of newcomers stayed with a host with whom they shared no origin-specific ties. Although the source materials do not allow for any comprehensive view of the role of social networks in supporting different migration circuits, the available evidence suggests that the operation of these networks was seldom limited to the narrow concept of chain migration. The fact that many employment ties appear to have been established prior to arrival suggests that social networks and contacts did play an important part in providing arrival modalities, but in a broader sense than that captured by the concept of chain migration, i.e. in the more diffuse sense of conveying migration information between different places.[11] To throw further light on the role of such channels of migration information in structuring different migration circuits, and to further explore the different speeds of change with which they adapted to the changing context of push and pull factors, it is now time to turn to a detailed discussion of the characteristics and evolution of the four main circuits distinguished above.

Intra-Provincial Rural-Born Migrants

In March 1819 at the age of seventeen, Catharina Cassiers moved to Antwerp from the nearby village of Merksem to work as a domestic servant. Her first position was with shopkeeper Martinus Peulinckx from Tienen, who was married to Isabella Cassiers from Merksem, probably a cousin or sister of Catharina. Catharina stayed with them for two years before she moved on to a position in another household for two more years. When she subsequently returned to Isabella's household in February 1823, she found her widowed mother, Catherina Van Volsem, and a third young Cassiers, Helena, living at the same address. In 1827 Catharina and her mother moved out to set up a shop in the third and later fourth town district, after which they were joined in 1836 by Helena. After their mother died in 1839, Helena married an Antwerp-born musician in 1840, while in 1844 the then forty-two-year-old Catherina moved out to marry Petrus Elst, a shopkeeper from Kalmthout, who had been living in Antwerp for almost forty years. Soon after, they were joined by thirteen-year-old Joseph Hoppenbrouwers from Kalmthout. Although no patronymic affinity exists, he was probably related to Petrus, as he had previously lived at the same address, and would remain with the newly formed couple until the age of twenty-three. By that time, Catharina and Petrus's only child, Mathilda, born in 1845, had died at the age of seven. After Joseph left in 1854, an eighteen-year-old relative, Cornelius Hoppenbrouwers from Kalmthout, would take his place, and was to stay with Catharina and Petrus at least until the next census.[12]

Immigrants like Catharina Cassiers, born in one of the villages of Antwerp's immediate hinterland, formed the most substantial and continuous contingent among the city's newcomers throughout the second half of the eighteenth and first half of the nineteenth centuries. While intra-provincial rural-born migrants supplied 40 per cent of all resident immigrants in the census of 1796, by 1855 they still made up 37 per cent of all admissions to the city hospital.[13] Several aspects of Catharina's example bear out the main features that characterized this intra-provincial migration circuit. One is a strong female component: throughout the period under consideration, intra-provincial rural-born migrants supplied the comparatively largest proportion of female migrants, at a level of around 70 men for every 100 women. Another is the life-cycle profile of Catharina and her sisters: more than any other circuit, that of intra-provincial rural-born migrants remained strongly dominated by young and single adults. Throughout the period in question, between 75 and 87 per cent of incoming women in this circuit were aged between fifteen and twenty-nine, as were 63 to 80 per cent of their male counterparts. The Cassiers' activities as domestic servants and shopkeepers are likewise representative of the overall unspecialized and service-oriented occupational profile of most rural-born intra-provincial newcomers.

The Cassiers' example is possibly most telling in its evocation of the manifold social, familial and affective ties that bound hinterland migrants to the city of Antwerp. Intra-provincial rural migrants were the most likely of all migrants to stay with an Antwerp-born host upon arrival or with someone from the same area of origin, and were most likely to marry an Antwerp-born spouse.[14] These ties also served as anchors: throughout the period under consideration, provincial migrants remained the most 'persistent' type of newcomers, i.e. those most likely to stay in town for the rest of their lives or in any case for a long period of time. If they emigrated, moreover, they were most likely to move to one of Antwerp's suburbs, indicative of a continued urban attachment, or to stay within provincial boundaries. While family ties might have been exceptionally strong in the Cassiers' case (the mother was even born in Antwerp), the regional migrant who knew absolutely no-one in town upon arrival would have been rare. Intra-provincial rural newcomers represented those migrants whose paths to the city were most strongly embedded in an amalgamate of social, commercial, political and legal relationships connecting the city with its hinterland. Already prior to moving house, most of them would have visited the town several times, would be familiar with it, and probably had a number of family members or acquaintances who lived there or had lived there before. Their migration trajectories built on a long tradition of population exchange between the city and its privileged area of recruitment, by which migration information was conveyed by a permanent coming and going of marketgoers, vendors, litigants, family visits and temporary migrants.

When observing with regard to nineteenth-century Huy that newcomers from nearby areas were those least likely to leave again, Michel Oris formulated two main explanations for their greater persistence. The first was that by nature of their proximity they would have been best informed on real opportunities, protecting them from false expectations. The other was that they were most familiar with and therefore most easily integrated into the urban fabric. While both explanations highlight the positive effects of the greater social embeddedness of regional migration patterns in terms of familiarity and information access, Oris also conceded that the higher emigration rate of longer-distance migrants was partly attributable to 'their capacities to pass from one basin to another according to the opportunities ... in terms of employment and salaries' – which, implicitly, short-distance migrants did not possess.[15] In that sense, the strong social ties connecting hinterland migrants to their regional capital can be seen as both enabling their migration and constraining their options. While hinterland connections provided migrants with valuable information and social backing, they necessarily constrained the options which they could consider, as they were oriented almost exclusively – such is the nature of a demographic basin – towards the city in question. Speaking of 'town' in the villages of the Antwerp Province invariably referred to Antwerp; if one considered moving to a town, it was a move to Antwerp which was contemplated. And that is exactly what a growing number of villagers did in the course of the nineteenth century, which would eventually result in a restructuring of migration dynamics.

Several factors acted together to make increasing numbers of hinterland migrants consider moving to Antwerp in the period under consideration. On the one hand, the growth of maritime activities increased the number of jobs accessible to unspecialized migrants – although the long-term absorptive capacities of the urban labour market were subsequently undermined by the increasing instability of maritime traffic. On the other hand, the build-up of rural pressure played a progressively more important role in the observed rise of migration intensity. Population density in the provincial countryside doubled from 56 persons per square km in 1755 to over 77 in 1800 and to 109 around the middle of the nineteenth century.[16] Together with growing population came a decline in the average farm size and an increase in agrarian rents, which was coupled with a process of peasant expropriation.[17] In addition, the growing competition from mechanized production delivered a final blow to those clusters of proto-industrial textile manufacture which had existed in the north-east and south of the province.[18] These rural difficulties were complemented by a substantial reduction of common lands under a government-led enclosure project devised in the 1830s, further jeopardizing the survival strategies of land-poor and landless villagers.[19]

While all provincial districts were confronted with growing levels of proletarianization, the scale of rural disintegration varied, as did the propensity to migrate. The stronger continuity in property and common rights acted as a brake on emigration from the sandy Campine regions, while the more fertile and commercialized districts of Mechelen and Antwerp produced much larger numbers of land-poor and landless villagers who were pressured to look elsewhere in the search for income opportunities.[20] These differences in social and economic structure explain much of the observed divergence in provincial migration intensity, the increase in which was much stronger for nearby villages than for the Campine district (above, Maps 4.7–10). In addition, differential patterns of migration intensity were also determined by the density of hinterland connections: while the relatively low intensity levels from the Campine area reflect a lower rate of urban-oriented emigration pure and simple, the low figures for the region around Mechelen were more likely the result of the interference of competing centres of attraction. Villages in the vicinity of Antwerp in turn had stronger relationships with the provincial capital than those in the Campine area or in the region around Mechelen, a tradition which was reinforced by the development of railways.[21] Better connected to town and confronted with profound processes of agrarian transformation, migration to Antwerp was therefore more easily considered an option in these villages, and was a more familiar element in the local repertoire of household coping strategies.

In this period of structural social change, the strong social embeddedness of hinterland trajectories was a mixed blessing for the migrants concerned. On the positive side, existing social connections were of great importance in facilitating job access in Antwerp's highly personally-mediated port labour market. While comparative advantages in terms of age and strength also played a role, existing recruitment carousels and (in)formal employment networks – from the hiring of domestic servants by word of mouth to the exclusive employment rules of the *naties* – were of prime importance in connecting hinterland workers with the expanding employment sectors of the nineteenth century. As the Cassiers' example illustrates, these connections could not only assure that migrants were well informed of, and had easy access to, actual employment options, but they also provided social support that could cushion the vulnerabilities of urban life. The two younger Cassiers sisters both worked in the shop of their brother-in-law at some point during their Antwerp residence, which provided some sort of fallback between other jobs,[22] while their mother found refuge in her daughters' households at an age when she was unlikely to make an adequate living on her own. Similarly, of the thirty-five newcomers from CS1819 who could be traced for longer than five years, eleven lived in with family members at some point in time. Hence, the existence of family and social networks to fall back on when out of work or facing temporary hardship was an important complement to migrant-friendly employment growth in enabling the observed rise of hinterland migrants' persistence during the late 1810s and 1820s. That their migratory behaviour was subsequently the least affected by the growing level of turnover in the 1840s and 1850s likewise indicates the presence of social safety nets that could buffer the growing instability of the port labour market. Outsiders who lacked these connections to urban society would have greater difficulty finding work and getting through the slack season, and would more readily have to move on elsewhere in case of unemployment.[23] In all likelihood, hinterland migrants also enjoyed easier access to public relief from the local Charity Office, which could be of additional help in a complex and vulnerable income-pooling.[24] In these respects, the density of migration channels between town and hinterland was a positive asset which helped intra-provincial newcomers to remain in town and to continue to display relatively persistent patterns of stay. On the other hand, however, these assets also implied unavoidable constraints. As the direction and intensity of these migration channels depended on existing hinterland relations, they were almost invariably of an intra-provincial nature, and displayed a great degree of path dependency and inertia. As much as enabling migrants' move to Antwerp, in other words, they constrained their options to move elsewhere. By nature of the embeddedness of their social networks, few intra-provincial migrants were likely to be informed of income opportunities in other places than the nearest regional centre. In addition, even if they were, they could not afford to move too far away from family, friends or acquaintances. As most intra-provincial migrants operated in the least specialized, socially mediated and most unstable segments of the urban labour market, access to social networks which could provide work and act as a safety net was nothing less than a lifeline. Because of the density of their migration channels, in other words, intra-provincial rural migrants were at once enabled to stay in Antwerp and constrained from moving elsewhere.

The constrained nature of their migration options and the embedded nature of their migration channels lent a strong degree of continuity to the migration patterns of intra-provincial rural-born newcomers. However, this does not mean that no change took place. Although patterns of hinterland migration showed a considerable degree of resilience and continuity, even these long-standing patterns displayed signs of adaptation and transformation in the long run. These dynamics of 'slow change' included a growing masculinization of the inflow, increasing levels of turnover, a gradual decline in the proportion of return migration, and a growing preference for suburban and urban destinations on leaving – which can be read as adaptations to an increasingly irregular and masculine port labour market on the one hand, and to growing constraints in the home villages on the other. Even as rising push forces and tenuous pull forces limited the room for manoeuvre of many rural migrants, migration remained a remarkably selective affair, dominated by young, single adults, who were best equipped to take advantage of urban opportunities, and who continuously devised new adaptive strategies in a highly constrained environment.

Internal Inter-Urban Migration

Migrants born in cities with more than 10,000 inhabitants situated in present-day Belgium or the Dutch provinces of North Brabant and Limburg supplied a more or less constant proportion of newcomers between the mid-eighteenth and mid-nineteenth centuries: between 16 and 23 per cent. Throughout the period in question, they recorded the largest proportion of direct immigrants, and also the highest rates of return when they left again. If they did not return to their birthplace, they moved predominantly to another large city of similar or greater size. Their migration trajectories thus clearly followed different routes from those of intra-provincial rural migrants. They frequently crossed provincial or even 'national' boundaries, but very rarely made the cross-over between town and countryside. Rather than moving along the various relationships which connected a town with its hinterland, these rural-born migrants moved along the commercial, legal and political pathways which connected Antwerp to the urban network of the Southern Low Countries.

The geographical connections underlying this network, however, were subject to important variations over time. While the proportion of migrants born in towns located in the Antwerp or Brabant provinces remained more or less constant – each province supplying between 20 and 33 per cent – the share of North Brabant towns in this inter-urban circuit declined considerably over time, from 15 per cent in 1796 to 7 per cent in 1855. In their stead, Flemish cities grew in importance, increasing their share from 8 per cent in 1796 to 33 per cent in 1855. By comparison, Walloon cities together never supplied more than 10 per cent. These geographical shifts in the inter-urban migratory network corresponded to the overall regional shifts which were observed for newcomers as a whole, where the cross-border Brabantine connection gradually gave way to a stronger western connection with the Flemish regions – an evolution which among other things points towards the growing integration of a national urban network in the new Kingdom of Belgium, aided by the precocious development of its railway network.[25] In addition, the fall in employment opportunities for textile workers in favour of port-oriented jobs might have been another factor contributing to the shift away from North Brabant towns – which had previously supplied an important number of textile workers – and in the direction of Flemish and larger towns.[26]

Except for the census of 1796, internal inter-urban male migrants outnumbered women, which contrasts markedly with the female predominance among intra-provincial rural-born migrants. They were also somewhat older, and more likely to move in family units, although most were still single adults. Their patterns of stay tended to bifurcate into either short-term stays – less than one year – or else long-term stays involving more than five or ten years of residence. As such, they were less engaged in life-cycle patterns of labour migration than their rural-born counterparts.[27] Their occupational profile also diverged strongly from that of the first circuit, and displayed a more specialized character. While in 1796 it resembled that of the locally-born population more than that of other immigrants, they maintained their strong orientation towards industrial activities, complemented by an important contingent of white-collar workers in later periods. A large proportion of male newcomers worked in (specialized) construction jobs, as shipwrights, cabinetmakers and metalworkers, in the production of less specialized durable consumer goods (tailors, shoemakers), or of luxury goods (printers, sculptors). The white-collar contingent was made up mainly of office clerks, civil servants and the professions – among whom there was a number of medical students. Women, in turn, were less oriented towards domestic service than their rural-born counterparts – although between 50 and 66 per cent still entered town as maids.[28] Seamstresses and other garment workers were second in line, a group virtually absent among rural-born migrants. The orientation towards textile production, which in 1796 had still been relatively marked, was rapidly discarded in the first decades of the nineteenth century.

Both wages and career possibilities could have been factors of attraction for these internal inter-urban migrants. The proliferation of shipbuilding, transport activities and construction work provided an important demand for carpenters and toolmakers like Jean-Baptiste Vanbelkom, a twenty-two-year-old cooper from Tilburg who moved to Antwerp in 1855 to work in the coopering workshop of Widow Persenaire at two francs per day – which was about the equivalent of 10 kg of rye bread, and double the modal wage of an unskilled worker.[29] The growth of commercial agencies and government administration in turn attracted quite a number of white-collar workers and government workers, such as Frans Joseph Mertens from Ghent, a civil servant in customs administration, who moved to Antwerp from the customs office in Rijkevorsel (Province of Antwerp) with his wife in 1853, and left again for another office in Kessenich (Province of Limburg) in 1855.[30] The growth of commercial wealth created an indirect demand for domestic servants and producers of luxury goods, such as coach builders, instrument makers and fashion workers, many of whom came from Brussels. Together with establishments like the Antwerp Museum of Fine Arts, its Academy and its medical school, the expansion of luxury trades reinforced the city's attraction as a centre of advanced learning for people like sixteen-year-old *ouvrier bijoutier* (jewellery worker) Antoine Hessels from Breda, who came to Antwerp in 1850 'sponsored by his parents to perfect his skill'.[31] The trajectory of Ludovica Pirotte from Brussels, a trader in lace work moving to Antwerp from Liège in January 1855 and leaving again for Paris in March 1855, in turn illustrates how business dealings sometimes brought inter-urban migrants to Antwerp for extremely temporary periods.[32]

We know very little of the nature of the migration channels along which these inter-urban migrants moved. More than any other circuit, inter-urban newcomers in 1829 were likely to stay with a professional lodging house keeper (24 per cent), which might hint at the relatively impersonal and upmarket nature of some of their migration networks. The Napoleonic *inscription maritime* appears to have been instrumental in establishing Antwerp's initial connection with skilled shipbuilders from Flemish cities, who continued to come on a less formal basis in later years.[33] Migration from cities in the larger Brabantine area, on the other hand, relied on a longer tradition which was more firmly embedded in the commercial, economic and political interactions between different cities in the erstwhile Duchy of Brabant.[34] Commercial or professional contacts might have acted as a recruitment channel for some migrants, while others might have relied on the guidance of family members or acquaintances living in Antwerp, and still others remained in the city after having been stationed there during their military service.[35]

Although they operated in less vulnerable segments of the local opportunity structure, internal inter-urban migrants were strongly influenced by the general tendency towards growing turnover and decreasing return migration of the 1840s and 1850s. The proportion of emigrants in this category who had stayed in town less than one year increased from 34 per cent in 1829 to 52 per cent in 1855 among men, and from 32 to 69 per cent among women. At the same time, the incidence of return migration decreased from 42 to 36 per cent, while the proportion of those moving on to a city of more than 20,000 inhabitants grew from 30 to 43 per cent. The underlying dynamic was a growing importance of stepwise migration as small-town migrants became increasingly likely to move on to a large city instead of returning home. This resulted in a growing level of population exchange between Antwerp and other towns and cities in the Southern Low Countries, in particular Brussels. The precise implications of this increase in turnover and mobility are hard to unravel. Both can be interpreted as a result of growing tensions in urban labour markets and/or widening action radii in the wake of increasing commercial and political integration. However, the observation that most inter-urban migrants were relatively specialized workers, who were often engaged in an inter-urban pattern of career migration and probably followed the lure of particular employment opportunities, does not mean that perspectives for them were necessarily rosy – the risks of old age, illness, accidents or high dependency ratios also loomed large for them. One in three non-native Belgian sojourners examined in 1855 had been born in a town of more than 10,000 inhabitants, and had largely ended up in Antwerp via inter-urban channels. One of them was Jean-Baptiste Van Dijck, born in Turnhout in 1813, who had moved to Antwerp at the age of twenty-six to work as a carpenter. He stayed for eleven years, then moved on to Brussels for six months, returned to Antwerp for three years, and went to live again in Turn-hout for another six months. In 1853 he once again returned to Antwerp, where in November 1854 he married the forty-year-old Antwerp-born widow Joanna Bommels. A few months later they applied for relief, as Jean-Baptiste's health problems jeopardized the income of the large household – Joanna had brought along four children between the ages of one and six from a former marriage. That the family's struggle for survival involved household tensions is revealed by an undated note in the margin mentioning that Jean-Baptiste had been jailed for beating his wife.[36] Some inter-urban migrants also moved to Antwerp to be nearer their families. After living in 's Hertogenbosch for more than sixty years, the dyer (*ouvrier teinturier*) Henry Frederick Krekel and his wife Agnes Ruys came to Antwerp to live with their son Louis Guillaume, a journeyman carpenter who had made the same journey in 1846 at the age of twenty-four, and had in the meantime married an Antwerp-born spouse.[37] Clearly, not all inter-urban migrants were transitory career migrants in the prime of their life. Some stayed behind and settled down, while others could be overtaken by the mishaps of life. If the risks of old age or illness struck, many inter-urban migrants, too, would be involved in a struggle for survival.

Long-Distance Foreign Migration: A Specialized Affair?

Antwerp received many different groups of migrants from beyond the boundaries of present-day Belgium and the adjacent Dutch provinces. The timing of these foreigners' presence was subject to different developments in the local opportunity structure, evolutions in Antwerp's transport connections, and the city's situation in a wider political-geographical context, which produced various shifts in the urban international migration field (Table 5.1). While 'foreign' Dutch migrants – i.e. from beyond the provinces of North Brabant, Zeeland and Limburg – were the most numerous foreign group at the end of the eighteenth century, they were overtaken by French newcomers in the Napoleonic era, and by German immigrants by the late 1820s. While they often operated in different economic sectors, most were upmarket and/or specialized migrants, who were recruited for very specific income or career opportunities, and were also quick to leave if prospects were better elsewhere.[38] The highly transitory nature of most migration patterns concerned and their marked tendency towards geographical specialization suggest that most foreign migrants moved along channels that were both very different from their shorter-distance counterparts and relatively specific for their own country or region of origin. Although their share in the total number of newcomers was comparatively small, looking at the movements of foreign newcomers in greater detail for each of the main subgroups separately therefore provides valuable indications on how different circuits of migration

involved different speeds of change. I will discuss these different groups in order
of appearance in Table 5.1.

Table 5.1: Origin of Long-Distance Foreign Newcomers, 1796–1850 (N).

	C1796I N Res.	CS1808–13 AYI	CS1815–19 AYI	CS1829 N In	FR1850 N In
France	65	441	110	29	88
German regions	124	102	82	85	200
Netherlands (*)	132	152	34	43	79
Luxemburg	26	0	2	0	7
British Isles	2	4	30	12	60
Italian regions	7	11	8	0	3
Switzerland	7	6	8	14	14
Scandinavia	4	2	4	3	11
Other	12	11	12	6	24
Total	379	729	290	192	486

* Excluding the provinces of North Brabant, Zeeland and Limburg.
Abbreviations: N Res.: number of recorded residents in the 1796 census in the first and
fourth town district; AYI: average yearly inflow; N In: recorded inflow.

Prior to the period under French revolutionary rule, Antwerp had recorded only
a handful of migrants from France. In 1796 barely 1 per cent of the recorded
immigrants had been born in France, of whom at least a quarter had only
recently entered town. Long-term French inhabitants came mainly from nearby
border regions, displayed no marked occupational specialization and revealed a
high proportion of mixed marriages.[39] Recent arrivals, on the other hand, came
from a more varied set of birthplaces, and consisted mainly of administrators of
the new government and their households, like the newly arrived thirty-year-old
Inspecteur-Général des Douanes from Châlons-sur-Saône, who took up residence
near the newly installed Customs office.[40] The later period of French rule would,
however, witness a pronounced increase in the presence of French immigrants in
Antwerp. Whereas in 1796 'old' and 'new' Frenchmen together provided only
about 100 inhabitants, the late Napoleonic era would record an average inflow
of more than 400 French-born newcomers each year, the majority of whom were
male. While some of these were government officials and clerks, or else merchants or tailors, most were naval workers from the northern coasts who travelled
between different French military shipyards via the state-organized labour allocation system of *inscription maritime*. Most arrived in batches of five to twenty,
were housed in one of the many *cabarets et logements militaires* that sprung up
near the naval shipyards and headquarters, and stayed up to eighteen months at
most. While most eventually left when the shipyards were dismantled, a number
of erstwhile naval workers remained behind, like the Besançon-born Pierre Conscience, an erstwhile *gardien volant de la marine* who in 1809 had contracted
marriage to a housemaid from nearby Brecht.[41] As the Napoleonic wars had a

disintegrating effect on many a soldier's or ex-soldier's family – by 1807 Pierre Conscience was orphaned and had lost his only brother in battle – the number of French naval workers who eventually stayed behind might have been greater than generally assumed, although the sudden fallback in employment opportunities made it difficult for them to keep body and soul together.[42]

Although the transition from French to Dutch rule drastically reduced the number of French newcomers to between 50 and 100 per year, the connections forged under Napoleonic rule were not cut off completely. Throughout the Dutch period, there was some continued seasonal migration of a handful of northern French shipwrights and construction workers, although the drying up of this recruitment channel over time suggests their gradual replacement by closer labour supplies, such as from Flemish cities like Ghent and Ostend (see above).[43] French traders, in turn, also maintained some migratory connection with Antwerp, but lagged behind in numbers as compared to other nationalities (see below). Instead, the Dutch period witnessed a further concentration on what can be loosely defined as 'cultural' jobs, or jobs in which the tone-setting allure of French culture provided a comparative advantage. Belgian theatre, for instance, would remain heavily influenced by French drama in the course of the nineteenth century, and employ many a French actor and director – both in elitist spheres and in more popular *variété* theatres and *concert-cafés*. Likewise, the strong reputation of French cooking in nineteenth-century bourgeois and aristocratic culture is well attested, while even popular culture was tempted by Parisian fashion.[44] Indicative of how cultural allure intertwined with migration patterns, the residence card registers of the Dutch period record a conspicuous number of French actors, cooks and tailors. By 1850 these were complemented by musicians, singers, barbers' assistants and waiters – who were to enhance the cosmopolitan appeal of the developing bourgeois leisure culture, for which Paris set the tone. By 1850, the 'cultural bias' in the occupational orientation of French newcomers was manifest: more than half were artists (actors, singers, musicians), fashion workers (barbers, tailors, milliners) or catering workers (cooks, waiters), while the remainder consisted mainly of upmarket traders and clerks. Among the eleven single women who submitted an occupation, we find one actress, three musicians, two maids and one brothel keeper – likewise jobs which were in different ways related to the French cultural sphere. Unlike their naval predecessors, these cultural workers were born in a variety of French regions, and had often arrived via Paris. They tended to be contracted for specific occasions, or hired to work in an upmarket establishment, like the *artistes dramatiques* and *artistes lyriques* who came to stage a performance in the city's royal theatre.[45] Some performed in less lavish places, like the threesome of Parisian musicians who were 'fed and boarded by Mr Prévillier, innkeeper in this town'.[46] Waiters, cooks and barbers' assistants in turn mostly ended up in one of the classy establishments in the central, upmarket districts around the Meir and Groenplaats, sometimes managed by a compatriot.[47]

The composition of the inflow of French newcomers to Antwerp over the course of the late eighteenth and first half of the nineteenth centuries was clearly influenced by the specific labour demand for specialized workers which the developing naval, and later commercial, centre entailed, and by the political-geographical context in which Antwerp operated. In the early decades of the nineteenth century, the relevant labour demand was primarily one for a large number of shipbuilders and related occupations to carry out Napoleon's naval ambitions, while in later years a – more modest – demand for cultural workers took the upper hand. Whereas the rapid large-scale imports of naval workers in the early years had required the interference of state-organized labour allocation mechanisms, these had little in common with the occupation-specific networks and cultural interactions, mediated by advertisements, theatres and private agencies, which channelled most cultural migrants in later decades.

The story of German immigration reads rather differently. At the end of the eighteenth century, there were scarcely more Germans living in Antwerp than there were Frenchmen. Like their French counterparts, they came mainly from towns and villages in border regions, did not reveal any pronounced occupational profile, and showed a high degree of residential dispersion, social variation and intermarriage with the local population.[48] The freeing of the Scheldt in 1795 would, however, set off a marked expansion of the German presence in Antwerp, as the city revived its potential as a favourably located hub for German transit trade and, in a later phase, for German emigration to the New World. Germans soon became not only the most numerous group of 'foreign' migrants in nineteenth-century Antwerp, but also those whose presence was most continuous. More than any other non-national migrants, they are regarded as having established a relatively closed colony, with its own schools, shops and meeting places. While this process of community-building gained momentum in the second half of the century, the period dealt with here is commonly regarded as the formative period of Antwerp's 'German colony'.[49] Exploring the background, recruitment channels and arrival modalities of German newcomers in the first half of the nineteenth century, therefore, provides further indications of the role and nature of social networks in the colony's formative years.

Although a number of German trading houses established or expanded their Antwerp bases immediately after the freeing of the Scheldt,[50] the adverse international situation of most of the French period would postpone the true take-off of the German commercial influx until the more stable conditions of Dutch rule. In the late Napoleonic period, most German newcomers – averaging 100 per year – were carpenters, joiners, blacksmiths, locksmiths and casual labourers destined for the shipyards and related activities, and they displayed patterns of stay which were comparable to those of their French colleagues. Most came from cross-border or north-western coastal areas which by 1811 were part either of the French Empire or of one of its satellite states. Although it is unclear whether the *inscription maritime* was extended to these areas, it is likely that most of these German naval workers were recruited via similar semi-official or military circuits.[51] As in the case of their French colleagues, some of the migration circuits of construction workers established under Napoleonic rule continued on a smaller and more voluntary basis in the Dutch period, with a number of German carpenters and stonecutters returning to Antwerp along well-structured paths of seasonal migration, often staying at the same address in consecutive years. Although none of their hosts was German-born, they all combined lodging activities with work in the construction sector, indicating the operation of employer-organized recruitment channels, possibly drawing on contacts laid by the conscription and *inscription maritime* of Napoleonic rule.[52] In the early Belgian period these migration patterns faded away: among the handful of German toolmakers and construction workers recorded in 1850 we find only specialized industrial workers, such as a *serrurier mécanicien* (locksmith) and an *ingénieur mécanicien* (mechanical engineer), recruited by the Cockerill shipyards. The disappearance of less specialized workers was, like their French counterparts, probably attributable to a geographic restructuring of labour demand and supply: while the industrialization of the Ruhr area provided closer opportunities for many German workers, local demand for construction labour became filled by a labour supply closer to Antwerp.

From the Dutch period onwards, construction workers were replaced by commission merchants, traders and office clerks from Frankfurt, Cologne, Hamburg and other main commercial centres as the most prominent and numerous group of German newcomers, destined to man the proliferating trading firms as Antwerp assumed its role as a prime transit centre for the German hinterland. Most of the *commis* were relatively young, and came to Antwerp to gain relevant experience and be trained in the business, while merchants and commission agents were generally somewhat older and tended to settle for a longer period with wife and children.[53] Their residence in Antwerp was often a phase in a multi-stop training and career trajectory via different trading centres, with Aachen, Frankfurt, Barmen and Brussels as the most popular destinations on leaving. While most worked for German companies, some of them were also housed with the company on their arrival in Antwerp. We find a fair number listing illustrious German trading families and companies as their hosts, such as Kreglinger, Lemmé, Bisschofsheim, Osterrieth & Schmidt and Coomans & Born.[54] The link between their origin and the trading activities of their employer was sometimes very clear, as in the case of the thirty-one-year-old office clerk from Freiburg, who arrived in Antwerp from New York in 1850, and was employed 'at the German emigration and expedition office of Mr Huger'.[55] Not all clerks or agents, however, were housed with their employers; an important number stayed in lodging houses or hotels, some of which appear to have specialized in accommodating this specific category of newcomers, although not run by Germans.[56] While heavily oriented towards German trade companies, then, German newcomers did not move along exclusively German networks. In 1829, only three out of twenty-five selected German clerks were staying with a compatriot, while another ten stayed with an Antwerp-born host, and the others with an array of other immigrants, in a variety of lodging arrangements. Neither were their employers always German. We find seventeen-year-old August Helmers from Lennep (Nordrhein-Westfalen) working for a French wine trader from Rembercourt (Meurthe & Moselle), while other German clerks entered the service of Mauroy & Junet, a trading firm of merchants from Mons (Hainaut).[57] Nor were all clerks employed by trading companies: two clerks from 1850 ended up working in a German bookshop on the main Groenplaats square, while in 1829 we find a number working for Antwerp-born shopkeepers, and two others for the German tailor Bücher. Once the connection between Antwerp and German office personnel had been established via the recruitment channels of German merchant companies, then, this specific labour supply also found its way to other, sometimes non-German, employers.

A similar mixed picture arises from the group of male and female domestic servants. On the one hand, their recruitment was in many cases clearly related to the existence and expansion of the German merchant colony and emigrant infrastructure, such as that of a twenty-three-year-old maid from Cologne, whom the foreigners' administrators in 1850 recorded as 'working in a lodging house for German emigrants in this town', or a forty-year-old servant from Delbrück (Nordrhein-Westphalia) who came to work in the Hotel de Cologne for her compatriot Kruburg. However, there was no necessary correlation between the nationality of servants and their employers. In 1829, for instance, we find two maids from Monschau and Imgenbroich working in the establishment of a French cook from Châlons-sur-Saône, and another one from Münster who came to serve the English trader Bingen from Doncaster.[58] A last group of German newcomers who entered the stage by the middle of the nineteenth century were occupied in the production of luxury goods, such as watchmakers, pressmen and painters,[59] or of specialized food products, like confectioners and pastry cooks. Most of these servants and artisans were probably actively recruited by their employers, via advertisements or existing job channels, which are difficult to reconstruct. Yet they were at least partly related to the movements of their commercial predecessors, in the sense that the latter's presence at once assisted the flow of migration information and created a derivative demand for certain German services and products. By mid-century, they were also supplemented by a

growing number of German emigrants who passed through the port of Antwerp
on their way to the New World. Their arrival was indicative of and instrumental
to a broadening of the migration channels connecting Antwerp to less resourceful Germans from a wider German hinterland, whose presence created additional
business opportunities for compatriots specializing in the 'emigrant trade', such
as shipping agents, lodging keepers, innkeepers and postal entrepreneurs.[60]

Although origin-networks clearly played a role in channelling German
migration – especially in an early phase – recruitment circuits were not origin-
exclusive. Many German clerks and traders, like servants and artisans, worked for
non-German employers and/or stayed with non-German hosts. Their recruitment channels had little to do with the marginal presence of their compatriots
in the eighteenth century, nor with the construction workers manning Napoleon's shipyards. Rather, they developed from newly established commercial
connections and opportunities, which were strong enough to attract a number
of aspiring career migrants prepared and able to move without the safeguard of
long-established migration paths or auxiliary social networks. As such, the commercial influx of the post-Napoleonic period displayed many similarities with
the recruitment channels of German trading personnel in late nineteenth-century Rotterdam, Antwerp's main transit rival. These came from various regions,
stayed in town for only a relatively short period – mainly less than one year – and
were housed by compatriots in only a small minority of cases. Evidence of chain
migration in this case was very limited, and Lesger et al. concluded that most were
recruited via internal company circuits of *organizational migration*: 'All of them
were aware of specific possibilities in certain Dutch cities and did not necessarily
need personal contacts and social networks to migrate'.[61] This was a situation
very different from the smaller provincial centre of Utrecht in the same period,
where the German population was heavily concentrated in a number of specific
retail niches (stoneware and clothing) and was virtually absent from wholesale
trade. Up to three in four German newcomers to Utrecht were recruited via origin-specific and occupation-specific chain migration circuits, as against at most
one in four of their Rotterdam counterparts.[62] This divergence in recruitment
patterns is explained by the dissimilar opportunity structure of the two cities,
as the expanding possibilities of transit trade in Rotterdam attracted a different
set of immigrants from those attracted by the more restricted opportunities in
Utrecht. In Utrecht, path-dependent trajectories from previous migrations were
much more important in maintaining contemporary recruitment than in the
case of Rotterdam: 'The presence of a large group, and the concentrated residential pattern generated an independent dynamic in the migration process that
transcended the trade possibilities and the opportunity structure of Utrecht.
The existence of a Westerwalder community in Utrecht was the reason more
Westerwalders moved to this town.'[63] Some of the community-specific dynam-

ics at work in Utrecht bore resemblance to the derivative demand for German products or personnel that attracted a growing number of housemaids, bakers and painters to Antwerp towards the end of our period. While the pioneering group of merchants and trade personnel had sufficient access to non-personal business information to guide their movements, a broader array of derivative workers for whom inter-personal networks were more important followed in their footsteps, accompanied by a growing number of would-be emigrants channelled to Antwerp via the expanding railway system.[64] In this sense, patterns of chain migration might have become more important as time wore on and the German colony became both larger and more socially diverse in the second half of the nineteenth century.

Let us now turn to a third major group of 'foreign' newcomers: Dutch men and women from beyond the Moerdijk. Like the Germans and the French, those recorded in the 1796 census were not very numerous and did not reveal any strong signs of ethnic clustering.[65] Coming mainly from large-city backgrounds (in particular Amsterdam, Rotterdam and Leiden),[66] their occupational profile seemed better-off than that of the locally-born or of the total migrant population, but was more or less comparable to that of urban-born migrants as a whole, with important proportions of traders, shopkeepers, artisans and domestic servants. While the Napoleonic era also witnessed the arrival of a number of Amsterdam and Rotterdam traders who were anticipating Antwerp's commercial opportunities, most 'foreign' Dutch newcomers in this period were mainly, like the French and the Germans, naval and construction workers. Their patterns of stay likewise resembled these other nationalities, arriving in groups of five to ten at a time, and moving into one of the lodging houses in the first or fourth districts.[67] The relatively small contingent of Dutch newcomers recorded in the late 1810s and 1820s represented mainly a continuation of earlier patterns, with a handful of traders, construction workers and producers of consumer goods mostly staying in town for a number of months. The observation that some Dutch carpenters stayed with the same carpenter/lodger as their German colleagues further confirms that the occupation-specific networks supporting the continued seasonal migration of construction workers were not dependent on shared geographical origins, but might well be traced back to the multinational links of the Napoleonic era. In addition, a handful of government officials came down from beyond the Moerdijk to reinforce the administration of the newly established United Kingdom of the Netherlands, displaying somewhat longer patterns of stay. The influx of women, meanwhile, continued on a par with their male compatriots. Most of these were recorded as being in domestic service and eight worked in the garment industries. It is possible that at least some of these seamstresses, and possibly also some servants, actually worked as prostitutes: they were all housed at inns and cabarets in the Kloosterstraat in the heart of the red-light district, and near the quayside and military barracks – which in that period housed more than 5,000 Dutch troops. In the years 1828–30 the inns at which they stayed are recorded as taking in single young women with a variety of occupations, some of whom had young children. Most of them stayed in town for one or two years, and then moved on to a different destination, while their migration trajectories – birthplace, last place of residence and next destination – often amount to a list of different garrison towns, such as Brussels, Dordrecht, Bruges, Gorcum, Namur, Den Bosch, Gouda and Utrecht. An alternative explanation is that they were soldiers' or sailors' wives or girlfriends, who accompanied their partners.[68] What is certain, in any case, is that their immigration pattern disappeared after Belgian independence, which confirms a certain connection with the Dutch military presence.

By mid-century, 'foreign' Dutch newcomers were a varied group of migrants drawn from upmarket commercial and artisanal milieus. Among them were seven merchants from Amsterdam and the Hague, such as twenty-year-old *commissionnaire expéditeur de marchandises* Joseph van Gelder from Amsterdam, who moved to Antwerp from Calcutta with his new wife and baby child,[69] and a shopkeeper-to-be from Leiden with 2,000 francs in his pocket (the equivalent of about as many daily wages of an unskilled male worker).[70] They arrived together with ten proprietors, four Amsterdam-born Jewish diamond workers, four painters, three teachers, three actors employed by the Royal Theatre, three students, two confectioners, a cigar maker employed at 100 francs per month, a furniture painter, coach painter, a range of other occupations, and thirteen domestic servants, who mainly served relatively well-off employers: three hotel keepers, two merchants, a diamond trader, a pharmacist, a captain and a cabinet maker, and four whose occupation remains unknown. With an average age of twenty-seven and mainly unmarried, most Dutch newcomers were well-off single migrants or specialist workers, who came to Antwerp with a view to specific employment, commercial or training opportunities, on a relatively short stop-over on a longer inter-urban career trajectory.[71]

However, the settlement examinations taken from Dutch-born sojourners in the same year remind us that below this coming and going of career migrants there was a less privileged stratum of permanent 'foreign' Dutch migrants. The examinations list forty-eight male sojourners and twenty-six female ones who had been born in one of the Dutch provinces north of the Moerdijk, and who had migrated to Antwerp at different points in time over the preceding decades. The observation that family migrants were clearly over-represented among those applying for relief confirms both the immobilizing effect of family migration and formation, and its adverse effect on social vulnerability.[72] However, it was not only in terms of family status that sojourners ranked higher on the vulnerability scale than newcomers. Most of them listed occupations which attest to a significantly lower degree of specialization, with casual labourer, sailor and carpentry worker as the most frequently cited male occupations. As with the internal inter-urban sojourners, military service appears to have been a migration-stimulating event for many Dutch sojourners too: nineteen men had spent several years in military service, which had often initiated their migration trajectory – a trajectory which sometimes reads like a miniature military history of the first half of the nineteenth century. Pierre Frederiks, for instance, born in IJsselstein (Utrecht) in 1793, entered Dutch military service in 1810 at the age of seventeen, changed to the French army in 1812, and to the Dutch again after Napoleon's defeat in 1814, where he stayed for another seven years – which probably brought him to Antwerp. From 1821 to 1823 he in any case claims to have worked in Antwerp as a casual labourer, after which he again went into military service for another six years. In 1829, finally, he settled down in Antwerp where he continued to work as a day-labourer, and where in 1842, at the age of forty-nine, he married a German woman from Breitenau (Nassau), and where he would eventually die in 1860.[73]

As with their French counterparts, the recruitment patterns of 'foreign' Dutch migrants were strongly influenced by the military and political connections which in certain periods existed between Antwerp and their country of origin. Fragmentary evidence indicates that military channels of allocation might have been an important catalyst for Antwerp-bound migration for part of the 'foreign' Dutch newcomers. By the latter part of the period studied, most newcomers were relatively specialized upmarket traders and artisans, who moved in response to specific employment opportunities, and in fact displayed little resemblance to their predecessors who figured in the relief administrators' books. While political and military connections had been important in recruiting some of the less specialized 'foreign' Dutch migrants to Antwerp in the early decades of the nineteenth century, by the later decades we find mainly a class of newcomers able to migrate more on the basis of their own means and knowledge of existing opportunities.

Smaller groups complemented Antwerp's palette of immigrant nationalities. The growth of a presence from the British Isles was closely related to the city's commercial development as a port town. While in 1796 only two residents from the British Isles were identified, and in the Napoleonic era they were virtually absent for understandable reasons, in the first years of Dutch rule they would come to supply thirty – almost exclusively male – newcomers per year, of whom some twenty were merchants, traders or proprietors, mostly from cities like London, Dublin and Dundee, and whose establishment would lay the foundation of British and Irish commercial activity in the following decades. By 1829, as with the Germans, the accent had shifted towards auxiliary clerks: among the twelve newcomers from the British Isles recorded that year, there were five office clerks, in addition to two proprietors and a variety of artisans. In 1850, one in two male newcomers was a trader, commission agent or proprietor. Other conspicuous groups were a group of nine students aged between sixteen and twenty-one – probably Roman Catholics – who all came to study at a private school, and three painters, who came to study at the Museum and Academy. Other male Britons at the time performed mainly specialized and sometimes particular jobs, such as that of mechanical engineer or dentist. The rare women were either accompanying their husbands or were independent proprietors; only two women from the British Isles entered town as domestic servants. Apart from the initial phase of settlement in the early years of Dutch rule, most immigrants from the British Isles, like other foreign career migrants, did not stay long.[74] On the lodging arrangements of these newcomers, the data are scarce. It is likely that most clerks and commission agents worked for British trading companies. This was explicitly so for two young clerks aged fifteen and seventeen from Manchester who came to work for the Clegg company in 1829, two *marchands de fruits et pommes de terre* from 1850 who were 'employed by Wray merchant based in Leeds' or a twenty-six-year-old commission agent from London who declared himself 'agent of English companies for the placement of manufactories'.[75] In both the Clegg and Wray cases, one of the two newcomers was a close relative of the employer. Like their German counterparts, however, such immigrants may have been employed by non-British employers too. Thus in 1850 we find, for instance, a British warehouse keeper working for Thomas Menge, and a *commis négociant* in the service of Van Reuth & Cy.[76]

The presence of Italians was much less related to commercial traffic than that of Germans, Britons or Dutch, and in fact decreased over the period. Those Italians that we encountered in the later eighteenth and first half of the nineteenth century were mostly artisans or traders corresponding to some of the classic occupational niches of certain Italian emigration regions: a handful of plaster figurine makers, a travelling musician and some stamp salesmen.[77] The figurine makers from the region of Lucca, who continued a tradition already present in the second half of the eighteenth century, generally arrived in a group of up to five at the same time, stayed at the same addresses in the first town district, and left within a period of two to five months, after which they moved on to new destinations. The traders in stamps, from the Alpine Trento region, generally stayed for a few months – the only exception being a shop assistant from Pieve Tessino who came to work for his compatriot Trossani for more than six years.[78] All in all, the evolution of the Antwerp opportunity structure had little influence on the inflow of Italians, who, if anything, continued mainly along eighteenth-century patterns. The evolution of a Swiss presence yields a somewhat more varied picture. Starting out with a collection of barkeeper, military sergeant, weaver, spinner, pelt dresser, seamstress and domestic servant in 1796, the Swiss presence in later periods was to evolve into a handful of pastry cooks and traders, and a number of casual labourers. The pastry cooks, of whom we find traces in the Napoleonic and Dutch periods as well as in 1850, all came from a set of villages in the canton of Graubünden, and were almost all employed by the same Swiss pâtissier Tschander, and later his widow, on the Grand Place.[79] Other Swiss migrants were either merchants or a mixture of artisans and construction workers who had probably ended up in these regions as soldiers – they in any case appeared only in the years after the Napoleonic wars, and had disappeared by 1850. By that time, the only Swiss newcomers were Tschander's pastry cooks, some traders and a number of painters for the Antwerp academy.

The residue of foreign migrants from other regions, who rarely provided more than 1 per cent of the total, formed a varied group of generally upmarket migrants. Noteworthy are the handful of commission merchants and clerks recruited from the Americas, such as nineteen-year-old commission merchant François Garay from Veracruz in 1815, eighteen-year-old office clerk Esteban Dela Lama from Buenos Aires in 1829, or the twenty-one-year-old *particulier* (private proprietor) from Rio de Janeiro in 1850 – symbolizing the role of increasing Atlantic interaction over this period.[80] Other conspicuous groups encountered in the residence card and foreigners' registers are a handful of Scandinavian deck officers and captains, quite a number of Central European painters and – possibly the most colourful one – an Algerian *limonadier* who came to Antwerp with his wife and children to open up a tavern in 1850.[81] Notwithstanding their diversity, most of these exotic migrants were attracted to Antwerp by the widening career or training opportunities which the increasing internationalization of the city's relations entailed.

At the end of the eighteenth century, then, Antwerp had harboured few foreign migrants within its city walls. The handful of French, German, 'foreign' Dutch and others who could be encountered in the streets came mainly from cross-border regions and displayed modest degrees of occupational specialization. Two main – and to a great extent discontinuous – developments would radically reshape the context of foreign recruitment patterns in the first half of the nineteenth century. The first was the imposed role of Antwerp as military spearhead of a powerful political structure which would at the height of its power reach out over the major part of the European continent. The other was the rapid expansion of commercial and maritime activity after the lifting of the Scheldt blockade, in particular from the Dutch period onwards. In the wake of the first development, large contingents of mainly construction workers were recruited to Antwerp from distant and less distant regions via state-organized systems of labour allocation. Some of the recruitment patterns forged in this period continued at a more modest and informal pace after the downfall of Napoleon, but eventually faded in the course of the second quarter of the nineteenth century. To a certain extent, the external influence of state-organized labour allocation mechanisms was repeated on a smaller scale under Dutch rule, when the stationing of more than 5,000 troops appears to have formed a channel via which several 'foreign' Dutch migrants ended up in Antwerp. More importantly for the further evolution of foreign recruitment patterns was the marked increase in commercial activity after the Napoleonic wars. The expansion of sizeable opportunities in international trade and commerce attracted a new type of specialized, wealthy and aspiring career migrants over sometimes great distances. Three main subgroups were identified among their ranks: commercial clerks and traders, highly skilled artisans, and cultural workers and artists. Patterns of chain migration do not appear to have been very important in these types of recruitment. All these migrants belonged to groups which by nature of their occupational specialization and socio-economic status had access to impersonal circuits of migration information (corporate employment opportunities, artisan organizations, advertisements, newspapers) and could afford to move without the support of family or social safety nets.

By nature of the discontinuity of the two main developments occasioning their attraction, recruitment patterns of foreign migrants in the first half of the nineteenth century showed relatively little continuity with earlier patterns. They arose relatively independently from a radically new navy-oriented and, later, commerce-oriented opportunity structure which had little to do with the situation in the second half of the eighteenth century. That these new recruitment patterns could arise without the help of pre-established connections was only possible because of: 1) the state-organized and semi-military nature of the first type's recruitment patterns (in this sense, the French state was probably the most powerful channel of 'corporate' recruitment conceivable); and 2) the wealthy and elitist nature of the migrants attracted by developing commercial opportunities – a group of well-informed and well-endowed upper-class migrants who operated along wide geographic horizons, who were prepared to take the risks of exploring new commercial opportunities and migration trajectories and who could build on the experience and information networks established elsewhere. The limited, non-path-dependent and well-informed nature of their movements explains why their migration was generally targeted at specific opportunities on the one hand and loose-footed on the other: as no strong ties existed with Antwerp except career possibilities, they were swift to move on if better opportunities arose elsewhere. This 'thin' migration context, determined almost exclusively by income opportunities, allowed this exclusive group of upmarket migrants to display very rapid rates of change, whereby they were swift to react and adapt to newly emerging or disappearing opportunities, unhindered by the inertia of highly embedded migration channels and social networks.

In a later phase, the growing presence of foreign migrant groups and the proliferation of transport facilities gave rise to a third main circuit of foreign migration materializing mainly in the second half of the nineteenth century. I am referring here to a derived demand for domestic servants, shopkeepers, bakers and the like which the establishment of new ethnic communities entailed. Although we have found little indications of ethnic clustering in the first half of the nineteenth century, existing research suggests that this became more important in the second half of the century – when German, (Eastern European) Jewish and other foreign presences developed into relatively closed 'colonies'. Some traces of this trend are observable in the foreigners' registers of 1850, which recorded a number of domestic servants employed in German emigrant lodging houses and merchant households. Possibly, this secondary channel of path-dependent ethnic-specific recruitment of less specialized workers grew in importance in the course of the second half of the nineteenth century, when the further expansion of Antwerp's emigrant trade and the proliferation of maritime and overland connections lowered the threshold for less resourceful long-distance migration.

Other Rural Migrants: A Question of Niches or Crises?

Throughout the whole period under consideration, around 30 per cent of newcomers were rural-born migrants from beyond the Antwerp provincial boundaries, but within the boundaries of present-day Belgium and adjacent Dutch provinces. Already when discussing the census results of 1796, it was observed that Antwerp's prime regional recruitment area extended into villages situated in neighbouring provinces, most notably Brabant, North Brabant and the two Limburg provinces – which together provided 80 per cent of extra-provincial rural-born migrants at the time. However, the regional composition of Antwerp's 'other rural-born migrants' would change considerably over time. By 1855 the share of the same four regions had shrunk to 50 per cent. The Walloon regions experienced an upsurge in their proportion of migrants in the French period, which fell back again in the course of the following decades. Instead, the provinces making up the erstwhile County of Flanders were to increase their share from only 10 per cent in the eighteenth and early nineteenth centuries to 38 per cent in 1855 – replicating the shifts observed for the internal inter-urban circuit, where Flemish cities also increased their importance over the same period. Some of these regions had more long-standing migratory connections to Antwerp than others. When exploring dynamics of change within the circuit of non-provincial rural recruitment, it is therefore useful to make a broad distinction between those regions which in the eighteenth century had already represented an extension of the prime provincial recruitment area, i.e. North

Brabant and Brabant, those regions which remained situated at the margins of the regional recruitment area – Limburg and Zeeland – and the relatively new recruitment regions of Wallonia and Flanders.

Rural-born migrants from the provinces of Brabant and North Brabant made up between 15 and 19 per cent of all newcomers between 1796 and 1829, and 12 per cent in 1855. As proposed when discussing the results from the 1796 census, most of the area resembled a secondary belt of regional recruitment. The specificities of transport routes, the absence of other big cities, and long-standing religious and cultural connections made Antwerp the 'nearest' large city for many villagers in North Brabant and (mainly eastern) Brabant. Migrants from these regions included many women among their ranks, and often travelled to Antwerp directly – typical characteristics of an urban demographic basin.[82] For many villagers in the Brabantine area, direct migration to Antwerp was a familiar behaviour in much the same ways as in the Antwerp Province itself, embedded in broader interactions between the town and its hinterland. Moreover, their occupational profile was more or less comparable to that of intra-provincial rural migrants, with important clustering in the sectors of domestic service, food industries, retail, tools and construction, and transport.[83] Much as in the case of their intra-provincial counterparts, it is plain that Antwerp's development into a port town greatly expanded the employment opportunities for unspecialized newcomers from the Brabantine countryside. As their home regions had already belonged to Antwerp's regional migration field in the eighteenth century, and predecessors had already tended to cluster in those sectors which experienced the largest expansion, they could capitalize on pre-existing connections and recruitment circuits to find a place in the city's rapidly changing urban labour market, allowing them to develop longer patterns of stay.[84] In addition, the supporting role of social networks was important in this respect. Given the long-standing nature of their migration patterns, migrants from the 'secondary' regional belt were also likely to have been acquainted with their destination beforehand, and to have known people who had lived there and who lived there still. Moreover, both their lodging arrangements and intermarriage patterns indicate that they too had well-developed connections with locally-born residents more or less comparable to their intra-provincial counterparts.[85] Hence, individual migration trajectories of the early decades of the nineteenth century, such as that of Catherina Verbist from Winksele (Leuven district), who came to work as a maid for an Antwerp fish vendor in 1829 and ended up marrying an Antwerp-born smith in 1833, speak not only of expanding employment opportunities, but also of manifold social and family links with the urban social structure.[86]

Although migration patterns from rural Brabant areas shared many characteristics with the first circuit of intra-provincial rural-born migrants, however, distance did take its toll. This was most evident as regards the *intensity* of Antwerp-bound migration from these areas, which averaged a level of 0.5 per thousand throughout the first half of the century, while the equivalent figure for rural villages within the Antwerp province increased to no less than 7 per thousand in 1850 (see above, Maps 4.7–10). Yet, there were important disparities within the Brabantine regions. Levels of migration intensity were highest – an average of 1 per thousand and village rates up to 5 per thousand – in the poor and relatively isolated Hageland area, with its high incidence of mainly temporary emigration, and long-standing connections to Antwerp.[87] Rates were in turn lowest for the areas around Brussels and 's Hertogenbosch, confirming that the influence of competing urban migration fields cut off the south-western and northernmost area of the erstwhile Duchy of Brabant from Antwerp's rural catchment area. At an intermediary level, several villages in the southern half of the Province of North Brabant recorded migration intensities of over 1 and 2 per thousand, while the weight of recruitment from the border belt shifted from east to west in the course of the nineteenth century. One factor in occasioning this shift was that the collapse of textile production made Antwerp comparatively less attractive for villagers from the eastern part of North Brabant, where rural textile production was relatively widespread.[88] Another factor was that the infertile sandy soils, small-scale subsistence farming and rural textile production in the east of the province made for greater resilience of local survival strategies and less likelihood of emigration, much as in the case of the Antwerp Campine.[89] The fertile polders along the coastal regions near Breda, in contrast, were exploited by larger-scale commercial landholdings, and recorded higher rates of population growth and proletarianization in the course of the nineteenth century, which would have made more villagers likely to emigrate. In addition, the direct road to Breda and the railway connection to Roosendaal (1854) provided a relatively smooth connection between the west of North Brabant and Antwerp's expanding port labour market.[90] Both landholding structures and differences in connectivity, then, appear to have shaped differential intensities of migration from Brabant areas. While migration to Antwerp was a familiar pattern in many villages, distance and landholding structures prevented it from proliferating to the same degree as in many closer provincial villages over the first half of the nineteenth century, causing the relative contribution of the Brabant provinces to decrease over time.

Although migrants from Brabant areas shared many characteristics with the first circuit of intra-provincial rural-born migrants, they moved along migration channels which were less dense and less exclusively oriented towards Antwerp. That the more limited social embeddedness of their migration patterns created weaker ties is illustrated by their changing migratory behaviour in the context of the increasingly unstable urban labour market of the 1840s and 1850s. While the number of Brabant immigrants expanded moderately between 1829 and 1850, their length of stay decreased considerably over this period, which was attributable to a growing number of female domestic servants who stayed in town less than one or two years.[91] This trend went hand in hand with an increasing level of mobility prior to and after the move to Antwerp, which was indicative of their growing involvement with stepwise patterns of migration via regional towns such as Turnhout or Breda to larger cities like Antwerp and Brussels.[92] Given that Brabant maids in 1850 were on average two years older than their predecessors in earlier decades, some of them formed part of a group which in earlier decades would have spent their whole service period in the regional town which now proved an intermediate step between their place of birth and Antwerp.[93] That they now decided to move on from, say, Turnhout to Antwerp, might be interpreted as resulting from rising constraints in the home region, or as a result of the growing yet fluctuating demand for housemaids, shop assistants and waitresses in the wake of Antwerp's commercial and maritime expansion.[94] Research like that of Hilde Bras on Zeeland maids has alerted us to the extent to which their moves were also guided by preferences and ambitions on the part of the maids themselves, and on the role played by the attractions of city life.[95] As improving means of transport and communications brought Turnhout and Breda nearer to Antwerp, and Antwerp in turn nearer to Brussels, maids' increasing mobility might also be interpreted as a result of widening horizons, which allowed them to pursue a more diverse urban experience.

In many ways, the rural regions of the provinces of Limburg and Zeeland can be considered something of a tertiary belt of regional recruitment. Immigrants from here share with Brabant and intra-provincial migrants an occupational profile primarily oriented towards casual labour, construction activities and domestic service, a high number of female migrants (mainly maids), and a relatively high proportion of direct migrants – at least in the early decades. They differ, however, in the low intensity of migration as a proportion of total population. In fact, the average migration intensity from the two Limburg provinces displays something of a declining trend over the period in question (from 0.5 per thousand in 1808–13 to 0.3 per thousand in 1850), which indicates that the region gradually tended to move out of Antwerp's orbit – possibly because of the interference from alternative – possibly German – destinations. Zeeland, in turn, became slightly more important as a region of origin only by the end of the period (0.2 per thousand in 1850). The region was like Limburg in that a large proportion of its recruits were female maids and woodworkers. A higher number of the latter were explicitly engaged in shipbuilding in the case of Zeeland. That Zeeland maids started moving to Antwerp in noticeable numbers in the 1850s can be seen as a reflection of the broadening of their action radius as described by Hilde Bras, and of the greater opportunities for domestic service in the developing port economy.[96] Both regions moreover displayed a high, and rising, level of turnover – especially as regards female immigrants – which paralleled the development described for migrants from the province of North Brabant.

The Walloon regions were largely outside Antwerp's rural recruitment sphere. Only in the period under French rule did the volume of Walloon immigration reach slightly higher proportions, but even then it did not involve more than 0.3 per thousand of the rural population. Throughout the first decades of the nineteenth century, a migration intensity of 0.1 per thousand was the norm – indicating that this was not an area with densely developed migration connections to Antwerp. Nevertheless, certain clusters of villages in the *arrondissements* of Charleroi, Waremme, Liège, Namur and Nivelles did send noteworthy numbers of migrants in specific periods, sometimes to an equivalent of more than 1 per thousand of their inhabitants each year. Most of these migrants revealed a very specific occupational profile. While Walloon migration was predominantly male throughout the period, the large majority of migrants consisted either of construction workers and casual labourers, who were recruited mainly from western parts of the Walloon area, or of straw hat makers, who came mainly from the district of Liège. The precise channels through which these migrants were recruited merit a closer look.

The recruitment of Walloon construction workers received an important boost during the period of Napoleonic rule, when on average more than 140 construction workers and casual labourers were recorded annually in the residence card registers – and up to 800 might have moved to Antwerp in peak years.[97] While most casual labourers were recruited from the district of Ath, stonecutters and bricklayers mainly came from the *arrondissements* of Soignies, Charleroi and Nivelles, in particular from the municipalities of Ecaussinnes, Soignies, Seneffe, Villers-la-Ville and Jodoigne. Carpenters, smiths and other construction workers came from a variety of Walloon regions. While the semimilitary recruitment channels of the Napoleonic era clearly played an important role in achieving these inputs, they did not come completely out of the blue. As early as in the 1796 census we find reference to the presence of twenty Walloon construction workers, mainly carpenters from Braine-l'Alleud (*arrondissement* of Nivelles) and stonecutters from Nivelles and Seneffe.[98] While the recruitment of casual labourers died out after Napoleonic rule, stonecutters and bricklayers from the region to the north of Charleroi continued to be recruited at a moderate rate after Dutch rule – attesting to a greater resilience of their migration channels and the importance of pre-existing connections. By the end of the Dutch period, when construction activity had again picked up, we find an increased number of stonecutters from Seneffe, Nivelles and Jodoigne, accompanied by a new inflow of *plafonneurs* mainly from the western part of the district of Namur (Fosses-la-Ville, Floreffe, Profondeville, Gembloux), from adjacent boroughs in the district of Charleroi (Farciennes, Châtelet) and from a pocket of boroughs on the border between the provinces of Liège and Brabant (Hélécine, Lincent). Their recruitment to Antwerp proceeded along well-established patterns of seasonal chain migration, supported by origin-based and occupation-based lodging arrangements and networks. One in three Walloon construction workers in 1829 stayed with someone from the same village, while most other hosts either came from areas nearby and/or were active in the same occupational branches.[99] They were mostly aged between twenty and thirty-five, and invariably arrived in spring and returned home in the autumn months.[100] As such, their recruitment to Antwerp was part of a strongly developed and well-attested (but little researched) tradition of seasonal migration from their areas of origin.[101] By the 1850s, however, they had disappeared, much like their French, Dutch and German counterparts,[102] most probably because of the development of better employment alternatives nearer to home, in particular in the wake of the early industrialization of the Charleroi area and the expansion of mining.

A second conspicuous group of Walloon migrants in early nineteenth-century Antwerp were the straw hat makers from the *communes* of Bassenge, Oupeye and Juprelle in the vale of the Geer on the border of the provinces of Liège and Limburg. While at the time of the 1796 census there was no trace of either Walloon straw hat makers or immigrants from these municipalities, by the Napoleonic era they were immigrating at a rate of twenty-two per year on average, and they continued to migrate at a somewhat slower rate in the following decades, and were still conspicuously present in the emigration registers by the middle of the century.[103] Almost exclusively male and aged between fifteen and thirty-seven, they arrived somewhere between January and March four or five at a time and stayed for four months on average, after which they returned home. Like the construction workers from the more western provinces, the Walloon straw hat makers were engaged in well-structured patterns of seasonal migration which took place in the context of broader household income-pooling, and which were supported by origin-specific and occupation-specific migration chains, in which family relations were also prominent.[104] The presence of this particular group of migrants in early nineteenth-century Antwerp reflected a very particular pattern of economic specialization in a set of villages in the Geer valley, which has been studied primarily in relation to their migration to the Netherlands. From the late eighteenth century onwards, an increasing number of inhabitants of these villages had started concentrating on the production of straw hats, inaugurating a specialization which would dominate their village economy throughout the nineteenth century. The production and marketing of these quality hats – expensive specimens cost the equivalent of three to four day's wages of a semi-skilled labourer in the early nineteenth century – involved an intricate combination of domestic and small factory production in the home villages, the emigration of a number of local manufacturers to different towns in the Netherlands, France, Germany and Belgium, and the seasonal recruitment of mainly male workers to the latter's *ateliers* during the spring months in order to perform the finishing tasks on the raw materials and semi-manufactured products which had been prepared at home throughout the winter. In these patterns of temporary and permanent migration and niche formation, village and family bonds were of great importance: most seasonal staff worked and stayed in the workplace of a fellow villager. The first straw hat makers from the Geer villages are thought to have turned up in Dutch towns in the later decades of the eighteenth century, and indications exist that temporary migration to Antwerp was already in place during the last years of the eighteenth century. These patterns were to intensify considerably in the first decades of the nineteenth century, and would be abandoned, together with the concomitant migration patterns, only by the close of the century, when changes in taste, and imports, would undermine the market for the straw hats from the Geer valley.[105] The presence and migration patterns of the straw hat makers from the Geer valley in the case of Antwerp corresponded completely to the patterns established for early nineteenth-century Dutch cities, whereby trained workers came to produce hats in the *ateliers* of an established fellow villager during the first months of the fashion season. Interestingly, Matheus Mathot – the employer and lodger of most migrants in Antwerp – was probably related to Bernard Mathot from Bassenge (1732–1817), who emigrated to Gouda in 1781 and became the founder of a whole family of straw hat making entrepreneurs in different nineteenth-century Dutch cities.[106]

Of course, not all Walloon migrants were either straw hat makers or construction workers – throughout the sources, other jobs performed by Walloon migrants, such as female domestic servants and seamstresses, are occasionally encountered. These were, however, never numerous, and the migrants concerned came from a variety of different places. There is little evidence that the movements of these other Walloon migrants were in any way stimulated or enabled by the channels used by their compatriots in building or hat making. The hatters' migration channels in fact represented very specific and exclusive patterns of chain migration, which were structured around particular niches. These niches were not only or even primarily a reflection of skill, but were also related to the origin of the materials used. They resulted in close-knit origin-specific and occupation-specific channels of migration, which were hardly accessible to outsiders, and which left room for only very limited interaction with urban society.

Prior to the middle of the nineteenth century, the Flemish countryside (in East and West Flanders) was unimportant as a supplier of newcomers to Antwerp. In the first decades of the century, migration intensity barely reached more than 0.1 per thousand for most Flemish areas. The only areas with which somewhat closer connections existed were the Scheldt districts of Dendermonde and Sint-Niklaas. Recruitment from the (shipbuilding) district of Dendermonde was strongly stimulated by the *inscription maritime* under French rule (0.4 per thousand), but waned in the years under Dutch rule. Only the Waasland region of the Sint-Niklaas district increased its importance among Antwerp newcomers in the period under Dutch rule, but did not rise above an intensity of 0.4 per thousand in 1829. This state of affairs changed dramatically in the 1850s, when the yearly number of Flemish rural newcomers increased more than sevenfold as compared to the 1820s. By 1850, the intensity of rural recruitment had increased significantly for all Flemish districts. With an average of 1.9 per thousand, the intensity of rural recruitment from the Sint-Niklaas district had by that time attained a level comparable to the Campine district of Turnhout in the 1830s and 1840s. In addition, the recruitment intensities from the districts of Oudenaarde (0.6 per thousand), Ghent (0.5 per thousand), and Eeklo (0.4 per thousand), grew to levels comparable to those of the provinces of North Brabant and Belgian Brabant in the same period. While urban migrants were able to move along existing inter-urban connections, most of the immigration by rural-born Flemings represented radically new trajectories. I have argued earlier that the devastating impact of the crisis of the 1840s, by which Flanders was disproportionately hard hit, was the prime underlying cause of this sudden increase in the rate of (often family) migration from the Flemish countryside to Antwerp. The precise mechanisms by which these crisis factors operated, however, were not straightforward.

An important caveat in this respect is that there was no linear correlation between the severity of the crisis and the number of immigrants arriving in Antwerp.[107] The district supplying most of the Flemish-born applicants for relief in Antwerp in 1855, that of Sint-Niklaas (33 per cent), was one where the linen industry had been the least predominant, while districts which were hardest hit by the crisis, such as those of Roeselare, Tielt and Kortrijk, sent only a marginal – though rising – number of newcomers to Antwerp. Of course, the district of Sint-Niklaas did suffer under the consequences of the agricultural and industrial crisis, but to a far lesser extent than some of the more inland Flemish regions.[108] Other factors than the crisis itself clearly played a role too. An obvious one is distance: Sint-Niklaas was the closest Flemish district to Antwerp. Although interactions with Flanders were underdeveloped, some migration connections between the Waasland region and Antwerp had existed in earlier periods, which could have provided a vehicle for intensified emigration in the 1840s and 1850s. However, the distance factor was not straightforward either, as this does not explain the relatively high proportion (24 and 16 per cent respectively) of rural-born Flemish sojourners from the districts of Ghent or Bruges. Here, the vicinity of an important city, which could operate as a gateway between intra-regional and inter-urban patterns of migration, appears to have been an important factor. Information on their migration trajectories from settlement examinations and emigration registers confirms that many Flemish rural migrants had arrived in Antwerp via a pattern of stepwise migration via a major Flemish town.[109] Flemish cities thus appear to have formed important gateways in structuring Antwerp-bound migration from a wide range of birthplaces in the Flemish countryside. As connections with Flemish cities had a longer tradition than those with the countryside, and had increased in importance over the first decades of the nineteenth century, they formed the prime node in channelling Flemish migration to Antwerp – aided by the further development of railways. Most Flemish newcomers in the 1840s and 1850s had therefore either been born in a city or had lived in one. This observation corresponds with the overall distinction in migration behaviour observed in the wake of the Flemish crisis, namely that cities supplied more cross-provincial migrants than rural regions. When they left, urban migrants were also more likely to leave for another Belgian province, while rural migrants were much more intensely engaged in migration to another country, mainly to the cross-border French regions, and to a lesser extent also to the Americas.[110]

While the number of migrants from the districts hardest hit by the collapse of linen production was comparatively limited, there are also few indications that Flemish newcomers were ex-linen workers. While the urban-born were predominantly engaged in semi-skilled toolmaking and construction, rural-born migrants clustered in unskilled service activities or worked as casual labourers.[111] Possibly, some of the unspecialized workers might formerly have been linen workers. However, in the twenty-nine instances where we have information on the occupations of one or both of the sojourners' parents, there are only three references to a textile job: two refer to a weaving father, one to a spinning mother. All the others refer to a variety of – sometimes skilled – occupations, from potter, ropemaker, carpenter, shoemaker, fisherman and baker to even a goldsmith. Most Flemish newcomers of the 1850s, therefore, came from, or via, cities, did not come from the districts which had been hardest hit by the linen crisis, and do not appear to have been former linen workers. Although growing push forces were evidently important as a prime factor in increasing the likelihood of migration, the precise mechanisms of selection which sent these groups of newcomers to Antwerp are more complex than the crisis alone allows for. Pre-existing connections between certain regions and cities clearly played a channelling role in recruiting certain groups of migrants to Antwerp. Rather than setting those hardest hit on the road to urban growth poles, it appears that extra-provincial Flemish migration took place via some displacement mechanism, whereby impoverished rural migrants would move at most to their regional capital, while more long-standing urban residents moved out to places where opportunities appeared better. The end result was in any case that Flemish newcomers were not an indiscriminate group of crisis victims, but rather a subset which was relatively well equipped to deal with port city life.

However, the observation that the Flemish were to a certain extent positively selected does not imply that their life in Antwerp was without difficulty. Their high dependency ratio and the absence of pre-existing social and recruitment networks must have made it relatively more difficult for them to find a job and to cover periods of unemployment in Antwerp's irregular port labour market. In the unstable labour market context of the 1840s and 1850s, which witnessed an increase in protective strategies by established groups, unconnected newcomers would experience difficulties accessing many labour market segments, difficulties which are reflected in the high proportion of Flemish migrants among relief applicants and hospital patients. In her study on migration to the mid-nineteenth-century Brussels suburb of Sint-Joost-ten-Node, De Metsenaere observed that Dutch-speaking newcomers – of which the Flemish made up an important share – were more likely to move in family units and via chain networks than French-speaking migrants, and more often ended up in alleys inhabited by people from the same villages, resulting in mono-dialect living quarters. Their residential segregation and strong origin-connections, in turn, made these alleys into 'ghettos of poor labourers, Dutch-speaking islands which are nevertheless representative for the proletariat of Sint-Joost'.[112] Of course, the Brussels situation is cross-cut by a linguistic cleavage which to a certain extent paralleled certain social stratifications. Although Flemish newcomers and the Antwerp population in principle spoke the same language, considerable differences in dialect would have existed. Many of the Flemish examined in the settlement indications, moreover, appear to have lived in the same streets and alleyways in the poor quarter of Sint-Andries.[113] As these also represent the streets where most of Antwerp's poorest residents lived, however, it is not clear whether chain migration dynamics played a role in this residential clustering.[114] Unfortunately, the data at hand do not allow us to explore Flemish newcomers' further trajectories in town or to assess the possible success of their migration. How they fared and how urban life treated these newcomers, operating between crisis and opportunity, is worth a separate study in itself.

Patterns of Adaptation: The Speeds of Change

A wide range of migrant groups has passed before our eyes. The great varieties in origin, occupational profile, migration trajectories and patterns of stay make it clear that the newcomers who passed through Antwerp's city gates between the mid-eighteenth and the mid-nineteenth centuries were anything but a homogeneous group. Within these great internal variations, however, a number of basic subgroups could be identified on the basis of certain shared characteristics. Intersections between the different circuits were rare, and were situated only at the margins. Thus small regional towns like Lier and Turnhout could function as gateways between intra-provincial and inter-urban patterns of migration, while regional capitals like Brussels, Ghent or Liège functioned as inter-urban gateways to Antwerp for distant rural migrants. On the whole, however, crossover was rare, and most migration took place along a handful of relatively closed circuits. The different groups of migrants moving along distinct circuits of recruitment have been shown to have reacted and adapted in very different ways to the radical changes in local opportunity structure which took place over the period under consideration. The speed and direction of these adaptations were at once a reflection of the objective room for manoeuvre of different migrant groups in terms of capacities, resources and household constraints, and of the different channels of migration along which they operated. As most short-distance migrants came from a rural setting with little occupational diversification and rising income constraints, their room for manoeuvre was substantially more limited than that of the wealthier and/or more skilled newcomers who moved over greater distances. On the whole, we found very little indication of chain migration or of occupation-specific or origin-specific networks structuring newcomers' trajectories to Antwerp. This does not mean that the meso level of migration processes is of little importance for understanding the evolution of migration patterns over the period. On the contrary, if the conception of migration channels is widened from the narrow concept of chains to the wider and more diffuse context of information dissemination and spatial interaction, these channels appear to have played an essential role in structuring and reinforcing differential patterns of adaptation.

I have in this respect already referred implicitly or explicitly to the distinction between 'dense' and 'thin' migration channels. Dense channels were characterized by a strong degree of embeddedness in broad spatial interactions to ensure the conveyance of migration information, such as, for instance, in the manifold legal, commercial, political and social relationships which connected a town with its hinterland. The constant movement of market-goers, vendors, litigants, administrators, family members and friends ensured a continuous and diffuse flow of information about existing opportunities along their routes. As these relationships were often built on a century-long tradition of information and population exchange, and existing routes of transport and communication between certain places and regions, the spatial scope of these information channels was very path-dependent and difficult to reshape. Thin channels of migration, on the other hand, were used by migrants who had access to very targeted and often exclusive sources of information on particular opportunities which were relevant to them, such as journeymen's associations, advertisements, newspapers or corporate placement mechanisms. Because they had direct access to these reliable sources of information, they had little need for the denser and embedded channels of information to be up to date on existing opportunities or to guide their movements. Moreover, the difference lies not only in a differential dependence on embedded channels as sources of information, but also in a differential dependence upon social networks in the context of survival strategies. The most vulnerable groups were generally those who not only had the poorest access to thin information channels, but were also in the greatest need of supportive social networks as a buffer against the calamities of life. The strongly embedded nature of the migration channels along which they generally operated, then, provided them with the possibility of maintaining these necessary contacts while moving. At the same time, they could not afford to move to places where the safety net of social connectedness was completely absent. In this sense, the embeddedness of their migration channels was at once an enabling and a constraining factor in their migration behaviour. While providing a supportive social infrastructure to their moves, dense migration channels by definition offered only a limited range of possible destinations. Upmarket migrants who had access to better and more exclusive sources of information and were less dependent on informal social networks to survive[115] had more options and more freedom to choose. As a result, the thin nature of their migration channels allowed them to make more considered migration decisions.

These distinctions between dense and thin migration channels, and the groups of migrants using them, are most readily applicable to the two extreme types of migrants considered in the above pages: intra-provincial rural-born migrants on the one hand and foreign international migrants on the other, in which case their objective room for manoeuvre was inversely proportional to the density of the migration channels used. But what about intermediate groups, groups that were more or less subject to the same objective constraints and opportunities but had access to different migration channels? In this context, the observed difference in the evolution of migration behaviour between rural-born people from North Brabant or the Hageland region on the one hand and from the province of Antwerp on the other is an interesting case in point. Migrants from the 'secondary' area of regional recruitment had more or less the same occupational profile, operated in more or less the same labour market segments, and displayed more or less the same migration behaviour in the late eighteenth and early nineteenth centuries as migrants from the city's prime demographic basin, yet they were far more affected by the overall tendency towards increasing mobility and turnover in the course of the 1840s and 1850s. Their intra-provincial counterparts, however, displayed a far greater continuity and persistence in their migration patterns throughout the period under consideration. The explanation for this divergence in migration behaviour is twofold. The lesser embeddedness of the migration channels from the secondary regional recruitment area due to a general distance-decay effect – reflected among other things in a far smaller intensity of recruitment – implied that their social networks and safety nets in town, although present, were less developed than those of their intra-provincial counterparts. As the growing instability of port-related employment in the course of the 1840s and 1850s increased the necessity of social support structures in order to survive in town, migrants from the secondary regional belt were at a comparative disadvantage as compared with intra-provincial newcomers with better developed connections. As competition for jobs increased, moreover, intra-provincial migrants would probably have been more successful in developing protective strategies via informal recruitment preferences and closing off certain branches from distant competitors. In this sense, the lesser embeddedness of the migration channels of North Brabant and Hageland migrants was a comparative disadvantage in the struggle for survival in an increasingly unstable port labour market. While regional migrants could (barely) overcome periods of unemployment by falling back on social networks and relief provisions, migrants from the secondary belt would in this case have been more readily forced to move on elsewhere. At the same time, however, there is a more positive complement conceivable to this comparative disadvantage. The fact that migrants from the North Brabant and Hageland areas travelled over longer distances and had more often moved to other places before coming to Antwerp also implied that their action radius was larger, that they had access to more diverse sources of information, and more destination options to consider and to compare. In this sense, their more complex migration experience and repertoire might have made them readier to move on if prospects in Antwerp deteriorated, whereas intra-provincial migrants had few alternatives to consider, and were more likely to attempt to stay put. Moving along highly embedded channels of migration for relatively unspecialized migrants could thus be a blessing as well as a curse, in the same ways as the lesser connectedness of other migrant groups at once forced them and enabled them to move elsewhere when employment opportunities deteriorated. Whether migrants themselves experienced the blessing or the curse is a question which cannot be answered on the basis of the source materials used here. Both circuits were evidently confronted with rising structural constraints and difficulties, but adapted and reacted to them in different ways. Which one of the two was better remains an open-ended question.

The implication of these observations is that a large degree of 'integration' of migrants and their circuits with the society of destination, in the form of a strong familiarity, a high degree of intermarriage, mixed family connections, long-term patterns of residence and so on, represents something of a trade-off with migrants' actual room for manoeuvre. As much as it might enhance their chances of survival or even betterment in local society, at the same time it limits their potential to move elsewhere. In turn, the truly wealthy and successful migrants do not need to be integrated with local society as nearly as their unskilled counterparts. In this sense, a great degree of integration should not necessarily be considered a measure of immigrant success – as it is often implicitly or explicitly taken to be – but rather a measure of the relative lack of alternatives. This conception of integration, moreover, is very different from patterns of niche or chain migration such as observed in the case of the Walloon construction workers or straw hat makers. Although supportive social relations are of essential importance in these specific channels, they differ from dense channels of recruitment in that they are not integrated with wider local society. As migration takes place along inner-circle networks, with virtually no connections to the host society, these circuits are relatively detached from their precise location, and are far less path-dependent and easier to transfer than their denser counterparts. Because of their close relationship to particular commercial ventures, especially in the case of the straw hat makers from the Geer valley, these migrants were also relatively 'selective' in terms of specific local opportunities. Given a sufficient insight into possible destinations, which appears to have been assured by the wide network of *fabriqueurs* along different Dutch, Belgian and French cities, moreover, their limited degree of integration makes such patterns apt to have been transplanted relatively easily when better options turned up elsewhere.

Unspecialized regional migrants thus tended to move along dense channels of migration which were the product of century-long spatial interaction and integration between town and countryside, and therefore very slow to change. This does not mean, however, that they were completely immobile, as the example of the Flemish immigrants to Antwerp demonstrates. The sudden increase in the number of rural-born Flemish newcomers to Antwerp in the 1850s represents a breaking-up of the regional context to which their movements had earlier been confined. This 'pioneering' behaviour of unspecialized migrants was instigated by the shock of famine and crisis which dramatically lowered the opportunity cost of exploring new migration options. In a situation where they had very little to lose, they were more easily prepared to face the risk of unfamiliar destinations. Even so, the Flemings who eventually arrived in Antwerp were only a relatively 'positive' selection out of the far greater group which was affected by the crisis. Even in a situation of extreme crisis, the most vulnerable groups could not mobilize the necessary information resources to escape from extreme poverty, famine and starvation, nor take the risk of cutting local ties and ending up without any support. Moreover, even those who did migrate to Antwerp in search of better opportunities were anything but well-off, and did not enjoy very good prospects in the inhospitable environment of mid-nineteenth century Antwerp. The forging of new channels of unspecialized migration thus unavoidably entailed a painful process of adaptation in which the initial absence of supportive structures represented an awkward drawback, and which was only contemplated when local income possibilities fell dramatically.

Similarly, the increasing mobility of rural migrants from the secondary belt of regional recruitment and of internal inter-urban migrants in the course of the 1840s and 1850s was a hallmark of growing attempts to adjust to a society where existing patterns of population exchange were increasingly invalidated by an uneven restructuring of rural and urban income opportunities. The result of these attempts at adjustment and readjustment was a growing rate of inter-urban mobility, swelling the insalubrious and overcrowded city and resulting in an overall increase of the urban population – although few were likely to stay where they were. Throughout the preceding pages, small towns have surfaced several times as the main accelerators in the process of increasing inter-urban mobility and, by extension, urbanization. Greater numbers of newcomers to small towns like Lier or Turnhout were likely to move on to larger cities than ever before, while rural migrants who had come to Antwerp directly were more likely to return to the countryside if they left again. While the latter group remained confined to the dense information channels of hinterland relations, small regional towns more readily appear to have functioned as gateways and nodes of information, widening up the migration horizons of their newcomers. Only a more extensive analysis of the evolution of stepwise and direct urban migration in nineteenth-century Belgium might substantiate these impressions as to the driving role of small towns as essential gateways and pacemakers to the increasing concentration of the country's population in large cities. Another interesting question in this respect is whether the observation that female domestic servants were in the vanguard of increasing involvement in inter-urban patterns of migration might be attributable to the access they had to 'thinner' inter-urban information channels via their employers.

The different degrees of adaptability of different migrant groups were a reflection of disparities in resources and skills, but also in the access to, and need for, specific migration channels. To a certain extent, the strong expansion and improvement in means of communication and transport in the course of the long nineteenth century would have a mitigating effect on inequalities in access to migration information, but not on inequalities in terms of objective room for manoeuvre and the need for supportive social networks. While the increasing possibilities of transport and communication would allow dense migration patterns to be reshaped and transformed at a far greater and accelerated pace than before, they would remain subject to the same structural constraints and possibilities as in earlier periods. While the increasing spatial integration of different regions in the world would allow dense channels of migration to break through the regional context to which they had been confined in times when horses were the fastest means of overland transport, it would eventually witness a reproduction of analogous patterns on a wider or more distant spatial scale, where transplanted networks would take over the functions of hinterland connections in providing a social safety net for the most vulnerable of migrant groups.

CONCLUSIONS

We have set out in this study to explore an old question from a new perspective. The relationship between migration and urban change in Europe's long nineteenth century has already been the subject of considerable scholarly attention and debate. While recent historiography has dismissed the once powerful image of urbanization as a one-off transfer of impoverished villagers to overcrowded cities, this work has instead stressed the complex nature of migration patterns, the strong degree of continuity with earlier migration traditions, and the relative success of urban migrants. Yet, however illuminating these revisions have been in many respects, it remains difficult to reconcile their emphasis on continuity and success with the speed and intensity of societal disruption that was taking place in Europe's long nineteenth century. This study therefore aimed to re-explore the dynamics of urban migration by combining an elaborate conceptual framework with an instructive case study in a way that could address and transcend the paradoxes of continuity and change, of structure and agency, and of winners and losers. The setting of the case study was the city of Antwerp in present-day Belgium between 1760 and 1860, when it changed from a medium-sized textile centre to a booming international port town – a setting which was deemed particularly relevant because of the profundity of societal change, and because of the availability of exceptionally rich source materials which allowed us to reconstruct the main dynamics and compositions of urban migration flows over a century-long period. What, then, has this specific case study taught us with regard to the relationship between migration and urbanization in the transition from pre-industrial to industrial society, and with regard to the limits, constraints and dynamics of migration as an adaptive strategy in periods of structural social change?

A first general dynamic that was confirmed by the case study is that push and pull conditions at macro level were a main determining force of migration change, by shaping the main constraints and opportunities within which households and individuals operated. As a nineteenth-century port town, Antwerp held considerably more opportunities for immigrant employment than it had done as a regional textile centre in the eighteenth century. The development of its port activities created high-end opportunities for skilled technicians and merchants from urban backgrounds while greatly expanding the range of jobs in services, retail and transport accessible to unspecialized rural newcomers. The migrant-friendly nature of its economic transformation was therefore an important precondition for the enlargement and intensification of Antwerp's migration field in the course of the nineteenth century. Pressure from conditions in the countryside, however, also mattered a great deal and became more important as time went on. While its effects in terms of stimulating migration and inhibiting return were initially more or less counterbalanced by the expansion of local employment opportunities, by the 1840s the structural disintegration of rural livelihoods was propelling more newcomers to Antwerp than the primarily temporary jobs of its maritime expansion could absorb. It was above all the changing balance between overall push and pull forces, then, which fed the growing levels of turnover and inter-urban mobility observed from the 1840s onwards – a trend which set the tone for decades to come, and which was characteristic of the uneven nature of social and economic transformation in the transition from pre-industrial to industrial society.

Another general observation is that history mattered. Although the transformation of socio-economic structures at a macro level was the prime delimiting force behind the evolution of patterns of migration, changing push and pull forces were accommodated within existing repertoires and patterns of recruitment. The important part played by existing patterns of migration in the shaping of constraints and opportunities was not only due to their role as conveyors of migration information, but also because of their links to local patterns of labour market segmentation, which shaped informal preferences and social and cultural norms with regard to suitable income activities. Established patterns of labour market segmentation therefore constitute a key factor in understanding why immigrants rather than the locally-born population took up the major share of port-related employment in the early decades of the nineteenth century. The long-standing patterns of recruitment that had connected certain groups of migrants with transport, services and retail activities from at least the mid-eighteenth century onwards helped migrants to fill up most of the expanding port-related employment in the nineteenth century. The migrant-friendly nature of Antwerp's conversion, then, was not only attributable to the specificities of a port town, but was helped by existing patterns of labour market segmentation. Unlike the situation in most other port towns, where migrants were mainly relegated to the lower paid and most unstable sectors, this path-dependent trajectory combined with the novelty of maritime activity to create a situation where migrants were able to occupy both the core and periphery of the new port labour market. We might therefore generalize by saying that the development of new economic activities is likely to enhance local opportunities for newcomers

– because of the absence of local vested interests and trained or suitable labour – in particular when the innovations are in some way linked to earlier migrant strongholds. Pre-existing patterns of labour market segmentation, then, were of great importance in shaping migrants' responsiveness and adaptability towards the changing local opportunity structure.

This brings us to a third major observation, with regard to the prime channelling role of the meso level of our explanatory framework. Rather than social networks alone, to which the meso level has often been reduced in migration analysis, the crucial role here appears reserved for the more broadly defined channels of migration *information*, which are often connected to patterns of labour market segmentation. Existing commercial, political, social, legal and other connections between different places and regions form important conveyor belts for migration information – which fact in itself reinforces the role of history as a structuring force. However, while existing patterns of migration play an important role in enabling migrants to seize newly developing opportunities, they are at the same time a constraining force, since they circumscribe the range of options open to migrants. The extent to which migrants are subject to the limits of existing patterns, however, is in turn shaped both by the objective room for manoeuvre of the migrants involved and the spatial information field in which they operate. An important distinction established in this respect in the Antwerp case is the one between 'dense' and 'thin' channels of migration information. Dense channels depended on broad, manifold and long-standing commercial, legal, political, cultural and social interactions between a town and its hinterland as the main conveyor belts for information on migration opportunities. Thin channels, in contrast, were wider in scope and more exclusive in nature, such as business networks, artisans' organizations or government administrations. As dense channels were embedded in century-old regional traditions, they were substantially more resilient and spatially specific than the thin channels of migration information, which were better able to shift between different possible destinations in accordance with changing opportunities. Migrants whose skills were in abundant supply and who relied on dense information channels had comparatively little room to explore various migration destinations. Better-off migrants whose skills were scarce and who were well informed about employment opportunities at different destinations, on the other hand, had considerably more room to pursue the best available migration options, irrespective of their familiarity with the different destinations and the presence of social contacts. As a result, the spatial room for manoeuvre of migrants on the lower end of the social ladder tends to be considerably more limited than that of their better-off counterparts. While history mattered, then, it mattered more for some than for others.

These differences in adaptability in turn conditioned dissimilar speeds of change with which migrant groups responded to changing constraints and opportunities. Change was slowest among the least specialized groups whose dependence on dense migration channels was largest. It was fastest and most opportunity-oriented among relatively skilled and better-off groups who had access to specialized and reliable information channels and who were less dependent on physical proximity to maintain their social contacts. These speeds of change go a long way in explaining the main and to a certain extent contradictory trends that governed the evolution of Antwerp's migration field in the course of the nineteenth century: a strong continuity (and intensification) of the contours of its demographic basin on the one hand, and various temporary enlargements of its long-distance recruitment range on the other. While the first was symptomatic of the limited horizon of its hinterland migrants in the face of rising migration pressures, the second was an illustration of the freer and more opportunity-oriented nature of the migration circuits along which most of its long-distance newcomers travelled. These different circuits of migration and their associated patterns of stay gave rise to very dissimilar relationships to wider urban society: most hinterland migrants travelling along dense circuits tended to become fairly integrated, while many of their longer-distance counterparts using thinner channels of migration information tended to be relatively dissociated. The resilience of regional migration circuits provided social and cultural ties which ensured that few rural migrants would have found themselves isolated or alienated after moving to town. At the same time, this embeddedness of regional migration circuits and their high degree of integration with urban society can be considered as much a blessing as a curse for the migrants involved. While enhancing immigrants' prospects in local society, they necessarily constrained their options with regard to the possibility of moving elsewhere. In this sense, the degree of integration with urban society should not necessarily be regarded as an indication of migrant success, but might equally be taken as revealing the limited range of alternative destinations.

Even in the context of highly resilient and dense patterns of hinterland migration, moreover, the changing conditions of push and pull at a general macro level brought about important transformations in the long run. The main shifts over time included an overall intensification of migration, a declining rate of return migration and a greater extent of urban settlement, either in town itself or in one of the rapidly expanding villages in its suburban belt – all of which can be related to declining rural income opportunities. Although the spatial horizon of hinterland migration remained relatively stable over time, then, the evolution of migrants' patterns of stay and further migration trajectories bear witness to different attempts at adjustment and readjustment to the changing conditions of labour demand and supply. Moreover, as the sudden appearance of immigrants from East and West Flanders in the late 1840s and 1850s demonstrates, abrupt crises could instigate a breakthrough in the spatial limitations of rural migrants' horizons and compel them to explore new migration destinations. Considering existing patterns of migration as sunk investments of social and cultural capital, it is easy to understand why and how infringements on life and labour cycles would be primarily countered by a growing involvement in established patterns and repertoires for the most vulnerable of migrant groups, which would eventually be abandoned only when they became truly untenable. In this sense, the relatively slow pace of adaptation in resilient patterns of migration along long-standing recruitment channels was also subject to different speeds of change, which were dictated by the evolution and contradictions of structural push and pull forces at a macro level.

The end result of these different patterns of adaptation at different speeds was a disintegration of the population exchange mechanisms which characterized early modern patterns of rural–urban migration, and a changing position of the migration experience in the life courses of the migrants involved. Rather than a temporary absence from home during the *belle saison* or a life-cycle phase of young adulthood, which was the experience of the majority of immigrants in the second half of the eighteenth century, the move to Antwerp became a temporary stop in increasingly complex migration trajectories, and/or a gateway to mainly urban or suburban patterns of residence. Migration in the time of the urban transition was, in other words, anything but a radically new one-off population transfer from countryside to towns, and was instead a path-dependent process of different patterns of adaptation at different speeds, which in different ways culminated in a greater proportion of the population living in and moving between cities. While existing migration circuits and social ties to a certain extent channelled and buffered the ongoing processes of adaptation, the macro conditions on which they had been built became increasingly invalidated by the dynamics of structural social change. These dynamics of continuity and change forced growing numbers of migrants to develop new strategies for adaptation, which eventually reshaped the spatial and economic contexts that had governed the dynamics of migration for several centuries.

A last crucial observation concerns the great degree of selectivity displayed by most newcomers. Notwithstanding the important challenges of adaptation which the changing push and pull forces and the limiting role of migration channels entailed, recruitment remained remarkably selective with regard to local labour demand throughout the whole period under consideration. Although crisis situations temporarily produced larger proportions of older and family migrants, the great majority of newcomers throughout the period under consideration consisted of young, single adults, who were best suited to the demands of city life and moved mainly to expanding port-related sectors. The implication is that immigrants did not occupy a secondary place in urban society. On the contrary, most newcomers were better suited to the rapidly changing local opportunity structure than the locally-born population. In turn, the constant inflow of suitable migrant labour was a vital condition to overcome the bottlenecks of a rapidly changing urban labour market and to buffer the irregular labour demand of a highly seasonal port economy. While most of the locally-born population remained unwilling or unable to shift from the production of textiles to the building of port infrastructure and the handling of cargo, then, migrant dockers and builders were the shock troops of Antwerp's maritime expansion. Their increased presence and changing patterns of stay in turn radically reshaped the face of the city. They redressed urban sex ratios, swelled the ranks of young adult residents, contributed to an increasingly international and exotic mix of residents and passers-by, and invigorated the quayside life, while their growing number and increasingly transient patterns of stay increased pressures on housing and relief provisions, and exacerbated problems of urban congestion. Although migrants' key role in the process of urban change may have been exceptionally large because of Antwerp's radical transformation, the case study has in any case exemplified the momentous role migrants could play as the facilitators and vehicles of urban change in the long nineteenth century. At the same time, it has also demonstrated the importance of considering all forms of movement, short and long, in and out, foreign and internal, so as to appreciate fully the huge and heterogeneous adaptive efforts involved, and to map adequately the crucial importance of mobility in urban economic development.

Do these observations on newcomers' key economic role imply that migration was successful from the perspective of the migrants? This appears to have been most straightforwardly the case for the upmarket newcomers whose move to the newly developing commercial centre held considerable opportunities for training and career advancement. The question is more difficult to answer for the less-endowed and less-specialized newcomers from the rural hinterland. The observation that migration remained more or less selective does not imply that it was necessarily a positive experience or that adaptation was painless. For one thing, the increasing instability of local employment required a growing flexibility of the labour supply, which was buffered by an increasing coming and going of newcomers. Although the growing complexity of migration patterns can in some instances be related to widening horizons, the increased flexibility of newcomers was primarily imposed on them by the diminishing absorptive capacities of the urban labour market. Furthermore, selectivity can be assumed to have been highest at the moment of arrival. Although most sources allow us to follow newcomers during the first months or years after arrival, the collection of a comprehensive set of longitudinal data on migrants' life courses before and after the move to Antwerp was beyond the limits of this study. What happened to migrants in later phases of their lives is therefore largely obscured from view. The declining possibilities of return, however, must have limited their options in dealing with the problems of old age or the calamities of life. In this sense, the oblique and selective view of the unenviable situation of poor longer-term migrants provided by the settlement examinations might well represent the sad sequel to the story of many initially 'selective' newcomers, but a conclusive answer has to await the mapping of migrants' longer-term life trajectories. Likewise, an analysis of the evolution of newcomers' various affective residential, cultural, demographic and social relationships with regard to Antwerp society might throw further light on the extent to which the changing patterns of migration and the transformation of the urban labour market also changed local perceptions of, and attitudes towards (different groups of) newcomers during the period under consideration.

While the question of success remains somewhat open-ended at an individual level of analysis, at a broader level of society the end assessment of migration as an adaptive strategy is unambiguously pessimistic. Those who were hardest hit by rising constraints were generally those least equipped to benefit from expanding opportunities – at home or elsewhere. The new opportunities which Antwerp's developing port activity entailed benefited primarily young, fit, male newcomers from the regional hinterland, but were of little avail to most of the locally-born ex-textile workers hit hard by the collapse of the city's industrial base or for older residents of their home villages who were equally confronted by rising push forces. Unskilled and regional migrants in turn had fewer options to pursue remunerative opportunities than specialized migrants with broad spatial horizons. Rather than providing alternatives to those most in need, then, migration reshaped and often reinforced the uneven distribution of the costs and gains of societal transformation, and the unequal relations between winners and losers. While all urban dwellers bore part of the social cost of increasing urban congestion and impoverishment, those groups who suffered most from the ongoing societal transformations generally had the least access to alternative sources of income. As a strategy to deal with the painful costs of social transformation at societal level, then, migration has a poor record.

In today's society, the vast improvements and advances in the means of communication and transport have markedly expanded people's access to different sources of information and the speed with which new spatial connections can be established, while the spatial level of societal transformation and adaptation has increasingly taken on international proportions. Notwithstanding the even greater speeds of social change which characterize our age, however, history remains of prime importance in channelling migratory movement, as for instance the influence of earlier colonial connections on the differential inflow to contemporary European countries testifies. At the same time, the continued need for proximity and supportive social networks remains a prime factor in guiding migration decisions, which is reflected amongst other things in patterns of clustered settlement among the most vulnerable of migrant groups. Probably now more than ever, migration is a strongly differentiated process, which connects certain groups with specific destinations and distinct labour market segments, from Mexican cleaners and Romanian lorry drivers to African doctors, Indian computer programmers and European microbiologists. At the same time, migration continues to be a markedly selective affair, leaving behind those with the poorest prospects. Understanding the causes and effects of migrants' movement requires that we look not only at the objective dynamics of push and pull which characterize the uneven and unequal development of global capitalism, but also at the very distinct circuits of recruitment which channel their movements and at the variable scope which dynamics at macro and meso level leave for individual and collective room for manoeuvre. At the same time, these different groups are part and parcel of one and the same increasingly globalizing but extremely segmented labour market – and are an essential element in its functioning. Migrants' role as the shock troops of economic change continues to be exploited, sometimes mercilessly, from the sweatshops of Guangzhou, over the building sites of Dubai, to the cleaning companies of London. From sweatshops to building sites, the inflow of migrants helps to overcome the potential bottlenecks in the expansion of labour-intensive industries, and to circumvent the resistance and inertia that employing established workers in these branches would entail. At the economic level, then, migrants today fulfil an ambiguous role similar to that of their counterparts in the urban transition of the long nineteenth century, somewhere between victims and actors of societal transformation, between vehicles and buffers of social change – an ambiguity which together with migrants' essential heterogeneity helps to explain the diverse and often contradictory attitudes to different groups of newcomers throughout the social and political spectrum.

APPENDIX I: SOURCE MATERIALS, SAMPLES AND CLASSIFICATIONS

1 Available Demographic Figures

Many contemporary and later documents give sometimes very detailed figures on population numbers and composition, yet their value and trustworthiness is often difficult to gauge, sometimes conflicting and at times limited. This appendix summarizes the figures that formed the basis of general demographic calculations throughout this book.[1]

Available Figures on Population Size

Several figures are available on Antwerp's population size – some more trustworthy than others. In the table below I have rendered those figures deemed most reliable, which were taken as the basis for further demographic calculations. The 'limited' population figures refer to figures targeting mainly the officially resident population ('*population de droit*' or 'actual' population), while 'extended' population figures tended to include some or all of the non-legal or temporary residents ('*population de fait*' or 'legal' population), such as soldiers, naval workers, sailors and visitors.[2]

Table AI.1: Available Figures on Antwerp's Population Size, 1755–1866.

Date	Year	Limited population	Extended population	Origin of figure
	1755	47,000	48,600	Nominal census[3]
	1784	52,000	53,800	Nominal census[4]
April	1796	50,700		Nominal census[5]
1 Jan.	1806	60,057		Official quasi-nominal census[6]
Sep.–May	1815–16	52,059		Entries in new population registers[7]
31 Dec.	1820	55,673	59,941	Quasi-nominal census[8]
1 Jan.	1830	71,849	77,199	Nominal census[9]
15 Oct.	1846	82,758	88,487	Nominal census[10]
31 Dec.	1856	100,982	102,761	Nominal census
31 Dec.	1866	117,268	123,571	Nominal census

Table AI.2: Origin of the Antwerp Population in Different Censuses, 1796–1866 (%).[11]

Location of birth	1796[12]	1830	1846	1856	1866
Antwerp	78	68	65 (69)	64 (67)	67
Immigrants	22	32	35 (31)	36 (33)	33
Antwerp Province	11	14	14	15	27
Other Belgian province	6	10	12	14	
Netherlands	5	6	5	4	4
Elsewhere	1	3	5	3	2
Total	100	100	100	100	100
Total (N)	47,361	71,849	88,487	102,761	117,269

Graph AI.1: Recorded Numbers of Births, Deaths, Immigrants and Emigrants per Year, 1780–1866.

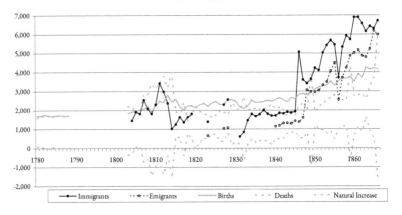

Birth and death figures for the years 1780–8 are derived from a retrospective table compiled under French rule in the year XIII,[13] and those for the years 1803–12 from a retrospective table compiled in 1827.[14] For the years 1813–15 I rely on the contemporary reports conserved in the municipal and provincial archives.[15] From 1815 I have used the figures collected in the 1914 yearbook, which correspond to the figures published in the yearly communal reports.[16] The figures between 1803 and 1815 in all probability include stillbirths, which, according to separate recording in the late 1810s, comprised around 6 per cent of all births. The number of immigrants for the years 1804–7 is based on the original enumeration in the registers, SAA, MA, 2668/1. For the years 1808–19, figures are extrapolated on the basis of my own sample CS1808–19 from SAA, MA, 2668/2–6. For the 1820s the yearly number of immigrants is estimated at around 2,200 per year 1820–6, and around 2,500 per year for 1827–9 – which is an upper-bound estimate based on the combined evidence of immigration registers and sporadic figures on the number of immigrants.[17] For the years 1831–40, figures are based on an extrapolation of the number of entries in the first-district register, and available aggregate figures for the years 1837 and 1840.[18] From 1841 onwards figures are taken from the yearly figures in the communal report.[19] As all these figures pertain to the *recorded* number of immigrants and emigrants, they represent lower-bound estimates of the true volumes of migration, of which the accuracy needs to be judged separately. From the 1840s onwards, the recorded immigration figures refer only to the number of newcomers added to the population books, and therefore employ, if anything, a stricter and lower-bound definition of immigration than the earlier residence card registers, underscoring the momentous increase over time. Although the 1846 peak – like the 1856 drop – is attributable in the first place to a 'recalibration' on the basis of the new census and concomitant population registration regime, the consistently higher level at which the figures for both immigrants and emigrants continued for the following years, reflected a reality of increasing overall mobility, which would continue well into the second half of the nineteenth century.

2 Source Samples and Databases

This research makes use of different sets of source materials and databases compiled from them (see Chapter 2). Reference to sources throughout the text and tables is generally limited to an abbreviation, with letters referring to the source materials, and digits to the years for which data have been retrieved (e.g. HA1855: sample from the hospital admissions (HA) to the St Elisabeth hospital in 1855). This section provides an overview of these different datasets in alphabetical order of the abbreviations used.

C1796: Census of 1796

Archival location: SAA, BZA, D 1–5, Telling Jaar IV.

    Sample: I selected all immigrants recorded in the *cahiers* from the first and fourth districts in a database, C1796I, containing 5,591 entries in total. As children below the age of twelve were not nominally recorded in the census (only their number was recorded), the selection only pertains to persons aged twelve or more. The selection was limited to the first and fourth districts because it is only for these districts that immigrants' place of birth – a vital piece of information for the mapping of recruitment patterns – was recorded. Although each of the town districts had its own specific socio-economic composition, taking the first and fourth district together (harbouring more than half of the urban population) yields a cross-section that does not diverge too much from that of the city as a whole in terms of wealth and occupational distribution, although the sample remains slightly biased towards the more proletarian elements of the urban population, and the total proportion of immigrants is somewhat below (26 per cent) that of the city as a whole (27 per cent).[20] The differences are, however, not such as to seriously distort the overall analysis, as most attention goes to differences between immigrants and non-immigrants: although the total reference group is modestly biased towards the less wealthy elements of the urban population, there is no reason to suspect that the main differences between immigrants and the locally born *within* this group would have differed substantially from the differences between the two groups within the city as a whole.

Information recorded: When available, address, name, sex, age, place of birth, occupation, year of arrival in Antwerp, marital status, spouse's place of birth and occupation, number of children under twelve. The varying level of education and zeal of the different enumerators led to a great variation in the quality and completeness of the information.

Confrontation with other sources: The results from C1796I could be subtracted from De Belder's results pertaining to all adult residents in the first and fourth districts, referred to as C1796DB(D1+4), to achieve separate figures for immigrants and native-born. This was possible thanks to the very 'raw' and detailed nature of the tables provided by De Belder in appendix, such as page-long tables recording the incidence of separate occupations – almost to the same level of detail as the original source – for each town district.[21] To compensate for counting errors,[22] results from C1796I were recalculated to De Belder's totals before subtracting them from C1796DB(D1+4).[23] These recalculated figures from C1796I are referred to as C1796I(cor). A recapitulative overview of the different data sources is as follows: C1796DB = figures relating to the total Antwerp population in the census of 1796 as analysed and published by De Belder; C1796DB(D1+4) = figures relating to the total population of the first and fourth town districts in the census of 1796 as analysed and published by De Belder; C1796I = figures relating to the total number of immigrants in the first and fourth town district as recorded by myself (N=5,591); C1796I(cor) = recalculation of the figures of C1796I to the total number of immigrants counted by De Belder (N=5,113) in order to subtract them from the totals from C1796-DB(D1+4) to arrive at separate and comparable distributions of the locally-born and immigrant populations of the first and fourth town districts.

C1830: Census of 1830

I have not carried out any original archival research on the census of 1830. Instead, intensive use was made of the data contained in the many detailed and valuable tables which Hannes provided in appendices to his doctoral research on the 1830 census,[24] such as a very detailed listing of recorded occupations of the adult population subdivided according to sex, town district and origin category (bijlage 3, pp. 20–132),[25] an overview of the origins of children under twelve years of age (bijlage 4, pp. 134–5), of foreign adult migrants' country of origin (bijlage 4, p. 136), of the origin of marriage partners of the 457 marriages concluded in 1830 (p. 8), and a detailed table on the marital status, sex, age (five-yearly categories) and origin of the 1,950 deaths of Antwerp-domiciled persons which had occurred in 1830 (bijlage 5, pp. 145–50). I have sometimes proceeded to a regrouping and processing of the relatively raw data contained in Hannes's tables in order to compare them with other source data, such as C1796.

CS: Residence Card Registers

Archival location: SAA, MA, 2668/1–18.

Sample: I have selected one in ten entries of the registers MA, 2668/2–6,[26] stretching from 1 August 1808 to 24 March 1820, yielding 2,227 cases; from the registers MA, 2668/7–17, stretching from 11 March 1828 to 26 October 1830, I have selected one in four entries of those registers available for 1828 and 1830, yielding 331 and 291 cases respectively, and all 1,674 entries in the residence card registers of 1829. All registers taken together, this amounted to a total sample of 4,523 entries, of which 4,461 referred to non-Antwerp-born,[27] and who were accompanied by 105 adult card-sharing companions.[28]

Recorded information: Date of recording in the register, name, sex, age (absent in MA, 2668/4), occupation, place of birth, last place of residence (absent in MA, 2668/4–6), details on identification documents. If available, information on further trajectories (remigration: destination and date, transfer to population books, moves, extensions, decease).

ER: Emigration Registers

Archival location: SAA, MA, 74780–9 (1821–80).

Recorded information: The emigration registers – at least for the period under consideration – only record date of emigration, name, last address in Antwerp and destination. For further details on the emigrants in question it is necessary to trace them in the population books via the address mentioned, and complement the data with the information recorded there (in particular: place of birth, age, occupation, household and marital situation, and – in the case of immigrants – date of arrival in Antwerp, and previous place of residence). This has been done only for a selection of recorded emigrants. See PB, below, for further details on the information from the population books.

Sample: All entries from the emigration registers in 1829 (829) and 1855 (2,700) have been retrieved, with reference to the address and destination. This database is referred to as ER1829 and ER1855. From this sample, 1/5 from ER1829 (166 cases) and 1/10 from ER1855 (240 cases[29]) have been looked up in the population books. As only the head of household was mentioned in the emigration registers, this yielded another 31 and 30 adult spouses respectively. The combined database on the emigrants looked up in the population books *and* their accompanying spouses is referred to as ERP1829 (N=197) and ERP1855 (N=270). After excluding Antwerp-born emigrants, the database of non-native emigrants is referred to as ERPI1829 (N=138) and ERPI1855 (N=217). In addition, the changing practice of population registration between 1829 and 1855 created a difference in 'target population' of the emigration registers. In both years, the emigration registers functioned as 'cancellation' registers for prior residents recorded in the population books who left Antwerp to live else-where. However, the function of the population books differed between the two years. In 1855, in principle, all residents – also temporary migrants – were to be recorded in the population books when they came to Antwerp, and thus would be recorded in the emigration registers when leaving again. In 1829, however, this was not the case. At that time, the residence card registers were still in place as an intermediary step between immigration and recording in the population books. That means that a specific category of emigrants is systematically absent from ER1829 – but not from ER1855 – i.e. short-term immigrants who came to Antwerp and left again without ever being recorded in the population books, but who were instead provided with a residence card. Because of this system-atic absence, ER1829 is biased towards long-term emigrants and Antwerp-born, and would not constitute a correct point of comparison with the – in princi-ple – exhaustive group of emigrants recorded in 1855. Luckily, the 'missing' category from ER1829 was present in another database collected for research, namely CS1829.[30] To correct for the source-specific bias of ER1829, then, the data concerning ERPI1829 were combined with the entries on the 555 recorded leavers from CS1829 (538 heads of household and 17 spouses), corrected by a weight factor to compensate for different sampling methods (ERPI1829*5), resulting in a database ERPI1829+ containing 1,245 virtual entries, which in reality only pertain to 693 different observations (555 from CS1829 and 138 from ERPI1829). Together, this database in principle records all (non-native) persons who left Antwerp in 1829 and declared their departure at the appropri-ate administration, which is the equivalent of the contents of ERPI1855, and thus provides a suitable ground for comparison.

FR: Foreigners' Records

Archival location: Conserved in a separate collection in the SAA under the name SAA, MA, Vreemdelingenzaken, Vreemdelingendossiers (MA 44248–787), from 1840 onwards, and consultable only on microfilm. The files still record the original numbering by the foreigners' administration, which is the number used when referring to specific files in the text (e.g. FR1850-7874) is *vreemdelingen-dossier* n°. 7874.

Note: Not all files in the *vreemdelingendossiers* pertain to 'fresh' arrivals. Some files, for instance, contain correspondence with details and information on non-national persons believed to reside or to have resided in Antwerp and believed, for instance, to have committed criminal offences. These files had nothing to do with newcomers, and thus have been left aside when collecting data.

Selection: All files from 1850 concerning 'fresh' arrivals. From the 916 files of which the administrative 'opening' by the Antwerp Mayor occurred in 1850, 767 concerned 'fresh' arrivals. After excluding Belgian-born newcomers (which for some reason or another did not or no longer had Belgian nationality) from this selection for reasons of source comparability, 758 files remain.

Number of valid entries: 758. Entries may relate to more than one person:

Number of files concerning newcomers: 758.

Number of adult newcomers recorded in these files (heads of household + companions):[31] 824.

Number of files concerning Dutch-born heads of household: 382.

Number of adult newcomers in files concerning Dutch-born heads of household: 424.

Recorded information: For all adult newcomers, sex, occupation and place of birth; for files concerning Dutch-born heads of households (N=382), all other information from the initial examination has been recorded (name, sex, age, marital status, occupation, employer, last place of foreign residence, date of entry in Belgium, previous places of residence in Belgium, date of entry in Antwerp, possible information concerning *conduite morale*, date of examination, eventual further information regarding remigration, re-immigration, marriage, etc.).

HA: Hospital Admissions to the St Elisabeth Hospital

Archival location: OCMWA, BG, Sint-Elisabeth Gasthuis (EG), 4, 15, 50, 52, 135, 146, 176, 177.

Selection: All admissions to the hospital in 1829 (3,167) and 1855 (5,237) – both paying and freely admitted patients.

Note: Corrected for double entries of remaining patients at the beginning of each month. A minor problem is that some persons were admitted to the hospital more than once per year, thus resulting in a minor number of double counts.[32]

Recorded information: Name, sex, birthplace.

Number of valid cases: 8,404 admissions, of whom 3,671 immigrants.

HISGIS: Data on the Population Size of Belgian Communes Published by HIS-GIS

The Belgian historical GIS project is a project hosted by the University of Ghent which, among others, provides map-based data on the population size of Belgian *communes* in different censuses since 1796/1800. These data on population size have been collected and published by Vrielinck,[33] and are consultable on-line via the HISGIS project at http://www.flwi.ugent.be/hisgis, where more details on

the collection methods can also be found. Eric Vanhaute and Torsten Wiedemann from the University of Ghent have been so kind to provide me with the
original Access database of the HISGIS data on the population size of Belgian
communes and *fusiegemeenten* (i.e. reclassified in accordance with the communal
boundaries of 1976) in the censuses from 1796 to 1866. These data have been
used to calculate the *intensity* of migration (number of immigrants to Antwerp
in relation to population size) from different Belgian *communes* and regions at
different points in time, by using the nearest population figure available (see
below, Appendix I.3).

IN1850

The origin composition of the gross inflow of newcomers in 1850 (IN1850) was
approximated by combining a range of different sources – among others with
an eye to intensity calculations. NSMP1850 mention 4,222 recorded immigrants in 1850, consisting of 2,217 immigrants from the Antwerp Province,
1,471 from another Belgian province and 534 from another country. While the
three origin categories employed in NSMP are too broad to compare meaningfully with earlier data from the residence card registers, the base figures from
NSMP could be distributed along the origin distribution reconstructed from
HA1855 to approximate the origin of newcomers in 1850 at a more detailed
spatial level. In addition, while foreign migration remained relatively underestimated in both HA1855 and NSMP1850, the FR1850 registers give us more
detailed information on this specific group. Therefore, the origin composition
of IN1850 was approximated as follows: the 2,217 intra-provincial newcomers
from NSMP1850 were distributed along origin according to the same proportions as the 927 intra-provincial migrants recorded in HA1855; the 1,471
inter-provincial newcomers according to the same proportions as the 705 inter-
provincial migrants recorded in HA1855; for the foreign migrants, the data
from FR1850 are retained. Although the method applied is necessarily approximate, the resultant figures can be considered fairly indicative vis-à-vis the 'real'
origin distribution of recorded newcomers in 1850.

NIDI: Data on the Population Size of Dutch Communes Published by NIDI

Erik Beekink from the Netherlands Interdisciplinary Demographic Institute
(NIDI) has been so kind to supply me with an electronic version of the data on
the population size of the Dutch *communes* as collected by the Dutch historian
Hofstee, and completed and corrected by NIDI.[34] This database is referred to as
NIDI, sometimes with reference to the base year(s) used, e.g. NIDI1830: data
from NIDI for the year (in this case census) of 1830. These data have been used
to calculate the *intensity* of migration (number of immigrants to Antwerp in

relation to population size) from different Dutch communes and regions at different points in time (below, Appendix I.3).

NSC and NSMP: National Statistical Publications (Censuses/Mouvement de la Population)

Different statistical publications from official government organizations, such as the Ministry for Internal Affairs, contain data which are relevant for the study of migration to Antwerp. The most important ones are the published census results (NSC) of 1846, 1856 and 1866, and the yearly or ten-yearly published *Mouvement de la population* (NSMP) in the eponymous publications from 1840 to 1850, and in the *Documents statistiques* from 1851 to 1860. See the *Statistique de la Belgique* titles in the Works Cited for full details.

PB: Population Books

Archival location: Population books are available for Antwerp from 1800 onwards, and are conserved at the communal archives in a separate collection, SAA, MA-BZA, which can only be consulted on microfilm. Five series have been consulted for research:

POPA: Population Books, 1800–15 (MA-BZA, B 1–10).
POPB: Population Books, 1815–29 (MA-BZA, B 11–40).
POPC: Population Books, 1830–46 (MA-BZA, B 41–82).
POPD: Population Books, 1846–56 (MA-BZA, B 83–124).
POPE: Population Books, 1856–66 (MA-BZA, B 125–65).

Information recorded: Although some columns tend to vary from series to series, the following information is generally available: name, age / date of birth, marital status, place of birth, date of arrival in Antwerp, date of moving to this particular address, previous address, date of moving out from the present address, destination or new address. Each series goes back to a census, when for each house all residents were recorded in the population books. Subsequent mutations were recorded in chronological order. Family members are recorded one after the other, and thus are generally easily identifiable. When moving into Antwerp, the previous place of residence is mentioned instead of previous address, but only at the *first* address.

Sample: No systematic sample has been taken from the population books, but they have been used for different record linkages, which are mentioned throughout the text.

SE: Settlement Examinations

Archival location: Three sources allowed us to retrieve settlement examinations:

OCMWA, BW, 933, contains 190 examinations taken from households headed by a Belgian sojourner and applying for relief in 1855.

OCMWA, BW, 946, contains 221 examinations taken from households headed by a Dutch-born sojourner and applying for relief between 1849 and 1851

OCMWA, BW, 947 III, contains 173 examinations of persons taken into the St Elisabeth hospital in 1850 or 1851 and belonging to a household headed by a Dutch-born sojourner.

Selection and information recorded: All information from these settlement examinations has been collected. Because of the specificity of the source, the quality and exhaustiveness of the information recorded in these examinations tends to vary markedly. Migration information on female migrants who are not heads of household, for instance, is generally absent. Moreover, even for men, information is sometimes limited to that which is strictly necessary to establish their settlement. The wealth of detail ranges from at most a birthplace on one side of the spectrum, to a very detailed description of all different migration trajectories since birth at the other side.

Database: Data on the 190 Belgian-headed households have been collected in a database named SEB1855, recording information on 328 adult individuals. The data on Dutch-headed households have been merged in one database, SENL1849–51, from which 39 duplicate households (i.e. occurring both in BW946 and BW947 III) have been removed, thus containing information on 355 households and 849 adult individuals. If the Belgian and Dutch data are used together for analysis, they are referred to as SE1849–55. Not all individuals on whom the settlement examinations convey information are necessarily immigrants. Of 849 individuals recorded in SE1849–55, 111 were born in Antwerp, but had lost their Antwerp settlement, for instance through marriage or emigration. When analysing patterns of immigration and migration trajectories, the analyses have been *a priori* limited to the 683 persons in SE1849–51 unambiguously identifiable as immigrants.

3 A Note on the Classification of Place Names

The *quality* of the ways in which the different sources record persons' place of birth and other place names tends to vary considerably from source to source, and from period to period. In general, the later the period, the more easily interpretable and the more reliable the recorded place names are – among other things because of the frequent mention of province or country next to the place name itself, and because of better-educated administrative personnel, which reduced spelling creativity. Sometimes we are informed of a region of origin without the actual place being specified, such as Meierij or Frankrijk, and so on, in which case they have been classified with the most local level of classification with which they could unambiguously be grouped, e.g. 'province of North Brabant' or 'France'. In addition, when there existed more than one place with the same name and ambiguity was too large to settle, some of these place names were classified as non-localized.[35] If place names proved really impossible to localize, they were classified as missing. Yet, most places were readily interpretable and could be correctly localized without many problems or ambiguities. These in turn had to be classified in order to allow further analysis. Eventually, the choice was made to use current administrative boundaries (as per 1 January 2005) as the main classification scheme, because the regime and boundary changes over the period under consideration were so many that it was impossible to use contemporary boundaries consistently as a systematic and *comparable* classification scheme. Luckily, the main geographical divisions of Belgium and the Netherlands (from, e.g. Counties and Duchies, over French *départements* to nineteenth- and twentieth-century provinces), and to a lesser extent of other countries too, are marked by a very strong continuity from the eighteenth to the twentieth centuries, so that today's boundaries can be used as a general classification scheme without producing too strong an anachronistic effect.[36] The classification scheme used contains different levels, from large grids to smaller grids, depending on the distance and density of migration. For European migrants, one common yardstick was devised, namely that of *region*. The basic idea here was to use geographical delimitations which were more or less comparable in size, so that it would be useful to compare them on one map. For Belgium and the Netherlands these regions are today's provinces, for France the *départements*, for Germany the *Regierungsbezirke* (subdivision of *Länder*), for Switzerland the *cantons*, for Italy the provinces (a level below *regioni*), for England and Wales the administrative counties ('metropolitan and non-metropolitan counties'), for Scotland its 'council areas', and for Ireland its counties. These 'regions' are a basic unit of analysis throughout the text, tables and maps. When comparisons are made between two regions (e.g. the region of origin of marriage partners, or region of origin compared with that of last place of residence), it is – unless specified otherwise – these units of analysis which are used to determine whether or not the two regions are 'the same region' or 'a different region'. In addition, an alternative geographical classification scheme was devised as research progressed, which transcends the limitations of purely administrative divisions and captures the main distinctions in the varied nature of Antwerp's recruitment patterns. This alternative classification scheme is used in alternation with purely administrative divisions and groups the most important areas of recruitment by means of so-called origin pyramids.[37] The logic of these divisions follows from the discussion on the characteristics of Antwerp's recruitment pattern in the second half of the eighteenth century as discussed in Chapter 3, and retains validity for the whole of the period in question. The use of these 'areas' of origin, rather than purely administrative divisions, at once facilitates and enhances the meaningfulness of further analysis on the relation between origin and other migration characteristics, such as, for example, occupation or length of stay.

As regards the distinction between *urban* and *rural* places, there was need for a standard which allowed diachronic comparisons without shifting places from one category to the other as time moved on. For this purpose, one classification was devised, on the basis of available population figures for 1800 and 1850. The basic distinction between urban and rural, unless explicitly mentioned otherwise, is the following: rural = every place with less than 5,000 inhabitants in 1800 *and* 1850; urban = every place with more than 5,000 inhabitants in 1800 *or* 1850.[38] The 5,000 benchmark was the lowest possible, as this was the benchmark used by Bairoch et al. For the densely populated Belgian and Dutch regions, this may however be considered a relatively appropriate lower limit for an 'urban' environment, in particular as the 'end' date is 1850, i.e. any place with more than 5,000 inhabitants in 1850 is considered urban. For some purposes, the 5,000 limit was considered too low, e.g. especially dealing with Flemish migrants and rural–urban trajectories. Here alternative measures at 10,000 or 20,000 inhabitants were also used – in which case this is always mentioned explicitly. The sources and classification method is in these cases the same as for the 5,000 benchmark, i.e. for the 10,000 benchmark: rural = every place with less than 10,000 inhabitants in 1800 *and* 1850; urban = every place with more than 10,000 inhabitants in 1800 *or* 1850; and for the 20,000 benchmark: rural = every place with less than 20,000 inhabitants in 1800 *and* 1850; urban = every place with more than 20,000 inhabitants in 1800 *or* 1850. Sometimes, intermediary categories are used, with: village = every place with less than 5,000 inhabitants in 1800 *and* 1850; medium-sized town = all places between a village and a large city; large city = more than 20,000 inhabitants in 1800 *or* 1850.

At various instances in the analysis, use is made of *migration intensity*, i.e. the number of immigrants (to Antwerp) from a specific geographical delimitation in relation to the total number of inhabitants living in this geographical delimitation at about the same time. This was calculated only for Belgium and the Netherlands, as these were the most important regions of origin, and adequate data were available by which to make the calculations. For Belgium, we could rely on the data on population size at the level of contemporary *fusiegemeenten* in the HISGIS project,[39] while for the Netherlands an analogous grouping at the level of (virtual) *fusiegemeenten* was carried out on the basis of the NIDI data.[40] One problem is, however, that censuses were not necessarily held at the same time in the Netherlands and Belgium.[41] In some years during which a census was carried out in Belgium, I have therefore used the corresponding figures from the Hofstee dataset (i.e. calculated on the basis of vital and growth trends),[42] i.e. for 1816 (derived from the 1815 census) and 1821 (which corresponds to the HISGIS 1820, which represents the situation on 1 January 1821). The greatest problem was to find an equivalent of the 1806 figures on the basis of which to calculate the 1796 intensity figures. This was eventually done by reducing the NIDI1816 figures by 5 per cent – the average difference between the 1806 and 1816 HISGIS figures. Of course, the resultant figures cannot be taken as precise. Moreover, the value of the original census figures tended to vary considerably over time. The comparability of the intensities through time is complicated further by the varying time-distance between migrants counted and population figures used (for instance CS1808–13 intensity calculated in relation to 1816 population figures, while CS1829 intensity calculated to 'nearer' 1830 population figures).[43] Yet, notwithstanding these caveats, the resultant figures are sufficiently relevant to provide an *indicative* measure of differences in migration intensity between different municipalities and regions, and over time.

Table AI.3: Overview of HISGIS/NIDI Base Figures used for Calculations.

Source	HISGIS base figures	NIDI base figures
C1796I	1806	1816 – 5%
CS1808–13	1816	1816
CS1812–13	1816	1816
CS1815–19	1820	1821
CS1829	1830	1830
NS1841–5	1846	–
NS1847–50	1856	–
FR1850	–	1850
IN1850	1846/56[44]	–

4 A Note on the Classification of Occupations

Most of the different sources produced in the wake of population registration and employed for the purpose of this study record occupational information on the person in question, under the heading *profession ou métier* or something similar – which pose fewer problems of identification than place names. More problems, however, arise in interpreting the entry. In general, the entry for 'occupation' in sources of population registration suffers from three major flaws. 1) Because occupational activities may change rapidly, but changes were not declared at the registry office, the occupations retained in population books and other sources may no longer correspond to reality, especially in the case of temporary unemployment, old age or multiple jobs, so that occupational information is sometimes more an indication of self-identity rather than a reflection of the actual activities in making a living.[45] 2) These problems are even greater in the case of women, as female employment – especially in the case of living-in daughters or married women – is generally omitted in the sources, or obscured by categories such as 'housewife' or 'daughter'. 3) Assessing the social and economic implications and scale of occupational activities solely on the

Table AI.4: Overview of Migrants' Regions of Birth, 1796–1855 (%).[46]

	C1796I	CS1808–11	CS1812–13	CS1815–20	CS1829	HA1829	ERPI1829+	SE1849–51	FR1850	HA1855	ERPI1855
Grand-Duchy Luxemburg	**0.5**	**0.0**	**0.0**	**0.1**	**0.0**	**0.7**	**0.0**	**0.0**	**0.9**	**0.1**	**0.0**
Belgium	**74.4**	**53.0**	**61.9**	**67.8**	**72.3**	**71.9**	**67.1**	**43.8**	**0.0**	**77.8**	**80.1**
Prov. Antwerp	47.6	13.9	22.5	33.2	43.0	40.1	41.3	24.9	0.0	44.2	44.9
Prov. Brabant	13.6	13.9	19.4	16.3	12.9	13.8	11.7	5.3	0.0	10.0	11.1
Prov. West Flanders	1.3	2.4	2.5	2.1	2.7	3.5	1.7	2.3	0.0	4.4	2.8
Prov. East Flanders	4.0	7.5	5.2	4.3	4.3	6.6	5.8	8.8	0.0	13.9	12.0
Prov. Hainaut	1.3	4.5	3.3	3.0	2.9	2.1	1.6	1.0	0.0	2.0	4.2
Prov. Liège	1.1	4.8	3.1	2.9	2.0	1.4	0.6	0.7	0.0	0.4	2.8
Prov. Limburg (B)	4.4	3.6	4.3	5.1	3.3	3.5	2.9	0.6	0.0	2.0	0.9
Prov. Luxemburg	0.1	0.4	0.4	0.1	0.0	0.2	0.0	0.0	0.0	0.1	0.5
Prov. Namur	0.7	2.1	1.2	0.6	1.1	0.7	1.5	0.1	0.0	0.6	0.9
Belgium Unspec.	0.2	0.0	0.0	0.1	0.1	0.0	0.0	0.0	0.0	0.0	0.0
Netherlands	**20.4**	**18.7**	**19.4**	**14.2**	**18.8**	**16.6**	**22.3**	**56.2**	**51.1**	**14.0**	**13.0**
Prov. Zealand	0.7	1.2	1.0	1.4	1.4	1.6	1.6	6.0	5.4	1.2	0.9
Prov. North Brabant	12.1	8.8	9.9	7.7	10.5	8.7	13.8	32.7	30.1	7.9	8.8
Prov. Limburg (NL)	4.5	1.4	2.9	2.6	4.4	1.5	2.7	7.6	5.5	2.1	1.4
Prov. North Holland	0.9	3.0	2.9	0.4	0.2	1.4	1.1	2.5	3.3	0.6	0.9
Prov. South Holland	1.1	3.1	2.1	1.5	1.4	2.1	1.1	4.7	4.4	1.0	0.5
Prov. Utrecht	0.2	0.3	0.0	0.1	0.2	0.2	0.6	0.9	0.6	0.3	0.0
Prov. Gelderland	0.4	0.8	0.2	0.3	0.7	0.4	1.5	0.4	0.6	0.4	0.5
Prov. Overijssel	0.1	0.0	0.4	0.0	0.1	0.1	0.0	0.3	0.1	0.1	0.0
Prov. Drenthe	0.0	0.0	0.0	0.0	0.0	0.0	0.0	0.1	0.0	0.0	0.0
Prov. Fryslân	0.1	0.0	0.0	0.1	0.0	0.1	0.0	0.6	0.6	0.1	0.0
Prov. Groningen	0.1	0.0	0.0	0.0	0.0	0.4	0.0	0.4	0.0	0.1	0.0
Netherlands Unspec.	0.3	0.3	0.0	0.0	0.0	0.1	0.0	0.0	0.4	0.0	0.0
France	**1.4**	**21.4**	**14.8**	**7.7**	**1.7**	**3.8**	**2.7**	**0.0**	**9.9**	**1.0**	**0.5**
Bretagne	0.1	1.3	0.8	0.3	0.0	0.1	0.0	0.0	0.2	0.1	0.0
Basse Normandie	0.0	1.4	1.6	0.3	0.1	0.0	0.5	0.0	0.0	0.0	0.0

Haute Normandie	0.0	3.7	2.3	0.3	0.1	0.1	0.0	0.0	0.7	0.0	0.0
Picardie	0.1	2.2	0.8	0.6	0.1	0.2	0.1	0.0	0.2	0.0	0.0
Nord – Pas-de-Calais	0.7	6.8	5.8	2.1	0.8	1.9	1.5	0.0	2.3	0.2	0.5
Pays-de-la-Loire	0.1	0.0	0.2	0.1	0.0	0.0	0.0	0.0	0.0	0.0	0.0
Centre	0.0	0.1	0.2	0.3	0.0	0.0	0.0	0.0	0.1	0.0	0.0
Ile-de-France	0.1	1.7	1.2	1.0	0.2	0.0	0.5	0.0	1.8	0.0	0.0
Champagne – Ardennes	0.1	0.8	0.4	0.0	0.1	0.1	0.0	0.0	0.2	0.1	0.0
Lorraine	0.0	0.5	0.6	0.4	0.1	0.0	0.1	0.0	0.2	0.1	0.0
Alsace	0.1	0.3	0.0	0.6	0.0	0.1	0.0	0.0	0.4	0.0	0.0
Bourgogne	0.1	0.0	0.0	0.1	0.0	0.1	0.0	0.0	0.1	0.0	0.0
Franche-Comté	0.0	0.1	0.0	0.1	0.0	0.0	0.0	0.0	0.2	0.0	0.0
Poitou – Charentes	0.0	0.1	0.0	0.4	0.1	0.1	0.0	0.0	0.4	0.0	0.0
Auvergne	0.0	0.1	0.0	0.3	0.0	0.1	0.0	0.0	0.0	0.0	0.0
Limousin	0.0	0.0	0.0	0.0	0.0	0.0	0.0	0.0	0.1	0.0	0.0
Rhône – Alpes	0.0	0.4	0.0	0.0	0.1	0.1	0.1	0.0	0.7	0.1	0.0
Aquitaine	0.0	1.3	0.4	0.1	0.1	0.3	0.0	0.0	0.5	0.0	0.0
Languedoc-Roussillon	0.0	0.1	0.0	0.0	0.0	0.0	0.0	0.0	0.6	0.0	0.0
Provence – Alpes – Côte d'Azur	0.0	0.0	0.0	0.3	0.0	0.0	0.0	0.0	0.2	0.0	0.0
France Unspec.	0.0	0.4	0.4	0.6	0.1	0.1	0.0	0.0	0.6	0.0	0.0
Germany	**2.6**	**5.0**	**3.3**	**5.8**	**5.1**	**2.6**	**4.7**	**0.0**	**24.4**	**3.5**	**4.6**
Schleswig – Holstein	0.0	0.1	0.2	0.8	0.2	0.6	0.2	0.0	0.9	0.4	0.0
Mecklenburg-Vorpommern	0.0	0.0	0.0	0.0	0.0	0.1	0.0	0.0	0.2	0.3	0.0
Brandenburg	0.0	0.5	0.0	0.0	0.0	0.0	0.0	0.0	0.5	0.0	0.0
Niedersachsen	0.2	0.8	0.4	1.1	0.4	0.9	0.3	0.0	2.9	0.7	0.5
Sachsen-Anhalt	0.0	0.0	0.0	0.0	0.2	0.0	0.3	0.0	0.1	0.0	0.0
Sachsen	0.1	0.0	0.2	0.0	0.1	0.0	0.0	0.0	0.2	0.0	0.0
Nordrhein – Westfalen	1.5	2.3	1.9	2.4	2.2	0.7	2.0	0.0	8.2	1.3	2.8
Hessen	0.1	0.5	0.2	0.8	0.9	0.1	0.5	0.0	2.7	0.2	0.9
Thüringen	0.0	0.0	0.0	0.0	0.0	0.0	0.0	0.0	0.2	0.1	0.0
Rheinland – Pfalz – Saarland	0.1	0.3	0.4	0.3	0.5	0.1	0.7	0.0	2.9	0.0	0.5
Baden – Württemberg	0.0	0.4	0.0	0.4	0.3	0.0	0.0	0.0	2.3	0.1	0.0

Bayern	0.0	0.1	1.2	0.0	0.2	0.1	0.2	0.0	0.0	0.0	0.0
Germany Unspec.	0.0	0.1	1.8	0.0	0.4	0.0	0.1	0.0	0.0	0.1	0.4
Other countries	**1.9**	**3.7**	**13.7**	**0.0**	**3.1**	**4.3**	**2.1**	**4.3**	**0.6**	**1.9**	**0.7**
Italy	0.5	0.5	0.4	0.0	0.0	0.2	0.0	0.6	0.4	0.5	0.1
Switzerland	0.5	0.3	1.7	0.0	1.6	0.2	0.8	0.6	0.0	0.4	0.1
Scandinavia	0.0	1.0	1.3	0.0	0.2	0.7	0.2	0.3	0.2	0.0	0.0
British Isles	0.0	0.6	7.4	0.0	1.1	1.3	0.7	2.1	0.0	0.3	0.0
Baltic States	0.0	0.1	0.5	0.0	0.0	0.1	0.1	0.0	0.0	0.3	0.1
Austria	0.0	0.0	0.4	0.0	0.0	0.2	0.0	0.1	0.0	0.0	0.0
Hungary	0.0	0.0	0.1	0.0	0.0	0.0	0.0	0.0	0.0	0.1	0.1
Czechia	0.0	0.0	0.1	0.0	0.0	0.0	0.0	0.1	0.0	0.0	0.0
Bulgaria	0.0	0.0	0.0	0.0	0.0	0.1	0.0	0.0	0.0	0.0	0.0
Poland	0.5	0.1	0.5	0.0	0.0	0.2	0.1	0.4	0.0	0.3	0.0
Russia	0.0	0.0	0.2	0.0	0.0	0.0	0.0	0.0	0.0	0.0	0.0
Portugal	0.0	0.0	0.0	0.0	0.0	0.0	0.0	0.0	0.0	0.0	0.0
Spain	0.0	0.0	0.1	0.0	0.1	0.0	0.1	0.0	0.0	0.0	0.0
Americas	0.5	0.9	0.2	0.0	0.1	1.0	0.2	0.1	0.0	0.1	0.0
Asia	0.0	0.0	0.5	0.0	0.1	0.2	0.0	0.0	0.0	0.0	0.0
Africa	0.0	0.0	0.2	0.0	0.0	0.0	0.0	0.0	0.0	0.0	0.0
Total	**100.0**	**100.0**	**100.0**	**100.0**	**100.0**	**100.0**	**100.0**	**100.0**	**100.0**	**100.0**	**100.0**
Valid Total (N)	216	2,099	816	683	1,226	1,342	1,669	723	485	777	4,766
Unknown / not localized	1	116	8	0	19	114	67	22	39	38	825
Grand total	217	2,215	824	683	1,245	1,456	1,736	745	524	819	5,591
(Antwerp-born)	53	3,022	0	0	295	1,711	0	38	11	9	0

basis of a registry entry remains very difficult. A 'trader', for instance, can be a very wealthy merchant or a small vendor, while a 'cooper' may be running a coopering workshop with ten employees, or might himself be one of these workers. This is an even greater problem when status specifications (for instance apprentice, journeyman, master, aid, assistant, etc.) are as good as absent, or mentioned unsystematically. These three major problems hamper the interpretation and usefulness of the occupational information retained in the sources used for research, and cannot be circumvented. Yet there are three main reasons why each of these major problems has comparatively less bearing on the results of this study. 1) As most of the sources used record information *at the time of arrival*, and sometimes explicitly refer to the employer for whom a newcomer comes to work, we can reasonably assume that the information on occupational activity is relatively up-to-date and is meaningfully related to the jobs which newcomers come (or at least intend) to perform in town, making the occupational information relatively adequate to map the 'pull' which emanated from the urban employment structure. 2) As in other sources, the information on the occupational activity of married women is generally wanting. However, as the large majority of incoming women were young and single adults, this only concerned a minor part of the female inflow. For the large majority of female newcomers, then, we are informed on the jobs which they came, or aimed, to perform. 3) The question on the socio-economic *level* at which certain activities are performed remains an intricate affair even in the sources employed for this research. Unfortunately, status specifications are generally very incomplete and unsystematic, and only CS1829 and FR1850 contain relatively systematic comments on employment status and scale. (The fact that almost all incoming men in 1829 were classified as journeymen, assistants, apprentices or aids is a strong indication that most newcomers were wage-dependents rather than independent entrepreneurs.) Although the socio-economic level of activity is a very relevant piece of information by which to gauge the social mobility over time, and to assess the manoeuvrability of migrants, the information on sector and skill which occupational specifications contain already provides a broad oblique division between highly skilled and relatively unskilled activities, and a prime indication of the manoeuvrability of different migrants. Moreover, information on sector and skill also helps to provide insight into one of the major questions of research, i.e. the relation between the occupational composition of the inflow and the developing port economy. Although the precise socio-economic level at which activities were undertaken often remains unknown when not linked with other sources of information, then, the information about occupation on arrival does generally allow us to determine the segments of the labour market in which newcomers operated, and by which they were attracted.

Occupations can be grouped and compared in many ways, depending on the specificities of the economy concerned, and on the questions and issues one wishes to research. In this research, I have given priority to an occupational classification scheme which allowed me to broadly distinguish port-related sectors from industrial export sectors and local maintenance sectors – which is also why it does not entirely correspond to the classification schemes used by De Belder, Hannes, or Lis.[47] The main distinction in the classification scheme is therefore that between (potentially) port-related sectors (transport workers and casual labour, trade and shipping, tools and construction), the production of consumer durables (in particular textiles and garment industries) and local maintenance sectors, such as retail (mainly shopkeepers and vendors, see below), local services and food industries, and domestic service. This basic classification scheme (level 1) has been further subdivided into detailed categories up to level four. Throughout the text and analysis, occupational groups have sometimes been reclassified along any of these four different levels in order to highlight main differences and trends. As status specifications were never consistently or systematically recorded in the sources, they do not form part of the general classification scheme applied. Available information was nevertheless retained and used in analysis where relevant (for instance in C1796 and C1830, and CS1829). Thanks to the detailed level of the tables given in appendix, the results produced by Hannes and De Belder could be reclassified according to this classification scheme in order to facilitate mutual comparisons and comparisons with other source materials.[48]

Table AI.5: Overview of Occupational-Category Levels 1–3.

Level 1	Level 2	Level 3
1. Primary sector	1. Primary sector	1. Primary sector
2. Domestic service	2. Domestic service	2.a. Domestic service (house)
2. Domestic service	2. Domestic service	2.b. Shop, bar & hotel assistants
2. Domestic service	2. Domestic service	2.c. Domestic service (institutional)
3. White-collar workers & proprietors	3.a. Officials	3.a. Officials
3. White-collar workers & proprietors	3.b. Office personnel	3.b. Office personnel
3. White-collar workers & proprietors	3.c. The professions	3.c. The professions
3. White-collar workers & proprietors	3.d. Clergy & proprietors	3.d. Clergy & religious personnel
3. White-collar workers & proprietors	3.d. Clergy & proprietors	3.e. Proprietors
4. Trade & shipping	4. Trade & shipping	4.a. Wholesale
4. Trade & shipping	4. Trade & shipping	4.b. Traders
4. Trade & shipping	4. Trade & shipping	4.c. Shipping
5. Transport workers & casual labour	5. Transport workers & casual labour	5.a. Freight handlers & trade workers

Level 1	Level 2	Level 3
5. Transport workers & casual labour	5. Transport workers & casual labour	5.b. Coachmen
5. Transport workers & casual labour	5. Transport workers & casual labour	5.c. Casual labour
5. Transport workers & casual labour	5. Transport workers & casual labour	5.d. Rail & ship workers
6. Retail, local services & food industries	6.a. Retailers	6.a. Retailers
6. Retail, local services & food industries	6.b. Catering	6.b. Catering
6. Retail, local services & food industries	6.c. Local services	6.c. Local services
6. Retail, local services & food industries	6.d. Food industries	6.d. Food & drink processing
7. Tools & construction	7.a. Carpentry	7.a. General carpentry
7. Tools & construction	7.a. Carpentry	7.b. Specialized carpentry
7. Tools & construction	7.c. Stone cutters & bricklayers	7.c. Stone cutters & bricklayers
7. Tools & construction	7.d. Smiths, founders & smelters	7.d. Smiths, founders & smelters
7. Tools & construction	7.z. Other	7.e. Finishing & decorating
7. Tools & construction	7.z. Other	7.f. Ropes, nets & sails
7. Tools & construction	7.z. Other	7.z. Other
8. Consumer durables	8.a. Textiles & lace	8.a.1. Textiles
8. Consumer durables	8.a. Textiles & lace	8.a.2. Lace & Embroidery
8. Consumer durables	8.b. Clothing & leather	8.b.a. Clothing
8. Consumer durables	8.b. Clothing & leather	8.b.b. Leather
8. Consumer durables	8.c. Wooden & metal goods	8.c. Wooden & metal goods
8. Consumer durables	8.d. Luxury & printing	8.d. Luxury & printing
8. Consumer durables	8.z. Other consumer durables	8.z. Other consumer durables
9. Other & miscellaneous	9.a. Chemical industries	9.a. Chemical industries
9. Other & miscellaneous	9.b. Refining & tobacco	9.b. Refining & tobacco
9. Other & miscellaneous	9.z. Miscellaneous	9.z. Miscellaneous
99. No occupation / mention	99. No occupation / mention	99. No occupation / mention
99. No occupation	99.a. Students	99.a. Students

APPENDIX II: ADDITIONAL TABLES PERTAINING TO CHAPTERS 3–5

Chapter 3

Table AII.1: Occupations of Immigrant Women in Relation to Age and Length of Stay, C1796I (%).[1]

C1796I	Age		Length of stay		Turnover rates	
	< 30	30 +	< 6 y	> 6 y	R1	R2
Domestic service	64	14	63	18	3,19	1,90
Clergy	1	3	1	3	0,71	0,26
Trade & retail	2	9	2	9	0,44	0,13
Catering & local services	2	5	2	5	0,72	0,18
Textiles	4	13	5	12	0,88	0,19
Lace	4	6	3	6	0,73	0,26
Clothing	5	7	5	7	1,19	0,32
Other	0	2	0	2	1,00	0,20
No occupation	17	41	19	39	0,73	0,23
Total	100	100	100	100	1,34	0,45
Valid total (N)	892	2,495	671	2,596		

Table AII.2: Occupations of Immigrant Men in Relation to Age and Length of Stay, C1796I (%).[2]

C1796I	Age		Length of stay		Turnover rates	
	< 30	30 +	< 6 y	> 6 y	R1	R2
Domestic service	16	6	16	6	2,59	1,52
White-collar workers	9	6	12	5	1,96	0,72
Trade, catering & services	6	14	7	14	0,79	0,28
Transport workers & casual labour	4	9	5	9	0,76	0,27
Food industries	10	8	8	8	0,82	0,39
Auxiliary status	8	4	8	4	1,13	0,84
Independent & unspecified	2	4	0	4	0,21	0,06
Tools & construction	9	16	13	16	1,03	0,36
Auxiliary status	6	7	7	7	1,39	0,54
Independent & unspecified	3	9	6	9	0,73	0,24
Textiles	13	10	8	11	0,94	0,29
Clothing & leather	12	7	9	8	1,27	0,42
Auxiliary status	4	1	3	1	1,55	1,00
Independent & unspecified	7	6	6	6	1,15	0,32

C1796I	Age		Length of stay		Turnover rates	
	< 30	30 +	< 6 y	> 6 y	R1	R2
Other & miscellaneous	17	18	17	17	1,14	0,38
No occupation	4	6	6	6	1,28	0,40
Total	100	100	100	100	1,15	0,42
Valid total	354	1,732	378	1,647		

Chapter 4

Table AII.3: Average Birthplace Distance of Male Immigrants, 1796–1829.[3]

	Occupational distribution (%)				Average birthplace distance (km)			
	C1796I	CS1808 –13	CS1815 –20	CS1829	C1796I	CS1808 –13	CS1815 –20	CS1829
Domestic service	8	6	14	15	49	127	88	60
White-collar workers	6	7	11	9	92	268	128	462
Trade & shipping	6	5	17	2	61	192	462	335
Transport workers & casual labour	8	12	12	9	48	87	107	64
Retail, local services & food ind.	18	8	9	8	64	93	87	65
Tools & construction	15	40	14	32	61	162	136	82
Consumer durables	22	15	12	14	98	126	134	106
Other & miscellaneous	12	6	9	9	50	61	165	66
No occupation	5	1	2	2	84	138	35	47
Total	100	100	100	100	69	143	175	117
Valid N	2.174	1.037	417	835				

Table AII.4: Length of Stay of Newcomers, 1808–29 (%).[4]

Length of stay	Men				Women			
	CS1808 –13	CS1815 –18	CS1819	CS1829	CS1808 –13	CS1815 –18	CS1819	CS1829
]0–1 year[	48	40	23	24	33	15	25	18
[1–2 years[	20	16	10	29	24	12	12	19
[2–5 years[	20	18	6	28	18	12	6	24
[5–10 years[	11	26	9	6	16	61	7	11
[10 years +[	0	–	51	13	10	–	50	28
Total	100	100	100	100	100	100	100	100
Complete observations (N)	488	153	30	306	167	45	33	230
Truncated observations (N)	548	183	34	529	134	173	53	609
Valid N	1,036	336	64	835	301	218	86	839

Table AII.5: Occupational Distribution of Male Newcomers and Immigrant Residents, 1829–30 (%).

	All Immigrants		AP		Other UK NL		Not UK NL	
	CS1829	C1830	CS1829	C1830	CS1829	C1830	CS1829	C1830
Primary sector	7	3	14	5	3	1	1	0
Domestic service	15	8	21	8	13	8	5	6
Office personnel	8	3	1	2	4	3	38	8
Officials, professions, clergy and proprietors	3	9	0	6	3	10	6	10
Trade & shipping	2	10	0	5	1	11	7	22
Transport workers & casual labour	9	16	14	22	8	14	3	8
Food industries	7	5	11	8	4	3	3	1
Retail & local services	1	10	2	11	1	10	0	7

	All Immigrants		AP		Other UK NL		Not UK NL	
	CS1829	C1830	CS1829	C1830	CS1829	C1830	CS1829	C1830
Tools & construction	32	17	21	15	44	19	21	17
Consumer durables	13	9	9	7	15	11	15	9
Other & miscellaneous	2	1	3	2	1	1	2	0
No occupation	2	9	2	9	2	9	0	12
All	100	100	100	100	100	100	100	100
Valid N	835	9,423	296	3,759	417	4,351	120	1,313

Abbreviations: AP: immigrants born in the Antwerp Province; Other UK NL: immigrants born in other parts of the then United Kingdom of the Netherlands; Not UK NL: immigrants from beyond the borders of the then United Kingdom of the Netherlands

Table AII.6: Relation between Place of Birth and Last Place of Residence, 1829–55 (%).[5]

	Men								Women								All							
	ERPI1829+				ERPI1855				ERPI1829+				ERPI1855				ERPI1829+				ERPI1855			
	SP	SR	OR	T	SP	SR	OR	T	SP	SR	OR	T	SP	SR	OR	T	SP	SR	OR	T	SP	SR	OR	T
Rural–Rural	48	16	7	71	47	10	5	63	47	22	10	79	32	19	13	65	48	19	8	75	33	20	12	64
Rural–Urban	–	3	7	10	–	5	10	15	–	1	3	4	–	10	13	24	–	2	5	7	–	8	12	20
Urban–Urban	13	–	3	15	13	3	–	17	11	1	–	12	3	–	4	7	12	1	1	14	8	–	4	12
Urban–Rural	–	–	3	4	–	5	–	5	–	–	4	4	–	–	4	4	–	–	3	4	–	1	4	5
Total	60	19	21	100	47	25	28	100	58	25	17	100	35	29	35	100	59	22	19	100	41	27	32	100
Valid N	258	82	88	428	28	15	17	60	222	94	66	382	24	20	24	68	480	176	154	810	52	35	41	128

Abbreviations: SP: same place; SR: same region; OR: other region; T: total.

Table AII.7: Length of Stay of Non-Native Emigrants, 1829 and 1855 (%).[6]

Length of stay (years)	ERPI1829+			ERPI1855		
	Men	Women	All	Men	Women	All
]0–1[	34	29	32	49	45	47
[1–3[	35	27	31	31	28	29
[3–5[	12	20	16	7	7	7
[5–10[	12	13	13	5	12	9
[10+[	7	11	9	7	7	7
Total	100	100	100	100	100	100
Valid N	606	621	1,227	95	121	216

Table AII.8: Relation between Place of Birth and Destination upon Leaving Antwerp, 1829 and 1855 (%).[7]

	Men								Women								All							
	ERPI1829+				ERPI1855				ERPI1829+				ERPI1855				ERPI1829+				ERPI1855			
	SP	SR	OR	T	SP	SR	OR	T	SP	SR	OR	T	SP	SR	OR	T	SP	SR	OR	T	SP	SR	OR	T
Rural–Rural	38	17	7	63	23	23	12	58	33	15	17	65	23	24	12	59	36	16	12	64	23	24	12	58
Rural–Urban	0	3	15	17	0	2	20	22	0	4	15	19	0	5	25	30	0	3	15	18	0	4	23	26
Urban–Urban	7	1	9	17	8	2	8	19	5	0	8	13	3	0	7	11	6	0	9	15	6	1	8	14
Urban–Rural	0	1	2	3	0	1	1	1	0	0	2	3	0	0	1	1	0	1	2	3	0	0	1	1
Total	45	21	33	100	32	27	41	100	38	19	42	100	26	29	45	100	42	20	38	100	29	28	43	100
Valid N	272	129	200	601	30	26	39	95	235	118	258	611	35	32	54	121	507	247	458	1212	62	61	93	216

Abbreviations: SP: same place; SR: same region; OR: other region; T: total.

Chapter 5

Table AII.9: Importance and Sex Ratio of the Four Major Recruitment Circuits, 1796–1855.[8]

	C1796I	CS1812–13	CS1815–20	CS1829	HA1855
IMPORTANCE (%)					
1 Intra-provincial rural-born	40	19	28	38	37
2 Internal inter-urban circuit	23	22	17	16	22
3 Long-distance foreign migration	9	26	22	13	12
4 Other rural migrants	28	33	33	33	29
Total	100	100	100	100	100
Valid N	4,743	485	716	1,668	2,099
SEX RATIO (N men for every 100 women)					
1 Intra-provincial rural-born	58	109	67	68	121
2 Internal inter-urban circuit	73	133	105	99	108
3 Long-distance foreign migration	86	166	468	226	205
4 Other rural migrants	54	188	125	114	78
All	62	151	125	100	111
Valid N	4,743	496	757	1,668	2,099

Table AII.10: Mean Age at Arrival for the Four Main Recruitment Circuits, 1796–1855.[9]

	C1796I		CS1808–11		CS1815–19		CS1829		FR1850/ ER1855	
	Men	Women	Men	Women	Men	Women	Men	Women	Men	Women
1 Intra-provincial rural-born	24.9	22.4	24.5	24.4	28.7	22.6	24.9	21.7	25.5	23.7
2 Internal inter-urban circuit	23.8	23.3	26.3	25.4	27.8	24.4	25.5	23.8	26.5	23.7
3 Long-distance foreign migration	26.8	22.6	29.9	31.4	29.7	26.6	25.9	26.1	29.6	28.3
4 Other rural migrants	25.0	22.2	27.4	24.8	28.0	24.5	25.0	23.5	30.1	32.2
All	25.0	22.7	28.0	28.1	28.7	24.2	25.2	23.0	27.2	25.0
Valid N	2,100	3,252	654	93	407	325	834	838	95	119

Table AII.11: Occupational Profile of the Four Major Recruitment Circuits, 1796–1855.[10]

	C1796				CS1808–13				CS1815–19				CS1829				FR1850/ ERPI1855			
Circuit number	1	2	3	4	1	2	3	4	1	2	3	4	1	2	3	4	1	2	3	4
MEN																				
Primary sector	■	-	-	-	■	-	-	+	■	-	-	+	■	-	-	-	+	-	-	-
Domestic service	+	o	-	o	-	+	-	+	o	■	o	+	o	-	-	o	o	■	■	■
White-collar & proprietors	o	o	o	o	o	+	-	-	-	o	o	o	-	o	o	-	o	■	■	+
Trade & shipping	o	-	o	o	-	-	■	-	■	■	■	-	■	o	o	-	+	-	-	-
Transport & casual labour	+	-	-	o	o	-	-	■	o	+	-	o	■	+	o	o	■	o	-	o
Retail, services & food industries	+	o	o	+	■	o	-	o	-	■	o	+	-	o	+	+	o	-	-	-
Tools & construction	-	o	o	o	-	+	+	o	-	-	o	-	-	o	+	-	■	■	■	o
Consumer durables	-	■	+	■	-	-	o	o	-	■	■	o	+	o	-	o	o	-	■	-
Other & miscellaneous	o	o	o	o	-	o	o	o	+	-	-	o	+	o	-	o	+	o	o	o
No occupation / no mention	o	-	■	o	-	+	-	o	+	■	■	o	+	-	o	o	+	-	o	o
Valid N	698	458	191	467	128	199	326	334	78	72	127	124	257	131	149	296	33	21	343	28
WOMEN																				
Domestic service	o	o	-	o	o	o	-	+	+	-	o	-	o	-	o	-	o	o	o	o
Trade & local services	o	o	-	o	-	o	■	o	-	■	-	+	■	-	+	+	-	-	+	■
Casual labour	-	-	-	-	■	+	■	-	-	■	-	o	-	o	o	■	o	o	-	+
Textiles & lace	o	+	o	o	+	+	-	-	-	■	o	-	■	■	o	-	-	■	-	-
Garment industries	-	+	o	o	-	+	-	-	-	-	o	■	■	■	o	■	-	■	-	-
Other & miscellaneous	+	o	-	-	o	-	-	-	-	-	■	-	o	+	+	-	+	o	+	-
No occupation / no mention	o	o	o	o	o	+	■	-	■	■	-	■	■	+	o	-	+	-	+	o
Valid N	1210	630	223	866	45	50	46	57	115	78	102	28	378	132	259	66	45	54	134	18

Symbols: ■ denotes very strong over-representation (LQ ≥ 1.5); + denotes moderate over-representation (LQ ≥ 1.2 and < 1.5); o denotes proportionate representation (LQ ≥ 0.8 and < 1.2); - denotes under-representation (LQ < 0.8). LQ: Location Quotient = % within subgroup / % of total (calculations for each period separately).

Table AII.12: Immigration and Emigration Trajectories of the Four Recruitment Circuits, 1829–55 (%).[11]

	1829					ERPI1855				
	1	2	3	4	All	1	2	3	4	All
IMMIGRATION TRAJECTORY: Relationship between birthplace and last place of residence										
Direct (same place)	58	65	50	61	60	44	48	29	36	41
Via a village	34	15	10	20	23	37	26	0	14	23
Via a medium-sized town	4	7	7	6	6	12	6	21	17	13
Via a large city	4	13	33	13	12	7	19	50	33	23
All	100	100	100	100	100	100	100	100	100	100
Valid N	635	272	189	569	1,666	41	31	14	42	128
EMIGRATION TRAJECTORY: Relationship between destination and place of birth (% of recorded leavers)										
Return to birthplace	44	43	29	44	42	28	36	32	24	29
To suburban belt	23	12	1	12	14	29	9	0	15	18
To other village	9	7	7	15	10	16	9	0	15	13
To medium-sized town	6	7	11	7	8	7	4	11	12	8
To large city	18	30	52	21	26	20	43	58	34	33
All	100	100	100	100	100	100	100	100	100	100
Valid N	457	230	175	354	1,210	83	47	19	67	216
EMIGRATION REGION										
Same place	44	43	28	44	41	28	36	32	24	29
Same region	34	15	7	14	21	51	21	0	13	28
Different region	22	42	65	42	38	22	43	68	63	43
All	100	100	100	100	100	100	100	100	100	100
Valid N	457	231	179	356	1,223	83	47	19	67	215

Source: for immigration trajectory 1829: CS1829; all other figures: ERPI1829+, ERPI1855.

Table AII.13: Turnover in the Four Major Recruitment Circuits, 1808–55 (%).[12]

% staying less than 1 year	CS1808–13		CS1815–19		CS1829		ERPI1829+		ERPI1855	
	M	W	M	W	M	W	M	W	M	W
1 Inter-provincial rural-born	29	23	29	16	21	16	24	28	42	33
2 Internal inter-urban	46	34	46	29	22	26	34	32	52	69
3 Long-distance foreign migration	51	41	45	26	31	17	41	22	77	38
4 Other rural migrants	53	30	31	14	25	18	45	31	43	49
All	48	33	37	19	24	18	34	29	49	46
Valid N	365	117	390	303	833	835	606	602	95	120

Migrants and Urban Change

Table AII.14: Relationship between Hosts and Newcomers, CS1829 (%).

Circuit of recruitment	Origin of host				Occupation of host				Of whom A E/C	Of whom E/C from SA	Of whom O from SA
	A	SA	Other	All	E/C	L	O	All			
MALE NEWCOMERS											
1 Intra-provincial rural-born	32	28	40	100	61	10	29	100	22	8	11
2 Internal inter-urban circuit	26	10	64	100	33	24	43	100	12	4	4
3 Long-distance foreign migration	26	16	59	100	43	21	36	100	8	11	6
4 Other rural migrants	21	19	59	100	54	16	29	100	13	15	3
Total	27	20	53	100	52	16	32	100	15	10	6
Valid N	91	70	181	342	177	53	110	340	52	35	22
FEMALE NEWCOMERS											
1 Intra-provincial rural-born	36	19	45	100	96	1	4	100	36	16	2
2 Internal inter-urban circuit	25	10	65	100	76	2	22	100	18	10	2
3 Long-distance foreign migration	24	10	67	100	62	5	33	100	0	10	0
4 Other rural migrants	30	12	58	100	89	3	8	100	27	10	1
Total	32	15	53	100	89	2	10	100	28	13	2
Valid N	102	48	169	319	287	6	31	324	91	41	31

Abbreviations: A: Antwerp-born; SA: same area; E: employer; C: colleague; E/C: employer or colleague; L: professional lodging keeper; O: other occupation

NOTES

For full details of the abbreviations relating to source data used below and in the figures, see Appendix I.2. For abbreviations relating to library holdings, see Works Cited.

Introduction

1. P. Bairoch, *De Jéricho à Mexico: Villes et économie dans l'histoire* (Paris: Gallimard, 1985), pp. 277–95; P. M. Hohenberg and L. H. Lees, *The Making of Urban Europe, 1000–1994* (London: Harvard University Press, 1995), pp. 217–26.
2. J. J. Jackson and L. P. Moch, 'Migration and the Social History of Europe', in D. Hoerder and L. P. Moch (eds), *European Migrants: Global and Local Perspectives* (Boston, MA: Northeastern University Press, 1996), pp. 52–69, on pp. 52–3.
3. For an overview, see L. P. Moch, *Moving Europeans: Migration in Western Europe since 1650* (Bloomington and Indianapolis, IN: Indiana University Press, 2003), pp. 22–101.
4. S. Hochstadt, *Mobility and Modernity: Migration in Germany, 1820–1989* (Ann Arbor, MI: University of Michigan Press, 1999); J. H. Jackson, *Migration and Urbanization in the Ruhr Valley, 1821–1914* (Atlantic Highlands, NJ: Humanities Press, 1997); C. G. Pooley and J. Turnbull, *Migration and Mobility in Britain since the Eighteenth Century* (London: UCL Press, 1998).
5. Jackson, *Migration and Urbanization*; A. Knotter, *Economische transformatie en stedelijke arbeidsmarkt: Amsterdam in de tweede helft van de negentiende eeuw* (Zwolle: Waanders, 1991); W. H. Sewell, *Structure and Mobility: The Men and Women of Marseille, 1820–1870* (Cambridge: Cambridge University Press, 1985); H. Van Dijk, *Rotterdam 1810–1880: Aspecten van een stedelijke samenleving* (Schiedam: Interbook International, 1976).
6. J. de Vries, 'Problems in the Measurement, Description and Analysis of Historical Urbanization', in A. van der Woude, A. Hayami and J. de Vries (eds), *Urbanization in History: A Process of Dynamic Interactions* (Oxford: Clarendon Press, 1990), pp. 43–60; M. Oris, 'Fertility and Migration in the Heart of the Industrial Revolution', *History of the Family*, 1:2 (1996), pp. 169–82; J. G. Williamson, *Coping with City Growth during the British Industrial Revolution* (Cambridge: Cambridge University Press, 1990), p. 24.
7. L. Lucassen, 'De selectiviteit van blijvers: Een reconstructie van de sociale positie van Duitse migranten in Rotterdam (1870–1885)', *Tijdschrift voor Sociale en Economische Geschiedenis*, 1:2 (2004), pp. 92–116; L. P. Moch, *Paths to the City: Regional Migration in Nineteenth-Century France* (Beverly Hills, CA: Sage Publications, 1983); M.

Schrover, *Een kolonie van Duitsers: Groepsvorming onder Duitse immigranten in Utrecht in de negentiende eeuw* (Amsterdam: Aksant, 2002); Sewell, *Structure and Mobility*.

8.   J. Long, 'Rural–Urban Migration and Socioeconomic Mobility in Victorian Britain', *Journal of Economic History*, 65:1 (2005), pp. 1–35; Williamson, *Coping with City Growth*, pp. 59–81.

9.   Cf. T. Engelen, 'Labour Strategies of Families: A Critical Assessment of an Appealing Concept', *International Review of Social History*, 47 (2002), pp. 453–64.

1 Explaining Migration

1.   D. Baines, *Emigration from Europe, 1815–1930* (London: MacMillan, 1991), pp. 11–14, 25, 28.

2.   H. Jerome, *Migration and Business Cycles* (New York: National Bureau of Economic Research, 1926).

3.   T. J. Hatton and J. G. Williamson, *The Age of Mass Migration: Causes and Economic Impact* (New York: Oxford University Press, 1998), for example, have proposed an econometric model centred almost exclusively on wage gaps to explain the rhythms and intensities of nineteenth-century transatlantic migration.

4.   P. Clark, 'The Migrant in Kentish Towns 1580–1640', in P. Clark and P. Slack (eds), *Crisis and Order in English Towns, 1500–1700: Essays in Urban History* (London: Routledge and K. Paul, 1972), pp. 117–63.

5.   A. L. Beier, 'Vagrants and the Social Order in Elizabethan England', *Past and Present*, 64 (1974), pp. 3–29.

6.   C. Lis and H. Soly, 'Policing the Early Modern Proletariat, 1450–1850', in D. Levine (ed.), *Proletarianization and Family History* (Orlando, FL: Academia Press, 1984), pp. 163–228, on pp. 164–5; C. Lis, H. Soly and D. Van Damme, *Op vrije voeten? Sociale politiek in West-Europa (1450–1914)* (Leuven: Kritak, 1985), pp. 41–9.

7.   E.g. R. Rommes, *Oost, west, Utrecht best? Driehonderd jaar migratie en migranten in de stad Utrecht (begin 16de–begin 19de eeuw)* (Amsterdam: Stichting Amsterdamse Historische Reeks, 1998), pp. 38–44.

8.   J. L. van Zanden, *The Rise and Decline of Holland's Economy: Merchant Capitalism and the Labour Market* (Manchester: Manchester University Press, 1993), p. 50.

9.   Knotter, *Economische transformatie*.

10. S. Amin and M. van der Linden, 'Introduction', in S. Amin and M. van der Linden (eds), *"Peripheral" Labour? Studies in the History of Partial Proletarianization* (Cambridge and New York: Cambridge University Press, 1997), pp. 1–7, on pp. 2–4; O. Hufton, *The Poor of Eighteenth-Century France* (Oxford: Clarendon Press, 1974), pp. 11–24.

11. A. Poitrineau, 'Aspects de l'émigration temporaire et saisonnière en Auvergne à la fin du XVIIIe et au début du XIXe siècle', *Revue d'Histoire Moderne et Contemporaine*, 9 (1962); J.-P. Poussou, 'Mobilité et migrations', in J. Dupâquier (ed.), *Histoire de la population française, Vol. 2: De la Rénaissance à 1789* (Paris: Presses Universitaires de France, 1988), p. 111.

12. Or in the least aspiring situations: '*manger hors de la région*, without further gain, was sufficient incentive to make an Auvergnat take to the road for up to nine months of the year', Hufton, *The Poor*, p. 73.

13. Cited in translation in J. Lucassen, *Migrant Labour in Europe, 1600–1900: The Drift to the North Sea* (London: Croom Helm, 1987), p. 96.

14. Ibid., pp. 30–4.

15. S. Sassen, *Guests and Aliens* (New York: The New Press, 1999), pp. xiv–xv.
16. C. Tilly, 'Transplanted Networks', in V. Yans-McLaughlin (ed.), *Immigration Reconsidered: History, Sociology and Politics* (London: Oxford University Press, 1990), pp. 79–995, on p. 84; P. Versteegh, 'The Ties that Bind: The Role of Family and Ethnic Networks in the Settlements of Polish Migrants in Pennsylvania, 1890–1940', *History of the Family*, 5 (2000), pp. 111–49, on pp. 116–19; S. A. Wegge, 'Chain Migration and Information Networks: Evidence from Nineteenth-Century Hesse-Cassel', *Journal of Economic History*, 58:4 (1998), pp. 957–87, on pp. 960–1.
17. Hufton, *The Poor*, pp. 95–7.
18. Wegge, 'Chain Migration', pp. 971–83.
19. Baines, *Emigration from Europe*, pp. 29, 31–8, 41–2, 50.
20. Ibid., p. 34; C. Tilly, 'Migration in Modern European History', in W. H. McNeill and R. S. Adams (eds), *Human Migration: Patterns and Policies* (Bloomington, IN, and London: Indiana University Press, 1978), p. 53.
21. Hufton, *The Poor*, pp. 95–6; M. Schrover, 'Potverkopers, vijlenkappers, winkeliers en stukadoors: Nichevorming onder Duitse migranten in de negentiende-eeuwse stad Utrecht', *Tijdschrift voor Sociale Geschiedenis*, 26:4 (2000), pp. 281–305.
22. Poitrineau, 'Aspects de l'émigration', pp. 11–15.
23. Cf. Hufton, *The Poor*, pp. 98–9.
24. Lucassen, *Migrant Labour*, p. 53.
25. Poitrineau, 'Aspects de l'émigration', pp. 11–15.
26. C. Lesger, L. Lucassen and M. Schrover, 'Is There Life Outside the Migrant Network? German Immigrants in 19th Century Netherlands and the Need for a More Balanced Migration Typology', *Annales de Démographie Historique*, 104:2 (2002), pp. 29–50, on pp. 30–7.
27. C. Lesger, 'Informatiestromen en de herkomstgebieden van migranten in de Nederlanden in de Vroegmoderne Tijd', *Tijdschrift voor Sociale en Economische Geschiedenis*, 3:1 (2006), pp. 3–23.
28. Moch, *Moving Europeans*, p. 16.
29. Lesger, 'Informatiestromen', pp. 8–9; J.-P. Poussou, *Bordeaux et le Sud-Ouest au XVIIIe siècle: croissance économique et attraction urbaine* (Paris: Touzot, 1983), pp. 80–1.
30. Poussou, *Bordeaux*, pp. 80–1.
31. Baines, *Emigration from Europe*, pp. 55–6.
32. Cf. also P. Kooij, 'Migrants in Dutch Cities at the End of the Nineteenth Century', in D. Menjot and J.-L. Pinol (eds), *Les immigrants et la ville: Insertion, intégration, discrimination (XIIe–XXe siècles)* (Paris: Harmattan, 1996), pp. 193–206.
33. T. G. Anderson, 'Proto-Industrialization, Sharecropping, and Outmigration in Nineteenth-Century Rural Westphalia', *Journal of Peasant Studies*, 29:1 (2001), pp. 1–30, on pp. 19–21.
34. R. Paping, 'Family Strategies concerning Migration and Occupations of Children in a Market-Oriented Agricultural Economy', *History of the Family*, 9:2 (2004), pp. 159–91, on pp. 169–70, and the original study: R. Paping, 'Gezinnen en cohorten: Arbeidsstrategieën in een marktgerichte agrarische economie: de Groningse kleigebieden, 1830–1920', in J. Kok (ed.), *Levensloop en levenslot: Arbeidsstrategieën van gezinnen in de negentiende en twintigste eeuw* (Groningen: Nederlands agronomisch instituut, 1999), pp. 17–88.
35. J. Kok, 'Choices and Constraints in the Migration of Families: The Central Netherlands, 1850–1940', *History of the Family*, 9:2 (2004), pp. 137–58, on pp. 146–7, and the

original study: J. Kok, 'Migratie als gezinsstrategie in midden-Nederland', in Kok (ed.), *Levensloop en levenslot*, pp. 89–156.

36. Cf. R. Skeldon, *Migration and Development: A Global Perspective* (Harlow: Longman, 1997), p. 8.

37. On wage formation in the early modern period, see R. S. DuPlessis, *Transitions to Capitalism in Early Modern Europe* (Cambridge and New York: Cambridge University Press, 1997), pp. 266–72.

38. Cf., among others, Baines, *Emigration from Europe*, p. 14; Kok, 'Choices and Constraints', pp. 147–52; J. Lucassen and L. Lucassen, 'Migration, Migration History, History: Old Paradigms and New Perspectives', in J. Lucassen and L. Lucassen (eds), *Migration, Migration History, History: Old Paradigms and New Perspectives* (Bern: Lang, 1997), pp. 9–38, on p. 16.

39. Kok, 'Choices and Constraints', pp. 145–6.

40. Paping, 'Family Strategies', pp. 171–2.

41. Cf. U. Pfister, 'Exit, Voice and Loyalty: Parent–Child Relations in the Proto-Industrial Household Economy', *History of the Family*, 9:4 (2004), pp. 401–23.

42. Cf. Engelen, 'Labour Strategies of Families', p. 458. See also below.

43. W. Gordon, '"What, I Pray You, Shall I Do with the Balance?" Single Women's Economy of Migration', *International Review of Social History*, 50:1 (2005), pp. 53–70.

44. H. Bras, *Zeeuwse meiden: Dienen in de levensloop van vrouwen, 1850–1950* (Amsterdam: Aksant, 2002); H. Bras, 'Maids to the City: Migration Patterns of Female Domestic Servants from the Province of Zeeland, the Netherlands (1850–1950)', *History of the Family*, 8:2 (2003), pp. 217–46.

45. Cf. Kok, 'Choices and Constraints', p. 146; M. Oris, 'The History of Migration as a Chapter in the History of the European Rural Family: An Overview', *History of the Family*, 8:2 (2003), pp. 187–215, on p. 194.

46. P.-A. Rosental, *Les sentiers invisibles: Espace, familles et migrations dans la France du 19e siècle* (Paris: Ecole des Hautes Etudes en Sciences Sociales, 1999).

47. Cf. P. Clark, 'Migrants in the City: The Process of Social Adaptation in English towns, 1500–1800', in P. Clark and D. Souden (eds), *Migration and Society in Early Modern England* (London: Hutchinson, 1987), pp. 267–94, on pp. 280–2; J. Ehmer, 'Worlds of Mobility: Migration Patterns of Viennese Artisans in the Eighteenth Century', in G. Crossick (ed.), *The Artisan and the European Town, ca. 1500–1900* (Aldershot: Scolar Press, 1997), pp. 172–99, on pp. 186–94; H. R. Southall, 'The Tramping Artisan Revisits: Labour Mobility and Economic Distress in Early Victorian England', *Economic History Review*, 44:2 (1991), pp. 272–96.

48. D. Farasyn, *De 18de eeuwse bloeiperiode van Oostende, 1769–1794* (Oostende: Stadsarchief, 1998).

49. R. G. Fuchs and L. P. Moch, 'Pregnant, Single, and Far from Home: Migrant Women in Nineteenth-Century Paris', *American Historical Review*, 95:4 (1990), pp. 1007–32.

50. M. van der Heijden, 'Contradictory Interests: Work, Parents, and Offspring in Early Modern Holland', *History of the Family*, 9:4 (2004), pp. 355–70, on pp. 365–7.

51. M. Neven, 'Retourmigratie in een plattelands samenleving tijdens de Industriële Revolutie: Het land van Herve (België) 1846–1900', *Tijdschrift voor Sociale en Economische Geschiedenis*, 1:1 (2004), pp. 47–75.

52. Cf. F. van Poppel and M. Oris, 'Continuities and Disparities in the Pattern of Leaving Home', in F. vand Poppel, M. Oris and J. Lee (eds), *The Road to Independence: Leaving*

Home in Western and Eastern Societies, 16th–20th Centuries (Bern: Lang, 2004), pp. 1–29.

53. Cf. Oris, 'The History of Migration', pp. 193–4.
54. Cf. Kok, 'Choices and Constraints', pp. 147–52.
55. Cf. T. Engelen, A. Knotter, J. Kok and R. Paping, 'Labor Strategies of Families: An Introduction', *History of the Family*, 9:2 (2004), pp. 123–36.
56. Oris, 'The History of Migration', pp. 196–7.
57. For a pioneering and inspiring multi-level integrative approach, see L. P. Moch, 'Dividing Time: An Analytical Framework for Migration History Periodization', in Lucassen and Lucassen (eds), *Migration*, pp. 41–56; Moch, *Moving Europeans*, pp. 13–18.
58. On the role of economic considerations in the movement of 'political' migrants or refugees, see Lucassen and Lucassen, 'Migration', pp. 14–17.
59. The framework proposed here bears many conceptual resemblances to the concept of 'family strategies' or the 'adaptive family economy', although it does not necessitate taking the household as prime unit of analysis. For a discussion of the concept in relation to the approach proposed here, see A. Winter, 'Patterns of Migration and Adaptation in the Urban Transition: Newcomers to Antwerp, c. 1760–1860' (PhD dissertation, Vrije Universiteit Brussel, 2007), pp. 32–3. On the usefulness and caveats of the concept in historical research, see, among others, Engelen et al., 'Labour Strategies of Families', pp. 123–5; L. Fontaine and J. Schlumbohm, 'Household Strategies for Survival 1600–2000: An Introduction', in L. Fontaine and J. Schlumbohm (eds), *Household Strategies for Survival 1600–2000: Fission, Faction and Cooperation* (Amsterdam: Cambridge University Press, 2000), pp. 1–17; A. Knotter, 'Problems of the "Family Economy": Peasant Economy, Domestic Production and Labour Markets in Pre-Industrial Europe', in M. Prak (ed.), *Early Modern Capitalism: Economic and Social Change in Europe, 1400–1800* (London: Routledge, 2001), pp. 135–60; J. Kok, 'The Challenge of Strategy: A Comment', *International Review of Social History*, 47 (2002), pp. 465–85.
60. A. Knotter and J. L. van Zanden, 'Immigratie en arbeidsmarkt te Amsterdam in de 17e eeuw', *Tijdschrift voor Sociale Geschiedenis*, 13:4 (1987), pp. 403–31, and its slightly revised English edition in van Zanden, *The Rise and Decline*, ch. 3.
61. E. Kuijpers, *Migrantenstad: Immigratie en sociale verhoudingen in 17e-eeuws Amsterdam* (Hilversum: Verloren, 2005), pp. 213–87. However, if informal social networks truly formed the core explanation for the observed patterns of occupational specialization, they must have operated first and foremost at the level of families, villages and local communities rather than regions, yet no empirical efforts have been made by Kuijpers to verify or refute the existence of such small-scale networks. That a pattern of specialization nevertheless emerges at a – very broadly defined – *regional* level might be taken as an indication that other, region-specific, factors might have been important too.
62. Lesger, 'Informatiestromen'.
63. J. Lucassen, *Naar de kusten van de Noordzee. Trekarbeid in Europees perspectief, 1600–1900* (Utrecht, 1984), pp. 159–68; van Zanden, *The Rise and Decline*, pp. 31–53, 70–1.
64. Agricultural and living conditions in Scandinavia were sufficiently marginal to establish a large difference between earning capacities at home and on the Amsterdam labour market. A Norwegian servant girl could, for instance, expect to earn 30–40 times higher wages in Amsterdam than in the Norwegian countryside: S. Sogner, 'Young in Europe around 1700: Norwegian Sailors and Servant-Girls Seeking Employment in Amster-

dam', in J.-P. Bardet, F. Lebrun and R. Le Mée (eds), *Mesurer et comprendre: Mélanges offerts à Jacques Dupaquier* (Paris: PUF, 1994), pp. 515–622, on p. 521.

65. Lesger, 'Informatiestromen', pp. 11–12; Sogner, 'Young in Europe', pp. 526–31.
66. Cf. E. Orrman, 'The Condition of the Rural Population in Late Medieval Society (c. 1350–1520)', in K. Helle (ed.), *The Cambridge History of Scandinavia, vol. 1: Prehistory to 1520* (Cambridge: Cambridge University Press, 2003), pp. 581–611, on pp. 595–7.
67. Although not all Scandinavian sailors necessarily planned to return, many of them undoubtedly did, and in that case they were better off gaining experience which was marketable at home than performing activities which offered no career perspectives on their return. Cf. Sogner, 'Young in Europe', p. 519: 'Maritime experience acquired on Dutch keel was regarded favourably by navy officers, and the absentees were as a rule on formal leave, and expected to return'.
68. C. Lesger, *Handel in Amsterdam ten tijde van de Opstand: Kooplieden, commerciële expansie en verandering in de ruimtelijke economie van de Nederlanden, ca. 1550–ca. 1630* (Hilversum: Verloren, 2001), pp. 33–5, 42, 68–75.
69. As eventually happened: Sogner, 'Young in Europe', p. 532.
70. A. Cottaar and L. Lucassen, 'Naar de laatste Parijse mode: Strohoedenmakers uit het Jekerdal in Nederland 1750–1900', *Studies over de sociaal-economische geschiedenis van Limburg* (2001), pp. 45–82.
71. P. Lourens and J. Lucassen, *Arbeitswanderung und berufliche Spezialisierung: Die lippischen Ziegler in 18. und 19. Jahrhundert* (Osnabrück: Vandenhoeck & Ruprecht, 1999).
72. Schrover, 'Potverkopers', p. 300.
73. Poitrineau, 'Aspects de l'émigration', pp. 11–23; A. Poitrineau, *Remues d'hommes: Essai sur les migrations montagnardes en France aux XVIIe et XVIIIe siècles* (Paris: Aubier Montaigne, 1983), pp. 126–30.
74. N. Green, *Ready-to-Wear and Ready-to-Work: A Century of Industry and Immigrants in the Women's Garment Trade in Paris and New York* (Durham: Duke University Press, 1998), pp. 188–218, quote on p. 217.
75. In principle the term refers to the totality of relevant opportunities, which can be expanded to include not only employment and housing opportunities, but also political, cultural, educational and matrimonial opportunities.
76. P. Bourdelais, 'Demographic Changes in European Industrializing Towns: Examples and Elements for Comparison', *History of the Family*, 5:4 (2000), pp. 363–72; R. Lee, 'Urban Labor Markets, In-Migration, and Demographic Growth: Bremen, 1815–1914', *Journal of Interdisciplinary History*, 30:3 (1999), pp. 437–74; Moch, *Moving Europeans*, pp. 131–43.
77. See, for instance, Lucassen, *Migrant Labour*, pp. 54–64; Poitrineau, *Remues d'hommes*.
78. Cf. R. Duroux, 'The Temporary Migration of Males and the Power of Females in a Stem-Family Society: The Case of 19th-Century Auvergne', *History of the Family*, 6:1 (2001), pp. 33–49.
79. J. Lucassen and R. Penninx, *Nieuwkomers: Immigranten en hun nakomelingen in Nederland, 1550–1985* (Amsterdam: Meulenhoff, 1985), p. 142; Schrover, 'Potverkopers'.
80. E. Morawska, *Insecure Prosperity. Small-Town Jews in Industrial America, 1890–1940* (Princeton, NJ: Princeton University Press, 1996). On the relationship between recruitment patterns and local opportunity structure, see also L. Lucassen and F. Vermeulen, *Immigranten en lokale arbeidsmarkt: Vreemdelingen in Den Haag, Leiden, Deventer en Alkmaar (1920–1940)* (Amsterdam, 1999).

81. Cf. Hufton, *The Poor*, pp. 97–8; J. G. Williamson, 'Coping with City Growth', in R. Floud and D. N. McCloskey (eds), *The Economic History of Britain since 1700, vol. I: 1700–1860*, 2nd edn (Cambridge: Cambridge University Press, 1994), pp. 332–56, on p. 339.

82. Clark, 'The Migrant in Kentish Towns'; P. Clark and D. Souden, 'Introduction', in Clark and Souden (eds), *Migration and Society*, pp. 11–48, on pp. 22–38.

83. Cf. Kok, 'The Challenge of Strategy', p. 475; Lucassen and Lucassen, 'Migration', pp. 19–20; L. Lucassen, 'A Blind Spot – Migratory and Travelling Groups in Western European Historiography', *International Review of Social History*, 38:2 (1993), pp. 209–35, on pp. 218–21. See also A. Winter, 'Vagrancy as an Adaptive Strategy: The Duchy of Brabant, 1767–1776', *International Review of Social History*, 49:2 (2004), pp. 249–78.

84. Possibly, one could try recourse to a formal econometric evaluation of wage patterns, but this would in any case be beyond the scope of the present study.

85. Cf. Oris, 'The History of Migration', pp. 194–5.

86. Cf. also Lucassen and Vermeulen, *Immigranten* .

87. Cf. S. Sassen, 'Immigration and Local Labor Markets', in A. Portes (ed.), *The Economic Sociology of Immigration: Essays on Networks, Ethnicity and Entrepreneurship* (New York: Sage, 1995), pp. 87–127.

88. Cf. Pooley and Turnbull, *Migration and Mobility*, p. 70: 'Even in the late-twentieth century the unskilled have difficulty gaining information about distant job opportunities'. On the adaptability of nation-wide artisan networks, see Southall, 'The Tramping Artisan'.

2 Migration in the Urban Transition

1. Among others, see Clark and Souden (eds), *Migration and Society*; S. Hochstadt, 'Migration in Preindustrial Germany', *Central European History*, 16:3 (1983), pp. 195–224; Hufton, *The Poor*, pp. 69–106; Kuijpers, *Migrantenstad*; Lucassen, *Migrant Labour*; Moch, *Moving Europeans*, pp. 22–101; D. Roche, *Humeurs vagabondes: De la circulation des hommes et de l'utilité des voyages* (Paris: Fayard, 2003); Tilly, 'Migration'.

2. Bairoch, *De Jéricho à Mexico*, pp. 264–71; J. de Vries, *European Urbanization, 1500–1800* (London: Methuen, 1984), pp. 175–98; Moch, *Moving Europeans*, pp. 44–6.

3. Hochstadt, 'Migration in Preindustrial Germany'; Moch, *Moving Europeans*, p. 44.

4. De Vries, *European Urbanization*, pp. 200–6; see also Moch, *Moving Europeans*, pp. 43–7.

5. De Vries, *European Urbanization*, pp. 196–7; A. Sharlin, 'Natural Decrease in Early Modern Cities: A Reconsideration', *Past and Present*, 79 (1978), pp. 126–38, on p. 138; A. van der Woude, 'Population Developments in the Northern Netherlands (1500–1800) and the Validity of the "Urban Graveyard" Effect', *Annales de Démographie Historique* (1982), pp. 55–75.

6. De Vries, *European Urbanization*, pp. 200 ff; Moch, *Moving Europeans*, pp. 43 ff.

7. P. Clark, 'Migration in England during the Late Seventeenth and Early Eighteenth Centuries', in Clark and Souden (eds), *Migration and Society*, pp. 213–52, on pp. 221–6; Clark and Souden, 'Introduction', pp. 22–35; Moch, *Moving Europeans*, pp. 47–9; Poussou, *Bordeaux*, pp. 63–150; Poussou, 'Mobilité et migrations', pp. 116–20; I. D. Whyte, *Migration and Society in Britain, 1550–1830* (Basingstoke: Macmillan, 2000), pp. 67–71. Compare with Kooij, 'Migrants in Dutch Cities'; J. Patten, 'Patterns of Migra-

tion and Movement of Labour to Three Pre-Industrial East-Anglian Towns', in Clark and Souden (eds), *Migration and Society*, pp. 77–106.

8. Moch, *Moving Europeans*, p. 47.

9. Poussou, 'Mobilité et migrations', pp. 116–18.

10. Cf. B. Blondé, *Een economie met verschillende snelheden: Ongelijkheden in de opbouw en de ontwikkeling van het Brabantse stedelijke netwerk, ca 1750–ca 1790* (Brussel: Paleis der Academiën, 1999), pp. 35–40.

11. Poussou, 'Mobilité et migrations', p. 118.

12. Among others, see Ehmer, 'Worlds of Mobility', pp. 188–94; Kooij, 'Migrants in Dutch Cities'.

13. Cf., for instance, L. Lucassen and B. de Vries, 'The Rise and Fall of a West-European Textile-Worker Migration System: Leiden, 1586–1700', in G. Gayot and P. Minard (eds), *Les ouvriers qualifiés de l'industrie (16e–20e siècle): Formation, emploi, migrations*, Révue du Nord, Hors série, Collection Histoire n° 15 (Lille: Université Charles-de-Gaulle, 2001), pp. 23–42.

14. Moch, *Moving Europeans*, pp. 46–7; Poussou, 'Mobilité et migrations', pp. 116–20.

15. Knotter and van Zanden, 'Immigratie en arbeidsmarkt'; Kuijpers, *Migrantenstad*; Lesger, 'Informatiestromen'; van Zanden, *The Rise and Decline*, ch. 3. See above, pp. 23–5, for the discussion on migrants in seventeenth-century Amsterdam.

16. Knotter and van Zanden, 'Immigratie en arbeidsmarkt'; Kuijpers, *Migrantenstad*, pp. 85–92; Patten, 'Patterns of Migration'; Poussou, 'Mobilité et migrations', pp. 117–19; Whyte, *Migration and Society*, pp. 68–81.

17. De Vries, *European Urbanization*, p. 203.

18. Cf., among many others, G. Grantham, 'Economic History and the History of Labour Markets', in G. Grantham and M. MacKinnon (eds), *Labour Market Evolution: The Economic History of Market Integration, Wage Flexibility and the Employment Relation* (London and New York: Routledge, 1994), pp. 1–26, on pp. 13–15; Hufton, *The Poor*; Knotter, 'Problems of the "Family Economy"'; Moch, *Moving Europeans*, pp. 68–70; J. Schlumbohm, 'Labour in Proto-Industrialization: Big Questions and Micro-Answers', in Prak (ed.), *Early Modern Capitalism*, pp. 125–34.

19. Moch, *Moving Europeans*, pp. 49–58, 68–70.

20. Van Zanden, *The Rise and Decline*, pp. 7–11 and *passim*.

21. For criticisms, see, for instance, A. Knotter, 'A New Theory of Merchant Capitalism?', *Review*, 20:2 (1997), pp. 193–210; C. Lis and H. Soly, 'Different Paths of Development: Capitalism in the Northern and Southern Netherlands during the Late Middle Ages and the Early Modern Period', *Review*, 20:2 (1997), pp. 211–42.

22. See A. Winter, *Divided Interests, Divided Migrants: The Rationales of Policies Regarding Labour Mobility in Western Europe, c. 1550–1914*, Working Paper 15 (London: Global Economic History Network – London School of Economics, 2005).

23. Hufton, *The Poor*, pp. 97–8.

24. Lucassen and de Vries, 'The Rise and Fall'.

25. P. Bairoch, 'The Impact of Crop Yields, Agricultural Productivity, and Transport Costs on Urban Growth between 1800 and 1910', in van der Woude et al. (eds), *Urbanization in History*, pp. 134–52; de Vries, *European Urbanization*, p. 39; A. van der Woude, A. Hayami and J. de Vries, 'Introduction: The Hierarchies, Provisioning, and Demographic Patterns of Cities', in van der Woude et al. (eds), *Urbanization in History*, pp. 3–19, on pp. 5–14; E. A. Wrigley, 'Brake or Accelerator? Urban Growth and Population Growth

before the Industrial Revolution', in van der Woude et al. (eds), *Urbanization in History*, pp. 101–12.

26. De Vries, *European Urbanization*, p. 39.

27. Bairoch, *De Jéricho à Mexico*, pp. 277–95; Hohenberg and Lees, *The Making of Urban Europe*, pp. 217–26.

28. P. M. Hohenberg, 'Urban Development', in D. H. Aldcroft and S. P. Ville (eds), *The European Economy, 1750–1914. A Thematic Approach* (Manchester and New York: Manchester University Press, 1994), pp. 284–312.

29. See, among others, N. F. R. Crafts, *British Economic Growth during the Industrial Revolution* (Oxford: Clarendon Press, 1985); J. de Vries, 'The Industrial Revolution and the Industrious Revolution', *Journal of Economic History*, 54:2 (1994), pp. 249–70.

30. Jackson, *Migration and Urbanization*, pp. 18–19; Jackson and Moch, 'Migration and the Social History of Europe', pp. 52–3.

31. S. H. Preston and E. van de Walle, 'Urban French Mortality in the Nineteenth Century', *Population Studies*, 32:2 (1978), pp. 275–97; R. Schofield, D. Reher and A. Bideau (eds), *The Decline of Mortality in Europe* (Oxford: Oxford University Press, 1991).

32. Moch, *Moving Europeans*, p. 131.

33. Williamson, *Coping with City Growth*, p. 24.

34. De Vries, 'Problems in the Measurement', pp. 52–60, quote on p. 58; Williamson, 'Coping with City Growth', pp. 337–8.

35. Jackson, *Migration and Urbanization*, pp. 190–1. See also Hochstadt, *Mobility and Modernity*, pp. 135–43; D. Langewiesche and F. Lenger, 'Internal Migration: Persistence and Mobility', in K. J. Bade (ed.), *Population, Labour and Migration in 19th- and 20th-Century Germany* (Leamington Spa etc.: Berg, 1987), pp. 87–100, on pp. 89–91, on the high turnover in urban migration in nineteenth-century Germany. On the continuity of artisan migration patterns (with high turnover among journeymen) in Germany and Austria, see J. Ehmer, 'Migration of Journeymen as Nineteenth-Century Mass-Migration', in R. Leboutte (ed.), *Migrations and Migrants in Historical Perspective: Permanences and Innovations* (Brussels: P.I.E. – Peter Lang, 2000), pp. 97–109.

36. Van Dijk, *Rotterdam*, p. 443.

37. Knotter, *Economische transformatie*, p. 294.

38. Jackson, *Migration and Urbanization*, pp. 203, 254.

39. Pooley and Turnbull, *Migration and Mobility*, pp. 93–125; C. G. Pooley and J. Turnbull, 'Migration and Urbanization in North-West England: A Reassesment of the Roles of Towns in the Migration Process', in D. Siddle (ed.), *Migration, Mobility and Modernization* (Liverpool: Liverpool University Press, 2000), pp. 186–214.

40. Pooley and Turnbull, *Migration and Mobility*.

41. E.g. S. Hochstadt, 'Migration and Industrialization in Germany, 1815–1977', *Social Science History*, 5:4 (1981), pp. 445–68; Hochstadt, *Mobility and Modernity*, pp. 135–6; Jackson, *Migration and Urbanization*, pp. 194–202. See also R. Leboutte, 'Le rôle des migrations dans la formation des bassins industriels en Europe, 1800–1914', in A. Eiras Roel and O. Rey Castelao (eds), *Les migrations internes et à moyenne distance en Europe, 1500–1900* (Santiago de Compostella: Xunta de Galicia & CIDH, 1994), pp. 443–82, on pp. 446–8.

42. Williamson, *Coping with City Growth*, pp. 59–81.

43. Long, 'Rural–Urban Migration'.

44. Sewell, *Structure and Mobility*, pp. 234–312.

45. Jackson, *Migration and Urbanization*; C. Lis and H. Soly, 'Neighbourhood Social Change in West European Cities', *International Review of Social History*, 38 (1993), pp. 1–30; Sewell, *Structure and Mobility*.

46. Cf. J. Kok, 'Comment on Pooley and Turnbull', *Annales de Démographie Historique*, 2 (2002), pp. 113–18, on pp. 114–15: 'more variation, either temporal, social or regional, may have surfaced when, instead of concentrating on specific moves, entire migration histories or trajectories would have been analysed more extensively'.

47. See also Pooley's comment on Kok's remarks: 'we may have understated the impact of change on particular localities and regions ... [as] the regional scale of analysis smoothed out variations and emphasized stability ... We were looking at gross migration flows – all moves over any distance over a lifetime – and in doing so necessarily ignored to some degree the impact of net differences in migration flows on particular localities. In this sense the conclusion of stability in gross movement ... does not contradict the evidence of change in net movement evidenced by aggregate census and similar sources.' C. G. Pooley, 'Reflections on Migration and Mobility', *Annales de Démographie Historique*, 2 (2002), pp. 125–7, on p. 126.

48. K. D. M. Snell, *Annals of the Labouring Poor: Social Change and Agrarian England, 1660–1900* (Cambridge: Cambridge University Press, 1985), pp. 15–66. See also A. Kussmaul, *Servants in Husbandry in Early Modern England* (Cambridge and New York: Cambridge University Press, 1981), pp. 11–29; Moch, *Moving Europeans*, pp. 111–14.

49. Moch, *Moving Europeans*, pp. 66–8, 109–10; P. Van den Eeckhout and J. Hannes, 'Sociale verhoudingen en structuren in de Zuidelijke Nederlanden, 1770–1840', in D. P. Blok (ed.), *Algemene geschiedenis der Nederlanden* (Haarlem: Fibula-Van Dishoeck, 1981), pp. 435–75, on pp. 458–9; C. Vandenbroeke and W. Vanderpijpen, 'Landbouw en platteland in de Zuidelijke Nederlanden, 1770–1844', in Blok (ed.), *Algemene geschiedenis*, pp. 183–209, on pp. 204–5.

50. Moch, *Moving Europeans*, pp. 115–20.

51. M. De Moor, 'Common Land and Common Rights in Flanders', in M. De Moor, L. Shaw-Taylor and P. Warde (eds), *The Management of Common Land in North West Europe, c. 1500–1850* (Turnhout: Brepols, 2002), pp. 113–41, on pp. 126–36; J. Humphries, 'Enclosures, Common Right, and Women: The Proletarianization of Families in the Late Eighteenth and Early Nineteenth Centuries', *Journal of Economic History*, 50:1 (1990), pp. 17–42; Snell, *Annals*, pp. 138–227; Vandenbroeke and Vanderpijpen, 'Landbouw en platteland', pp. 184–5.

52. Moch, *Moving Europeans*, pp. 114–15; C. Ó Gráda, *Black '47 and Beyond: The Great Irish Famine in History, Economy, and Memory* (Princeton, NJ: Princeton University Press, 1999).

53. C. Tilly, 'Demographic Origins of the European Proletariat', in Levine (ed.), *Proletarianization and Family History*, pp. 1–85, on pp. 30–6.

54. Moch, *Moving Europeans*, pp. 111–19.

55. Knotter, *Economische transformatie*; S. Pollard, 'Labour in Great Britain', in P. Mathias and M. M. Postan (eds), *The Cambridge Economic History of Europe, Vol. VII, Part 1* (Cambridge: Cambridge University Press, 1978), pp. 97–179; J. L. van Zanden, *De industrialisatie van Amsterdam, 1825–1984* (Bergen: Octavo, 1987).

56. Pollard, 'Labour'; E. Vanhaute, '"De meest moordende van alle industrieën": De huisnijverheid in België omstreeks 1900', *Tijdschrift voor Sociale Geschiedenis*, 20:4 (1994), pp. 461–83.

57. Cf. Knotter, *Economische transformatie*; R. Lee, 'The Socio-Economic and Demographic Characteristics of Port Cities: A Typology for Comparative Analysis?', *Urban History*, 25:2 (1998), pp. 147–72, on pp. 159–64; C. Lis, *Social Change and the Labouring Poor: Antwerp, 1770–1860* (New Haven, CT: Yale University Press, 1986), pp. 27–62.
58. Cf. Lis, *Social Change*.
59. Baines, *Emigration from Europe*, pp. 44–5.
60. On the selectivity of 'stayers', see, for instance, Lucassen, 'De selectiviteit van blijvers'. A less unambiguously positive view on the effect of migration on social mobility is found in J. Kok and H. Delger, 'Success or Selection? The Effect of Migration on Occupational Mobility in a Dutch Province, 1840–1950', *Histoire et Mesure*, 13 (1998), pp. 289–322.
61. J.-C. Perrot, *Genèse d'une ville moderne: Caen au XVIIIe siècle* (Paris: Mouton, 1975), pp. 145, 153–65.
62. Jackson, *Migration and Urbanization*, pp. 72–86, 190–1.
63. Cf. de Vries, 'Problems in the Measurement', p. 59. See also D. Baines, 'Internal and Medium-Distance Migrations in Great-Britain, 1750–1900', in Eiras Roel and Rey Castelao (eds), *Les migrations internes*, pp. 127–46, on pp. 129–30, 132; Hochstadt, *Mobility and Modernity*, pp. 114–34; P. E. White, 'Internal Migration in the Nineteenth and Twentieth Centuries', in P. E. Ogden and P. E. White (eds), *Migrants in Modern France: Population Mobility in the Later Nineteenth and Twentieth Centuries* (London: Unwyn Hyman, 1989), pp. 13–33, on pp. 18–19.
64. Or, as one keen observer has reflected on the high incidence of in- and outmigration in mid-nineteenth century Brussels: 'If migration was one of people's "homely adjustments" to circumstances, then it is clear from the evidence on hand that there was a lot of re-adjusting going on'. S. de Schaepdrijver, *Elites for the Capital? Foreign Migration to Mid-Nineteenth-Century Brussels* (Amsterdam: PDIS, 1990), p. 23.
65. The phrase is from Pollard, 'Labour', pp. 117–18.
66. Van Zanden, *The Rise and Decline*, p. 7; J. L. van Zanden, 'Do we Need a Theory of Merchant Capitalism?', *Review*, 20:2 (1997), pp. 255–67, on pp. 264–5. An important consideration, which cannot be discussed further here, is whether some of the mechanisms of a 'spatial separation between reproductive costs and productive use of labour' via migration did not continue on a wider spatial international level. Cf. also Winter, *Divided Interests*, pp. 47–9.
67. In strict terms, his theory does not require that these patterns should necessarily have changed in form, or even in content. Because in essence the same developments that brought forth a closed labour market under 'industrial capitalism', engendered a 'deruralization of the countryside': the geographical space between town and country under industrial capitalism no longer separates two different modes of production; all is now equally part and parcel of the same 'system'. So what matters for his theory is not whether people continued to move as they did before, but rather that they now moved within the same 'closed labour market'.
68. Van Zanden, *The Rise and Decline*, pp. 14–15, and restated in van Zanden, 'Do we Need a Theory'.
69. This was even less likely given that an increased labour supply in cities, other things being equal, would have contributed to a *decline* in the reward for labour. Power relationships and collective labour action probably counted for a great deal as well – but that is another discussion. See also van Zanden, 'Do we Need a Theory', p. 261.
70. Van Zanden does refer to the importance of 'internal dynamics' creating new conditions as a force bringing about change, in particular referring to increasing proletarianization,

but does this only directly in relation to proto-industrial developments, and does not elaborate on possible implications for migration patterns: van Zanden, *The Rise and Decline*, pp. 12–14.

71. A. Chatelain, *Les migrants temporaires en France de 1800 à 1914* (Lille: Université de Lille III, 1976); U. Herbert, *A History of Foreign Labor in Germany, 1880–1980: Seasonal Workers, Forced Laborers, Guest Workers* (Ann Arbor, MI: University of Michigan Press, 1990); Langewiesche and Lenger, 'Internal Migration'; Lucassen, *Naar de kusten*, pp. 200–4, 222 ff; Moch, *Moving Europeans*, pp. 120 ff.

72. See, for instance, R.-A. M. Harris, *The Nearest Place that Wasn't Ireland: Early Nineteenth Century Irish Labor Migration* (Ames, IA: Iowa State University Press, 1994).

73. De Vries, *European Urbanization*, p. 39; A. Lottin and H. Soly, 'Aspects de l'histoire des villes des Pays-Bas méridionaux et de la Principauté de Liège (milieu du 17e siècle à la veille de la Révolution Française)', in J.-P. Poussou (ed.), *Etudes sur les villes en Europe Occidentale (milieu du 17e siècle à la veille de la Révolution Française)* (Paris, 1981), p. 217; D. Morsa, 'L'urbanisation de la Belgique (1500–1800): Taille, hiérarchie et dynamique des villes', *Revue du Nord*, 79:320 (1997), pp. 303–30, on p. 310.

74. Lottin and Soly, 'Aspects de l'histoire', p. 218; Morsa, 'L'urbanisation de la Belgique', pp. 309, 330.

75. P. Deprez and C. Vandenbroeke, 'Population Growth and Distribution and Urbanisation in Belgium during the Demographic Transition', in R. Lawton and R. Lee (eds), *Urban Population Development in Western Europe from the Late Eighteenth to the Early Twentieth Century* (Liverpool: Liverpool University Press, 1989), pp. 220–57; P. M. M. Klep, *Bevolking en arbeid in transformatie: Een onderzoek in Brabant, 1700–1900* (Nijmegen: SUN, 1981); Lottin and Soly, 'Aspects de l'histoire'; Morsa, 'L'urbanisation de la Belgique'; H. Van der Wee, 'Industrial Dynamics and the Process of Urbanization and De-Urbanization in the Low Countries from the Late Middle Ages to the Eighteenth Century. A Synthesis', in H. Van der Wee (ed.), *The Rise and Decline of Urban Industries in Italy and in the Low Countries (Late Middle Ages–Early Modern Times)* (Leuven: Leuven University Press, 1988), pp. 307–82.

76. M. Carlier, 'Migration Trends in the Towns of Flanders and Brabant (15th–18th Century)', in *Le migrazioni in Europa secc. XIII–XVIII: Atti della Venticinquesima Settimana di Studi, 3–8 maggio 1993* (Prato: Instituto Internazionale di Storia Economica 'F. Datini', 1994), pp. 355–70, on pp. 359–60; Klep, *Bevolking*, pp. 58–65; Lottin and Soly, 'Aspects de l'histoire', pp. 225–6.

77. D. Morsa, 'Sociale structuren en identiteiten in de Belgische steden in het licht van recente werken', *Tijdschrift van het Gemeentekrediet*, 47:184 (1993), pp. 37–60, on p. 49; D. Morsa, 'Les immigrants dans les villes des principautés belges (17e–18e siècles)', in Menjot and Pinol (eds), *Les immigrants et la ville*, pp. 171–91, on p. 175.

78. Klep, *Bevolking*, p. 63.

79. J. De Belder, C. Gijssels, C. Vandenbroeke and L. van der Straeten, *Arbeid en tewerkstelling in Antwerpen 1796: Een socio-professionele en demografische analyse: Werkdocumenten* (n.p., 1985); C. Gyssels and L. van der Straeten, *Bevolking, arbeid en tewerkstelling in West-Vlaanderen (1796–1815)* (Gent, 1986); C. Gyssels and L. van der Straeten, *Bevolking, arbeid en tewerkstelling in de provincie Antwerpen op het einde van het ancien régime* (n.p., [1990]), p. 84; L. Jaspers and C. Stevens, *Arbeid en tewerkstelling in Oost-Vlaanderen op het einde van het ancien régime* (Gent, 1985), pp. 83–4; J. Verbeemen, 'Mechelen in 1796: Demografische en sociaal-economische studie', *Handelingen van de Koninklijke*

Kring voor Oudheidkunde, Letteren en Kunst van Mechelen (1954), pp. 135–79, on p. 140.

80. Bairoch, *De Jéricho à Mexico*, p. 288; de Vries, *European Urbanization*, p. 45; Deprez and Vandenbroeke, 'Population Growth', p. 233.

81. Deprez and Vandenbroeke, 'Population Growth', pp. 233, 235.

82. Ibid., pp. 226, 233; R. J. Lesthaeghe, *The Decline of Belgian Fertility, 1800–1970* (Princeton, NJ: Princeton University Press, 1977), p. 38.

83. M. Bruwier, 'Ondernemers en zakenlieden', in J.-M. Duvosquel and H. Hasquin (eds), *België onder het Frans bewind, 1792–1815* (Brussel: Gemeentekrediet, 1993), pp. 229–51; J. Dhondt, 'L'industrie cottonière gantoise à l'époque française', *Revue d'Histoire Moderne et Contemporaine*, 2 (1955), pp. 233–79; P. Lebrun, M. Bruwier, J. Dhondt and G. Hansotte, *Essai sur la révolution industrielle en Belgique, 1770–1847* (Bruxelles: Palais des Académies, 1979); J. Mokyr, *Industrialization in the Low Countries, 1795–1850* (New Haven, CT, and London: Yale University Press, 1976); H. Van der Wee, 'La "révolution industrielle" en Belgique, 1800–1850. Un survol', in B. Van der Herten, M. Oris and J. Roegiers (eds), *La Belgique industrielle en 1850: Deux cents images d'un monde nouveau* (Deurne: Crédit Communal, 1995), pp. 29–32, on pp. 31–2; K. Veraghtert, 'De economie in de Zuidelijke Nederlanden 1790–1970', in Blok (ed.), *Algemene geschiedenis*, pp. 127–39, on pp. 128–9.

84. J. De Belder, 'Stad en platteland: Inleiding tot de problematiek', *Taal en Sociale Integratie*, 4 (1981), pp. 169–82, on pp. 173–4.

85. Deprez and Vandenbroeke, 'Population Growth', pp. 230–3; J. Kruithof, 'De demografische ontwikkeling in de 19de eeuw', in *Bouwstoffen voor de geschiedenis van Antwerpen in de 19de eeuw: Instellingen, economie, kultuur* (Antwerpen: Lloyd Anversois, 1964), pp. 508–43, on pp. 509–12.

86. De Belder, 'Stad en platteland', pp. 172–5.

87. C. Vandenbroeke, *Sociale geschiedenis van het Vlaamse volk* (Leuven: Kritak, 1984), pp. 25–30, 127–50. It was the Flemish social and economic development of the eighteenth century which formed the original inspiration for Mendels's well-known thesis on proto-industrialization: F. Mendels, 'Proto-Industrialization: The First Phase of the Industrialization Process', *Journal of Economic History*, 32:1 (1972), pp. 241–61; F. Mendels, *Industrialization and Population Pressure in Eighteenth-Century Flanders* (New York: Arno Press, 1981).

88. H. Coppejans-Desmet, 'Bevolking en tewerkstelling in transformatie op het Vlaamse platteland (einde 18de–midden 19de eeuw)', *Tijdschrift van het Gemeentekrediet*, 48:190 (1994), pp. 15–34, on pp. 18–24, 32–4; De Belder, 'Stad en platteland', pp. 175–6; G. Jacquemyns, *Histoire de la crise économique de Flandres, 1845–1850* (Bruxelles, 1929); H. Van der Wee and K. Veraghtert, 'De economie van 1814 tot 1944', in *Twintig eeuwen Vlaanderen* (Hasselt: Heideland-Orbis, 1978), pp. 130–211, pp. 144–8.

89. De Belder, 'Stad en platteland', p. 177; Vandenbroeke, *Sociale geschiedenis*, pp. 177–8. See also Mokyr, *Industrialization*, pp. 245–6.

90. Jacquemyns, *Histoire*, pp. 381–6. Even if we allow the true number of emigrants to have been double the number recorded (cf. ibid, p. 386, n. 1), emigration levels remained comparatively small.

91. T. Feys, 'Radeloosheid in crisistijd: Pogingen van de Belgische autoriteiten om een deel van de arme bevolking naar de Verenigde Staten te sturen, 1847–1856', *Belgisch Tijdschrift voor Nieuwste Geschiedenis*, 34:2 (2004), pp. 195–230; D. Musschoot, *Wij gaan naar Amerika: Vlaamse landverhuizers naar de Nieuwe Wereld 1850–1930* (Tielt: Lan-

noo, 2002); L. Schepens, *Van vlaskutser tot franschman: Bijdrage tot de geschiedenis van de Westvlaamse plattelandsbevolking in de negentiende eeuw* (Brugge, 1973), pp. 111–90; J. Stengers, *Emigration et immigration en Belgique au 19e et 20e siècles* (Bruxelles: Académie royale des sciences d'outre-mer, 1978), pp. 36–61.

92. V. Aelbrecht, 'L'immigration ouvrière belge à Tourcoing durant le Second Empire', *Belgisch Tijdschrift voor Nieuwste Geschiedenis*, 21:3–4 (1990), pp. 351–81; De Belder, 'Stad en platteland', p. 177; Deprez and Vandenbroeke, 'Population Growth', p. 232; N. Dhordain and D. Terrier, 'Accumulation de la main-d'oeuvre et comportements délinquants: Les villes du textile dans la région lilloise au cours des années 1860', *Revue du Nord*, 84:347 (2002), pp. 691–721; Moch, *Moving Europeans*, pp. 132–6; L. Schepens, 'Émigration saisonnière et émigration définitive en Flandre Occidentale au 19e siècle', *Revue du Nord*, 56 (1974), pp. 427–31; C. Vandenbroeke, 'Migraties tussen Vlaanderen en Noord-Frankrijk in de 19de en 20ste eeuw', *Frans-Nederlands Jaarboek* (1993), pp. 157–68.

93. E. Mahaim, *Les abonnements d'ouvriers sur les lignes de chemins de fer belges et leurs effets sociaux* (Bruxelles, 1910); B. Van der Herten, 'La révolution industrielle stimulée par une révolution des communications', in Van der Herten et al. (eds), *La Belgique industrielle*, pp. 41–8; Van der Wee and Veraghtert, 'De economie', pp. 138–9, 157–61.

94. T. Eggerickx and M. Poulain, 'Les phases du processus d'urbanisation en Belgique', in *Croissance démographique et urbanisation: Politiques du peuplement et aménagement du territoire* (Paris: PUF, 1993), pp. 83–94, on pp. 85–8; A. H. Kittell, 'The Revolutionary Period of the Industrial Revolution: Industrial Innovation and Population Displacement in Belgium, 1830–1880', *Journal of Social History*, 1:2 (1967), pp. 119–48.

95. Whereby in particular Flemish newcomers appear as a new (or strongly expanded) immigrant group in many places from the late 1840s onwards. See M. De Metsenaere, 'Migraties in de gemeente Sint-Joost-ten-Node in het midden van de negentiende eeuw: Methodologische inleiding tot de studie van de groei en verfransing van de Brusselse agglomeratie', *Taal en Sociale Integratie* (1978), pp. 81–152, on pp. 121–9; C. Dumont, *Migrations intérieures et immigration dans le bassin industriel de Charleroi 1800–1866* (Bruxelles: ARA, 1994), pp. 181–3, 198–9; Eggerickx and Poulain, 'Les phases', pp. 86–8; K. Lambert, 'Industrialisatie in een plattelandsgemeente. Effecten op bevolking en arbeid te Sleidinge, 1820–1914', *Revue Belge d'Histoire Contemporaine* (1984), pp. 381–419, on pp. 389–91; Oris, 'Fertility and Migration', pp. 171–2; S. Pasleau, 'Les migrations internes en Belgique: Ruptures et continuités du XVIIe au XXe siècle', in Eiras Roel and Rey Castelao (eds), *Les migrations internes*, pp. 179–204, on pp. 188–90; M. Poulain, M. Foulon, A. Degioanni and P. Darlu, 'Flemish Immigration in Wallonia and in France: Patronyms as Data', *History of the Family*, 5:2 (2000), pp. 227–41; P. Van den Eeckhout, 'Determinanten van het 19de-eeuwse sociaal-economische leven te Brussel: Hun betekenis voor de laagste bevolkingsklassen' (PhD dissertation, Vrije Universiteit Brussel, 1980), pp. 70–5; P. Van den Eeckhout, 'De rekrutering van de Brusselse armenbevolking in relatie met de afstotingsmechanismen in het gebied van herkomst', *Taal en Sociale Integratie*, 4 (1981), pp. 235–7.

96. Deprez and Vandenbroeke, 'Population Growth', pp. 235 ff.; see also E. C. Vollans, 'Urban Development in Belgium since 1830', in R. P. Beckinsale and J. M. Houston (eds), *Urbanization and its Problems: Essays in Honour of E. W. Gilbert* (Oxford: Blackwell, 1968), pp. 171–93.

97. Bourdelais, 'Demographic Changes'; C. Desama, 'Démographie et industrialisation: Le modèle verviétois (1800–1850)', *Revue du Nord* (1981), pp. 147–55; R. Leboutte,

Reconversions de la main d'ouvre et transition démographique. Les bassins industriels en aval de Liège, 17e–19e siècles (Paris: Les Belles Lettres, 1988); Oris, 'Fertility and Migration'; M. Oris, 'L'impact d'une dépression économique sur le champ migratoire d'une grande ville industrielle: L'expérience de Seraing entre 1857 et 1900', *Revue du Nord*, 79:320–1 (1997), pp. 531–48; S. Pasleau, 'Structures démographiques d'un faubourg industriel de Liège: Grivegnée en 1856', *Belgisch Tijdschrift voor Nieuwste Geschiedenis*, 16:3–4 (1985), pp. 397–432; S. Pasleau, 'L'immigration des travailleurs à Seraing durant la seconde moitié du 19e siècle', *Annales de Démographie Historique* (1993), pp. 227–50.

98. Immigrants' disproportionately high birth rates appear to have been related not only to their favourable age structure, but also to their relatively low average age of marriage, supported by the expansion of industrial opportunities. See, in particular, Oris, 'Fertility and Migration', and the other cited studies.

99. Cf. De Belder, 'Stad en platteland'.

100. M. De Metsenaere, *Taalmuur: Sociale muur? De negentiende-eeuwse taalverhoudingen te Brussel als resultaat van geodemografische en sociale processen* (Brussel: VUBPress (Centrum voor Interdisciplinair Onderzoek naar de Brusselse Taaltoestanden), 1988); de Schaepdrijver, *Elites for the Capital?*. See also Y. Leblicq and M. De Metsenaere, 'De groei', in J. Stengers and A. André (eds), *Brussel: Groei van een hoofdstad* (Antwerpen: Mercatorfonds, 1979), pp. 167–77, on pp. 173–7.

101. Most importantly, see Coppejans-Desmet, 'Bevolking'; J. Dhondt, 'Notes sur les ouvriers industriels gantois à l'époque française', *Revue du Nord*, 36:142 (1954), pp. 309–24; Kittell, 'The Revolutionary Period'; Klep, *Bevolking*; Kruithof, 'De demografische ontwikkeling'; Lis, *Social Change*.

102. Figures derive from a confrontation between J. De Belder, 'Elementen van sociale identiteit van de Antwerpse bevolking op het einde van de 18de eeuw: Een kwantitatieve studie', 2 vols (PhD dissertation, Rijksuniversiteit Gent, 1974), who studied the 1796 census, and J. Hannes, 'Bijdrage tot de ontwikkeling van een kwantitatief-kritische methode in de sociale geschiedschrijving' (PhD dissertation, Rijksuniversiteit Gent, 1969), who examined the 1830 census results. I am very grateful to both scholars for allowing me to access and quote their invaluable unpublished PhD research. See also Chapters 3 and 4 for more detailed analyses of these census results.

103. Lis, *Social Change*. Both the marginalization of female employment and the growing irregularity of demand for mainly unskilled labour were socio-economic characteristics that Antwerp shared with many port cities in the same period, and that can be attributed both to specificities of the nineteenth century and the particularities of port activity. See A. Knotter, 'Poverty and the Family Income Cycle: Casual Laborers in Amsterdam in the First Half of the 20th Century', *History of the Family*, 9:2 (2004), pp. 221–37; Lee, 'The Socio-Economic'; R. Lee and R. Lawton, 'Port Development and the Demographic Dynamics of European Urbanization', in R. Lawton and R. Lee (eds), *Population and Society in Western European Port Cities, ca. 1650–1939* (Liverpool: Liverpool University Press, 2002), pp. 1–36, on pp. 5–18.

104. On the origin of these and other demographic figures used here, see Appendix I.1.

105. See above, p. 36.

106. P. Lombaerde, 'De militaire werken van Louis-Charles Boistard en Simon Bernard te Antwerpen tijdens het Eerste Keizerrijk', *Belgisch Tijdschrift voor Militaire Geschiedenis*, 25 (1984), pp. 285–328, on pp. 306–9. If we could consistently subtract the deaths of 'foreigners having died in the hospitals or other places' for these years, which were some-

times mentioned alongside the numbers of 'normal' deaths, the result might actually show an undercurrent of modest birth-surplus, as the excess mortality due to immigrants resulted in a temporary 'Sharlin-effect': cf. Sharlin, 'Natural Decrease'. The observable increase in birth rates in the later French period (1806–15) is somewhat distorted by the inclusion of stillbirths for these years, but nevertheless remains marked, and is partly a reflection of the strong population expansion recorded for this period – and possibly also of the presence of a large number of soldiers.

107. Cf. Schofield et al. (eds), *The Decline of Mortality*.
108. Crude birth rates in Belgium for the period 1846–55 and 1856–65 averaged 28.7 and 31.1 per 1,000 respectively; crude death rates for the periods 1847–56 and 1857–66 averaged 23.4 per 1,000 for both periods. See R. Andre and J. Pereira-Roque, *La démographie de la Belgique au XIXe siècle* (Bruxelles: Université Libre de Bruxelles, 1974), pp. 21, 71.
109. Lee, 'The Socio-Economic'; Lee and Lawton, 'Port Development'.
110. Available birth- and death-figures for the period 1803–15 include stillbirths. For the periods 1755–84 and 1785–95, the average number of births and deaths is based only on the available figures for 1780–8. For the period 1796–1805 the averages are based on the available figures for the years 1802–5. Rates are calculated per 1,000 inhabitants of the respective mid-populations. Population figures and rates from 1755 to 1846 refer to the *legal* population, those thereafter to the *actual* population. The exceptionally high birth rate recorded for the period 1816–20 might partly be attributable to the large difference between legal (used as reference) and actual population in this period. The net residual increase for the period 1840–6 probably lay somewhat higher than suggested here (and that of the period 1830–9 somewhat lower), as the 1840 population size retained for calculations was probably somewhat overrated.
111. For sources, see Appendix I.1. Rates are calculated per 1,000 inhabitants of the respective mid-populations. Population figures and rates 1806–46 are based on *legal* population figures, those thereafter on *actual* population figures. Gross mobility calculations are based on the figures presented on immigration and net migration. 'Persistence' is measured as the percentage ratio between net migration and immigration, 'yield' as the percentage ratio between net migration and gross mobility.
112. A sample from the emigration registers of 1829 and 1855 showed that at least 85 and 87 per cent respectively of emigrants recorded in these years were people who had immigrated to Antwerp at an earlier stage (ERPI+1829, ERPI 1855).
113. See Appendix I.1.
114. Cf. Knotter, *Economische transformatie*, p. 294; Van Dijk, *Rotterdam*.
115. F. Daelemans, 'Bronnen voor het historisch-demografisch onderzoek van het hertogdom Brabant tijdens het ancien régime: Enkele kritische nota's', in F. Daelemans (ed.), *Bronnen en methoden van de historische demografie voor 1850* (Brussel: ARA, 1984), pp. 45–73, on pp. 57–60.
116. Local registration activities under the *ancien régime* were very selective, often aimed either at privileged groups – in order to establish their prerogatives, as in the case of burgher books – or at groups considered marginal and/or potentially subversive, such as poor immigrants, vagrants and boarding-house lodgers, with an eye to keeping them in check. Other potential sources on migration for this period, like marriage registers, also remain selective and biased towards a selective group of 'settling' migrants. See A. Winter, 'Patterns of Migration', pp. 127–35, for a discussion of these earlier sources.
117. On the role of the 'revolutionary' concept of nationhood and citizenship in making the registration of population (and the identification of the *étranger*) a prime objective of

the emergent state bureaucracy, see M.-C. Blanc-Chaléard, 'Des logiques nationales aux logiques ethniques', *Le Mouvement Social*, 188 (1999), pp. 3–16; L. Lucassen, 'The Domination of the National Category: A Review of Some Recent Studies on (Im)migration and Nation Building', *Immigrants and Minorities*, 14:3 (1995), pp. 319–31; G. Noiriel, *Le creuset français: Histoire de l'immigration, XIXe–XXe siècles* (Paris: Seuil, 1988).

118. See Winter, 'Patterns of Migration', pp. 129–34, for a discussion of the legislative background to these different measures.

119. SAA, MA-BZA, D 1–5; SAA, MA-BZA, B 1–82.

120. H. Balthazar, J. De Belder, J. Hannes and J. Verhelst, *Bronnen voor de sociale geschiedenis van de 19e eeuw (1794–1914)* (Leuven: Nauwelaerts, 1965), pp. 19–21.

121. See Winter, 'Patterns of Migration', pp. 134–6. Emigration registers exist on a continual basis from 1820 onwards (SAA, MA, 74780), but provide only summary information. See Appendix I.2.

122. SAA, MA, 2668/1–18. We know that registration continued for the periods missing thanks to the entries' numeration, original inventories and references in linked sources (See Appendix I.1).

123. Although in some cases, for instance in Paris, they must have existed, but might not have been conserved. Cf. *Pasinomie: collection complete des lois, arêtes et règlements généraux qui peuvent être invoqués en Belgique* (1789–), 1st series, vol. 10, pp. 250–4: 13 Messidor VIII (01/07/1800). Unfortunately, explicit normative guidelines on the compilation of these immigration registers in the Antwerp case could not be retrieved, which means that they had to be inferred from confronting national legislation and fragmentary local decrees with knowledge of local practice elsewhere and the analysis of the different sources produced. See Winter, 'Patterns of Migration', pp. 136–42.

124. Such security cards were for instance issued to the male Parisian population in 1794 with *Pasinomie*, 1st series, vol. 4, pp. 431–2: 19=19/09/1792. See, for instance, O. Faron and C. Grange, 'Un recensement parisien sous la révolution: L'exemple des cartes de sûreté de 1793', *Mélanges de l'école française de Rome: Italie et Mediterranée*, 111:2 (1999), pp. 795–826; M. Reinhard, 'Connaissance de la population de la France pendant la Révolution', in M. Reinhard (ed.), *Contributions à l'histoire démographique de la révolution française, 2me série* (Paris: Commission d'histoire économique et sociale de la Révolution Française, 1965), pp. 7–18. They were distributed in Antwerp for the first time in 1796 in concurrence with the census, when they appear to have been intended as some sort of mini-passport for travelling within the borders of the canton. Cf. SAA, MA, 673/1, *Extract ... 3 Germinal IV (23/03/1796)*; *Proclamatie ... 3 Fructidor IV (21/08/1796)*; RAA, PA, A 131/30. A new round of *cartes de sûreté* were distributed in 1798, this time explicitly intended as a requisite identity document for all inhabitants, as a measure of enhancing overall registration and control. Cf. SAA, MA, 673/1, *Extrait ... 8 Messidor VI (26/06/1798)*. Keeping an additional register for providing new entrants with such documents, would amount to a *de facto* immigration register, and this would explain why the first volume in the immigration register series, from 1803 to 1808, bears the title of 'Registre aux Cartes de Sûreté' – although it only deals with immigrants. That the two succeeding volumes changes their names to 'Registre d'hôtel et de cartes de sûreté', attests to their conflation with other legislative requirements on the registration of movement.

125. This altered use was eventually confirmed by the switch to the term 'Registre de permis de séjour' from 1811 onwards – while continuity in function and practice with the previous volumes was evident, among other things by continual numbering. The only reference to the term of *permis de séjour* in national legislation is limited to Paris (*Pasi-*

nomie, 1st series, vol. 10, pp. 250–4: 13 Messidor VIII (01/07/1800)), but limiting the theoretically general *cartes de sûreté* to certain immigrant groups has been known to have happened elsewhere at certain moments: see *Pasinomie*, 1st series, vol. 6, p. 574: 23 Messidor III (11/07/1795); 2nd series, vol. 1, p. 21: 03/02/1814; *Nederlandse Staatscourant*, 78 (31 March 1815).

126. The only normative text I have retrieved that explicitly deals with the matter, a draft instruction by the hand of the mayor dated 29 August 1806, ordered all non-local persons of both sexes arriving in Antwerp 'with the intention of setting up residence or for a temporary stay' to present themselves to the police office the day after their arrival to receive a temporary security card in return for their passports (SAA, MA, 464/3, n°. 2: Bureau de police du 29 aout 1806). The comprehensive scope of the residence card registers is confirmed by the list of new enrolments in the population books between 1801 and 1805 in SAA, V, 1812 (the only such list preserved for the first half of the nineteenth century): all of the people listed there had previously been issued with a *carte de sûreté*.

127. The 1806 instruction (see previous note) stated that when a residence card holder wished to leave town again, he or she was to exchange the card for a new passport at the central police station. Alternatively, he or she could be transferred to the population registers after a while – the 1806 instruction spoke of one year. The benchmark of one year corresponds to the time after which a *domicile de fait* was generally considered acquired. See *Pasinomie*, 1st series, vol. 1, pp. 150–1: 1920/04/1790, art. 6; pp. 195–6: 30/05/06/1790, art. 2; vol. 5, pp. 501–5: 24 Vendémiaire II (15/10/1793), Titre V, art. 4; vol. 7, p. 79: 10 Vendémiaire IV (02/10/1795), Titre III, art. 4; vol. 10, p. 20: 22 Frimaire VIII (13/12/1799), art. 6. From practice it is clear that eventual transfers to the population registers did not observe strict criteria in terms of length of stay, but were probably decided more or less on an *ad hoc* basis and as a result of certain administrative preoccupations. See Winter, 'Patterns of Migration', pp. 139–40.

128. Referred to in the margins of the population books with 'par autorisation'. In the 1810s, such direct inscriptions *par autorisation* were rare in the population books, and they became markedly more frequent in the 1820s.

129. See Winter, 'Patterns of Migration', pp. 140–2, for a discussion of possible criteria.

130. The conserved residence card registers of 1828–30 recorded only a maximum of 1,800 newcomers per year, while fragmentary reports mention a recorded number of newcomers of 2,300 in 1827 and 2,600 in 1828 (RAA, PA, J 158–9). See Appendix I.1.

131. This could be established on the basis of fragmentary registers retained at district level. SAA, MA, 2672, 73958; MA 2668/19–25; 450/170. See also Appendix I.1.

132. However, by ordering all residents with their *habitation effective* in the *commune* to be included in the population registers, the new instructions (*Pasinomie*, 3rd series, vol. 16, pp. 390–5: 30/06/1846) did not solve the inherent ambiguity of residence in a migratory context. See R. Leboutte and R. Obotela, 'Les registres de population en Belgique: Genèse d'une technique administrative et d'une source de démographie historique', *Handelingen van de Koninklijke Commissie voor Geschiedenis*, 154:3–4 (1988), pp. 285–305, on pp. 293–4. Separate nominal lists of new registrations to the population registers – the functional successor to the previous 'immigration registers' – are available only from 1894 onwards: SAA, MA, 74656–8.

133. F. Caestecker, *Alien Policy in Belgium, 1840–1940: The Creation of Guest Workers, Refugees and Illegal Aliens* (New York: Berghahn Books, 2000), pp. 4–8; S. Vervaeck, *Gids voor sociale geschiedenis. Bronnen voor de studie van immigratie en emigratie. Hedendaagse*

tijden, deel 1: Archiefbronnen bewaard in het Algemeen Rijksarchief (Brussel: ARA, 1996), pp. 25–7.

134. SAA, MA, 44248–44787.

135. In particular the non-declaration of life-events – the registration of which had previously been the exclusive domain of the Church – was propagated as a form of passive resistance against the new 'godless' order in the early years of French rule. However, this form of 'silent resistance' appears to have been strongest in the turbulent 1790s. By the time of the ascendancy of Napoleon, anti-French feelings had subsided a great deal, and by the early 1800s the civil registry began to proceed rather smoothly in the Southern Netherlands. Likewise, early censuses and population registers were flawed by the unwillingness, ignorance and lack of resources of the populace as well as of many local authorities – more so in rural than in urban areas – yet benefited from an increasing professionalization of local administration in the early nineteenth century. See Balthazar et al., *Bronnen*, pp. 19–20; A. Cosemans, 'Volkstellingen, burgerlijke stand en memoires in Brabant onder het Franse Regime en in het Verenigd Koninkrijk (1795–1829)', *Handelingen van de Zuidnederlandse Maatschappij voor Taal- en Letterkunde en Geschiedenis*, 17 (1963), pp. 47–66, on pp. 62–4; Leboutte and Obotela, 'Les registres', pp. 287–8; J. Mertens, 'Burgerlijke stand en bevolkingsregisters', *Vlaamse Stam: Tijdschrift voor Familiegeschiedenis* (1974), pp. 525–39, on p. 529; M. Poulain, 'Du registre de population aux statistiques de migration interne en Belgique: Critique des sources et correction des données', *Population et Famille*, 45:3 (1978), pp. 1–45, on p. 4. Of course, the sources emanating from the registrars' office cannot account for conscious attempts to evade registration, but those who wanted to remain unnoticed, like young men hoping to avoid conscription (cf. S. Vrielinck, *De territoriale indeling van België (1795–1963): Bestuursgeografisch en statistisch repertorium van de gemeenten en de supracommunale eenheden (administratief en gerechtelijk): Met de officiële uitslagen van de volkstellingen* (Leuven: Universitaire Pers, 2000), pp. 2058–61), would have been well advised to avoid the military stronghold and relatively well-policed city of Antwerp altogether.

136. Registration practice, for instance, benefited greatly from the presence of a Commissaire Général de Police from 1808 onwards, who answered directly to the Ministre de Police Générale and was explicitly charged with the control of newcomers: *Pasinomie*, 1st series, vol. 10, pp. 319–23: 5 Brumaire IX (27/20/1800); *Pasinomie*, 1st series, vol. 13, pp. 258–9: 23 Fructidor XIII (10/09/1805); R. Boumans, *Het Antwerps stadsbestuur voor en tijdens de Franse overheersing* (Brugge: De Tempel, 1965), pp. 536–7. I have found many incidences of control and even prosecution to compel compliance with registration rules, through passport control at the city gates and police raids (e.g. RAA, PA, F 75B, 130/10, 131/23; PA, F 9; SAA, MA, 445/1, n°. 1; 464/3, n°. 2; 673/1; 673/2, n°. 1). However, these measures were most rigorous only in certain periods of heightened military concern. In 1811 we learn that the control of passports was by that time limited to voyagers entering the city in coaches or carriages, and that people on foot could easily slip through: RAA, PA, A 75 B. A selected reading from the regular reports from the Antwerp Mayor to the Prefect and the Ministre de Police Générale (RAA, PA, F 53–9; PA, A 126/7; SAA, MA, 465) indicates that arrests of strangers provided with insufficient identity documents within the Antwerp city walls, for instance by police patrols and visits to lodging houses, were relatively frequent – some ten every fortnight in 1811 – but were seldom followed by any punishment. In 1832 – also a period of political unease – we found reference to a round-up of *sans-papiers*, which likewise did not yield much result: SAA, MA, 2635, 24/11/1832. Although stronger than elsewhere,

and stringent at times of heightened concern, then, the manpower of the relevant local authorities remained too small to establish full compliance to registration rules solely by active control or repressive measures.

137. The 1818 Antwerp act even stated explicitly that the local authorities would provide no services whatsoever to persons who neglected to declare changes in residence: RAB, PK Antw 2001 B, 231, n°. 34, art. 8. In turn, there are no indications that the risk of refusal might have deterred people from declaring their arrival to the Antwerp authorities: local authorities had few reasons to refuse residence even to the humblest of newcomers, as the specificities of poor relief organization meant that they rarely bore the brunt of immigrants' insolvency anyway (see below).

138. G. Engbersen, 'De illegale vreemdeling', in J. Burgers and G. Engbersen (eds), *Illegale vreemdelingen in Rotterdam* (Meppel: Boom, 1999), pp. 11–29, on pp. 11–13.

139. E. Hélin, 'Aux confins de la démographie historique et de l'histoire sociale: Mesurer les migrations', *Belgisch Tijdschrift voor Nieuwste Geschiedenis*, 21:3–4 (1990), pp. 605–38, on p. 613. SAA, MA, 673/1, *Besluyt ...* 05/07/1831, art. 3, only obliges 'fathers and sons older than sixteen' to provide themselves with a 'security card'. Women were demonstrably under-represented in the early years of the residence card registers, which appear to have been considered fully applicable to immigrating women only after 1811; female domestic servants in particular are all but absent from the previous registers, making the early registers badly suited to exploring gender-specific patterns of migration.

140. For instance, newcomers who came to Napoleonic Antwerp via purely coercive or military channels of recruitment, such as the import in 1804 of several hundreds of convicts from Bicêtre and Brest to work as forced labourers in the construction of the new arsenal, or the deployment of three *bataillons de l'Escaut* on shipbuilding activities, did not leave any trace in the residence card registers: C. Epin, *Les ouvriers des arsenaux de la Marine sous Napoléon, vivre et survivre en travaillant pour l'état* (Paris: l'Herminette, 1990), pp. 41–9; Lis, *Social Change*, p. 42; Lombaerde, 'De militaire werken', p. 294. Epin's study illustrates how alternative sources produced by defence or maritime institutions can be deployed to shed more light on these particular groups.

141. D. Hanson, 'Une source d'histoire sociale: Les listes d'habitants dressées par la police, à Liège de 1797 à 1930', *Annuaire d'Histoire Liégoise*, 20:44 (1979), pp. 115–64, on p. 159; Hélin, 'Aux confins', p. 610; Leboutte and Obotela, 'Les registres', p. 295; Poulain, 'Du registre', pp. 4–30; J. Stengers, 'Les mouvements migratoires en Belgique aux 19e et 20e siècles', in *Les migrations internationales de la fin du 18e siècle à nos jours* (Paris: CNRS, 1980), pp. 283–317, on p. 284; M. G. Termote, 'Statistiques migratoires directes: Le registre de population' *Migrations intérieures: Méthodes d'observation et d'analyse* (Paris: Centre National de la Recherche Scientifique, 1975), pp. 157–64, on p. 160. The Antwerp administration also frequently complained that recorded emigration figures were tenuous because many residents left town without making a formal declaration: *Rapport sur l'administration et la situation des affaires de la ville d'Anvers* (Anvers: Stad Antwerpen, 1836–1915), 1837, p. 13; *Rapport ... d'Anvers*, 1840, p. 10.

142. For a discussion of settlement legislation in the Southern Low Countries, see A. Winter, 'Caught between Law and Practice: Migrants and Settlement Legislation in the Southern Low Countries in a Comparative Perspective, c. 1700–1900', *Rural History*, 19:2 (2008), pp. 137–62. See also D. Van Damme, 'Onderstandswoonst, sedentarisering en stad-platteland-tegenstellingen: Evolutie en betekenis van de wetgeving op de onderstandwoonst

in Belgie (einde achttiende tot einde negentiende eeuw)', *Belgisch Tijdschrift voor Nieuwste geschiedenis*, 21:3–4 (1990), pp. 483–534.

143. *Pasinomie*, 1st series, vol. 5, pp. 501–5: 24 Vendémiaire II (15/10/1793), Titre V, art. 4; 2nd series, vol. 4, pp. 481–5: 28/11/1818, arts 8, 13; 3rd series, vol. 15, pp. 13–24: 18/02/1845; vol. 19, pp. 334–6: 28/06/1849; *Exposé de la situation du royaume: Statistique générale de la Belgique (Période décennale de 1851–1860)* (Bruxelles: Ministre de l'Intérieur, Imp. Th. Lesigne, 1863–5), 100Q ff.

144. OCMWA, BW, 933, 946, 947 III.

145. These were predisposed towards 'invalid' poor – the old and disabled – and single-parent families and households with many children, the most vulnerable family- and life-cycle phases: Lis, *Social Change*, pp. 102–14. Possibly because of their household structure, these sources often concern sojourners who had typically already spent some time in Antwerp, and were also likely to stay on for a long time.

146. To be sure, social selection played a role in the composition of the hospital's population. Although the city hospital catered to a variety of both insolvent and paying patients, higher-middle and upper classes were all but absent from the public hospital, which in perception and practice remained a provision for the poorer sections of the urban population. These poorer sections who could not afford home treatment, however, made up the bulk of the urban – and immigrant – population. Among these groups, the risk and frequency of illness was high for all ages and both sexes: young adults aged between 16 and 35 made up between 40 and 50 per cent of the hospital's population in the nineteenth century, as opposed to only some 10 per cent for the over-66: L. Vermeiren, 'Van gasthuis tot ziekenhuis: De negentiende eeuw (tot 1925)', in *750 jaar St.-Elisabethgasthuis te Antwerpen, 1238–1988* (Brussel: Gemeentekrediet, 1988), pp. 145–226, on pp. 173–4, 182–8.

147. OCMWA, BG, EG 1–66 (men), 131–85 (women).

148. De Belder, 'Elementen'; Hannes, 'Bijdrage'; Lis, *Social Change*.

149. For more details on the selection and sampling methods used, see Appendix I.2.

150. *Rapport ... d'Anvers*, 1837–60; *Statistique de la Belgique: Population. Mouvement de l'état civil pendant l'année [1841–50]* (Bruxelles: Imprimerie de Vandooren Frères, 1843–51); *Documents statistiques publiés par le département de l'Intérieur avec le concours de la Commission centrale de statistique, 1851–1867* (Bruxelles, 1857–69), and various published census results.

3 Migration to a Regional Textile Centre

1. K. Degryse, 'The Artistocratization of the Antwerp Mercantile Elite (17th–18th Century)', in C. Lesger and L. Noordegraaf (eds), *Entrepeneurs and Entrepreneurship in Early Modern Times: Merchants and Industrialists within the Orbit of the Dutch Staple Market* (Den Haag: Stichting Hollandse Historische Reeks, 1995), pp. 35–42; C. Lis, 'Sociale politiek in Antwerpen, 1779: Het controleren van de relatieve overbevolking en het reguleren van de arbeidsmarkt', *Tijdschrift voor Sociale Geschiedenis*, 2 (1976), pp. 146–66, on pp. 152–3; Lis, *Social Change*, pp. 6–16; L. Michielsen, 'De handel', in *Antwerpen in de achttiende eeuw: Instellingen, economie, cultuur* (Antwerpen: De Sikkel, 1952), pp. 94–122; A. K. L. Thijs, 'De geschiedenis van de suikernijverheid te Antwerpen (16de–19de eeuw): Een terreinverkenning', *Bijdragen tot de Geschiedenis*, 62 (1979), pp. 23–50; A. K. L. Thijs, 'The River Scheldt Closed for Two Centuries, 1585–1790', in F. Suykens (ed.), *Antwerp: A Port for All Seasons* (Deurne: MIM, 1986), pp. 169–278,

on pp. 172–202; A. K. L. Thijs, *Van 'werkwinkel' tot 'fabriek': De textielnijverheid te Antwerpen (einde 15de–begin 19de eeuw)* (Brussel: Gemeentekrediet, 1987), pp. 180–5.

2. Blondé, *Een economie*, pp. 102–4; De Belder, 'Elementen', vol. 1, pp. 23–45; H. Soly, 'Social Aspects of Structural Changes in the Urban Industries of Eighteenth-Century Brabant and Flanders', in Van der Wee (ed.), *The Rise and Decline*, pp. 241–60, on pp. 249–50.
3. B. Blondé, 'Economische groei en armoede in de pruikentijd: Een voorbeeld van de Brabantse steden, 1750–1780', in C. Reyns (ed.), *Werkgelegenheid en inkomen* (Antwerpen: UFSIA, 1996), pp. 343–58; Blondé, *Een economie*, pp. 168–245; B. Blondé and H. Deceulaer, 'The Port of Antwerp and its Hinterland: Port Traffic, Urban Economies and Government Policies in the 17th and 18th Centuries', in R. Ertesvåg, D. J. Starkey and A. Tove Austbø (eds), *Maritime Industries and Public Intervention* (Stavanger: Maritime Museum, 2002), pp. 21–44; H. Deceulaer, 'Urban Artisans and their Countryside Customers: Different Interactions between Town and Hinterland in Antwerp, Brussels and Ghent', in B. Blondé, E. Vanhaute and M. Galan (eds), *Labour and Labour Markets between Town and Countryside (Middle Ages–19th Century)* (Turnhout: Brepols, 2001), pp. 218–35, on pp. 221–9; Klep, *Bevolking*, pp. 97–104, 315–16, 319–21; P. M. M. Klep, 'Urban Decline in Brabant: The Traditionalization of Investments and Labour (1374–1806)', in Van der Wee (ed.), *The Rise and Decline*, pp. 261–86, on pp. 281–4; R. Van Uytven, 'Brabantse en Antwerpse centrale plaatsen (14de–19de eeuw)', in *Het stedelijk netwerk in België in historisch perspectief (1350–1850): Een statistische en dynamische benadering* (Brussel: Gemeentekrediet, 1992), pp. 29–79, on p. 47.
4. Klep, *Bevolking*, p. 63.
5. C. Bruneel, 'Bijdrage van de poorterboeken tot de historische demografie: Kritische bedenkingen bij het voorbeeld van Antwerpen', *Tijdschrift van het Gemeentekrediet*, 172 (1990), pp. 101–10.
6. J. Verbeemen, 'Immigratie te Antwerpen', *Mededelingen van de Geschied- en Oudheidkundige Kring voor Leuven en omgeving Lustrumuitgave: De Brabantse stad* (1959), pp. 81–100.
7. Blondé, *Een economie*, pp. 133–6, 275–80. Blondé's figures are based on the place of origin of new burghers between 1745 and 1784, and are mostly concerned with identifying relative inter-urban interactions within the Brabant urban network. He does not provide absolute numbers, or a detailed table of his results. H. Deceulaer, *Pluriforme patronen en een verschillende snit: Sociaal-economische, institutionele en culturele transformaties in de kledingsector in Antwerpen, Brussel en Gent, ca 1585–ca 1800* (Amsterdam: Stichting Beheer IISG, 2001), p. 57; Deceulaer, in 'Urban Artisans', has also remarked on the very limited and amputated nature of the main Antwerp hinterland in the eighteenth century.
8. For more details on the sources and sampling method used, see Appendix I.2. Although a number of ambiguities in the information recorded (for example non-localized birthplaces, approximate ages and periods of stay, and unclear occupations), the interference of the exceptional political circumstances of the late 1790s, and the selectivity of the sample hamper the exactness of the calculations, the findings are sufficiently indicative to provide insight into migrants' backgrounds and their positions within urban society as a whole. A first discussion of the census data in relation to migration patterns in the second half of the eighteenth century was rendered in A. Winter, 'De microcontext van stedelijke groei: Posities en trajecten van immigranten op de Antwerpse arbeidsmarkt in de tweede helft van de achttiende eeuw', *Stadsgeschiedenis*, 1:2 (2006), pp. 122–47.

9. Before the division of the Netherlands in the Eighty Years War, the northern Dutch province of North Brabant belonged to the Duchy of Brabant too. After the division, the 'curtailed' Duchy retained its name.

10. A large city is defined as a city with more than 20,000 inhabitants in 1800 *or* 1850, a rural place is defined as a place with less than 5,000 inhabitants in 1800 *and* 1850, and all places with a size in between are considered as intermediate towns. See Appendix I.3 on more details of geographical classifications used.

11. See Appendix I.3.

12. Jaspers and Stevens, *Arbeid*, pp. 82–7, 89–129; Lucassen, *Naar de kusten*, pp. 42–3; D. Van Overmeire, 'Bevolking, arbeid en strukturele mutaties in het Land van Waas in de 19de eeuw', *Annalen van de Koninklijke Oudheidkundige Kring van het Land van Waas*, 92 (1989), pp. 177–212; M.-A. Wilssens, *Bevolkingsdruk en boerenverstand: Evolutie van de levensstandaard in het Waasland in de 18de eeuw* (Brussel: Gemeentekrediet, 1992).

13. C. Bruneel, 'Economie en samenleving in de eeuw van de Verlichting', in R. Van Uytven (ed.), *De geschiedenis van Brabant van het hertogdom tot heden* (Zwolle: Waanders, 2004), pp. 479–513, on pp. 492–5; Lucassen, *Naar de kusten*, pp. 48–51.

14. Class intervals include the lower boundary value and exclude the upper boundary value.

15. Turnhout's own competing basin, like that of Lier, was in all probability relatively small. Blondé's research on the servicing areas of Brabant cities in the second half of the eighteenth century, among others on the basis of burgher books and information on the grain market to which peasants brought their produce, has demonstrated how the servicing areas of both cities were cut off by the relatively greater attraction of Antwerp as an urban centre: Blondé, *Een economie*, pp. 138–40.

16. Klep, *Bevolking*, pp. 28–31; E. Vanhaute, *Heiboeren: Bevolking, arbeid en inkomen in de 19de-eeuwse Kempen* (Brussel: VUBPress, 1992), pp. 27–34; E. Vliebergh and R. Ulens, *Het Hageland: Zijne plattelandsche bevolking in de 19de eeuw: Bijdrage tot de studie der economische en sociale geschiedenis* (Brussel, 1919).

17. Even in these villages, however, at most 25 per cent of the total population was employed in non-agrarian activities in the eighteenth century, and never full time. Gyssels and van der Straeten, *Bevolking ... Antwerpen*, pp. 132–7; Klep, *Bevolking*, pp. 215, 226; R. Van Uytven, 'Peiling naar de beroepsstructuur op het Brabantse platteland omstreeks 1755', *Bijdragen tot de Geschiedenis*, 55 (1972), pp. 172–203, on pp. 190–4; Vanhaute, *Heiboeren*, pp. 130–2.

18. A. Kappelhof, 'Toenemende spanningen', in Van Uytven (ed.), *De geschiedenis van Brabant*, pp. 529–37, on p. 531; M. Schrover, 'The Demographic Consequences of Changing Employment Opportunities: Women in the Dutch Meierij in the Nineteenth Century', *History of the Family*, 2:4 (1997), pp. 451–79, on pp. 472–3.

19. Blondé, *Een economie*, pp. 143–52, 168–230; Vanhaute, *Heiboeren*, pp. 34–6.

20. Klep, *Bevolking*, pp. 28–9.

21. Vliebergh and Ulens, *Het Hageland*; see also Van Uytven, 'Peiling', pp. 194–7; and M. Van Dijck and W. Peeters, 'Algemene karakterschets van Vlaams-Brabant: Eenheid en verscheidenheid', in J. De Maeyer and P. Heyrman (eds), *Geuren en kleuren: Een sociale en economische geschiedenis van Vlaams-Brabant, 19de en 20ste eeuw* (Leuven: Peeters, 2001), pp. 21–39, on pp. 26–7, on the relatively backward situation of rural Hageland.

22. Until well into the twentieth century, the region was focused more on the Campine areas than on the western part of Brabant, and remained largely untouched by the agrarian and commercial developments in the Brussels hinterland: Blondé, *Een economie*, pp. 135–6, 147; Van Dijck and Peeters, 'Algemene karakterschets', pp. 26, 34–6.

23. Blondé, *Een economie*, p. 149; Vanhaute, *Heiboeren*, pp. 34–6.
24. See the origin pyramids below, pp. 108–9. Regional centres in the home region would then have functioned as an intermediary gateway between rural–urban migration streams of a strongly intra-regional nature, and inter-regional streams that were more of an inter-urban nature. Although the information on origins from the census does not allow us to establish whether migrants had moved directly from their place of birth or via some intermediate move, it is unlikely that migrants from the city's direct hinterland, with very large contingents of rural-born migrants, had moved to other urban centres – which were sparse in the regions east of the Scheldt – before coming to Antwerp.
25. Poussou, *Bordeaux*, pp. 76–7.
26. Blondé, *Een economie*, pp. 128–30.
27. Cf. Klep, *Bevolking*, p. 63.
28. C. Bruneel, 'Les migrations entre villes et campagnes: L'exemple des Pays-Bas méridionaux', in *Le migrazioni in Europa secc. XIII–XVIII* (Prato: Instituto Internazionale di Storia Economica 'F. Datini', 1994), pp. 501–32, on pp. 523–5; R. Mols, *Introduction à la démographie historique des villes d'Europe du 14e au 18e siècle*, 3 vols (Louvain: Bibliothèque de l'Université, 1954–6), vol. 2, pp. 183–99; D. Souden, 'Migrants and the Population Structure of Later Seventeenth-Century Provincial Cities and Market Towns', in P. Clark (ed.), *The Transformation of English Provincial Towns, 1600–1800* (London: Hutchinson, 1985), pp. 133–68, on p. 152; J. Verbeemen, 'De werking van economische factoren op de stedelijke demografie der XVIIe en der XVIIIe eeuw in de Zuidelijke Nederlanden', *Belgisch Tijdschrift voor Filologie en Geschiedenis*, 34 (1956), pp. 680–700.
29. The equivalent proportions were 40.3 per cent for Lier and 34.0 per cent for Mechelen according to Gyssels and van der Straeten, *Bevolking ... Antwerpen*, p. 84. Verbeemen, 'Mechelen in 1796', p. 140, gives the slightly divergent figure of 32 per cent for Mechelen. The figure for Antwerp was 27.2 per cent (De Belder, 'Elementen', vol. 1, p. 89). For Brussels, the estimated equivalent was 34 per cent. A. Cosemans, *Bijdrage tot de demografische en sociale geschiedenis van de stad Brussel, 1796–1846* (Brussel: Gemeentekrediet, 1966), records an immigrant percentage of only 21 per cent in the Brussels census of 1796, but this percentage is based on data for only five of the eight city sections (from which the immigrant-rich seventh section is missing), and is unjustly calculated against the total population *including* children under the age of 12, whose origins were not recorded in the census. Moreover, for some of the five sections included in the calculations the number of immigrants is impossibly low, implying that immigrants were not always consistently marked as such in the census or that Cosemans miscounted. For the first section, for instance, Cosemans counts a total of only 322 persons born outside Brussels in a total population of 8,269 (among whom 2,084 children below the age of 12), i.e. an improbably low 5.2 immigrant percentage among the over-12 population: Cosemans, *Bijdrage*, pp. 1–25, 81. In the census of the year XI (1803) – i.e. seven years after the 1796 census – R. Bruyninckx and M. De Metsenaere, 'De rekrutering van de Brusselse bevolking op basis van de telling van het jaar XI', *Taal en Sociale Integratie*, 4 (1981), pp. 183–98, on p. 187, find a total of 3,611 immigrants in an over-12 population of 7,622, i.e. an immigrant percentage of 47 per cent, for the very same first section. When Cosemans's immigrant percentage is recalculated for the four other sections for which data are available, it amounts to 34 per cent – which might still constitute an underestimate.

30. Jaspers and Stevens, *Arbeid*, pp. 83–4, records 26.8 per cent of the adult population of Ghent and 24 per cent of that of Sint-Niklaas as having been born elsewhere.
31. Ibid., pp. 82–7, 89–129; Lucassen, *Naar de kusten*, pp. 42–3.
32. While the total proportion of immigrants in the adult population of rural villages in the *arrondissementen* of Ghent East and Sint-Niklaas was only 26 and 27 per cent respectively, in the *arrondissementen* of Antwerp East, Antwerp West and Turnhout East these proportions were 48, 42 and 48 per cent respectively. Only the *arrondissement* of Turnhout North, where only 28 per cent of the village populations lived in a place other than that of their birth, revealed a high immobility. Gyssels and van der Straeten, *Bevolking ... West-Vlaanderen*, pp. 81–8.
33. Klep, *Bevolking*, pp. 47–8, 52–4, 103–4.
34. See the discussion above, pp. 23–5.
35. Lucassen and de Vries, 'The Rise and Fall', pp. 26–38.
36. W. P. McCray, 'Creating Networks of Skill: Technology Transfer and the Glass Industry of Venice', *Journal of European Economic History*, 28:2 (1999), pp. 301–33.
37. Cf. Ehmer, 'Worlds of Mobility', pp. 182–3; Van Uytven, 'Peiling', pp. 190–1. It is worth noting that when I use the term 'unspecialized' I do not necessarily imply that the activities involved did not demand skill, but rather that these were occupations which were widely practised in town and country alike. In turn, 'specialized' occupations are occupations which are rarely found, and which generally show some correlation with population size. In general, there is a broad correlation between 'specialized' and 'specialist' (i.e. skilled) occupations, but not necessarily so.
38. Ehmer, 'Worlds of Mobility', p. 181; Kuijpers, *Migrantenstad*, pp. 283–4; Lucassen and Penninx, *Nieuwkomers*, pp. 96–9, 135–6.
39. Van Zanden, *The Rise and Decline*, p. 50.
40. Ehmer, 'Worlds of Mobility', pp. 183–4.
41. Lesger, 'Informatiestromen', pp. 21–2. See also Hufton, *The Poor*, pp. 95–7, 101.
42. That origin-specific skills generally interacted with informal preferences in practice is well illustrated by the discussion of the causes of the origin-specific occupational clustering in seventeenth-century Amsterdam, above, pp. 23–5.
43. Van Uytven, 'Peiling', pp. 182–90.
44. B. Blondé and R. Van Uytven, 'De smalle steden en het Brabantse stedelijke netwerk in de Late Middeleeuwen en de Nieuwe Tijd', *Lira elegans*, 6 (1999), pp. 129–82, on pp. 168–82; P. van Dun, '"De Brouwerijen hebben hier van oudts (...) altijdts goede neeringhen gehadt"', in J.-M. Goris (ed.), *Bier, wijn en jenever in de Kempen* (Herentals-Roosendaal: Centrum voor de studie van land en volk van de Kempen, 2002), pp. 69–90; Vliebergh and Ulens, *Het Hageland*.
45. A. K. L. Thijs, *De zijdenijverheid te Antwerpen in de zeventiende eeuw* (Luik: Pro Civitate, 1969), pp. 14–17; Thijs, *Van 'werkwinkel'*, pp. 152, 180–5, 215–18, 370–80, 392, and passim. In his analysis of the relationship between occupation and economic position, De Belder found that textile production was by far the poorest branch in town. No less than 79 per cent of all people working in the production of textiles and lace belonged to households that possessed no real estate or property liable to taxation, as against an urban average of 60 per cent: De Belder, 'Elementen', vol. 2, pp. 219–28, 251–8, 281–8, 315–25, 336–8.
46. Lis, *Social Change*, pp. 14–16; Thijs, *Van 'werkwinkel'*, pp. 168–70, 180–5, 400–1.
47. Source: C1796DB (D1+4) and C1796I (cor).

48. Klep, *Bevolking*, p. 224; Thijs, *Van 'werkwinkel'*, pp. 370–2, 389–92. Those rare immigrant women who did carry out lacework came predominantly from an urban background or had come to the city at a very young age.
49. Van Uytven, 'Peiling', p. 192.
50. Cf. Thijs, *Van 'werkwinkel'*, p. 369.
51. As with immigrant lace workers, an important proportion of immigrant seamstresses was urban-born. The great importance of women in the garment trades might also have been a reflection of changes in fashion and consumption which were mostly situated in the domain of women's clothing. Cf. Deceulaer, *Pluriforme patronen*, pp. 191–6, 211–30. On eighteenth-century French-oriented fashion developments, see I. van Damme, 'Zotte verwaandheid: Over Franse verleiding en Zuid-Nederlands onbehagen, 1650–1750', in R. de Bont and T. Verschaffel (eds), *Het verderf van Parijs* (Leuven: Universitaire Pers Leuven, 2004), pp. 187–204. It is remarkable that immigrant men working in the sector had often immigrated as children with their parents. On the presence of tailors and shoemakers in the Brabant countryside, see Van Uytven, 'Peiling', pp. 185, 188–9.
52. Among others, see Moch, *Moving Europeans*, pp. 46–7; Souden, 'Migrants', p. 152.
53. Unfortunately, the occupational denominations do not allow us consistently to distinguish different groups of transport workers. The identification of freight handlers in general and *natie* members in particular in the census of 1796 is hampered by the abolition of the *naties* by the French in 1795 – to be restored in a new form soon after – and the combination of different occupations. Cf. F. Prims, *Geschiedenis van het Antwerpsche turfdragersambacht* (Antwerpen: Veritas, 1923), pp. 334–42. Consequently, the number of identifiable *natie* gangers in 1796 undoubtedly underrates their true number. See H. Deceulaer, 'Arbeidsregulering en loonvorming in de Antwerpse haven, 1585–1796', *Tijdschrift voor Sociale Geschiedenis*, 18 (1992), pp. 22–47, on p. 27, n. 20. Drivers might equally well be engaged in transport to and from Antwerp as in transporting goods within the city walls, for instance from the quayside to warehouses, or from brewers to inns, but a distinction between inter-urban 'coachmen' and intra-urban 'carters' cannot be made on the basis of occupational denomination. In spite of this occupational obscurity, it is clear that migrants were strongly represented both in inter-urban and extra-urban transport activities, and in both the core and the periphery of these highly polarized labour markets.
54. Consequently, those immigrants that did work in shipping came from places situated along water routes to Antwerp's southern quadrant, such as Mechelen, Rupelmonde, Duffel, Rumst and Brussels. To understand why almost no immigrants with a background in shipping came to Antwerp, one needs to appreciate the depressed state of the sector: in the eighteenth century Antwerp's shipping activities had further declined in importance, and had become limited to minor inland waterway routes. The shipmaster's guild had been marked by a continual loss of members, and the number of masters that actually owned a vessel appears to have hit rock bottom at 21 or 22 in 1791. Blondé and Deceulaer, 'The Port of Antwerp', pp. 33–5, 40; Thijs, 'The River Scheldt', pp. 227 ff.
55. Coach lines often departed and arrived in front of inns, which functioned as important nodes in the transportation and storage or reception of goods and people, and often specialized in connections with specific regions: B. Blondé, 'De transportwegen en de economische ontwikkeling in de regio Antwerpen – Mechelen – Lier (1710–1790)', *Bijdragen tot de Geschiedenis*, 78:1–4 (1995), pp. 93–105; J. Van Hout, 'De Antwerpse herbergen, 1750–1850' (Licentiaat dissertation, Katholieke Universiteit Leuven, 1981), pp. 140–2. Overland transport was stimulated in the whole of Brabant by the consider-

able expansion of paved roads in the eighteenth century: B. Blondé, 'Aux origines de la révolution des transports: L'exemple des chaussées "belges" au dix-huitième siècle', in S. Curveiller and D. Clauzel (eds), *Les champs relationnels en Europe du Nord, 18ième–20ème siècles: Deuxième colloque européen de Calais* (Balinghem: Cache, 1998), pp. 17–40; Blondé, *Een economie*, pp. 168 ff.

56. Although the *natiegasten* typically worked at the job too, their 'core' position also served as an investment on which profits were realized by means of their corporate monopoly and the low wages of subcontracted 'peripheral' workers. In some minor instances, membership even functioned merely as an investment – members could receive half of the income of a 'substitute' – but in most cases this was discouraged: G. Asaert, G. Devos and F. Suykens (eds), *The 'Naties' in the Port of Antwerp: Six Centuries of Activity in City and Port* (Tielt: Lannoo, 1993), pp. 17–30; Blondé and Deceulaer, 'The Port of Antwerp', pp. 37–40; Deceulaer, 'Arbeidsregulering'.

57. Among those who could be identified as *natie* members, immigrants were more numerous than the locally born, while the proportion of immigrants among other transport workers and casual labourers – most of whom worked at the docks and warehouses – was somewhat lower but nevertheless marked. Existing research on the basis of burgher books has also demonstrated the important immigrant presence within the Antwerp *naties*: among new residents purchasing citizenship between 1751 and 1795, more than 10 per cent identified themselves as 'transport workers', and the proportion among new burghers from the Campine areas was even greater. Cf. the confrontation of the figures from Blondé and Deceulaer, 'The Port of Antwerp', p. 40, with those of Verbeemen, 'Immigratie te Antwerpen', pp. 99–100, and J. Verbeemen, 'Emigratie uit de Antwerpse Kempen', *Oudheid en Kunst*, 36 (1953), pp. 3–68. Likewise, the majority of *natie* gangers in the later eighteenth century appears to have been recruited from among rural, and in particular Campine, immigrants: Blondé and Deceulaer, 'The Port of Antwerp', p. 44, n. 131. On the importance of social networks in the organization of port work, see Deceulaer, 'Arbeidsregulering', pp. 26–8, 42.

58. Because membership of the butchers' guild was contingent upon the exploitation of one of the (numerically) limited stalls in the *Vleeshuis* (Meat Hall), this had created a quasi-hereditary system: F. Smekens, 'Ambachtswezen en "nieuwe nijverheid"', in *Antwerpen in de achttiende eeuw*, pp. 64–94, on p. 68. Among fishmongers, a similar system was in operation.

59. Antwerp's mercers' guild had undergone considerable expansion in the eighteenth century, at a pace much faster than population growth: B. Blondé and H. Greefs, 'Werk aan de winkel: De Antwerpse meerseniers: Aspecten van kleinhandel en verbruik in de 17de en 18de eeuw', in G. Devos (ed.), *De lokroep van het bedrijf: Handelaars, ondernemers en hun samenleving van de zestiende tot de twintigste eeuw: Liber amicorum Roland Baetens* (Antwerpen: UFSIA, 2001), pp. 207–29, on pp. 211–13. Although it is difficult in the Antwerp case to disentangle the possible pull of new market opportunities from the potential push of rising employment constraints in other sectors, similar increases in the number of retailers have in other cases been related to a 'consumer revolution' taking place in the eighteenth century, which was among other things associated with a growing importance of hinterland markets for urban retailers: as distribution chains and consumption rates proliferated in the countryside, urban retailers increasingly catered for rural customers, either via pedlar middlemen or via urban 'shopping' by rural customers. Cf. B. Blondé, 'Winkelen te Lier: Een onderzoek naar de afbakening van het Lierse hinterland in de achttiende eeuw', in *Het stedelijk netwerk in België in historisch perspectief*

(1350–1850) (Brussel: Gemeentekrediet, 1992), pp. 111–24; Deceulaer, 'Urban Artisans'; H. Deceulaer, 'Consumptie en distributie van kleding tussen stad en platteland: Drie regionale patronen in de Zuidelijke Nederlanden (zestiende – achttiende eeuw)', *Tijdschrift voor sociale geschiedenis*, 28:4 (2002), pp. 439–68; E. Steegen, *Kleinhandel en stedelijke ontwikkeling: Het kramersambacht te Maastricht in de vroegmoderne tijd* (Maastricht, 2006), pp. 328–37.

60. Lucassen and Penninx, *Nieuwkomers*, pp. 142–3; Schrover, 'Potverkopers'.
61. Cf. Clark, 'Migrants in the City', pp. 273–4; Hufton, *The Poor*, pp. 100, 104; Moch, *Moving Europeans*, p. 50.
62. On the problems of terminology, see Blondé and Greefs, 'Werk aan de winkel', pp. 214–15. On the cost and capital outlay involved in setting up a shop, see I. K. Ben-Amos, *Adolescence and Youth in Early Modern England* (New Haven, CT: Yale University Press, 1994), pp. 217 ff.; Steegen, *Kleinhandel*, pp. 237–51; B. Willems, 'Krediet, vertrouwen en sociale relaties: Kleine producenten en winkeliers te Antwerpen in de 18de eeuw' (PhD dissertation, Vrije Universiteit Brussel, 2006), pp. 191–267. The role of gender in immigrants' observed predilection towards retailing and trading activities is difficult to gauge. Most of the women shopkeepers were married (67 per cent) or widowed (28 per cent), but their husbands worked in the distribution sectors in only a minority of cases (18 per cent) and exercised a variety of trades. A similar relative 'independence' is noticeable among female caterers, whose husbands – when still alive – worked in the same trade in only 24 per cent of cases; 38 per cent if brewers are added. Whether these female retail activities constituted a primary or secondary contribution to the household income-pooling is, however, impossible to establish on the basis of the census data alone.
63. Cf. Knotter, *Economische transformatie*, p. 23.
64. And remains controversial: Blondé, *Een economie*, pp. 50–1; Knotter, *Economische transformatie*, pp. 23–7.
65. Bruneel, 'Bijdrage', pp. 101–4.
66. Cf. Smekens, 'Ambachtswezen'. Possibly, in the shipmasters', tailors' and shoemakers' trades, migrant-unfriendly regulations might also have played a role in producing their evident under-representation.
67. Deceulaer, 'Arbeidsregulering'; Smekens, 'Ambachtswezen', pp. 68–70.
68. Although some were able to play an important role: Smekens, 'Ambachtswezen', p. 72 ff.; Thijs, *Van 'werkwinkel'*, pp. 322–3.
69. On entry costs, see Smekens, 'Ambachtswezen', pp. 69–70.
70. The strongest incidences of occupational clustering on the basis of place of origin are to be found among urban migrants. Brussels, for instance, in itself supplied twenty of the ninety-seven recorded male garment workers in the first and fourth districts. Apart from the capital's important supply of garment (and also textile) workers, however, there are only fifteen incidences of a particular place supplying more than five (and never more than ten) male workers in a particular occupational sector (out of 2,174 recorded male immigrants in total). As most of these places were nearby or urban centres supplying a great number of migrants, these figures hardly add up to a pattern of local specialization. The only notable exception is provided by the seven stonecutters from the *commune* of Seneffe in Hainaut, whose specialization fitted in with a well-established local tradition of quarrying and stonecutting in a handful of villages to the south-west of Nivelles, and with their concomitant (often temporary) export of skilled stone workers. See Dumont, *Migrations intérieures*, pp. 79, 181; Lucassen, *Naar de kusten*, pp. 310–17. Among female immigrants, high incidences of certain occupations from certain places were more fre-

quent, but – given their undifferentiated occupational structure – were not necessarily related to clear-cut incidences of local specialization.

71. Although they did supply an important number of brewing workers, Tienen, Hoegaarden and surrounding villages were not predominant in the sector; neither was their supply limited to this particular branch.

72. Cf. also Thijs, *Van 'werkwinkel'*, pp. 322–3.

73. The example of baker Jacques Smeyers, discussed below, indicates that family-based networks could play an important role in the move to Antwerp and the development of a career. Similar examples abound in the burgher books, where many 'chains' of namesake fellow villagers acquiring citizenship spaced over time are identifiable. One such is the Wouters family, who supplied six of the sixty new burghers born in the Campine village of Lille in the fifty years preceding the census, four of whom were entered as *natiegast*. See for instance Verbeemen, 'Emigratie uit de Antwerpse', esp. pp. 32–3.

74. For instance, the seven persons from Herentals surnamed Verbuecken who acquired citizenship between 1746 and 1796 consisted of two bakers, a schoolmaster, a carpenter, a case-maker and two persons whose occupation is unknown, and the three Van Laer burghers from Beerse counted included a *natie* member, a physician and a shopkeeper. See Verbeemen, 'Emigratie uit de Antwerpse', pp. 9, 24–5.

75. Comparing the origin of living-in with that of other household members offers a potentially fruitful inroad to the mapping of social networks, but even then one would probably miss out on the most important facets of these networks that centre upon the first weeks or months after arrival. In any case, this comparison demands a household-based analysis of the census information that could not be pursued within the limits of the present research. A detailed search to identify potential kin and family members living in town might also offer new perspectives for research, but this requires a view of the total immigrant population in all city districts, which also fell beyond the scope of present research.

76. A very wealthy elite (8 per cent) and a second group of moderately wealthy households (9 per cent) were identified on the basis of their subjection to two extraordinary tax levies in 1794 and 1796. A third intermediary group (22 per cent) did not possess any fortunes, but did have recourse to some limited independent means in the form of real estate (land tax) and/or an independent economic activity in trade or industry (patent tax). A fourth, propertyless, group (61 per cent) did not have any of these and was solely dependent on wage labour for its income. The latter was composed of autonomous households (49 per cent) on the one hand and persons living-in with households from the first three categories (12 per cent) on the other hand – mostly domestic servants. De Belder related this wealth classification to the 1796 census occupational structure, yet the occupational classification used by him to do so is not readily comparable with the one used in the present study. De Belder, 'Elementen', vol. 2, pp. 219–28, 251–8, 281–8, 315–25, 336–8. See also Appendices I.2 and I.4.

77. As a general rule, I have retained only explicit references to a dependent work position such as journeyman, attendant, servant, aid, worker, boy, apprentice or assistant (e.g. *garçon charpentier, aide cabaretière, ouvrier lapidaire, garçon de bureau*, etc.) as denoting persons in an explicitly subordinate position. All occupations without reference to status (such as 'tailor') or with an explicit reference to an independent position ('master baker'), have been grouped separately as 'independent or unspecified'. By the nature of the source, the proportion of 'subordinate' workers provides only a strict minimum

of the true number of 'dependent' workers, as the different census executors proceeded with varying accuracy and criteria with regard to the status specifications of occupations: status references figure, for instance, much less frequently in the *cahiers* of the fourth district than in those of the first. While the proportion of explicitly subordinate workers therefore cannot be taken even as an indication of the total proportion of wage-dependent workers in the labour force, it does provide a measurement of *relative* differences in the overall proportion of subordinate workers, for instance between the locally born and immigrants, as there is no reason to suspect that the mention or otherwise of occupational status was in any way dependent on origin or any other characteristic of the recorded inhabitant rather than on the varying assessment and accuracy of the different census clerks.

78. De Belder, 'Elementen', vol. 1, p. lxi.
79. In each wealth category but the very rich, moreover, immigrants were disproportionately present among patent holders, i.e. independent masters and entrepreneurs in industry or trade, and thus the economically most active groups.
80. Source: De Belder, 'Elementen', vol. 1, pp. 13–14, 103, 126–33. The table excludes children under the age of twelve. On the wealth classification scheme, see note 76 above.
81. The apparently greater persistence of propertyless persons living in independent households might in turn be attributable to an overall greater persistence of married persons and/or a transfer of erstwhile single servants marrying and setting up an independent – propertyless – household.
82. As the age of immigration is calculated by subtracting the recorded age at the time of the census from the information concerning length of stay, the preciseness of the figures suffers from being rounded off twice. Of course, the resultant figures do not represent the ages of *all* incoming migrants in the second half of the eighteenth century, as both older immigrants and short-stayers stood less chance of being recorded alive and present at the time of the census, and patterns of seasonal migration in particular are largely obscured from the census's view. Nevertheless, the data are of indicative value to identify the main features of life-cycle related migration patterns.
83. Clark, 'The Migrant in Kentish Towns', p. 124; Patten, 'Patterns of Migration', p. 80; R. Schofield, 'Age-Specific Mobility in an Eighteenth-Century Rural English Parish', in Clark and Souden (eds), *Migration and Society*, pp. 253–66; Souden, 'Migrants', p. 142; P. Spufford, 'Population Movement in Seventeenth-Century England', *Local Population Studies*, 4 (1970), pp. 41–50; Whyte, *Migration and Society*, pp. 40–3.
84. Hohenberg and Lees, *The Making of Urban Europe*, pp. 92–4; Moch, *Moving Europeans*, pp. 49–58, 68–70.
85. The census books typically only mention a calendar year to indicate immigrants' length of stay in the city. To correct for the distortions emanating from a strong tendency to approximate – especially the years ending in –6 (i.e. '10, 20, 30 ... years ago'), and to a lesser extent those in –0, are greatly over-represented – the calculations presented make use of a ten-yearly moving average.
86. These figures are the result of extrapolating a small number of migrants (N=169) recorded as having arrived in 1796, by means of a very approximate multiplicator factor derived from the monthly distributions and turnover rates observed in the censuses of 1808–20 and retaining an arbitrary census date of 15 April. Unfortunately, the small empirical basis, the exceptional political circumstances (the establishment of employees and representatives of the newly installed French regime, for instance, probably inflated the number of recent immigrants) and the impreciseness as to the actual census date

and scope (the census stretched over several weeks, and the administrative treatment of temporary migrants is unknown) hamper the validity of these extrapolations. For details, see Winter, 'Patterns of Migration', pp. 208–9.

87. To a certain extent, men's apparently limited participation in medium-term patterns of migration might have been affected by the turbulent political context of the late 1780s and early 1790s and the under-registration of men of conscription age. In addition, the male predominance among the small number of 1796 arrivals suggests that men were more involved in short-term seasonal patterns of migration (yet is also partly attributable to the predominantly male influx of representatives of the new French regime) which unfortunately remain largely obscured from the census's view.

88. That Antwerp's attraction as a vocational centre was relatively limited in the eighteenth century was also observed by B. De Munck, 'Leerpraktijken. Economische en sociaal-culturele aspecten van beroepsopleidingen in Antwerpse ambachtsgilden, 16de–18de eeuw' (PhD dissertation, Vrije Universiteit Brussel, 2002).

89. See, for instance, Souden, 'Migrants', pp. 148–9.

90. The overall social implications of the shift in female employment in relation to length of stay remains difficult to gauge, not the least because of the great increase in the proportion of housewives 'without occupation'.

91. However, the value of the parameters is marred by a lack of status specifications, which make it difficult to separate masters from journeymen. See note 77 above. The proportional increase of textile workers was due to a marked stability in absolute terms, without significant changes in occupational status, while the apparent stability of clothing and leather workers reflected a minor decline in absolute terms.

92. Due to the specificities of the semi-independent employer position of a *natiegast*, being a *natie* member may be considered an entrepreneurial undertaking.

93. Although credit networks were probably of importance, it is impossible that poor or propertyless migrants should have been able to have access to such sums. See I. K. Ben-Amos, 'Failure to become Freemen: Urban Apprentices in Early Modern England', *Social History*, 16 (1991), pp. 155–72, on pp. 164–6; Ben-Amos, *Adolescence*, pp. 217 ff.; Deceulaer, 'Arbeidsregulering'; Steegen, *Kleinhandel*, pp. 237–51; Willems, 'Krediet', pp. 191–267.

94. SAA, MA-BZA, D4, cahier 5, n°. 626.

95. Verbeemen, 'Emigratie uit de Antwerpse', p. 45.

96. SAA, MA-BZA, D4, cahier 16, n°. 2477; and Verbeemen, 'Emigratie uit de Antwerpse', p. 45.

97. Verbeemen, 'Emigratie uit de Antwerpse'. He was not recorded in the conserved files of the first and fourth districts in 1796.

98. SAA, MA-BZA, D1, cahier 13, n°. 1349.

99. De Munck, 'Leerpraktijken', pp. 297–8. For Leuven, analogous observations were made for the same period: M. Laureys, 'Bijdrage tot de sociale geschiedenis van het Leuvens ambachtelijke milieu. Het ambacht van de timmerlieden, de houtbrekers en de molen-makers' (Licentiaat dissertation, Katholieke Universiteit Leuven, 1980), pp. 137 ff., 196.

100. Fragmentary evidence indicates that, in the second half of the eighteenth century, carpenters in Antwerp received modal summer wages which were double (24–26.5 stivers) those paid to agricultural labourers in the vicinities of the town (12 stivers), and which were between 20 and 33 per cent higher than those paid to their colleagues in Campine villages (20–2 stivers): cf. Klep, *Bevolking*, p. 100; E. Scholliers, 'Prijzen en lonen te Ant-

werpen en in het Antwerpse (16e–19e eeuw)', in C. Verlinden (ed.), *Dokumenten voor de geschiedenis van prijzen en lonen in Vlaanderen en Brabant, Deel II* (Brugge: De Tempel, 1965), pp. 641–1056, pp. 982, 989, 1031. Female domestic servants, in turn, could in Antwerp – while being boarded, lodged and clothed – earn a yearly wage (between 36 and 54 guilders) which was the equivalent of between 150 and 200 summer's day's wages (5–6 stivers) of a female agricultural labourer in the surroundings of the city: ibid., pp. 989, 997, 1043.

101. De Belder, 'Elementen', vol. 1, p. lxi, 14.
102. Even if some of the marriages contracted after entry may have involved remarriages, and some of the migrants widowed at the time of the census may have been married at the time of arrival.
103. Immigrants as a whole revealed a much higher proportion of married and widowed persons than the locally-born population, but this was attributable to the specificities of their age structure. I have compensated for biases emanating from age differences by excluding all persons younger than twenty from the comparison (the youngest age-group distinguished by De Belder is that of age 12–20), and assuming they were all unmarried – which is a simplification with an unavoidable but demonstrably small margin of error. When the comparison is limited to persons aged twenty or more, the marital status of immigrants and non-immigrants was comparable, with around 60 per cent of men and 50 per cent of women recorded with a resident spouse at the time of the census. Marriages were considered to have occurred in Antwerp if spouses had immigrated at a different date, or when an immigrant had married an Antwerp-born spouse. Married couples who had immigrated at the same point in time were considered to have been married prior to arrival.
104. E.g. B. Van de Putte, 'Homogamy by Geographical Origin: Segregation in Nineteenth-Century Flemish Cities (Gent, Leuven, and Aalst)', *Journal of Family History*, 28:3 (2003), pp. 364–90, on pp. 364–5, 369, 379–80.
105. In addition, the age at immigration and the overall birthplace distance – at least for rural migrants – also appear to have been negatively related to the probability of marrying a locally-born person, which would confirm the role of 'familiarity' as an explanatory factor.
106. This is even more worth noting since we have seen that 'settled' immigrant men were often better-off than the majority of those born locally. It is striking in this respect that the lowest incidences of mixed marriages were recorded in those sectors with the biggest entrepreneurial opportunities for rural migrants, like the distribution sectors and food industries. Shopkeepers, for instance, one of the best-off immigrant groups, were among those to display the least tendency for marrying a locally-born bride. Of all male shopkeepers who had contracted marriage in Antwerp, only 25 per cent had married an Antwerp-born bride, as against 46 per cent of immigrant men on average. See in this respect the remarks by M. H. D. van Leeuwen and I. Maas, 'Endogamy and Social Class: An Overview', in M. H. D. van Leeuwen, I. Maas and A. Miles (eds), *Marriage Choices and Class Boundaries: Social Endogamy in History* (Cambridge: Cambridge University Press, 2005), pp. 1–25, on p. 10. The marked preference towards immigrant spouses might in these cases have fulfilled a function in the expansion of immigrants' social and commercial networks in the rural hinterland, which were of particular relevance to their occupational undertakings. Rural migrants in any case displayed a much stronger predilection for partners born in the same place, district and region than their urban-born

counterparts – but to what extent this was the result of 'positive' or 'negative' choices cannot be determined on the basis of the collected census materials.

107. For the definition of 'region', see Appendix I.3.
108. See B. Van de Putte, M. Oris, M. Neven and K. Matthijs, 'Migration', in M. van Leeuwen and I. Maas (eds), *Endogamy and Social Class in History* (Amsterdam: Cambridge University Press, 2005), pp. 179–218, on pp. 201–16.
109. Lucassen and de Vries, 'The Rise and Fall'.
110. Thijs, *Van 'werkwinkel'*, pp. 306–23, 394–6.
111. Lis, 'Sociale politiek', pp. 152–7; Thijs, *Van 'werkwinkel'*, p. 397. Textile and clothing workers were in any case not considered to be in short supply: nine in twelve of the occupations enlisted as 'unwanted' in 1781 – button makers, wool spinners, cotton spinners, knitters, diamond-mill turners, silk winders, weavers, rope makers, agricultural labourers, wig makers, lace makers and seamstresses – were jobs in the textile or clothing sectors; see SAA, V, 177.
112. Thijs, 'The River Scheldt', pp. 184–6.
113. Blondé, *Een economie*.

4 Migration to a Port in the Making

1. To explain the absence of industrial investments in Antwerp at a time when nearby Ghent set out on a precocious path of textile mechanization is a difficult exercise in counterfactual history. Existing analyses indicate that alternative investment opportunities in Antwerp's developing commercial and maritime activities after the reopening of the Scheldt diverted funds from a capital-intensive mechanization along Ghent lines. See, in this respect, Lis, *Social Change*, pp. 17–26; C. Lis and H. Soly, *Een groot bedrijf in een kleine stad: De firma de Heyder en Co. te Lier, 1757–1834* (Lier: Liers Genootschap voor Geschiedenis, 1987); H. Greefs, 'Foreign Entrepreneurs in Early Nineteenth-Century Antwerp', in Lesger and Noordegraaf (eds), *Entrepreneurs and Entrepreneurship*, pp. 101–17; H. Greefs, 'Enkele zwaartepunten in het onderzoek naar ondernemerschap en ondernemersstrategieën te Antwerpen gedurende de periode 1794–1870', *Belgisch Tijdschrift voor Filologie en Geschiedenis*, 76 (1998), pp. 419–42.
2. Lis, *Social Change*, pp. 17–26; Thijs, *Van 'werkwinkel'*, pp. 185–7.
3. K. Veraghtert, 'From Inland Port to International Port, 1790–1914', in Suykens (ed.), *Antwerp*, pp. 279–422, on pp. 293–6.
4. L. De Kesel, 'Structurele ontwikkeling van de haven', in *Bouwstoffen voor de geschiedenis*, pp. 124–69, on pp. 124–5; M. Jennes, 'De Franse scheepswerven Danet & Co te Antwerpen (1802–1807)', in P. Lombaerde (ed.), *Antwerpen tijdens het Franse keizerrijk 1804–1814: Marine-arsenaal, metropool en vestingstad* (Antwerpen: Simon Stevinstichting, 1989), pp. 33–40, on p. 33; K. Jeuninckx, 'De havenbeweging in de Franse en Hollandse periode' *Bouwstoffen voor de geschiedenis van Antwerpen*, pp. 94–123, on pp. 94–5; Veraghtert, 'From Inland Port', pp. 289–92.
5. L. Baudez, 'Prefect d'Herbouville (1800–1805) en het herstel van de haven van Antwerpen', *Sirene*, 44:172 (1993), pp. 21–5; G. Beetemé, *Anvers: Métropole du commerce et des arts*, 2 vols (Anvers: Frans Beerts, 1888), vol. 2, pp. 4–6; A. Fischer, *Napoléon et Anvers (1800–1811)* (Antwerpen: Loosbergh, 1933), pp. 25, 31–3; Jeuninckx, 'De havenbeweging', p. 96; Lis, *Social Change*, p. 21; F. Prims, *Geschiedenis van Antwerpen, Volume IX: Met Oostenrijk en onder de Franschen (1715–1814). Boek 2: De economische orde* (Antwerpen: Standaard, 1947), pp. 145–1848.

6. Cited in Fischer, *Napoléon*, pp. 51–2.
7. L. Baudez, 'De zeeprefectuur van Antwerpen tijdens het Franse bewind, 1803–1814', *Belgisch tijdschrift voor militaire geschiedenis*, 30:4 (1993), pp. 233–61; Beetemé, *Anvers*, vol. 2, pp. 25–9; De Kesel, 'Structurele ontwikkeling', pp. 125–6; Fischer, *Napoléon*, pp. 125, 186; A. Himler, 'De Antwerpse haven vanaf de Franse periode', *Tijdschrift van het Gemeentekrediet*, 47:185 (1993), pp. 33–56, on pp. 35–7; P. Lombaerde, 'De bouwgeschiedenis van het scheepsarsenaal te Antwerpen', in Lombaerde (ed.), *Antwerpen tijdens*, pp. 41–56; Veraghtert, 'From Inland Port', p. 292.
8. Beetemé, *Anvers*, vol. 2, pp 7–22; De Kesel, 'Structurele ontwikkeling', pp. 126–7; G. Devos, 'Inwijking en integratie van Duitse kooplieden te Antwerpen in de 19de eeuw', in H. Soly and A. K. L. Thijs (eds), *Minderheden in Westeuropese steden (16de–20ste eeuw)* (Brussel: Belgisch Historisch Instituut te Rome, 1995), pp. 135–56, on pp. 138–9; Jeuninckx, 'De havenbeweging', pp. 94–102; K. Veraghtert, 'The Antwerp Port, 1790–1814', in J. M. van Winter (ed.), *The Interactions of Amsterdam and Antwerp with the Baltic Region, 1400–1800* (Leiden: Nijhoff, 1983), pp. 193–9.
9. Lis, *Social Change*, p. 22; Prims, *Geschiedenis van Antwerpen, Volume IX*, pp. 146–7; Veraghtert, 'From Inland Port', pp. 296–300.
10. Baudez, 'De zeeprefectuur', pp. 246–8; Epin, *Les ouvriers*, pp. 19, 22–3, 77–85, 177–82; Himler, 'De Antwerpse haven', pp. 35–7.
11. Epin, *Les ouvriers*, p. 23; Jeuninckx, 'De havenbeweging', pp. 105–6; Veraghtert, 'From Inland Port', pp. 301–2.
12. Source: Veraghtert, 'De havenbeweging te Antwerpen tijdens de negentiende eeuw: Een kwantitatieve benadering', 4 vols (PhD dissertation, KUL, 1977), vol. 1, pp. 8, 15, vol. 4, p. xxv.
13. Asaert et al. (eds), *The 'Naties'*, pp. 142–6; Beetemé, *Anvers*, vol. 2, pp. 73–82; De Kesel, 'Structurele ontwikkeling', pp. 127–8; R. Demoulin, *Guillaume Ier et la transformation économique des provinces belges (1815–1830)* (Liège: Faculté de Philosophie et Lettres, 1938), pp. 338–57; G. Devos, 'Over scheepsmakelaars en beunhazen: Een onderbelicht aspect van de maritieme bedrijvigheid te Antwerpen (1801–1867)', in Devos (ed.), *De lokroep van het bedrijf*, pp. 243–55; Himler, 'De Antwerpse haven', pp. 37–8; Jeuninckx, 'De havenbeweging', pp. 105–6, 110–11; Lis, *Social Change*, p. 28; K. Veraghtert, 'De havenbeweging', vol. 2, 39–53; Veraghtert, 'From Inland Port', pp. 302, 310–21.
14. A great part of the relatively high incoming tonnage in the years 1816 and 1817 consisted of grain imports in response to the harvest failure of 1816.
15. Beetemé, *Anvers*, vol. 2, pp. 51–72; Jeuninckx, 'De havenbeweging', pp. 110–11; Lis, *Social Change*, pp. 27–8; F. Prims, *Geschiedenis van Antwerpen, Volume X: Nederlandsche en eerste Belgische periode (1814–1914). Boek 2: De economische orde* (Antwerpen: Standaard, 1949), pp. 10–14; Veraghtert, 'De havenbeweging', vol. 2, 32–8, 67–82; Veraghtert, 'From Inland Port', pp. 302–5, 308–9.
16. Beetemé, *Anvers*, vol. 2, pp. 82–9; Lis, *Social Change*, pp. 24–5; Veraghtert, 'From Inland Port', pp. 306–7.
17. Beetemé, *Anvers*, vol. 2, pp. 96–100; Lis, *Social Change*, pp. 28–30; Veraghtert, 'From Inland Port', pp. 329–37.
18. M. Goossens, 'Een negentiende-eeuws heidedorp in transformatie: Kalmthout: 1835–1910', *Bijdragen tot de Geschiedenis*, 67 (1982), pp. 197–261, on p. 206; F. H. Mertens and K. L. Torfs, *Geschiedenis van Antwerpen, sedert de stichting der stad tot onze tyden, Zevende deel* (Antwerpen: Rederykkamer de Olyftak, 1846), pp. 393–4; J. H. S. M.

Veen, 'Spoorwegontwikkeling in het gebied van het voormalige hertogdom Brabant, 1835–1870', *Bijdragen tot de Geschiedenis*, 78:1–4 (1995), pp. 53–66.

19. Veraghtert, 'From Inland Port', pp. 349–51, 387–92.
20. J. Everaert, 'Antwerpen als emigratiehaven: De overzeese landverhuizing naar Amerika (1830–1914)', *Mededelingen*, 26 (1982), pp. 55–67, on p. 56; Feys, 'Radeloosheid'; E. Spelkens, 'Antwerp as a Port of Emigration, 1843–1913', in *Two Studies on Emigration through Antwerp to the New World* (Brussel, 1976), pp. 51–139; Veraghtert, 'From Inland Port', pp. 356–7. These emigrants were not recorded in the population registers or emigration registers.
21. Lis, *Social Change*.
22. Ibid., pp. 40–62, based mainly on a longitudinal analysis of newcomers recorded in the residence card registers of 1817, complemented by the 1830 census as collected by Hannes to shed light on employment opportunities, and the relief recipients' list of 1855 to illustrate the further evolution of the urban migration field.
23. The average birthplace distance of newcomers increased from 61 km in C1796I, over 103 km in CS1812–13, and 124 km in CS1815–20, to 133 km in HA1855. At the same time, the median birthplace distance remained fairly constant between 40 and 50 km, attesting to the continuation and intensification of regional patterns of migration (below).
24. These observations diverge from the contention by Lis, *Social Change*, pp. 46–7, that Antwerp's recruitment area grew smaller in the second quarter of the nineteenth century. She based this proposition on an analysis of the birthplaces of immigrant heads of households and their spouses figuring on the list of families receiving permanent poor relief in 1855, of whom 57 per cent were born in the province of Antwerp, and another 15 per cent in that of Brabant – as against 51 and 18 per cent respectively in the residence card registers of 1817 (ibid., Appendix 4, pp. 177–8). That the relative importance of regional migration would have expanded over this period is, however, not corroborated by other sources: in HA1855, ERPI1855 and NSC1856 the corresponding proportion of migrants from the province of Antwerp was only 44, 45 and 42 per cent respectively (as against 40, 41 and 44 per cent in HA1829, ERPI1829+, and C1830), while migrants from Brabant made up another 10–11 per cent (as against 12–14 per cent in 1829). Rather, it is likely that nearby migrants in this period were over-represented on poor relief lists by reasons of the criteria applied by the poor relief administration, and that these lists therefore do not constitute a representative source by which to view the whole of the city's migration field.
25. Military recruits and forced prison labourers made up almost half of the workforce of the Antwerp arsenal in the Napoleonic period (Epin, *Les ouvriers*, pp. 31–55, 82–5), but they were not recorded in the immigration registers. Only civilian naval workers (*ouvriers militaires civils*), who made up the other, more specialized, half of shipyard workers and who were mainly recruited via the *inscription maritime* (see below), were duly recorded in this specific source. In addition, women and short-distance migrants were evidently under-recorded in the earlier registers. While the sources used therefore undervalue the scale of labour mobilization in this period, they do provide ample demonstration of the importance of naval-related labour demand in inducing the sudden and radical expansion of Antwerp's migration field.
26. The proportion of long-distance migrants might be somewhat inflated due to the under-registration of regional migrants in the early registers. Nevertheless, it is clear that there was a strong and disproportionate increase in the absolute number of long-distance

migrants which was indicative of a sudden expansion of Antwerp's migration field – the more so considering that military naval workers were not even recorded in the registers.

27. While the global picture is distorted by an under-registration of regional and female migrants, the disproportionate absence of women among long-distance migrants is manifest enough to indicate their continued predilection towards shorter-distance movements.

28. Epin, *Les ouvriers*, pp. 19, 22–3, 77–85, 177–82. The Antwerp mayor even spoke of '6,000 Frenchmen employed in the different administrations of the Government', and another '3 to 4,000 *ouvriers militaires civils*': SAA, MA, 2222/1, n°. 3. In addition, Lucassen, *Naar de kusten*, pp. 294–5, estimated on the basis of the French *enquête* on migrant labour from 1811 that a total of some 800 to 1,000 carpenters, labourers, masons and sawyers yearly came to the Département des Deux Nèthes to work on Antwerp's naval shipyards and construction sites as seasonal workers.

29. The last Antwerp-based ship repairer had closed down halfway through the eighteenth century, and no local tradition of shipbuilding remained. In 1803 the city had only two operating shipbuilders capable of instructing apprentice shipwrights – at least one of which, the more important one, was a recent immigrant from Baulon in Bretagne: Epin, *Les ouvriers*, pp. 18–19, 57–66, 173; C. Everaert-Vermoortel, *Antwerpen als krijgshaven van Napoleon I* (n.p., 1959), pp. 9, 17–18; Jennes, 'De Franse scheepswerven', pp. 34, 36.

30. Lis, *Social Change*, pp. 32–4.

31. Everaert-Vermoortel, *Antwerpen*, p. 9.

32. In return, at least in theory, the *inscrits* were exempt from all other public duties, and received a pension in the case of old age or disability. Epin, *Les ouvriers*, pp. 31–5; N. Hampson, 'Les ouvriers des arsenaux de la marine au cours de la Révolution Française (1789–1794)', *Revue d'Histoire Economique et Sociale*, 39 (1961), pp. 287–329, 442–73, on pp. 288–93; P. Villiers and P. Culerrier, 'Du système des classes à l'inscription maritime: Le recrutement des marins français de Louis XIV à 1952', *Revue Historique des Armées*, 2 (1982), pp. 44–53, on pp. 45–9. Additional 'useful' workers could be levied by *levées extraordinaires*, generally organized at departmental level: see *Pasinomie*, 1st series, vol. 2, pp. 134–7: 31/12/1790=07/01/1791; vol. 7, pp. 138–43: 3 Brulaire IV (25/10/1795); vol. 12, pp. 5–7: 7 Ventôse XI (26/02/1803). With the annexation to France in 1795, the *inscription maritime* had been extended to the Belgian coastal regions in a period during which heavy levies, downgraded prerogatives and arrears in payment had greatly reduced the popularity of the system, and when the use of force appears to have become a familiar device in rounding up the necessary shipyard levies: Epin, *Les ouvriers*, pp. 35–9; Mertens and Torfs, *Geschiedenis van Antwerpen*, p. 85.

33. This was recorded more or less systematically only in the second and third volumes of the *Registres*, and even then not always, so that the resultant percentages represent lower limits. The most frequently mentioned types of proof of identity provided by male and female immigrants in CS1808–11 were passports (56 per cent), *certificats d'activité à la marine* (18 per cent) and *certificats de bonne conduite* (9 per cent).

34. Such as in the case of the Hainaut stonecutters from the villages to the north of Mons and Charleroi (see note 70 to Chapter 3 and below, pp. 177–8).

35. In CS1808–13, 412 different places of birth in present-day Belgium and Netherlands were identified for 971 migrants, of which 183 corresponded to one of the 606 different places recorded as birthplaces for the immigrants in C1796I.

36. Examples of forced levies for naval activities in Antwerp are, for instance, found in RAAnd, DP, 374, 428. In 1811 the departmental governor indicated that the 250–300 Walloon day-labourers and navvies who came to Antwerp annually to work in naval construction activities were recruited by military engineers, and possibly most of the other Walloon construction workers were too. Cited in Lis, *Social Change*, p. 42; Lucassen, *Naar de kusten*, pp. 291–3.

37. Cf. Baudez, 'De zeeprefectuur', p. 261; Fischer, *Napoléon*. On the increasing role of French fashion tastes in the seventeenth- and eighteenth-century Southern Netherlands, see also van Damme, 'Zotte verwaandheid'.

38. Although prostitution was legal, it does not figure as an occupation in the *Registres*. Many seamstresses, however, are marked with a cryptic sign 'N' in the margin. In later population books, most overt prostitutes would be referred to as seamstress (*naaister, couturiere*), sometimes also accompanied by the N-sign. An example is, for instance, the population books for the Haringvliet (at the centre of the urban red-light district) in the middle of the nineteenth century, where we find many young single 'seamstresses' living together in the same house with one barkeeper or *cabaretière* (see SAA, MA-BZA, B 1–124).

39. Cf. SAA, MA, 2222/2, n°. 3; Epin, *Les ouvriers*, p. 85; Lis, *Social Change*, p. 42.

40. The inflow of men from the French north coast and the Walloon areas collapsed drastically, from an average of 239 and 217 per year in CS1808–13 to 33 and 71 in CS1815–20 respectively, while nevertheless maintaining an immigrant proportion that remained well above that of the closing years of the *ancien regime*, indicating a mitigated continuation of the migration links forged in the Napoleonic period.

41. Beetemé, *Anvers*, vol. 2, p. 54; Greefs, 'Foreign Entrepreneurs'; SAA, MA, 2668/5, n°. 9250, 17/07/1815 (William Wood).

42. Class intervals include the lower boundary value and exclude the upper boundary value.

43. In 1829 alone no less than 71 male German newcomers were recorded in the (selective) residence card registers, of whom 35 worked as office clerks, in addition to seven carpenters, three printers, three merchants, and small numbers in a variety of other occupations. Virtually all female compatriots recorded in the same year worked as domestic servants (11 out of 15).

44. This development is reflected less in published census data, which actually indicate a restoration of Dutch predominance among non-national immigrant residents in the 1850s and 1860s, than in dynamic sources such as aliens' records, which more fully capture the continued importance of other nationalities – in particular Germans – over the same period. That the latter's importance was reflected less in the cross-sectional census results, therefore, appears to have had more to do with different patterns of stay and accumulation effects than with the absence of foreigners from farther afield.

45. Only the cross-border regions of North Brabant, Limburg and Zealand supplied important numbers of rural-born and of (single) women, while the few women moving along long-distance channels were mostly married housewives accompanying their husbands.

46. The average yearly inflow (AYI) of newcomers from within the Brabantine region evolved from 1,255 in CS1812–13, experienced a setback to 704 in the early years of Dutch rule (CS1815–20), but then again expanded markedly to well above 1,109 recorded in CS1829 – which probably recorded only around three-quarters of newcomers – and to 2,901 in IN1850.

47. In the 1830 census, immigrants born within the Antwerp province (10,087) still convincingly outnumbered those born in other provinces of later Belgium (6,958). By the time of the 1846 census, the respective figures were 12,596 and 10,430, while by 1856 they had come up to par with 15,600 versus 14,528. Unfortunately, from 1866 onwards the published census results no longer distinguish migrants born in the Antwerp province from other Belgian migrants. In any case, between 1830 and 1866, inter-provincial migrants had more than doubled in number (+109 per cent), while those from the Antwerp province had increased by slightly more than half (+55 per cent). See Appendix I.1.

48. Patients born in the former County of Flanders almost doubled their proportion of immigrant admissions to the St Elisabeth hospital from 10 per cent in 1829 to 18 per cent in 1855. By this year the province of East Flanders alone accounted for 41 per cent of Belgian patients born outside the province of Antwerp, as against only 21 per cent in 1829, thus becoming more important as a recruitment region than the province of Brabant (30 per cent in 1855 as against 45 per cent in 1829). In the emigration registers, too, Flemish migrants supplied a substantially larger share (15 per cent) in 1855 than they did in 1829 (8 per cent), surpassing the number of emigrants from Brabant (12 per cent in 1829 and 11 per cent in 1855). Their increased presence also emerges from the settlement examinations of Belgian-born sojourners in 1855, 28 per cent of whom were born in the provinces of East and West Flanders, supplying two-thirds of all relief applicants from outside the province of Antwerp.

49. The five most frequently cited places of origin supplied only 31 per cent of all Flemish patients admitted to St Elisabeth hospital in 1855, which constituted a concentration percentage below even that of the Campine hinterland.

50. On the calculations applied, see Appendix I.3.

51. Class intervals include the lower boundary value and exclude the upper boundary value. Source: CS1808-13, CS1815-20, CS1829, IN1850, HISGIS, NIDI. On intensity calculations, see Appendix I.3.

52. Source: C1796DB, C1796DB(D1+4), C1796I(cor), C1830.

53. Relatively little is known about the precise organization of dock labour around 1830, but there is no doubt that the majority of dock workers were employed on only a casual basis. Cf. Asaert et al. (eds), *The 'Naties'*, pp. 142–50; Prims, *Geschiedenis van Antwerpen, Volume X*, pp. 15–16, 49–50; K. Van Isacker, *De Antwerpse dokwerker, 1830–1940* (Antwerpen: Nederlandse Boekhandel, 1966), pp. 17–19. See also Lis, *Social Change*, pp. 61–2, 157–8.

54. Lis, *Social Change*, pp. 24–6.

55. Although some specific tasks at the docks – like the sorting and loading of fruit – provided some opportunities for female casual labour, women occupied a very weak position in the dock labour market. Cf. Van Isacker, *De Antwerpse dokwerker*, pp. 46–8.

56. On the whole, female activity in informal local service activities was probably greater than was measured by the occupational data of the 1830 census. It is with respect to this grey zone of 'informal activities' that occupational census data are likely to have been least adequate, and that under-registration was probably strongest. Cf. Lis, *Social Change*, p. 33.

57. Deceulaer, *Pluriforme patronen*, pp. 203–30.

58. Lis, *Social Change*, pp. 23–6, 31 ff.

59. Although no equivalent figures are readily available for later censuses, the proportion of migrants in the urban labour force increased even further in the following decades, parallel to the growth of their share in the overall population and the growing levels of temporary migration (see below).

60. In the 1830s the modal nominal summer wage for agricultural labourers in the surround-ings of Antwerp was only around 40 per cent of the modal nominal summer wage of carpenter journeymen and bricklayers in the city: Klep, *Bevolking*, p. 100; Scholliers, 'Prijzen', p. 1049.

61. Asaert et al. (eds), *The 'Naties'*, pp. 141 ff.

62. Available evidence at census and company level suggests that most of Ghent's nineteenth-century textile workers were born within the city: Dhondt, 'Notes sur les ouvriers'; P. Scholliers, *Wages, Manufacturers and Workers in the Nineteenth-Century Factory: The Voortman Cotton Mill in Ghent* (Oxford: Berg, 1996), pp. 105–9.

63. Cf. de Schaepdrijver, *Elites for the Capital?*; S. Hahn, 'Vienna: A Nexus between East and West', in L. Nilsson (ed.), *Capital Cities: Images and Realities in the Historical Develop-ment of European Capital Cities* (Stockholm: Stads- och Kommunhistoriska Institutet, 2000), pp. 60–4; A. Steidl, *Auf nach Wien! Die Mobilität des mitteleuropäischen Hand-werks im 18. und 19. Jahrhundert am Beispiel der Haupt- und Residenzstadt* (Wien: Oldenbourg Wissenschaftsverlag, 2003), pp. 156–245. See also Lee, 'Urban Labor Mar-kets', p. 451.

64. Compare, for instance, with Knotter, 'Poverty and the Family'; Lee, 'Urban Labor Mar-kets'; Lee and Lawton, 'Port Development', pp. 11–20, and following note.

65. Cf. J. Bruggeman and P. van de Laar, 'Rotterdam als migrantenstad aan het einde van de negentiende eeuw', in P. van de Laar (ed.), *Vier eeuwen migratie: Bestemming Rotterdam* (Rotterdam: MondiTaal, 1998), pp. 146–70, on pp. 156–9; G. S. Jones, *Outcast Lon-don: A Study in the Relationship between Classes in Victorian Society* (Oxford: Clarendon Press, 1971), pp. 136–46; Knotter, *Economische transformatie*, pp. 135–8; Lee, 'Urban Labor Markets', p. 457.

66. Klep, *Bevolking*, pp. 99–104.

67. Lis, *Social Change*, p. 48.

68. J. D. Post, 'Famine, Mortality, and Epidemic Disease in the Process of Modernization', *Economic History Review*, 29:1 (1976), pp. 14–37, on p. 15.

69. C. Lis, 'Verarmingsprocessen te Antwerpen, 1750–1850' (PhD dissertation, Vrije Uni-versiteit Brussel, 1975), p. 183; Scholliers, 'Prijzen', pp. 941–56.

70. The proportion of male newcomers from the province of Antwerp aged thirty or more leapt from 20 per cent in the Napoleonic era – a proportion more or less comparable with patterns observed for the later eighteenth century – to 38 per cent on average in the early years of Dutch rule, with a peak of 47 per cent in 1818, while the propor-tion of recorded family migration increased from virtually nil to almost 10 per cent in 1818 and 1819 – but the true proportion of family migration probably suffered from an under-registration of card-sharing companions. They also stayed longer: the proportion of intra-provincial newcomers who were still present in town one year after their arrival increased from around 60 per cent in the late French period to an average of around 70 per cent for the early Dutch period. Interestingly, the longest extension of stay was noted for immigrants who arrived in 1816, where the average length of stay of recorded leavers shot up to 402 days as against 338 days among the 1812–13 cohort. Among intra-pro-vincial newcomers, the respective median lengths of stay were 265 days in 1816 and 196 in 1812–13.

71. Already in 1819, the proportion of male newcomers aged thirty or more subsided from peak values of 43 and 44 per cent in CS1817 and CS1818 to only 33 per cent in CS1819 – a proportion comparable to that in CS1815 and CS1816. Among women, the propor-tion of the over-thirties came down from 16 to 14 per cent. In CS1829, more than 95

per cent of newcomers were recorded as single, while only 21 per cent of men and 23 per cent of women were aged thirty or more – with a median age of 23. Although the registers by this time were probably biased towards young and single migrants, with family migrants more readily recorded in the population books directly, the available evidence points towards a quick post-crisis restoration of the predominance of young and single migrants.

72. Making a comparison with the eighteenth century is more difficult, as figures on gross inflow and outflow are lacking up to 1804. However, even if we assume gross inflow in the 1780s and 1790s to have averaged only 1,000 per year – less than half of the levels recorded in the 1820s – the proportion of immigrants staying longer than five years could not have exceeded 33 per cent in the period.

73. While shipping volumes fell from 130,000 tonnes in 1829 to 46,000 in 1831, the number of recorded newcomers fell from over 2,500 to 600, and would only regain its previous levels by the end of the 1830s. This drop was definitely not attributable to falling levels of migration control, as the insecure situation increased overall suspicion and control measures towards newcomers in the early 1830s (cf. SAA, MA, 2668/18; MA, 2635; and many sources in RAA – see the references in note 136 to Chapter 2).

74. Also office work appears to have been – at least by the late 1820s – a highly temporary occupation, especially so for German clerks and office workers (see below, pp. 164–5).

75. For the 1817 cohort, see Lis, *Social Change*, pp. 59–62. For the 1819 cohort, see Winter, 'Patterns of Migration', pp. 276–7: fifteen out of sixty-seven male newcomers in CS1819 were present and identifiable up to the census of 1830: twelve of them still performed more or less the same job in 1830 as on arrival, while those shifts which had taken place, from cloth trimmer via shopkeeper to warehouse keeper, or from labourer via domestic servant to coach proprietor, were in the direction of port-related activities. By 1830, eight worked in port-related sectors (three as labourers and the others as a coach driver, journeyman cooper, sail-maker, *natiebaas* and warehouse keeper), while another five worked in supportive or maintenance sectors (two hired servants, a barkeeper, a butcher boy, and a plasterer's mate) – confirming the tangible possibilities for settlement which employment in these sectors offered in the 1820s.

76. Of the nineteen women from 1819 traceable up to the 1830 census, fourteen had entered town as domestic servants. Seven of them were still in service in 1830, of whom all but one remained a domestic servant for as far as they could be traced throughout the registers, which was often until the next census in 1846. The chance that they would eventually marry and form a household had by that time become rather slim – in their case, domestic service had clearly become a lifetime situation. On the other hand, for many female immigrants domestic service was still only a life-cycle phase. By 1830 six prior domestic servants had become housewives without recorded occupation, while another one had become a shopkeeper. In addition, only the garment trades and casual labour offered intermediary or alternative income opportunities, between which shifts occurred regularly. On the shift from life-cycle to lifetime service in nineteenth-century England, see S. McIsaac Cooper, 'Service to Servitude? The Decline and Demise of Life-Cycle Service in England', *History of the Family*, 10:4 (2005), pp. 376–86.

77. Winter, 'Patterns of Migration', pp. 279–80: of all single newcomers from CS1819 still present in 1830, 75 per cent of men and 44 per cent of women had married.

78. Only 19 per cent of all married newcomers would again leave Antwerp between 1817 and 1830, as against 43 per cent of those who remained unmarried: Lis, 'Verarmings-processen', pp. 195, 217–19.

79. Hannes, 'Bijdrage', p. 87.
80. CS1819-155.
81. CS1819-46.
82. Between 13 and 16 per cent of all births in Antwerp between 1830 and 1860 were illegitimate (Kruithof, 'De demografische ontwikkeling', p. 524), which was a comparatively large proportion in a Belgian context: Lesthaeghe, *The Decline*, pp. 122–3.
83. Newcomer Jean François Van Walderen, for instance, lived with his partner Marguerite Heuren for almost ten years and had two 'illegitimate' children with her, before they eventually married in the 1830s (CS1819-077).
84. Cf. R. G. Fuchs, *Poor and Pregnant in Paris: Strategies for Survival in the Nineteenth Century* (New Brunswick, NJ: Rutgers University Press, 1992); Fuchs and Moch, 'Pregnant, Single'; J. Van Bavel, 'Family Control, Bridal Pregnancy, and Illegitimacy: An Event History Analysis in Louvain, Belgium, 1846–1856', *Social Science History*, 25:3 (2001), pp. 449–79, on p. 472.
85. Two of the six children of unmarried mothers from CS1819 died in the first year, while the child of Thérèse van Nuffel disappeared from the population registers when she returned to work as a domestic servant (CS1819-81).
86. Based on the analysis of Hannes, 'Bijdrage', pp. 78–9, and bijlage 5, 144–9 of the 1,757 deaths recorded by the civil registry in 1830.
87. Of the 611 newcomers from 1817 traced by Lis in the population registers, 67 were to die before the 1830 census. Similarly, at least eight of the 86 newcomers from CS1819 are recorded as having eventually died in Antwerp.
88. See, for instance, M. Oris and G. Alter, 'Paths to the City and Roads to Death: Mortality and Migration in East Belgium during the Industrial Revolution', *Belgisch Tijdschrift voor Nieuwste Geschiedenis*, 31:3 (2001), pp. 453–95.
89. The proportion of recorded leavers who returned to their place of birth or last place of residence in CS1815–29 was 51, 57 and 49 per cent for those who left within one (N=470), three (N=230) or five years (N=81) after arrival, but only 25 per cent for those who stayed between five and ten years (N=12), and only 22 per cent among those who stayed longer than ten years (N=9). The fall-off in the proportion of return-migrants over time was strongest among women, where the respective proportions fell from 53, 59 and 39 per cent to 17 and 20 per cent.
90. A new royal theatre hall had been built in 1834, while the 1840s witnessed, among other things, a reorganization and expansion of the city's Academy for Fine Arts, the re-opening of a completely refurbished Museum of Fine Arts, and a proliferation of musical and cultural associations: Mertens and Torfs, *Geschiedenis van Antwerpen*, pp. 504–12.
91. Veraghtert, 'From Inland Port', pp. 387–92.
92. Cited by Lis, *Social Change*, p. 35.
93. While 'cultural' occupations such as actors, musicians, *garçons coiffeur* and *garçons de café* were, for instance, the most numerous among French immigrants recorded in FR1850, most British newcomers were wholesale traders, proprietors or (better-off) students; Germans mainly supplied commission merchants, office clerks and painters; and newcomers from Holland and Utrecht provided a number of varied white-collar workers, proprietors and merchants, in addition to a handful of Amsterdam-born diamond workers. Finally, a number of Swiss *patissiers* and *confiseurs* catch the eye, as do a handful of Scandinavian merchants and sailors. See Chapter 5.
94. De Schaepdrijver, *Elites for the Capital?*, pp. 49, 64–6, 72–80. See also De Metsenaere, *Taalmuur*, pp. 160–2.

95. As with FR1850, data on re-migration is very fragmentary in the case of the Brussels aliens' records, and cannot be treated as representative for the whole group. Cf. de Schaepdrijver, *Elites for the Capital?*, p. 62.
96. NSMP1841–50. Note that cross-sectional data on migrant composition, which record only the net 'residual' of gross immigration figures mentioned here, assign greater weight to inter-provincial migration over intra-provincial migration in this period (see note 47 above), which may be indicative of different patterns of stay as well as different levels of accuracy in the reports used.
97. De Metsenaere, 'Migraties', pp. 121–9; Dumont, *Migrations intérieures*, pp. 181–3, 198–9; Oris, 'Fertility and Migration', p. 171; Poulain, et al., 'Flemish Immigration'; Van den Eeckhout, 'Determinanten', pp. 70–5; Van den Eeckhout, 'De rekrutering', pp. 235–7.
98. Of all Flemish-born men recorded in the emigration registers of 1855 (ERPI1855), no less than 60 per cent had been aged thirty or more at the time of their arrival, while 38 per cent had arrived with wife and/or children, as against only 24 per cent and 19 per cent respectively of those born in the province of Antwerp.
99. See note 48 above.
100. ERPI1855 and ERPI1829+. Even in the group of intra-provincial migrants, this proportion grew from 25 to 31 per cent. Among women, the trend is less clear. If at all, the sources show an increase in the proportion of women immigrating at an age between fifteen and nineteen, which might be related to an increase in the proportion of family migration, or to a lowering of the age of domestic servants.
101. Even allowing for a certain under-registration of family migration in CS1829, this indicates an important expansion of the phenomenon of older-age and family migration among Brabantine newcomers.
102. Cf. Van Isacker, *De Antwerpse dokwerker*, pp. 28–9.
103. In both years, the proportion which had been in town longer than ten years was very small, confirming that most re-migration took place in the first years after arrival.
104. To a certain extent, this decline also reflected the increased mobility before coming to Antwerp: complemented with the partial data on emigrants' previous place of residence, the (minimal) proportion of return migration declined from 51 to 45 per cent – which again is symptomatic of the increasing complexity of migration trajectories both before and after the stay in Antwerp.
105. Motivated by lower costs of living in the *banlieues*, these moves can be considered part of intra-urban survival strategies as the growing town became physically more integrated with the villages on its outskirts. On intra-urban mobility as a survival strategy, see, for instance, J. Kok, K. Mandemakers and H. Wals, 'City Nomads: Changing Residence as a Coping Strategy, Amsterdam 1890–1940', *Social Science History*, 29:1 (2005), pp. 15–43.
106. Of rural-born maids emigrating in 1855, 35 per cent chose an urban destination, as against only 20 per cent in 1829.
107. The male to female ratios here refer to the city's 'actual' (*population de fait*) rather than 'legal' (*population de droit*) population, where they were slightly lower – 85:100 and 89:100 respectively. The differences in sex ratios between the legal and actual populations recorded in the censuses are attributable to the masculine character of most of the city's actual residents who were not considered part of the legal population, such as soldiers and sailors. See Appendix I.1.

108. Most of the houses available, moreover, were old and small: most dated back to the late Middle Ages and sixteenth century, and dwellings with only one or two rooms were no exception: Lis, *Social Change*, pp. 64–8.

109. Ibid., p. 65; S. Van Houtven, 'Een studie naar de buurt en haar conflictregulerende werking: De Antwerpse Seefhoek anno 1879' (Licentiaat dissertation, Vrije Universiteit Brussel, 2005), pp. 42–4. Or, as the director of the Charity Bureau testified in 1860: 'The fifth district greatly resembles a hut camp, and so many hovels are built with such shoddy materials that after a few years they fall into decay'. Cited in Lis, *Social Change*, p. 65.

110. Sojourners' households were, for instance, strongly over-represented in the fourth – and poorest – town district, where many resided in the large Boeksteeg ghetto. An important proportion lived in the developing fifth district. In the third and most upmarket district, sojourners were heavily under-represented, while those from the second district clustered predominantly in the paupers' ghetto of Paradise Street and adjacent streets.

111. C. Lis, 'Woontoestanden en gangsaneringen te Antwerpen in het midden van de negentiende eeuw', *Belgisch Tijdschrift voor Nieuwste geschiedenis*, 1:1 (1969), pp. 93–131; Lis, *Social Change*, pp. 68–80.

112. Jackson, *Migration and Urbanization*, pp. 253–63.

113. Interestingly, Jackson never measures return movement as an actual return to one's place of birth or last place of residence, but solely in terms of settlement size and region.

114. SE1849–55. Valid observations: 278 (ever) married male sojourners and 266 male sojourners' parents.

115. The proportion was lowest among sojourners who had married after arriving in Antwerp (3 per cent), which attests to the role of the city in broadening marriage horizons. Even among those who had married before coming to Antwerp, however, the proportion of same-place marriages was substantially smaller (28 per cent) than among their parents. If the comparison is extended to include the region rather than place of birth, rates of geographical endogamy remained substantially higher for sojourners' parents (80 per cent) than for sojourners themselves (40 per cent) – although the proportion married to a bride from the same region of birth was substantially higher for those married before coming to Antwerp (66 per cent) than for those who had married in Antwerp (18 per cent).

116. Data on parents' mobility might have been somewhat underrated due to ignorance or simplifications on the part of their children, especially concerning the birthplace of deceased mothers.

117. Cf. Bras, *Zeeuwse meiden*, pp. 81–103; V. Piette, *Domestiques et servantes: Des vies sous condition* (Bruxelles: Académie Royale de la Belgique, 2000). I hope to pursue the particular case of female servants' mobility in a separate study.

118. SEB1855-154.

119. Hufton, *The Poor*; Lis, *Social Change*.

5 Circuits, Networks and Trajectories

1. Although setting the limit between rural and urban at 10,000 inhabitants creates a grey zone of small-town migrants grouped on either side of the distinction, it is contended that a more detailed – and therefore necessarily more complicated – classification according to population size would have contributed relatively little to the analysis of

the basic distinction between rural and urban. An alternative would have been to make a three-pronged classification with benchmarks at 5,000 and 20,000 or 50,000, but this would have substantially increased the number of categories, and would have obscured the main distinctions. The main contention is that one basic distinction between rural and urban – with an unavoidable grey area – is of prime importance, and further distinctions in terms of population size can be applied within the context of this broader subdivision. As the proportion of migrants from settlements with between 5,000 and 15,000 inhabitants – more or less the grey area in this context – is relatively small, they do not strongly interfere with the main characteristics of the 'rural' and 'urban' recruitment circuits. To distribute the grey area somewhat evenly between both categories, the benchmark was eventually put at 10,000 inhabitants instead of 5,000. Putting the benchmark at 5,000 would have resulted in a relatively 'pure' rural category, but the weight of persons from small-towns would have made too much of an amalgam of the 'urban' category. Moreover, given the densely populated nature of some rural regions, in particular Flanders, many rural villages had more than 5,000 inhabitants without representing an urban environment as such. In this respect, too, a benchmark at 10,000 was more appropriate than one at 5,000. Limiting the first circuit to the Province of Antwerp – instead of including adjacent areas whose migrants displayed some regional characteristics – is in turn motivated by the striving for a diachronically consistent view of developments within the quintessentially regional recruitment circuit, without having to account for spatial shifts in the outer areas of the 'demographic basin'. As we have seen, these 'outer' areas of Antwerp's regional recruitment area, located in the provinces of Brabant, North Brabant, Limburg and eventually also East Flanders, tended to shift somewhat in importance and immigrant profile throughout the period in question, while being mainly outside the regional recruitment area at other times. Excluding these provinces from the first category was therefore motivated by a striving for diachronic consistency in the definition of the quintessentially regional recruitment circuit. The main purpose of including the cross-border regions of North Brabant, Limburg and Zeeland in the third 'internal' circuit is to single out movements within an urban inter-regional circuit that was already present in the eighteenth century, and which is to be distinguished from longer-distance urban circuits that were mainly a reflection of Antwerp's increasing international interactions in the course of the nineteenth century. In addition to a mainly regional, at best national, network of cities, Antwerp also became a node in an international network of 'super-cities'. Connections with cities in Limburg (Maastricht), North Brabant ('s Hertogenbosch, Tilburg and Breda) and Zeeland (Vlissingen and Middelburg) clearly belonged to the first network and not to the second one, and were already strongly developed in the second half of the eighteenth century, while those with Dutch cities situated further away, such as Amsterdam, Rotterdam or Groningen, belonged mainly to the second group, and increased considerably only in the wake of Antwerp's developing port activities. That the third circuit has not been subdivided further between rural-born and urban-born is in turn justified by the observation that most long-distance migrants were born in cities anyway. Most rural-born 'foreign' migrants came from cross-border provinces included in the fourth category. The group of rural-born long-distance migrants would have made up too small a subgroup, while their inclusion does not strongly distort the profile of predominantly inter-urban international migrants. Finally, although the fourth circuit might give the impression of being a residual category, it consisted of a number of meaningful subgroups, which will be discussed separately.

2. Lis, *Social Change*, p. 69.
3. R. Skeldon, *Population Mobility in Developing Countries: A Reinterpretation* (London and New York: Belhaven Press, 1990), pp. 158–9, on an analogous two-step migration process to contemporary Lima.
4. Addresses in the sources were typically mentioned only with reference to the district and house number, without reference to the street name. The numbering of houses within town districts, however, was subject to several renumberings, and identifying each of the different house numbers mentioned in the sources with specific streets at specific points in time would have represented a very time-consuming operation that fell beyond the scope of this study.
5. The place of origin and occupation of hosts and their spouses were looked up in the population registers for one in two newcomers in 1829: 880 hosts were looked up, 687 were found. When comparing the geographic origins of host and newcomer, I have differentiated between hosts who were born in Antwerp, those who were born in the same area as the migrant in question and those who were born elsewhere. The definition of 'same area' employed here was distance-sensitive: for migrants born within the provinces of Antwerp, Brabant and North Brabant, the relevant areas correspond to today's *arrondissementen*, for other migrants from within the then Kingdom of the Netherlands, they correspond to today's provinces, and for other more distant migrants, they correspond to today's countries. Thus a Frenchman lodging in a Frenchman's house is classified as staying with someone from the same area, even if one came from the Département du Nord and the other from the Pyrenees. For more nearby migrants, finer grids were applied so as to remain meaningful, but they nevertheless remain relatively broad.
6. One caveat which merits being mentioned here is the relatively small number of foreign-born migrants in CS1829 (51 male and 21 female valid observations for which we can establish the relationships between host and newcomer). The patterns exposed for this particular circuit in terms of the relationship between newcomer and host therefore need not have been completely representative of their later and more numerous compatriots in the 1850s. However, there are few indications that the incidence of 'same area' linkages between foreign immigrants and hosts would have increased very strongly.
7. All hosts of migrants recorded as servant were classified as employer, while hosts who worked in the same sector (bakers versus baker journeymen, butchers versus butcher boys, carpenters versus joiners, etc.) were also classified as colleague or employer. Because it was not always possible on the basis of the material available to rule out the employment relationship between newcomer and host (colleague or employer), these two categories have been grouped together.
8. All hosts recording independent catering and lodging activities (*logeur, cabaretier, vendeur de bière, tenant maison de pension, hotelier*, etc.) in the population books, either as first or secondary occupation, were considered keepers of professional lodgings.
9. Where this relationship was obvious, such as in the case of *garçons de café* or *aides cabaretières*, hosts were classified as employer instead of professional lodging-keeper. In some minor instances where hosts were classified as lodging-keepers, such as a bookkeeper in a large hotel, the matter was less clear.
10. Cf. Jackson, *Migration and Urbanization*, pp. 269–73.
11. Cf. Lesger, 'Informatiestromen'.
12. CS1819-154 and population registers.

13. Only during the period of Napoleonic and early Dutch rule did this particular circuit record somewhat lower proportions, because of the relatively high numbers of foreign-born migrants present during these periods.

14. While 24 per cent of immigrant brides were likely to marry an Antwerp-born groom in 1830, this was 29 per cent for immigrants born within the province of Antwerp. This preference was less outspoken among men (35.5 and 35.3 per cent respectively).

15. M. Oris, 'La transition de la mobilité au 19e siècle: L'expérience de Huy-sur-Meuse (Belgique), entre 1847 et 1900', *Annales de Démographie Historique*, 84:10 (1993), pp. 191–225, on pp. 218–19.

16. If the number of rural inhabitants is set against total productive surface – i.e. excluding forests, wastelands, rivers and built-up areas – the respective densities in 1846 were as high as 221 in the district of Antwerp, 241 in that of Mechelen and 184 in that of Turnhout: Klep, *Bevolking*, pp. 57–60, 412–13.

17. E. Vanhaute, 'Eigendomsverhoudingen in de Belgische en Vlaamse landbouw tijdens de 18de en de 19de eeuw', *Belgisch Tijdschrift voor Nieuwste geschiedenis*, 24:1–2 (1993), pp. 185–226, on pp. 195, 217.

18. Klep, *Bevolking*, pp. 57–8; Lis, *Social Change*, pp. 50–1; Vanhaute, *Heiboeren*, pp. 130–3.

19. Between 1834 and 1856 the total surface of common lands in the province of Antwerp was halved from 32,000 to 16,000 hectares: E. Van Looveren, 'De privatisering van de gemene gronden in de provincie Antwerpen: Vier case-studies', *Bijdragen tot de Geschiedenis*, 66 (1983), pp. 189–216.

20. In the more remote district of Turnhout, the tendency towards peasant expropriation and marginalization was less outspoken than in other areas of the Antwerp Province: in 1846, 88 per cent of its rural population still owned farmland, while 37 per cent held sufficient land to derive the whole household income from agrarian activities. Nevertheless, also here a negative trend was evident. While in the middle of the eighteenth century peasants had still owned around 85 per cent of the cultivated land, by the middle of the nineteenth century this was only 70 per cent: Vanhaute, 'Eigendomsverhoudingen', p. 217. In the villages of Dessel and Rijkevorsel, the proportion of landless households increased from 5 and 10 per cent respectively in the mid-eighteenth century to 22 and 33 per cent a century later. The stronger continuity in property and common rights, however, enabled greater 'flexibility of the rural organization of survival', which, according to E. Vanhaute, 'Processes of Peripheralization in a Core Region: The Campine Area of Antwerp in the "Long Nineteenth Century"', *Review*, 16:1 (1993), pp. 57–81, on pp. 71–6, allowed most of the increasing pressure to be integrated within the existing repertoire of peasant survival strategies. That levels of emigration remained relatively low in these villages is confirmed by his exploration of local population registers, showing that average yearly emigration rates amounted to no more than 1 per cent between 1830 and 1910, of which at most 0.5 per cent was directed towards urban centres. Vanhaute, *Heiboeren*, pp. 62–8; Vanhaute, 'Processes of Peripheralization', pp. 66–8. In Kalmthout in the district of Antwerp, in contrast, emigration rates amounted to an average of 10 per cent around the middle of the nineteenth century. Goossens, 'Een negentiende-eeuws heidedorp', pp. 209, 234. By 1846, the proportion of land under leasehold had grown to 46 and 72 per cent respectively in the districts of Antwerp and Mechelen. At the same time, only one in two households held land, 72 and 62 per cent of which respectively was too small to secure a family income: Vanhaute, 'Eigendomsverhoudingen', p. 217. See also Lis, *Social Change*, p. 50.

21. In 1836 the line Antwerp–Mechelen was completed, while in 1854 a railway connection to Roosendaal linked up the villages to the north of the city. In 1855, a railway connection between Kontich and Lier, and between Lier and Turnhout, would open up the more eastern part of the province: Veen, 'Spoorwegontwikkeling', p. 64. See also Goossens, 'Een negentiende-eeuws heidedorp', p. 206.

22. A similar pattern was later repeated in the household of Catharina Cassiers, where Joseph and Cornelius Hoppenbrouwers – possibly orphaned relatives of Petrus Elst or stepchildren from a former marriage – made themselves useful in Petrus's shop before setting up an independent household themselves.

23. Cf. Lis, *Social Change*, pp. 150–62.

24. Although settlement legislation allowed for relief transfers from any one municipality to the other if both agreed on the transfer, it is likely that villages in the near surroundings of Antwerp had better-developed routine arrangements in this respect. As early as the middle of the eighteenth century traces are found of separate arrangements between the poor administrators of Antwerp and the local authorities of places like Mechelen, Lier, Gierle, Turnhout, and Deurne and Borgerhout on the relief transfers for sojourners: E. Pais-Minne, 'Weldadigheidsinstellingen en sociale toestanden', in *Antwerpen in de achttiende eeuw*, pp. 156–86, on p. 162; Winter, 'Caught between Law and Practice', pp. 145–6. The fact that intra-provincial migrants were over-represented on the poor relief lists (in 1855, 72 per cent of migrants on the poor relief lists were born in the provinces of Antwerp and Brabant according to Lis, *Social Change*, p. 46) also points in the same direction.

25. The shift is, for instance, reflected in the birthplace top 10 of internal inter-urban migrants over the period in question. Whereas in 1796 the top 10 listed four cross-border towns ('s Hertogenbosch, Tilburg, Breda, Maastricht) and not a single Flemish one, by 1855 only nearby Breda – the only Dutch city connected by a direct railway line – succeeded in maintaining its position, while the three other Dutch towns had been replaced by Flemish ones (Gent, Brugge, Aalst). The fact that Brussel, Turnhout, Lier and Mechelen invariably figured in the top 5 attests to the central importance of provincial and metropolitan connections.

26. Except for textile production, the small-sized regional centres in the southernmost province of the Netherlands did not possess any marked degree of occupational differentiation and specialization. Neither the production of luxury goods nor port-related construction activities had any strong tradition in the area. Kappelhof, 'Toenemende spanningen', p. 535; K. F. E. Veraghtert, 'Van ambachtelijke nijverheid naar industriële produktie', in H. F. J. M. van den Eerenbeemt (ed.), *Geschiedenis van Noord-Brabant, Deel 1: Traditie en modernisering, 1796–1890* (Amsterdam: Boom, 1996), pp. 223–40, on pp. 230–40. By 1850, most newcomers from Dutch cities in the cross-border provinces had a relatively unspecialized occupational profile, which showed many resemblances to their rural-born counterparts. In contrast, Flemish cities were more familiar with port activities, while especially Brussels had a strong edge in the production of luxury goods.

27. Or, more correctly, to the extent they were spending their young adult years working as domestic servants, apprentices or journeymen, this did not keep them in the same place for several years in a row.

28. Although they were somewhat more likely to serve in a merchant family and less likely to work in a farmers' household than rural-born intra-provincial maids, there was no large difference in the occupational profile of their employers: the largest proportion ended up

working for people in the retail and distribution sector, while the rest mainly worked in the households of traders, civil servants, doctors or other privileged residents.

29. FR1850, 7738. Compare with the wages compiled by Lis, *Social Change*, pp. 36–7, 175–6. It was, however, somewhat below the standard summer wage for carpenters in Antwerp (*c*. 2.5 francs): cf. Klep, *Bevolking*, p. 100; Scholliers, 'Prijzen', p. 1049.

30. ER1855-1030; POPD, 1–626.

31. He left again for Breda in 1851, but he would later turn up in Antwerp again in 1862 as an overseer of the Engineering Corps (*Surveillant du génie*). FR1850, 7573.

32. ER1855-560; POPD, 4–262.

33. While the first Flemish shipbuilders were recruited under Napoleonic rule via the *inscription maritime*, we still find a considerable number of caulkers, shipwrights and metalworkers from Ostend, Bruges, Ghent and Aalst in later years.

34. Cf. Blondé, *Een economie*; Blondé and Van Uytven, 'De smalle steden'.

35. E.g. CS1819-10, 42, 46, 155. The – selective – trajectories of urban-born sojourners as distilled from SE1849–55 indicate that military service might have been an important migration catalyst for several young men: 33 of 78 inter-urban male sojourners had spent several years of their youth in military service – from four up to ten years – at least half of whom had been stationed in Antwerp during part of that time. Possibly, military recruitment mechanisms continued to play an important role in channelling some of Antwerp's more distant urban newcomers in the 1840s and 1850s. In the absence of existing research on the social implications of military service in this period it remains difficult to establish the precise role of military service as a catalyst for migration.

36. SEB1855-123.

37. SENL1849-51:305–6.

38. We know from other sources that the relatively 'liberal' Kingdom of Belgium came to function as a safe haven for quite a number of political exiles, which might have constituted an additional attraction to foreign newcomers – but less so in Antwerp than in Brussels. In the case of Antwerp, we found little indication of political motives for moving – most political refugees *avant la lettre* turned to Brussels, which was the intellectual and political heart of the country. Caestecker, *Alien Policy*; S. de Schaepdrijver, 'Vreemdelingen in *Vilette*: De buitenlandse aanwezigheid in het negentiende-eeuwse Brussel', in Soly and Thijs (eds), *Minderheden in Westeuropese*, pp. 115–34, on pp. 119–20.

39. Of the 47 pre-1790 immigrants, 21 had married after their arrival (4 had been married prior to arrival, 14 were still unmarried at the time of the census, and 8 were widowed). Of these, 11 had married a local-born spouse, i.e. one in two, which was about the contemporary average. If they married a fellow immigrant, it was never a compatriot.

40. SAA, MA-BZA, D 1, cahier 14, n°. 1473.

41. And would later father the Flemish romantic writer Henri Conscience: E. De Bock, *Hendrik Conscience en de opkomst van de Vlaamsche romantiek* (Antwerpen: De Sikkel, n.d.), pp. 34–40; E. Willekens, *Hij leerde zijn volk lezen: Profiel van Hendrik Conscience 1812–1883* (Antwerpen: Stichting Hendrik Conscience, 1982), pp. 29–32.

42. Due to the paucity of re-migration registration in the early years of the *Registres*, this could not be verified through the residence card registers – only a thorough analysis of the origins of migrants in the 1815/16 census could throw further light on the matter.

43. Most probably, the toolmakers and construction workers of the Dutch period moved along paths which had been paved by the Napoleonic *inscription maritime*. They almost invariably came from the Département du Nord, Picardy or Brittany, i.e. the same regions which had provided most of the naval workers under Napoleon. In addition, at least four

of the twenty-four French newcomers in CS1815–16 produced a *congé militaire* or a *congé maritime* in return for their residence card. Little evidence has been found on the lodging arrangements of these construction workers: two shipwrights from Bordeaux and Cherbourg respectively were found staying with the journeyman carpenter Cassart from Gesves (Namur) in 1829, indicating the existence of occupation-specific (but not origin-specific) networks (CS1829-780, CS1829-1391). The other six construction workers recorded that year, however, stayed with a shopkeeper (2), innkeeper (2), labourer (1) – none of whom was a compatriot – and in a family house (1), indicating that other lodging arrangements were important too.

44. F. Sartorius, 'De Fransen in België in de 19de eeuw', in A. Morelli (ed.), *Geschiedenis van het eigen volk. De vreemdeling in België van de prehistorie tot nu* (Leuven: Kritak, 1993), pp. 152–5; P. Scholliers, *Arm en rijk aan tafel: Tweehonderd jaar eetcultuur in België* (Antwerpen: EPO, 1993), pp. 65–71. See also van Damme, 'Zotte verwaandheid' on the French cultural allure in the eighteenth century. Up until the middle of the nineteenth century, the lustrous city theatre – built in 1834 – would present exclusively French plays: Mertens and Torfs, *Geschiedenis van Antwerpen*, pp. 511–12.

45. FR1850-7569, 7980, 7985, 7986, 7988, 7990, 7992, 8163.

46. FR1850-8101, 8103.

47. In 1819, the 23-year old cook Jean Gilles Nerandau from Paris came to work in the restaurant of Joan Lange from Brighton for a year and a half, after which he returned to the French capital (CS1819-78). Likewise, in 1850 a 23-year old waiter from Cappy (Somme) and a 23-year old cook from Les Andelys (Eure) came to work in the restaurant of their compatriot Bertrand in the Meir, while another waiter was hired by *Sr. Léonard tenant café suisse sur la Place Verte* (FR1850-7727, 7728, 7614).

48. Only 2.6 per cent of all immigrants recorded in the 1796 census were born in a place within the boundaries of present-day Germany, mainly from a variety of cities and villages close to the Limburg borders. While most women were either maids, spinners or 'housewives', German men worked in a variety of occupations. With 17 per cent recorded as trader, merchant or shopkeeper, they had an orientation towards trade activities which was only slightly more marked than that of the immigrant population as a whole. In addition, a considerable number worked in local industries such as textile production, leather manufacture or tobacco processing. Of the 38 Germans who had married after arrival, 21 (9 men and 12 women) had married an Antwerp-born spouse, while 17 (12 men and 5 women) had married a fellow immigrant – from a variety of different places – but none of whom was a fellow German.

49. Cf. Devos, 'Inwijking en integratie'; G. Pelckmans, 'De Duitse kolonie te Antwerpen en haar invloed op de Antwerpse samenleving (19e eeuw – 1914)' (Licentiaat dissertation, Katholieke Universiteit Leuven, 1994); G. Pelckmans and J. Van Doorslaer, *De Duitse kolonie 1796–1914* (Kapellen: Pelckmans, 2000).

50. Like the Kreglinger brothers from Karlsruhe, who in 1795 established the illustrious Kreglinger Company on the Antwerp *Grand Place,* at that time occupied mainly with transit trade in colonial wares, and which together with its spin-offs would remain one of the city's prime commercial players in the nineteenth and twentieth centuries: Beetemé, *Anvers*, vol. 2, pp. 11–12; Pelckmans, 'De Duitse kolonie', pp. 7–8.

51. While recruitment from cross-border regions in Nordrhein-Westfalen might have partly built upon earlier connections, Bremen and Hamburg were notable newcomers in the birthplace top 5. However, only two of thirty Germans whose proof of identity was recorded in the residence card registers produced a naval certificate.

52. All construction workers of 1828–30 whose host was traced in the population books, appeared to stay with a colleague or employer who combined his work with keeping a lodginghouse, such as carpenter/lodging keeper Petrus Truyts from Boechout, who lodged at least two (POPB, 3-998). That this specific migrant group moved along well-structured patterns of seasonal migration, is confirmed by the presence of the same persons in consecutive years at the same address.
53. Cf. Devos, 'Inwijking en integratie', pp. 138–40.
54. CS1829-75, FR1850-7900, 7464, 7814, 7618, CS1829-1228. Compare with Beetemé, *Anvers*, vol. 2, pp. 54–7, 121–2.
55. FR1850-7879.
56. By the end of the Dutch period the inn of Sannes in the Borzestraat and the house of Muls in the Beggaardenstraat appear to have been places where many stayed: the first housed at least five German office clerks and one trader at different times in 1829 and the first months of 1830, while the second housed five. Sannes was born in Antwerp and his wife in Ostend, while Muls came from Oosterhout (North Brabant) and his wife from Antwerp. (POPB, 3-190; POPB, 3-279/80)
57. CS1829-81, CS1829-599. Cf. Beetemé, *Anvers*, vol. 2, pp. 65–6.
58. CS1829-1536, CS1829-1537, CS1829-1371. (Although it should be noted that the French cook's wife was born in Monschau).
59. A noticeable subgroup here was formed by artist painters (15 per cent) many of whom came to work or to study at the Antwerp Academy and Museum of Fine Arts.
60. Everaert, 'Antwerpen'; J. Everaert, E. Joos and R. Vervoort, *Landverhuizers: Antwerpen als kruispunt van komen en gaan* (Antwerpen: Pandora, 2002). The growing stream of hapless German emigrants would in the second half of the later decades of the nineteenth century entail a residue of would-be leavers, people who became stranded in Antwerp on their way to New York, and who mainly settled down near the station. This movement also provided the basis of Antwerp's important Jewish colony, which was fed from the 1880s onwards by the growing stream of eastern & central European Jews fleeing the adverse economic and anti-semitic conditions of the Russian and Habsburg Empires – some of whom eventually remained in Antwerp: V. Ronin, *Antwerpen en zijn "Russen". Onderdanen van de tsaar, 1814–1914* (Gent: Stichting Mens & Cultuur, 1993); L. Saerens, *Vreemdelingen in een wereldstad: Een geschiedenis van Antwerpen en zijn Joodse bevolking (1880–1944)* (Tielt: Lannoo, 2000), pp. 5–28.
61. Lesger et al., 'Is There Life', pp. 33–8, 41–4, quote on p. 44.
62. Ibid., pp. 38–41; Schrover, 'Potverkopers'; Schrover, *Een kolonie van Duitsers*.
63. Lesger et al., 'Is There Life', pp. 41–3, quote on p. 43.
64. A similar 'broadening' of migration streams from skilled pioneers to less skilled 'followers' was for instance noted for seventeenth-century Leiden by Lucassen and de Vries, 'The Rise and Fall'.
65. Women were in the majority: in the first and fourth districts we find 53 men and 79 women. Two out of three of those who married after arrival wed an Antwerp-born spouse, or else married a fellow immigrant who did not belong to the same migration circuit.
66. 81 per cent of men and 75 per cent of women were born in a city with more than 20,000 inhabitants, while the triad of Amsterdam (33 per cent), Rotterdam (12) and Leiden (8) supplied more than half of the total.
67. Like the Germans but unlike the French, however, none of them had naval identity documents with them. Although the channels along which they were recruited might have

been less formal or compelling than those mobilized by the *inscription maritime*, they were oriented towards the same navy-related labour demand. A second, much smaller group (14 per cent) was made up of tailors and shoemakers, who also moved in patterns of seasonal migration. Possibly, they were related to the military presence, and worked in the production of uniforms and army apparel.

68. In the settlement examinations of the 1850s there are for instance many examples of immigration by the wives of soldiers stationed in Antwerp, albeit for a later period (mainly 1830s and 1840s). E.g. SE1849-55-131, 160, 179, 155, 157, 69, 42, 21, 286.
69. FR1850, 7808.
70. FR1850, 7650. Compare with the wages collected by Lis, *Social Change*, pp. 36–7, 175–6.
71. 60 per cent of men and 44 per cent of women had moved in from elsewhere than their place of birth, while 40 per cent of men and 34 per cent of women left within one year after their arrival, 76 and 62 per cent respectively within two years of stay. When they left, they rarely returned home: 75 per cent of men and 89 per cent of women moved on to a place other than their place of birth, while only 39 and 11 per cent respectively moved somewhere where they had lived earlier. Brussels was the most popular destination, followed distantly by Amsterdam and Rotterdam.
72. Twelve men had moved in as children with one or more family members, and another twelve as married couples. Taken together, this makes one in two male sojourners as having moved in as a family unit, whereas the equivalent proportion of newcomers in FR1850 was only 23 per cent. Among women, the ratios were comparable: 50 vs. 33 per cent. In addition, those who had not been married at the time of arrival, had married – mostly an Antwerp-born spouse – by the time they ended up in the city hospital or applied for relief – at least as far as men are concerned (of 25 men who had married after their arrival, 14 had wed an Antwerp-born spouse, and 11 another immigrant, none of whom belonged to the same migration circuit). By nature of the source, women who had married an Antwerp-born spouse would not turn up in the settlement examinations.
73. SE1849-55, 363.
74. In the 1820s, 47 per cent left within one year after arrival, and 80 per cent stayed less than two years.
75. CS1829-93, 495; FR1850, 7870, 7872, 7862.
76. FR1850, 7521, 7851.
77. See, for instance, Lucassen, *Naar de kusten*, pp. 352–3; A. Radeff, 'Des migrations contraintes? Migrants et voyageurs alpins et appenins vers 1800', *Travaux et recherches de l'Université de Marne-la-Vallée*, 7 (2001), pp. 117–42.
78. CS1812-229.
79. While in the French and Dutch period, most of these *garçons confiseurs* and *ouvriers pâtissiers* were involved in multi-stop migration trajectories which brought them via Bruges, Mechelen, Ghent, Brussels and Rotterdam, by 1850 this had mainly evolved into a direct migration trajectory between Graubünden and Antwerp. Aged between sixteen and thirty-nine and housed by their employer, they revealed different patterns of stay. While 28-year old journeyman pastry cook Jan Lowy from Campovasto stayed with his employer for little less than a year before moving on to Brussels in June 1830, his 37-year old colleague from Brail would stay for two years in 1850 before returning home, while their 19-year old colleague from Fuldera would stay with Widow Tschander for more than seven years before returning to his home village.
80. CS1815-58, CS1829-1035; FR1850-7608.

81. FR1850-7968.
82. Data from the residence cards of 1808–11 and 1828–30 indicate that the proportion of direct rural-born migrants from Belgian (Flemish) Brabant and North Brabant was comparable to, or even higher than among intra-provincial rural born migrants. In 1808–11 62 per cent of male migrants from C1 had come directly from their place of birth, while among rural-born migrants from Flemish Brabant and North Brabant the proportion was the same (the data for 1808–11 on women are too scarce). In CS1828–30, the proportion of direct migrants was 52 and 61 per cent respectively for men and women from C1, and 59 and 66 per cent respectively for rural-born men and women from Flemish and North Brabant.
83. Although the precise setting could vary, all Brabant rural-born migrants had in common that they came from a background with little occupational diversification outside agriculture. The only notable exceptions being the brewing industry in the minor centres of the Hageland region, and proto-industrial (mainly textile) activity in the districts of Eindhoven and 's Hertogenbosch, which had, however, been on a declining trend since the early eighteenth century: Kappelhof, 'Toenemende spanningen', pp. 532–3.
84. According to the attrition tables, 37 per cent of men and 75 per cent of women from CS1815–19 stayed in town longer than five years, while the respective figures for CS1828–30 were 37 and 52 per cent – notwithstanding the unappealing conditions of the first years after independence.
85. Of rural Brabantine newcomers, 34 per cent lodged with an Antwerp-born host in 1829, a level more or less comparable with that of intra-provincial newcomers. Their level of intermarriage with the local-born population was also comparable: of all such immigrants present in 1796 who had married after arrival, 49 per cent of men and 61 per cent of women had wed an Antwerp-born spouse.
86. CS1829-388.
87. Cf. Van Dijck and Peeters, 'Algemene karakterschets'; Vliebergh and Ulens, *Het Hageland*. Via the Dijle and Demer rivers and the paved road between Mechelen and Liège, and later the railway between Tienen, Leuven and Mechelen (1837) the area was relatively well connected to Antwerp: Veen, 'Spoorwegontwikkeling', p. 64.
88. Cf. Kappelhof, 'Toenemende spanningen', p. 531; Schrover, 'The Demographic Consequences', pp. 472–3; L. G. J. Verberne, *Noord-Brabant in de negentiende eeuw tot omstreeks 1870: De sociaal-economische structuur* (Nijmegen: De Koepel, 1947), pp. 23–6. With 35 per cent of men and 30 per cent of women active in textile production, immigrants from this area had in 1796 been engaged in this labour market segment to levels comparable or even higher than those of the local-born population.
89. See, for instance, Schrover, 'The Demographic Consequences' on a specific way of coping with rising constraints in these regions.
90. Cf. A. H. Crijns and F. W. J. Kriellaars, 'Het traditionele patroon van de agrarische sector', in van den Eerenbeemt (ed.), *Geschiedenis van Noord-Brabant*, pp. 205–9; T. Engelen and P. M. M. Klep, 'Een demografisch traditionele samenleving', in van den Eerenbeemt (ed.), *Geschiedenis van Noord-Brabant*, pp. 61–76; Kappelhof, 'Toenemende spanningen', pp. 531–3; K. A. H. W. Leenders, 'Naar de climax van het gesloten landschap', in van den Eerenbeemt (ed.), *Geschiedenis van Noord-Brabant*, pp. 142–51; P. Meurkens, *Bevolking, economie en cultuur van het Oude Kempenland* (Bergeijk: Stichting Eicha, 1985).
91. Between the emigration registers of 1829 and 1855, the median length of stay for this particular group of migrants plummeted from 926 to 518 days. This drastic drop was

solely attributable to a radical change in women's patterns of stay: whereas in 1829 only 31 per cent of women stayed less than one year, and 45 per cent less than two years, by 1855 these proportions had shot up to 50 and 75 per cent respectively to attain a turnover rate which was even greater than that of men.

92. Whereas in CS1828–30, 74 per cent of maids had come to Antwerp directly, in FR1850 this had decreased to 44 per cent, with many having instead travelled via one of the intermediate centres situated between Antwerp and North Brabant, such as Turnhout, Breda, or Bergen-op-Zoom. In addition, they were more likely to move on to a new destination when they left Antwerp: of the fourteen maids whose following destination was listed in CS1828–30, eight returned to their birthplace, and eleven to a place in which they had resided prior to coming to Antwerp. In 1850 on the other hand, we find twelve of twenty-six recorded leavers moving on to a place in which they had never lived before, mainly to Brussels (4), Mechelen (2), and Berchem (2).

93. On the existing migration connections between the south-east of North Brabant and the Turnhout region, see Schrover, 'The Demographic Consequences', pp. 470–3.

94. Two in three of the female servants from North Brabant arriving in Antwerp in 1850 were employed by either merchants (22 per cent), shopkeepers (24) or innkeepers (22) – three occupations whose fate was directly related to the traffic of goods and people.

95. Bras, *Zeeuwse meiden*; Bras, 'Maids to the City'.

96. Bras, *Zeeuwse meiden*, pp. 93–114; Bras, 'Maids to the City'.

97. Cf. Lucassen, *Naar de kusten*, p. 295.

98. These construction workers represented 37 per cent of all Walloon men recorded in the 1796 census.

99. Four stonecutters from the *communes* of Seneffe and Nivelles stayed with Adrien Colinet from Arquennes (*commune* de Seneffe), recorded in the population books as stonecutter and lodging house keeper. Six other colleagues from the broughs of Seneffe and Jodoigne stayed with François Joseph Creton, stonecutter from Saint-Rémy-Geest (*commune* de Jodoigne), while we find six stonecutters from the same boroughs lodged with Johannes Libert, stonecutter from Feluy (*commune* de Seneffe). All but one of the thirteen *plafonneurs* recorded in 1829, in turn, stayed either with Jean Parfonry, innkeeper from Bas-Hélécine (*comm.* Hélécine), or the widowed labourer Aldegonda Sergeant from Jurbise (next to Soignies).

100. In some rare instances they are recorded as staying through the winter and spending two consecutive seasons in town. Only in one exceptional case have two brothers been recorded as staying longer than a year and a half: 15-year-old and 19-year-old Nicholas and Maximilién Lénain from Farciennes stayed with Jean Parfonry between March 1829 and November 1833, possibly because they were family or for training purposes.

101. The movement of stonecutters from the villages to the north of Charleroi, for instance, was closely associated with the existence of a number of important quarries in the region. Cf. Dumont, *Migrations intérieures*, pp. 79, 181; Lucassen, *Naar de kusten*, pp. 310–17.

102. That they were virtually absent from the hospital admission list of 1855 could be attributed to the specificity of the source, which is more likely to record medium-term or long-term stayers than seasonal migrants. However, in the emigration registers of 1855, where they should normally turn up, we found no trace of them. Yet there were no Walloon construction workers in the sample (1/10), and we found only one record in the total of 2,730 emigrants who headed for one of the *communes* cited above (Ecausinnes). It is still possible that these seasonal migrants by nature of the brevity of their stay remained largely outside the realm of migration registration which now had to pass via

the population books, and that they were recorded elsewhere or failed to be registered altogether. On the other hand, the emigration registers did record a large number of other seasonal migrants, as has already been amply documented elsewhere. Although the issue cannot be cleared up solely on the basis of the source materials used here, it appears that the recruitment of Walloon construction workers had fallen off by the 1850s.

103. In the early Dutch period their average yearly inflow decreased somewhat to around fourteen per year, while in CS1829 we found nine. The continued presence of straw hat makers in Antwerp in later decades is attested by their record in the emigration register of 1855, although they were probably less numerous then than in earlier periods. By then their origin appears to have shifted somewhat from the villages of Bassenge, Roclenge and Wonck to the adjacent cluster of Slins and Houtain-Saint-Siméon (ER1855-1200; PB1846-1856, 3–406).

104. While in the Napoleonic period most were lodged with Antoine Dautreppe, a *garçon plafonneur* from Floreffe (Prov. Namur), from 1817 onwards virtually all stayed in the house of Matheus Mathot, a straw hat maker from Bassenge, who was recorded as early as 1809. Moreover, the migrants themselves were often related to each other, and turn up regularly in the database at different points in time – an indication of the well-established seasonal nature of their migration pattern.

105. Cottaar and Lucassen, 'Naar de laatste Parijse mode'.

106. Ibid., pp. 56–7.

107. This was established by comparing the total number of Flemish immigrants per district – rural-born and urban-born – recorded in the hospital admission lists and settlement examinations of 1855 on the one hand, with the percentage of the rural-born population in those districts engaged in linen industry in 1843–4 on the basis of Jacquemyns, *Histoire*, pp. 53–4, as a measure of the effect of the subsequent collapse of linen production on the local economies.

108. Van Overmeire, 'Bevolking'. See also Jacquemyns, *Histoire*.

109. Of all rural-born Flemish sojourners examined in 1855, 71 per cent had lived in a place of more than 5,000 inhabitants before coming to Antwerp, and more than half had spent some time in a city of more than 20,000 inhabitants, mainly Ghent, Brussels, or Sint-Niklaas. Flemish newcomers born in cities had also often come to Antwerp via one or more intermediary stops. A similar picture arises from the emigration registers. Of all Flemish emigrants from 1855 whose last place of residence could be traced, only one in three had come to Antwerp directly from their place of birth, versus one in two of those born in the province of Antwerp. In turn, 41 per cent had travelled via a city of more than 5,000 inhabitants, as against only 22 per cent of intra-provincial migrants. The intertwining of rural and urban trajectories of recruitment is also reflected by the generally comparable proportions of urban and rural migrants which different districts supplied: districts supplying an important proportion of urban migrants, also supplied an important number of rural migrants.

110. Cf. Jacquemyns, *Histoire*, pp. 384–6.

111. Although the small number of cases and their social selectivity hamper the value of the results, as the only – selective – insight in Flemish occupations by mid-century is provided by the settlement examinations of 1855, where applicants' and their parents' occupations were listed. Urban-born migrants recorded a variety of semi-skilled and skilled occupations such as blacksmiths, locksmiths, shipwrights and coopers, while rural-born migrants performed less skilled activities in the retail & food industries, transport and

construction sectors. The training requirements of the skilled workers precludes the possibility that many of them would have been linen workers in earlier times.

112. De Metsenaere, 'Migraties', pp. 136–47.
113. In particular the Vliersteeg (4), Rijkenhoek (4), Arme Beukelaerstraat (3), Ridderstraat (3), Schuitstraat (3) and Boeksteeg (2).
114. On the Boeksteeg ghetto, see Lis, *Social Change*, pp. 71–2.
115. Or, more correctly, whereby the maintenance of social networks is much less dependent on physical proximity, as their greater access to different information channels also allows them to maintain family and social connections over greater distances.

Appendix I

1. For an extensive discussion of the problems, trustworthiness and historical value associated with these and alternative source materials, please see Winter, 'Patterns of Migration', Appendix I, pp. 1–34.
2. On the distinction, see Vrielinck, *De territoriale indeling*, pp. 2083–4, 2100.
3. Blondé, *Een economie*, pp. 255–60; Klep, *Bevolking*, p. 349. The 'extended' figure includes the military garrison.
4. F. Blockmans, 'De bevolkingscijfers', in *Antwerpen in de achttiende eeuw*, p. 395; Blondé, *Een economie*, pp. 255–6; Klep, *Bevolking*, p. 349. The 'limited' and 'extended' figures respectively exclude and include the military garrison.
5. Blondé, *Een economie*, pp. 256–7, 271; De Belder, 'Elementen'. The census probably excluded transitory residents.
6. Vrielinck, *De territoriale indeling*, p. 1668; also retained by Klep, *Bevolking*, pp. 400–3. Possibly, this result for Antwerp was (partly) based on a nominal registration of the population, as one district-list dated 1806 has been conserved in the communal archives: cf. SAA, MA-BZA, B, 1. The figure more or less corresponds to contemporary estimates of around 62,000 inhabitants (see SAA, MA, 2222/1, n°. 3), among whom '6,000 Français employés dans les différentes administration du Gouvernement', and another '3 à 4,000 ouvriers militaires civils (au moins d'autant étrangers qui travaillaient aux bassins et aux fortifications) … qui n'étaient pas portés sur le registres de population', which might have formed the basis for the estimate of Torfs, cited by F. Prims, *Antwerpen in 1830* (Antwerpen: Voor God en 't Volk, n.d.), p. 8.
7. We know that between September 1815 and May 1816 census activities were carried out in Antwerp, which would form the basis of a new series of population registers: SAA, MA-BZA, B, 11–30. Agnes Smits retrieved all the original entries in the population registers, and arrived at a total of 52,059 – which is the equivalent of the *population de droit* at the time: A. Smits, 'Demografische toestanden van de stad Antwerpen in de jaren 1810–1820' (Licentiaat dissertation, Katholieke Universiteit Leuven, 1962), p. 42. The figure corresponds to a contemporary estimate of 52,000 inhabitants by the Antwerp Mayor in October 1815, due to the departure of French officials and naval workers: SAA, MA, 2222/2, n°. 3 (see also previous note).
8. Vrielinck, *De territoriale indeling*, p. 1668; see also SAA, MA, 2222/1, n°. 4 (25/07/1821). There are several indications that the Antwerp authorities proceeded to an elaborate updating and control operation of the existing information in the population registers in 1820/1 by means of a general house-to-house visit, which was probably done in response to the census instructions, and formed the basis of the eventual census result of 59,941 communicated to the provincial authorities. The target population probably included

the military and other transitory population. In contrast, the retrospective table in Stad Antwerpen – Bevolkingsdienst, *Volksbeschrijvende en geneeskundige statistiek. Jaarboek over 1914* (Antwerpen: Gust Janssens, 1915), p. 3, cites a population of 55,673 in 1821. The strong divergence between this figure and the 1821 census result is probably attributable to the difference between 'legal' and 'factual' population.

9. The Dutch authorities proceeded to the organization of a uniform and simultaneous enumeration of the population representing the situation as per 1 January 1830 on the basis of uniform nominal registers and general instructions on a national scale. The nominal registers composed for the purpose of the census were here too designed to form the basis of generally held population registers – as was also the case in Antwerp (SAA, MA-BZA, B, 41–82). Legal initiative: *Pasinomie*, 2nd series, vol. 14, pp. 220–1: 29/09/1828; vol. 15, p. 322: 03/03/1829. The overall dedicated preparation, organization and supervision of the census operation and the presence of general and uniform instructions gave the operation the allure of a relatively 'scientific' national census for the first time, whose overall results were more reliable and accurate than any figures produced before in a general 'national' census. In Antwerp, 77,199 people were officially recorded as present (including the military garrison; Vrielinck, *De territoriale indeling*, p. 1668), but Hannes found only 71,849 persons recorded as initial entries in the new population registers: Hannes, 'Bijdrage', bijlage 3 (51,944 persons older than 12) + bijlage 4.1 (19,905 children under 13). Similar differences between the 'actual' population counted in the census and the 'legal' population recorded in the population registers were also encountered elsewhere: J. Block, 'Bijdrage tot de studie van de bevolking van Gent op 1-1-1830: Poging tot reconstructie van de volkstelling van 1829 te Gent' (Licentiaat dissertation, Rijksuniversiteit Gent, 1979), p. 23. An alternative figure of 72,962 'legal' inhabitants cited in a special publication by the city council in 1951 (*Antwerpen's bevolking gedurende 120 jaar* (Uitgeverij Ontwikkeling, 1951)) was probably manipulated in order to fit into the official census results: Hannes, 'Bijdrage', p. 48.

10. From 1846 onwards, national censuses were held on a regular – typically ten-yearly – basis, which have a very good overall reputation. The censuses took place under the auspices of the Commission Centrale de la Statistique, and were conducted on a uniform and simultaneous basis by specially trained censors. The enumeration of the population proceeded on the basis of nominal 'household cards', which in turn formed the basis for newly compiled population registers. The accuracy of the counting itself was very high, and the results were published in contemporary reports, and can be found, among other places, in Vrielinck, *De territoriale indeling*, p. 1668.

11. Source: C1796DB, C1796I, C1830, NSC1846, NSC1856, NSC1866. Figures from NSC1846 and NSC1856 pertain to the city's actual population, those from other censuses to the legal population. Figures between brackets approximate the composition of the city's legal population for those years.

12. As the 1796 census distinguishes migrants from non-migrants only for persons aged twelve or more, the 27 per cent immigrants calculated by De Belder, 'Elementen', vol. 1, p. 89, pertains only to the adult population. To arrive at a figure comparable with later censuses, I have distributed the total number of children along origin according to the distribution as observed by Hannes, 'Bijdrage', bijlage 4, for the 1830 census.

13. SAA, MA, 482: Lijst met aantal geboorten en sterften 1780–9. Although the birth figures do not completely correspond to those of Blockmans, 'De bevolkingscijfers' – part of the difference possibly lay in the inclusion or exclusion of stillbirths, and of the parish

of Notre Dame du Sud – the retrospective table provides sufficient indication of the general dimensions of the 'natural regime' at the end of the eighteenth century.

14. SAA, MA, 482: BS. Staat van het Getal geboorte, overlijden, huwelijken en echtsscheidingen, 19/02/1827.

15. SAA, MA, 2222/1, n°. 2: 'Mouvement de la population de cette ville', 1806–11; SAA, MA, 482: Three-monthly reports on the number of births and deaths, 1812–14; RAA, PA, J 176: 'Mouvement de l'état civil', 1815.

16. Stad Antwerpen – Gezondheidsdienst, *Volksbeschrijvende en geneeskundige statistiek*, p. 3; *Rapport ... d'Anvers*.

17. RAA, PA, J 158–9 records 2,299 immigrants and 1,038 emigrants for 1827 and 2,568 and 1,067 respectively for 1828; RAA, PA, J 175/A records 1,391 immigrants and 660 emigrants for 1823. Although most of the residence card registers of the 1820s have been lost, indications on numbering and contemporary inventories allow us to assume that the number of lost registers between 24 March 1820 and 1 March 1828 amounted to 29 or 30, and that they were similar in outlook to those preserved for the years 1828 and 1829, i.e. recording around 400 card-holders per volume – thus amounting to a total of 11,600–12,000 lost entries. Added to the known number of recorded immigrants in the preserved registers between 1 March 1828 and 31 December 1830 (i.e. 2,971), this amounts to a total of around 15,000 entries between 1 January 1820 and 31 December 1829, or an average of 1,500 per year, which is in line with numbers recorded in the auxiliary residence card register that has been conserved for the first town district (SAA, MA, 73958). With only 1,296 recorded entries between 11 March and 31 December 1828 in MA, 2668/7–10, the total number of recorded newcomers in the residence card registers in 1828 – when correcting for missing volumes and additional household members – at most amounted to around 1,700 – which is still substantially below the 2,568 recorded immigrants mentioned for the same year in RAA, PA, J 158–9. We know from other sources that immigration registers lost their exhaustive character in the 1820s, and were applied only for a subset of migrants, while other newcomers were directly recorded in the population records (see Chapter 2). Hence, the figures derived from the 1820s residence card registers undervalue the true volume of recorded migration. The provincial figures for 1827 and 1828 might in turn have overstated the number of immigrants to bring the intermediate population figures in line with the census results of 1 January 1827 and 31 December 1829. Assuming that there rests some sense in these figures, however, they in any case concerned peak years in the 1820s. Therefore, a general average of 2,200 is taken as an upper estimate for the average number of recorded immigrants per year for the period 1820–6, the RAA, PA, J 158–9 are retained for 1827 and 1828, and the number of newcomers is estimated at 2,500 for 1829.

18. The available aggregate recorded number of immigrants for this period can be found in RAA, PA, J 158 for the years 1837 (2,011) and 1840 (1,721), which correspond well to the figures extrapolated on the basis of the first district register SAA, MA, 73958, namely 1,944 and 1,769 respectively.

19. *Rapport ... d'Anvers*, retained by Kruithof, 'De demografische ontwikkeling'. For the year 1846, see the correction by Hannes, 'Bijdrage', p. 54.

20. The most substantial differences in occupational profile between the joint first and fourth districts as against the city as a whole concerned a relatively lower participation in domestic service (3.7 percentage points below average), religious personnel (-2.1 per cent), and agricultural activities (-1.7 per cent), and a somewhat greater participation in textile and lace production (+5.8 per cent), retail and trade (+1.6 per cent), and

transport activities (+0.8 per cent). The very wealthy (-1.8 per cent) and the moderately wealthy (-1.2 per cent) remain under-represented in the merging of the first and fourth districts. See De Belder, 'Elementen', vol. 1, pp. 44–5, 227–38.

21. Of particular use in this respect were his detailed overview of recorded occupations of the Antwerp adult population, subdivided according to sex, town district and wealth class (De Belder, 'Elementen', vol. 2, pp. 190–369); an overview of the marital status (unmarried, married or widowed) of the Antwerp adult population, subdivided according to sex, town district and wealth class (ibid., vol. 2, pp. 1–14); and an overview of the age structure of the Antwerp population (0–11, 12–20, and then ten-yearly groups), subdivided according to sex, town district and wealth class (ibid., vol. 2, pp. 15–77). De Belder also provided an overview of adult immigrants per occupational group, subdivided according to sex, town district and wealth class, but the occupational grouping of this table was unfortunately too broad to be of use for this research. Nevertheless, this table was of great value to be able to juxtapose and compare my data with those of De Belder, and to calculate differences in wealth status between immigrants and local-born.

22. I counted 5,591 immigrants (2,174 men and 3,417 women) in the first and fourth town districts, while De Belder only found 5,113 of them (2,041 men and 3,072 women) in the same files, a difference attributable to a different focus and *modus operandi*. While De Belder was very careful to register only original entries – that is of persons recorded present at the time of the census itself, and to disregard sporadic (and soon forfeited) attempts to update the information when people subsequently moved house (e.g. crossed-out or added names), I was not, for two reasons: 1) the original census files are no longer accessible, but only black-and-white photocopies, on which differences in ink colour and handwriting – which formed De Belder's prime guidelines for the distinction between initial entries and later additions ('Elementen', vol. 2, pp. 16–17) – are much less discernible. The only corrective I could and did employ without problems was to exclude those few persons recorded who had arrived in Antwerp after the census – identifiable by their 'timing of entry' – and to exclude double entries. I refrained from any other arbitrary exclusions; and 2) in my research the prime purpose was to gain a general view of the profile of Antwerp's immigrants at the end of the eighteenth century. In withholding only those living in the first and fourth districts, I necessarily built in a general margin of error concerning how representative the results were. This would not be magnified by the occasional 'false positive' inclusion of those few persons who had moved into the first or fourth district only at a later point of time, having first belonged to the groups (from the second, third or fifth districts) under-represented in the selection. In her graduation thesis on Antwerp's immigrants in the 1796 census – which was otherwise of very limited use – Caroline Beyers arrived at a total number of migrants for the first and fourth districts that did not differ much from mine, viz. 5,413, whilst using a similar 'broad' focus. C. Beyers, 'Onderzoek naar migratie: onbegonnen werk? Migratie in Antwerpen aan de hand van de volkstelling van het jaar IV' (Licentiaat dissertation, Rijksuniversiteit Gent, 2001), p. 28.

23. This implied multiplying all the results from C1796I with a ratio of 5113/5591 in order not to inflate the number of migrants (calculated separately for men and women, by multiplying with a ratio of 2041/2174 and 3072/3417 respectively). This of course assumes that the *relative* composition of my 'inflated' group of immigrants, in terms of age, occupation and the like, was comparable to the *relative* composition of the 'true' number of immigrants in the first and fourth districts counted by De Belder. This was not necessarily the case: as the female bias in the different numbers of migrants recorded

by De Belder and myself indicates, the 'extra' immigrant group probably consisted to an important extent of domestic personnel, which is plausible in that this involves one of the most mobile (also intra-urban) subgroups of the urban population. However, there was no possibility at hand to measure this bias seriously, so there was no firm ground on which further corrections could be applied. Moreover, as this involves a subgroup (domestic servants) of a subgroup (my 'extra' female immigrants), the possible numerical effect on the overall distribution was limited. In any case, as the resultant figures are unavoidably imprecise to a limited degree, they are less adequate for comparing very small or specific categories, yet sufficiently indicative for comparing larger groups.

24. Hannes, 'Bijdrage'.
25. In this table as elsewhere, Hannes distinguished six origin categories: Antwerp-born; immigrants from surrounding municipalities; from other places in the Province of Antwerp; from another Belgian province; from the present-day Netherlands; and other foreigners.
26. Because SAA, MA, 2668/1 does not record places of birth – a vital piece of information for the analysis of migration patterns – it has been left out from analysis.
27. In some periods, the *Registres* also recorded immigrating Antwerp-born migrants. For reasons of comparability of the figures, these are left out from all analyses unless mentioned explicitly.
28. In the case of family migration, residence cards were issued only to the heads of household, providing only one entry in the *Registre*. Typically, only the number and relation of card-sharing companions are mentioned (e.g. 'with wife and two children'). In CS1808–29 there was only one instance where male and female spouses were recorded separately when they arrived in town together. The normal course was to provide only one card for a married couple with or without children, at least if they entered town together. Children are included only in calculations concerning the absolute number of immigrants, but left out from further analysis – as they in principle did not fall under the legislation of residence cards. Information on spouses or other adult companions – i.e. a total of 105 in CS1808–30 – is retained for other calculations too (i.e. they form a separate entry in the census databases) as the *Registres* rarely contain any further specification of these companions. Moreover, comparisons with other sources demonstrate that accompanying family members were not always duly recorded in the *Registres*: of 87 migrants in CS1819 identified by default as single migrants from the *Registres* and transferred to the population registers, five appeared from the latter source to have immigrated with family members not mentioned in the *Registres* – three men had immigrated with their wives and children, one with his wife, and one female immigrant had entered town with her illegitimate infant. This means that family migration was sometimes disguised as solitary migration, and thus under-recorded. Even when this under-registration is corrected for, however, the number of immigrants arriving in a household context remained only a very small minority, so these lacunae did not greatly distort the eventual results.
29. Thirty persons could not be identified in the population books, and were therefore treated as missing.
30. This is not completely comparable, as ER1829 refers to all persons who *left* in 1829, while CS1829 records all persons who *entered* in 1829. Some of the recorded leavers from CS1829 thus left in 1830 or 1831. However, they compensate for the persons from earlier censuses who might have left in 1829 and who are not recorded in the sample. In that sense, this small 'shift' should not have distorted our data on the migra-

tion behaviour of emigrants around 1829. The only distortion which might have had an influence is that the revolution of October 1830 might have encouraged people to leave who might in normal circumstances have stayed (cf. the net loss of Antwerp population in the early 1830s), thus resulting in a shortening of lengths of stay which was not typical for emigrants in 1829. If anything, this distortion would have resulted in an *under*estimation of the lengths of stay calculated on the basis of ERPI+1829, which then only emphasizes the downward trend observable in length of stay between ERPI+1829 and ERPI1855.

31. Families or (sometimes) trading partners are, for instance, grouped together in one file and one examination.

32. These 'double counts' could have been avoided by a detailed checking and juxtaposing of the names of different entries, but this would have required a very large time effort for relatively minor corrections, which would not have affected the main thrust of results. As all groups in principle stood an equal chance for multiple admissions, there is no reason why these double counts should have distorted the overall results.

33. Vrielinck, *De territoriale indeling*, part 3.

34. A full coverage of these data and further explanation on how they have been compiled is found in: E. Beekink and P. van Cruyningen, *Demografische databank Nederlandse gemeenten* (Den Haag: NIDI, 1995).

35. The general rule is that in these cases priority was given to the nearest and most familiar place, assuming that administrators would have explicitly mentioned so if it were the more distant place that was meant. For instance 'Berchem' was assumed to be Berchem next to Antwerp rather than the East Flemish Berchem in the *commune* of Kluisbergen, and so on. Yet in some instances (e.g. 'Lille' – the city in the north of France or the Campine village?) ambiguity was too large to settle, so these places were categorized as non-localized. As these ambiguities were relatively few, the impact of possible mis-classifications was minimal, and if anything might have underestimated longer-distance recruitment.

36. Here and there, some very minor corrections have been made which deviate from current provincial boundaries in Belgium, mainly to correct for certain anachronisms and political-administrative particularities (e.g. Zwijnaarde was classified with East Flanders, and Voeren/Fourons with Liège, while Brussels Capital Region, Flemish Brabant and Walloon Brabant, unless specified differently, were grouped together in one Brabant Province as was the case prior to the state reform of 1995).

37. The divisions used are as follows: Suburban belt: those municipalities on the outskirts of the city that today belong to the *fusiegemeente* Antwerpen; Other arr. Antwerp: other municipalities within the boundaries of today's *arrondissement* Antwerpen; Antwerp Campine: all municipalities of today's *arrondissement* of Turnhout, and those municipalities in today's *arrondissement* of Mechelen that are to the east of Mechelen itself; North Brabant: today's province of North Brabant in the Netherlands; Dijle-Demer-Gete region: today's *arrondissement* of Leuven, the lower part of the *arrondissement* Tongeren (excluding the *fusiegemeenten* Lanaken, Maasmechelen and Voeren), and the lower part of the *arrondissement* Hasselt (the *fusiegemeenten* Gingelom, Sint-Truiden, Nieuwerkerken, Halen, Herk-de-Stad, Hasselt and Diepenbeek); the Senne region: today's *arrondissement* of Halle-Vilvoorde, the Brussels Capital Region and the municipalities of Bornem, Sint-Amands, Puurs, Willebroek and Mechelen; Other Limburg: all other Belgian municipalities within the boundaries of today's province of Limburg, and all municipalities within today's province of Limburg in the Netherlands; East and

West Flanders: today's provinces; Walloon regions: all other Belgian municipalities (i.e. within today's provinces of Hainaut, Namur, Liège, Luxembourg and Brabant-Wallon); Other Netherlands: all other Dutch municipalities; German border regions: today's *Bundesland* of North Rhine-Westphalia, the *Regierungsbezirken* Koblenz and Trier in the Rhineland, and *Regierungsbezirk* Weser-Ems in Lower Saxony; French North Coast: today's *régions* of Nord–Pas-de-Calais, Picardy, Upper and Lower Normandy, and Brittany; France (other): all other municipalities within the present-day boundaries of France; Other: all other places.

38. The population figures allowing this classification were derived from P. Bairoch, J. Batou and P. Chèvre, *La population des villes européennes, 800–1850: Banque de données et analyse sommaire des résultats* (Publications du Centre d'histoire économique internationale de l'Université de Genève 2, Genève: Droz, 1988), and supplemented for Belgium and the Netherlands with the HISGIS and NIDI population figures.

39. The HISGIS data also render the official census results per contemporary *gemeente*, yet as their boundaries tended to switch and vary from time to time, they do not provide a sufficiently continuous measurement by which to calculate migration intensity. Therefore, use was made of the HISGIS data recalculated for the boundaries of contemporary *fusiegemeenten* (see HISGIS on further details of the recalculation procedure).

40. The NIDI data record only the original census results at the level of original municipal boundaries – which were subject to considerable changes from one census to the next. To allow for a consistent comparison of population size and migration intensity over time, it was necessary to recalculate the different figures at a somewhat larger level in much the same way as the HISGIS data were recalculated to the level of contemporary *fusiegemeenten*. In line with HISGIS procedures, the main operational method I used in the Dutch case was that of the 'lowest common multiple', i.e. to find a delimitation which more or less covered the mutual shifts in municipal boundaries of its constituent parts. By grouping some village-level data together at the level of artificial Dutch *fusiegemeenten* (for further details on the groupings applied, see Winter, 'Patterns of Migration', Appendix 3, pp. 52–3), I could absorb most of the shifts in municipal boundaries, and create a series of population figures at a relatively detailed local level which allowed a consistent comparison of migration intensity both through time and between the HISGIS and NIDI data. These population figures at *fusiegemeente* level were the basis for calculations and maps on migration intensity.

41. The earliest Dutch census for which the NIDI data give information is that of 1815, while HISGIS starts in 1806 (data are available for 1800, but the census of 1806 is the earliest with more or less reliable results). Between 1815 and 1830, no further censuses were carried out in the Netherlands, while we have data for the 1818 and 1820 censuses in Belgium.

42. When Hofstee collected his data on the population size of Dutch municipalities, he started from the census results, and recalculated intermediate year-to-year population figures on the basis of available data on vital and growth trends, so that the NIDI-data provide more or less a continual series of population figures.

43. The discrepancy if of course greatest for the 1796 census figures – ten years apart from the 1806 census figures. As the 1796 census is a cross-sectional source, referring to the *accumulated* number of migrants living in the first and fourth districts, *diachronic* comparisons in terms of migration intensity with later *dynamic* sources on the number of newcomers per year are precluded anyway, so that this was not so much of a problem.

The greatest function of calculating the migration intensity for C1796I was to provide a measure to compare *geographical* differences in migration intensity at that time. The precise measure against which this was calculated was not so important, as long as it was more or less the same for all *communes* concerned.

44. The HISGIS base figure to compare with IN1850 is calculated as the mean between the 1846 and 1856 figures. A more elaborate calculation could have been used to calculate the population on 1 January 1850 on the basis of the growth trend between the 1846 and 1856 results, but given the overall only indicative nature of the figures, this was superfluous.

45. Cf. Balthazar et al., *Bronnen*, pp. 23, 28–9.

46. For reasons of brevity, the table has grouped some 'regions' (for instance the French *départements* and the German *Regierungsbezirke*) together in larger units.

47. On Lis's classification scheme, see Lis, *Social Change*, Appendix II, pp. 172–4.

48. There is only one exception to the reclassification potential of the occupational data given by Hannes and De Belder and that is the data which pertain to the trade sectors, where the authors have applied their own simplification to a wide array of diverse terms cited in the sources (*vendeur, debiteur, marchand, boutiquier, mercier*, etc.), so that wholesalers cannot be distinguished from more modest traders when integrating the two databases. While they were almost all listed separately by De Belder, Hannes appears to have grouped them with other traders under the term 'merchant' – yet given the potentially ambiguous use of the terms *marchands* and *négociants* in the original sources themselves, any distinction in this respect might have been arbitrary. When integrating the two databases, there is therefore no other option than to follow the 'lowest common factor' of the categorizations employed, which means distinguishing between trade and wholesale on the one hand (all 'traders' who were not explicitly identified as retailers), and retail on the other (grouping all those who were explicitly identified as catering to a local market, such as *boutiquiers, détaillant, visverkoper, fruitverkoper, melkboer*, etc.).

Appendix II

1. The ratios between the number of arrivals between 1796 and 1787 and the number of arrivals between 1786 and 1777 (R1) and the ratio between the number of arrivals between 1796 and 1787 and the number of earlier arrivals (R2) function as parameters for turnover.

2. See previous note.

3. As the data for 1796 are census data, they are not fully comparable with later data retrieved from residence card registers.

4. Only 39 per cent of entries in CS1808–29 record the actual date of re-departure, while 25 per cent end their observations with the date when the bearer was 'transferred to the population registers', 13 per cent with some other event occurring after arrival (e.g. a change of address or an application for a new card), and 23 per cent record no information later than the time of entry. Hence, a lot of values for length of stay refer only to the minimum length of stay. To approximate overall patterns of stay with reference to both complete and truncated observations, use was made of attrition tables to calculate 'transition chances' per month and per year. For more details on this statistical procedure, see R. Lesthaeghe, *Onderzoeksmethoden in mens- en maatschappijwetenschappen: Een inleiding, vol. 2* (Brussel: VUB, 1994), pp. 47–54.

5. Data pertain to trajectories prior to arrival in Antwerp. Last place of residence refers to the place from which the move to Antwerp was made. Distinction between rural and urban here is set at 20,000 inhabitants.

6. Data here pertain to non-native emigrants, and are not readily comparable to the length of stay calculated for newcomers from CS1808–29.

7. Distinction between rural and urban here is set at 20,000 inhabitants.

8. Because of the specificity of the source, the sex ratio in HA1855 cannot be considered representative of immigrants as a whole. As a partial corrective, NSC1846 gives the following sex ratios for the city's actual population: Antwerp-born residents: 87:100; immigrants born within the province of Antwerp: 72:100; those born in another Belgian province: 143:100; those born elsewhere: 132:100. The equivalent figures from C1830 are 88:100; 67:100; 70:100; and 98:100 respectively, and those from C1796 are 82:100; 60:100; 72:100; 56:100.

9. Values for the third circuit in the last two columns are based on FR1850, those for the other circuits on ERPI1855. The averages for C1796I include persons who moved in as children, whereas the CS and FR data pertain only to adult newcomers.

10. In the last four columns (FR1850/ER1855) the data for circuit 3 are based on FR1850, those for the other three circuits on ERPI1855. For CS1808–13 women's occupations only those from CS1812–13 are taken into consideration.

11. Of intra-provincial return migrants (circuit 1) grouped under 'return to birthplace', 12 and 10 per cent respectively re-migrated to a commune in the suburban belt. The boundaries between villages, medium-sized towns and large cities in the trajectories are set at 5,000 and 20,000 inhabitants respectively (Appendix I.4).

12. Based on attrition tables including missing and truncated values.

WORKS CITED

Archival Sources

Openbaar Centrum voor Maatschappelijk Welzijn, Antwerp (OCMWA)

Bureel van weldadigheid (BW)
  933, Renseignements concernant le domicile de secours des indigens belges, 1854–9.
  946, Indigents étranger à la Belgique, 1844–58.
  947, Indigents étranger à la Belgique, 1847–52.

Burgerlijke godshuizen (BG)
  858–75, Register van kennisgeving omtrent de onderstandswoonst van patiënten in het
    St-Elisabeth Gasthuis, 1849–1928.
  876–85, Staten van kennisgeving omtrent de onderstandswoonst van vreemdelingen in
    het St.-Elisabeth Gasthuis, 1859–1937.
  Sint-Elisabethgasthuis (EG)
  1–47, Inkomboeken behoeftige mannen, 1804–1925.
  48–66, Inkomboeken betalende mannen, 1804–1925.
  131–74, Inkomboeken behoeftige vrouwen, 1804–1928.
  175–85, Inkomboeken betalende vrouwen, 1804–1928.

Rijksarchief, Antwerp (RAA)

Archief van het departement van de Twee Neten en van de provincie Antwerpen (PA)
  A 126/3–126/14, Policie – Algemeene Policie – Inrichting – Personeel, Jaar III – 1818.
  A 131/23–132/19, Reispassen, 1792–1811.
  F 8–9: Vreemdelingen: briefwisseling, 1815–60.
  F 53–9, Gemeentelijke politie: verslagen, Jaar X – 1836.
  F 75, Politie: Reglementen, 1810–19.
  J 158, Bevolking, 1779–1857.
  J 159, Tienjaarlijkse tafels, 1792–1861.
  J 168–83, Statistieken. Bevolking, 1795–1860.

Rijksarchief, Anderlecht (RAAnd)

Dijleprefectuur (DP)
  374, Levée d'ouvriers pour le port d'Anvers, 1810–11.
  428, Levées d'ouvriers pour les ports d'Anvers et d'Ostende au service de l'armée, an XII-
    1806.

Rijkarchief, Beveren (RAB)

Archief van het Parket bij de Rechtbank van Eerste Aanleg te Antwerpen, Neerlegging 2001
　　B (PK Antw 2001 B), 231–2, Gemeentereglementen Antwerpen, 23 fructidor IX
　　(10/09/1801) – 1870.

Stadsarchief, Antwerp (SAA)

Modern Archief (MA)
　　445/1, Organisatie politie, 1790–1840.
　　450/170, Register der verblijfsvergunningen, wijk 5, 1844–6.
　　464/3, Personen onder politietoezicht: staten en briefwisseling, 1801–36.
　　465, Kopijboek van politierapporten aan de Ministre de la Police Générale, 1811.
　　482, Burgerlijke stand en bevolking, verscheidene documenten, 1780–1848.
　　673/1, Paspoorten en vreemdelingen, verscheidene documenten, 1820–45.
　　673/2, Vreemdelingen: lijsten, briefwisseling, paspoorten, 1820–45.
　　2222/1–2, Bevolking: Besluiten, reglementen, registerhouding, bewijzen aangiften,
　　　　statistieken, an 3-1848.
　　2635, Register der processen-verbaal van de Commission de Sûreté Publique, 1832–5.
　　2668/1–6, Registers der verblijfsvergunningen, 1803–20.
　　2668/7–18, Registers der verblijfsvergunningen, 1828–30.
　　2668/19–25, Registers der verblijfsvergunningen, vierde wijk, 1826–56 (1846).
　　2672, Register der verblijfsvergunningen, eerste wijk, 1811–21.
　　44248–787, Vreemdelingenzaken, Vreemdelingendossiers (1840–1910).
　　73958, Register der verblijfsvergunningen, eerste wijk, 1827–41.
　　74656–8, Registers van inschrijving, 1894–1901.
　　74780–9, Registers van vertrek, 1821–80.

Modern Archief, Bevolkingszaken (MA-BZA)
　　D1–5, Telling Jaar IV.
　　B, 1–10, Bevolkingsregisters, 1800–15 (POPA).
　　B, 11–40, Bevolkingsregisters, 1815–29 (POPB).
　　B, 41–82, Bevolkingsregisters, 1830–46 (POPC).
　　B, 83–124, Bevolkingsregisters, 1846–56 (POPD).
　　B, 125–16, Bevolkingsregisters, 1856–66 (POPD).

Privilegekamer (PK), 927–9, Gebodboeken, 1762–94.

Vierschaar (V)
　　177, Domicilie-boeck alias Poortersboek, 1780–95.
　　1812, Register der in- en uitwijking, 1801.

Published Primary Sources

Antwerpen's bevolking gedurende 120 jaar (Uitgeverij Ontwikkeling, 1951).

Documents statistiques publiés par le département de l'Intérieur avec le concours de la Commission centrale de statistique, 1851–1867 (Bruxelles, 1857–69).

Exposé de la situation du royaume: Statistique générale de la Belgique (Période décennale de 1851–1860) (Bruxelles: Ministre de l'Intérieur, Imp. Th. Lesigne, 1863–5).

Nederlandse Staatscourant, 78 (31 March 1815).

Pasinomie: collection complete des lois, arêtes et règlements généraux qui peuvent être invoqués en Belgique (1789–).

Rapport sur l'administration et la situation des affaires de la ville d'Anvers (Anvers: Stad Antwerpen, 1836–1915).

Scholliers, E., 'Prijzen en lonen te Antwerpen en in het Antwerpse (16e–19e eeuw)', in C. Verlinden (ed.), *Dokumenten voor de geschiedenis van prijzen en lonen in Vlaanderen en Brabant, Deel II* (Brugge: De Tempel, 1965), pp. 641–1056.

Stad Antwerpen – Gezondheidsdienst, *Volksbeschrijvende en geneeskundige statistiek. Jaarboek over 1914* (Antwerpen: Gust Janssens, 1915).

Statistique de la Belgique: Population. Relevé décennal. 1831 à 1840. Mouvement de l'état civil de 1840 (Bruxelles: Imprimerie de Vandooren Frères, 1842).

Statistique de la Belgique: Population. Mouvement de l'état civil pendant l'année [1841–50] (Bruxelles: Imprimerie de Vandooren Frères, 1843–51).

Statistique de la Belgique: Population. Récensement Général (15 octobre 1846) (Bruxelles: Ministre de l'Intérieur, 1849).

Statistique de la Belgique: Population. Récensement général (31 décembre 1856) (Bruxelles: Ministre de l'Intérieur, Imprimerie Th. Lesigne, 1861).

Statistique de la Belgique: Population. Récensement général (31 décembre 1866) (Bruxelles: Ministre de l'Intérieur, Imprimerie Th. Lesigne, 1870).

Secondary Sources

Aelbrecht, V., 'L'immigration ouvrière belge à Tourcoing durant le Second Empire', *Belgisch Tijdschrift voor Nieuwste Geschiedenis*, 21:3–4 (1990), pp. 351–81.

Amin, S., and M. van der Linden, 'Introduction', in S. Amin and M. van der Linden (eds), *"Peripheral" Labour? Studies in the History of Partial Proletarianization* (Cambridge and New York: Cambridge University Press, 1997), pp. 1–7.

Anderson, T. G., 'Proto-Industrialization, Sharecropping, and Outmigration in Nineteenth-Century Rural Westphalia', *Journal of Peasant Studies*, 29:1 (2001), pp. 1–30.

Andre, R., and J. Pereira-Roque, *La démographie de la Belgique au XIXe siècle* (Bruxelles: Université Libre de Bruxelles, 1974).

Antwerpen in de achttiende eeuw: Instellingen, economie, cultuur (Antwerpen: De Sikkel, 1952).

Asaert, G., G. Devos and F. Suykens (eds), *The 'Naties' in the Port of Antwerp: Six Centuries of Activity in City and Port* (Tielt: Lannoo, 1993).

Baines, D., *Emigration from Europe, 1815–1930* (London: MacMillan, 1991).

—, 'Internal and Medium-Distance Migrations in Great-Britain, 1750–1900', in Eiras Roel and Rey Castelao (eds), *Les migrations internes*, pp. 127–46.

Bairoch, P., *De Jéricho à Mexico: Villes et économie dans l'histoire* (Paris: Gallimard, 1985).

—, 'The Impact of Crop Yields, Agricultural Productivity, and Transport Costs on Urban Growth between 1800 and 1910', in van der Woude et al. (eds), *Urbanization in History*, pp. 134–52.

Bairoch, P., J. Batou and P. Chèvre, *La population des villes européennes, 800–1850: Banque de données et analyse sommaire des résultats* (Publications du Centre d'histoire économique internationale de l'Université de Genève 2, Genève: Droz, 1988).

Balthazar, H., J. De Belder, J. Hannes and J. Verhelst, *Bronnen voor de sociale geschiedenis van de 19e eeuw (1794–1914)* (Leuven: Nauwelaerts, 1965).

Baudez, L., 'De zeeprefectuur van Antwerpen tijdens het Franse bewind, 1803–1814', *Belgisch tijdschrift voor militaire geschiedenis*, 30:4 (1993), pp. 233–61.

—, 'Prefect d'Herbouville (1800–1805) en het herstel van de haven van Antwerpen', *Sirene*, 44:172 (1993), pp. 21–5.

Beekink, E., and P. van Cruyningen, *Demografische databank Nederlandse gemeenten* (Den Haag: NIDI, 1995).

Beetemé, G., *Anvers: Métropole du commerce et des arts*, 2 vols (Anvers: Frans Beerts, 1888).

Beier, A. L., 'Vagrants and the Social Order in Elizabethan England', *Past and Present*, 64 (1974), pp. 3–29.

Ben-Amos, I. K., 'Failure to become Freemen: Urban Apprentices in Early Modern England', *Social History*, 16 (1991), pp. 155–72.

—, *Adolescence and Youth in Early Modern England* (New Haven, CT: Yale University Press, 1994).

Beyers, C., 'Onderzoek naar migratie: onbegonnen werk? Migratie in Antwerpen aan de hand van de volkstelling van het jaar IV' (Licentiaat dissertation, Rijksuniversiteit Gent, 2001).

Blanc-Chaléard, M.-C., 'Des logiques nationales aux logiques ethniques', *Le Mouvement Social*, 188 (1999), pp. 3–16.

Block, J., 'Bijdrage tot de studie van de bevolking van Gent op 1-1-1830: Poging tot reconstructie van de volkstelling van 1829 te Gent' (Licentiaat dissertation, Rijksuniversiteit Gent, 1979).

Blockmans, F., 'De bevolkingscijfers', in *Antwerpen in de achttiende eeuw*, pp. 395–412.

Blok, D. P. (ed.), *Algemene geschiedenis der Nederlanden* (Haarlem: Fibula-Van Dishoeck, 1981).

Blondé, B., 'Winkelen te Lier: Een onderzoek naar de afbakening van het Lierse hinterland in de achttiende eeuw', in *Het stedelijk netwerk in België in historisch perspectief (1350–1850)* (Brussel: Gemeentekrediet, 1992), pp. 111–24.

—, 'De transportwegen en de economische ontwikkeling in de regio Antwerpen – Mechelen – Lier (1710–1790)', *Bijdragen tot de Geschiedenis*, 78:1–4 (1995), pp. 93–105.

—, 'Economische groei en armoede in de pruikentijd: Een voorbeeld van de Brabantse steden, 1750–1780', in C. Reyns (ed.), *Werkgelegenheid en inkomen* (Antwerpen: UFSIA, 1996), pp. 343–58.

—, 'Aux origines de la révolution des transports: L'exemple des chaussées "belges" au dix-huitième siècle', in S. Curveiller and D. Clauzel (eds), *Les champs relationnels en Europe du Nord, 18ième–20ème siècles: Deuxième colloque européen de Calais* (Balinghem: Cache, 1998), pp. 17–40.

—, *Een economie met verschillende snelheden: Ongelijkheden in de opbouw en de ontwikkeling van het Brabantse stedelijke netwerk, ca 1750–ca 1790* (Brussel: Paleis der Academiën, 1999).

Blondé, B., and H. Deceulaer, 'The Port of Antwerp and its Hinterland: Port Traffic, Urban Economies and Government Policies in the 17th and 18th Centuries', in R. Ertesvåg, D. J. Starkey and A. Tove Austbø (eds), *Maritime Industries and Public Intervention* (Stavanger: Maritime Museum, 2002), pp. 21–44.

Blondé, B., and H. Greefs, 'Werk aan de winkel: De Antwerpse meerseniers: Aspecten van kleinhandel en verbruik in de 17de en 18de eeuw', in Devos (ed.), *De lokroep van het bedrijf*, pp. 207–29.

Blondé, B., and R. Van Uytven, 'De smalle steden en het Brabantse stedelijke netwerk in de Late Middeleeuwen en de Nieuwe Tijd', *Lira elegans*, 6 (1999), pp. 129–82.

Boumans, R., *Het Antwerps stadsbestuur voor en tijdens de Franse overheersing* (Brugge: De Tempel, 1965).

Bourdelais, P., 'Demographic Changes in European Industrializing Towns: Examples and Elements for Comparison', *History of the Family*, 5:4 (2000), pp. 363–72.

Bouwstoffen voor de geschiedenis van Antwerpen in de 19de eeuw: Instellingen, economie, kultuur (Antwerpen: Lloyd Anversois, 1964).

Bras, H., *Zeeuwse meiden: Dienen in de levensloop van vrouwen, 1850–1950* (Amsterdam: Aksant, 2002).

—, 'Maids to the City: Migration Patterns of Female Domestic Servants from the Province of Zeeland, the Netherlands (1850–1950)', *History of the Family*, 8:2 (2003), pp. 217–46.

Bruggeman, J., and P. van de Laar, 'Rotterdam als migrantenstad aan het einde van de negentiende eeuw', in P. van de Laar (ed.), *Vier eeuwen migratie: Bestemming Rotterdam* (Rotterdam: MondiTaal, 1998), pp. 146–70.

Bruneel, C., 'Bijdrage van de poorterboeken tot de historische demografie: Kritische bedenkingen bij het voorbeeld van Antwerpen', *Tijdschrift van het Gemeentekrediet*, 172 (1990), pp. 101–10.

—, 'Les migrations entre villes et campagnes: L'exemple des Pays-Bas méridionaux', in *Le migrazioni in Europa secc. XIII–XVIII* (Prato: Instituto Internazionale di Storia Economica 'F. Datini', 1994), pp. 501–32.

—, 'Economie en samenleving in de eeuw van de Verlichting', in Van Uytven (ed.), *De geschiedenis van Brabant*, pp. 479–513.

Bruwier, M., 'Ondernemers en zakenlieden', in J.-M. Duvosquel and H. Hasquin (eds), *België onder het Frans bewind, 1792–1815* (Brussel: Gemeentekrediet, 1993), pp. 229–51.

Bruyninckx, R., and M. De Metsenaere, 'De rekrutering van de Brusselse bevolking op basis van de telling van het jaar XI', *Taal en Sociale Integratie*, 4 (1981), pp. 183–98.

Caestecker, F., *Alien Policy in Belgium, 1840–1940: The Creation of Guest Workers, Refugees and Illegal Aliens* (New York: Berghahn Books, 2000).

Carlier, M., 'Migration Trends in the Towns of Flanders and Brabant (15th–18th Century)', in *Le migrazioni in Europa secc. XIII–XVIII: Atti della Venticinquesima Settimana di Studi, 3–8 maggio 1993* (Prato: Instituto Internazionale di Storia Economica 'F. Datini', 1994), pp. 355–70.

Chatelain, A., *Les migrants temporaires en France de 1800 à 1914* (Lille: Universite⊠ de Lille III, 1976).

Clark, P., 'The Migrant in Kentish Towns 1580–1640', in P. Clark and P. Slack (eds), *Crisis and Order in English Towns, 1500–1700: Essays in Urban History* (London: Routledge and K. Paul, 1972), pp. 117–63.

—, 'Migrants in the City: The Process of Social Adaptation in English Towns, 1500–1800', in Clark and Souden (eds), *Migration and Society*, pp. 267–91.

—, 'Migration in England during the Late Seventeenth and Early Eighteenth Centuries', in Clark and Souden (eds), *Migration and Society*, pp. 213–52.

Clark, P., and D. Souden (eds), *Migration and Society in Early Modern England* (London: Hutchinson, 1987).

—, 'Introduction', in Clark and Souden (eds), *Migration and Society*, pp. 11–48.

Coppejans-Desmet, H., 'Bevolking en tewerkstelling in transformatie op het Vlaamse platteland (einde 18de–midden 19de eeuw)', *Tijdschrift van het Gemeentekrediet*, 48:190 (1994), pp. 15–34.

Cosemans, A., 'Volkstellingen, burgerlijke stand en memoires in Brabant onder het Franse Regime en in het Verenigd Koninkrijk (1795–1829)', *Handelingen van de Zuidnederlandse Maatschappij voor Taal- en Letterkunde en Geschiedenis*, 17 (1963), pp. 47–66

—, *Bijdrage tot de demografische en sociale geschiedenis van de stad Brussel, 1796–1846* (Brussel: Gemeentekrediet, 1966).

Cottaar, A., and L. Lucassen, 'Naar de laatste Parijse mode: Strohoedenmakers uit het Jekerdal in Nederland 1750–1900', *Studies over de sociaal-economische geschiedenis van Limburg* (2001), pp. 45–82.

Crafts, N. F. R., *British Economic Growth during the Industrial Revolution* (Oxford: Clarendon Press, 1985).

Crijns, A. H., and F. W. J. Kriellaars, 'Het traditionele patroon van de agrarische sector', in H. F. J. M. van den Eerenbeemt (ed.), *Geschiedenis van Noord-Brabant, Deel 1: Traditie en modernisering, 1796–1890* (Amsterdam: Boom, 1996), pp. 187–210.

Daelemans, F., 'Bronnen voor het historisch-demografisch onderzoek van het hertogdom Brabant tijdens het ancien régime: Enkele kritische nota's', in F. Daelemans (ed.), *Bronnen en methoden van de historische demografie voor 1850* (Brussel: ARA, 1984), pp. 45–73.

De Belder, J., 'Elementen van sociale identiteit van de Antwerpse bevolking op het einde van de 18de eeuw: Een kwantitatieve studie', 2 vols (PhD dissertation, Rijksuniversiteit Gent, 1974).

—, 'Stad en platteland: Inleiding tot de problematiek', *Taal en Sociale Integratie*, 4 (1981), pp. 169–82.

De Belder, J., C. Gijssels, C. Vandenbroeke and L. van der Straeten, *Arbeid en tewerkstelling in Antwerpen 1796: Een socio-professionele en demografische analyse: Werkdocumenten* (n.p., 1985).

De Bock, E., *Hendrik Conscience en de opkomst van de Vlaamsche romantiek* (Antwerpen: De Sikkel, n.d.).

De Kesel, L., 'Structurele ontwikkeling van de haven', in *Bouwstoffen voor de geschiedenis*, pp. 124–69.

De Metsenaere, M., 'Migraties in de gemeente Sint-Joost-ten-Node in het midden van de negentiende eeuw: Methodologische inleiding tot de studie van de groei en verfransing van de Brusselse agglomeratie', *Taal en Sociale Integratie* (1978), pp. 81–152.

—, *Taalmuur: Sociale muur? De negentiende-eeuwse taalverhoudingen te Brussel als resultaat van geodemografische en sociale processen* (Brussel: VUBPress (Centrum voor Interdisciplinair Onderzoek naar de Brusselse Taaltoestanden), 1988).

De Moor, M., 'Common Land and Common Rights in Flanders', in M. De Moor, L. Shaw-Taylor and P. Warde (eds), *The Management of Common Land in North West Europe, c. 1500–1850* (Turnhout: Brepols, 2002), pp. 113–41.

De Munck, B., 'Leerpraktijken: Economische en sociaal-culturele aspecten van beroepsopleidingen in Antwerpse ambachtsgilden, 16de–18de eeuw' (PhD dissertation, Vrije Universiteit Brussel, 2002).

de Schaepdrijver, S., *Elites for the Capital? Foreign Migration to Mid-Nineteenth-Century Brussels* (Amsterdam: PDIS, 1990).

—, 'Vreemdelingen in *Vilette*: De buitenlandse aanwezigheid in het negentiende-eeuwse Brussel', in Soly and Thijs (eds), *Minderheden in Westeuropese*, pp. 115–34.

de Vries, J., *European Urbanization, 1500–1800* (London: Methuen, 1984).

—, 'Problems in the Measurement, Description and Analysis of Historical Urbanization', in van der Woude et al. (eds), *Urbanization in History*, pp. 43–60.

—, 'The Industrial Revolution and the Industrious Revolution', *Journal of Economic History*, 54:2 (1994), pp. 249–70.

Deceulaer, H., 'Arbeidsregulering en loonvorming in de Antwerpse haven, 1585–1796', *Tijdschrift voor Sociale Geschiedenis*, 18 (1992), pp. 22–47.

—, *Pluriforme patronen en een verschillende snit: Sociaal-economische, institutionele en culturele transformaties in de kledingsector in Antwerpen, Brussel en Gent, ca 1585–ca 1800* (Amsterdam: Stichting Beheer IISG, 2001).

—, 'Urban Artisans and their Countryside Customers: Different Interactions between Town and Hinterland in Antwerp, Brussels and Ghent', in B. Blondé, E. Vanhaute and M. Galan (eds), *Labour and Labour Markets between Town and Countryside (Middle Ages–19th Century)* (Turnhout: Brepols, 2001), pp. 218–35.

—, 'Consumptie en distributie van kleding tussen stad en platteland: Drie regionale patronen in de Zuidelijke Nederlanden (zestiende – achttiende eeuw)', *Tijdschrift voor sociale geschiedenis*, 28:4 (2002), pp. 439–68.

Degryse, K., 'The Artistocratization of the Antwerp Mercantile Elite (17th–18th Century)', in Lesger and Noordegraaf (eds), *Entrepeneurs and Entrepreneurship*, pp. 35–42.

Demoulin, R., *Guillaume Ier et la transformation économique des provinces belges (1815–1830)* (Liège: Faculté de Philosophie et Lettres, 1938).

Deprez, P., and C. Vandenbroeke, 'Population Growth and Distribution and Urbanisation in Belgium during the Demographic Transition', in R. Lawton and R. Lee (eds), *Urban Population Development in Western Europe from the Late Eighteenth to the Early Twentieth Century* (Liverpool: Liverpool University Press, 1989), pp. 220–57.

Desama, C., 'Démographie et industrialisation: Le modèle verviétois (1800–1850)', *Revue du Nord* (1981), pp. 147–55.

Devos, G., 'Inwijking en integratie van Duitse kooplieden te Antwerpen in de 19de eeuw', in Soly and Thijs (eds), *Minderheden in Westeuropese*, pp. 135–56.

— (ed.), *De lokroep van het bedrijf: Handelaars, ondernemers en hun samenleving van de zestiende tot de twintigste eeuw: Liber amicorum Roland Baetens* (Antwerpen: UFSIA, 2001).

—, 'Over scheepsmakelaars en beunhazen. Een onderbelicht aspect van de maritieme bedrijvigheid te Antwerpen (1801–1867)', in Devos (ed.), *De lokroep van het bedrijf*, pp. 243–55.

Dhondt, J., 'Notes sur les ouvriers industriels gantois à l'époque française', *Revue du Nord*, 36:142 (1954), pp. 309–24.

—, 'L'industrie cottonière gantoise à l'époque française', *Revue d'Histoire Moderne et Contemporaine*, 2 (1955), pp. 233–79.

Dhordain, N., and D. Terrier, 'Accumulation de la main-d'oeuvre et comportements délinquants: Les villes du textile dans la région lilloise au cours des années 1860', *Revue du Nord*, 84:347 (2002), pp. 691–721.

Dumont, C., *Migrations intérieures et immigration dans le bassin industriel de Charleroi 1800–1866* (Bruxelles: ARA, 1994).

DuPlessis, R. S., *Transitions to Capitalism in Early Modern Europe* (Cambridge and New York: Cambridge University Press, 1997).

Duroux, R., 'The Temporary Migration of Males and the Power of Females in a Stem-Family Society: The Case of 19th-Century Auvergne', *History of the Family*, 6:1 (2001), pp. 33–49.

Eggerickx, T., and M. Poulain, 'Les phases du processus d'urbanisation en Belgique', in *Croissance démographique et urbanisation: Politiques du peuplement et aménagement du territoire* (Paris: PUF, 1993), pp. 83–94.

Ehmer, J., 'Worlds of Mobility: Migration Patterns of Viennese Artisans in the Eighteenth Century', in G. Crossick (ed.), *The Artisan and the European Town, ca. 1500–1900* (Aldershot: Scolar Press, 1997), pp. 172–99.

—, 'Migration of Journeymen as Nineteenth-Century Mass-Migration', in R. Leboutte (ed.), *Migrations and Migrants in Historical Perspective: Permanences and Innovations* (Brussels: P.I.E. – Peter Lang, 2000), pp. 97–109.

Eiras Roel, A., and O. Rey Castelao (eds), *Les migrations internes et à moyenne distance en Europe, 1500–1900* (Santiago de Compostella: Xunta de Galicia & CIDH, 1994).

Engbersen, G., 'De illegale vreemdeling', in J. Burgers and G. Engbersen (eds), *Illegale vreemdelingen in Rotterdam* (Meppel: Boom, 1999), pp. 11–29.

Engelen, T., 'Labour Strategies of Families: A Critical Assessment of an Appealing Concept', *International Review of Social History*, 47 (2002), pp. 453–64.

Engelen, T., and P. M. M. Klep, 'Een demografisch traditionele samenleving', in van den Eerenbeemt (ed.), *Geschiedenis van Noord-Brabant*, pp. 61–76.

Engelen, T., A. Knotter, J. Kok and R. Paping, 'Labor Strategies of Families: An Introduction', *History of the Family*, 9:2 (2004), pp. 123–36.

Epin, C., *Les ouvriers des arsenaux de la Marine sous Napoléon, vivre et survivre en travaillant pour l'état* (Paris: l'Herminette, 1990).

Everaert, J., 'Antwerpen als emigratiehaven. De overzeese landverhuizing naar Amerika (1830–1914)', *Mededelingen*, 26 (1982), pp. 55–67.

Everaert, J., E. Joos and R. Vervoort, *Landverhuizers. Antwerpen als kruispunt van komen en gaan* (Antwerpen: Pandora, 2002).

Everaert-Vermoortel, C., *Antwerpen als krijgshaven van Napoleon I* (s.l.: [eigen beheer], 1959).

Farasyn, D., *De 18de eeuwse bloeiperiode van Oostende, 1769–1794* (Oostende: Stadsarchief, 1998).

Faron, O., and C. Grange, 'Un recensement parisien sous la révolution: L'exemple des cartes de sûreté de 1793', *Mélanges de l'école française de Rome: Italie et Mediterranée*, 111:2 (1999), pp. 795–826.

Feys, T., 'Radeloosheid in crisistijd: Pogingen van de Belgische autoriteiten om een deel van de arme bevolking naar de Verenigde Staten te sturen, 1847–1856', *Belgisch Tijdschrift voor Nieuwste Geschiedenis*, 34:2 (2004), pp. 195–230.

Fischer, A., *Napoléon et Anvers (1800–1811)* (Antwerpen: Loosbergh, 1933).

Fontaine, L., and J. Schlumbohm, 'Household Strategies for Survival 1600–2000: An Introduction', in L. Fontaine and J. Schlumbohm (eds), *Household Strategies for Survival 1600–2000: Fission, Faction and Cooperation* (Amsterdam: Cambridge University Press, 2000), pp. 1–17.

Fuchs, R. G., *Poor and Pregnant in Paris: Strategies for Survival in the Nineteenth Century* (New Brunswick, NJ: Rutgers University Press, 1992).

Fuchs, R. G., and L. P. Moch, 'Pregnant, Single, and Far from Home: Migrant Women in Nineteenth-Century Paris', *American Historical Review*, 95:4 (1990), pp. 1007–32.

Goossens, M., 'Een negentiende-eeuws heidedorp in transformatie: Kalmthout: 1835–1910', *Bijdragen tot de Geschiedenis*, 67 (1982), pp. 197–261.

Gordon, W., '"What, I Pray You, Shall I Do with the Balance?" Single Women's Economy of Migration', *International Review of Social History*, 50:1 (2005), pp. 53–70.

Grantham, G., 'Economic History and the History of Labour Markets', in G. Grantham and M. MacKinnon (eds), *Labour Market Evolution: The Economic History of Market Integration, Wage Flexibility and the Employment Relation* (London and New York: Routledge, 1994), pp. 1–26.

Greefs, H., 'Foreign Entrepreneurs in Early Nineteenth-Century Antwerp', in Lesger and Noordegraaf (eds), *Entrepreneurs and Entrepreneurship*, pp. 101–17.

—, 'Enkele zwaartepunten in het onderzoek naar ondernemerschap en ondernemersstrate-gieën te Antwerpen gedurende de periode 1794–1870', *Belgisch Tijdschrift voor Filologie en Geschiedenis*, 76 (1998), pp. 419–42.

Green, N., *Ready-to-Wear and Ready-to-Work: A Century of Industry and Immigrants in the Women's Garment Trade in Paris and New York* (Durham: Duke University Press, 1998).

Gyssels, C., and L. van der Straeten, *Bevolking, arbeid en tewerkstelling in West-Vlaanderen (1796–1815)* (Gent, 1986).

—, *Bevolking, arbeid en tewerkstelling in de provincie Antwerpen op het einde van het ancien régime* (n.p., [1990]).

Hahn, S., 'Vienna: A Nexus between East and West', in L. Nilsson (ed.), *Capital Cities. Images and Realities in the Historical Development of European Capital Cities* (Stockholm: Stads– och Kommunhistoriska Institutet, 2000), pp. 60–4.

Hampson, N., 'Les ouvriers des arsenaux de la marine au cours de la Révolution Française (1789–1794)', *Revue d'Histoire Economique et Sociale*, 39 (1961), pp. 287–329, 442–73.

Hannes, J., 'Bijdrage tot de ontwikkeling van een kwantitatief-kritische methode in de sociale geschiedschrijving' (PhD dissertation, Rijksuniversiteit Gent, 1969).

Hanson, D., 'Une source d'histoire sociale: Les listes d'habitants dressées par la police, à Liège de 1797 à 1930', *Annuaire d'Histoire Liégoise*, 20:44 (1979), pp. 115–64.

Harris, R.-A. M., *The Nearest Place that Wasn't Ireland: Early Nineteenth Century Irish Labor Migration* (Ames, IA: Iowa State University Press, 1994).

Hatton, T. J., and J. G. Williamson, *The Age of Mass Migration: Causes and Economic Impact* (New York: Oxford University Press, 1998).

Hélin, E., 'Aux confins de la démographie historique et de l'histoire sociale: Mesurer les migra-tions', *Belgisch Tijdschrift voor Nieuwste Geschiedenis*, 21:3–4 (1990), pp. 605–38.

Herbert, U., *A History of Foreign Labor in Germany, 1880–1980: Seasonal Workers, Forced Laborers, Guest Workers* (Ann Arbor, MI: University of Michigan Press, 1990).

Himler, A., 'De Antwerpse haven vanaf de Franse periode', *Tijdschrift van het Gemeentekrediet*, 47:185 (1993), pp. 33–56.

Hochstadt, S., 'Migration and Industrialization in Germany, 1815–1977', *Social Science History*, 5:4 (1981), pp. 445–68.

—, 'Migration in Preindustrial Germany', *Central European History*, 16:3 (1983), pp. 195–224.

—, *Mobility and Modernity: Migration in Germany, 1820–1989* (Ann Arbor, MI: University of Michigan Press, 1999).

Hohenberg, P. M., 'Urban Development', in D. H. Aldcroft and S. P. Ville (eds), *The European Economy, 1750–1914. A Thematic Approach* (Manchester and New York: Manchester University Press, 1994), pp. 284–312.

Hohenberg, P. M., and L. H. Lees, *The Making of Urban Europe, 1000–1994* (London: Harvard University Press, 1995).

Hufton, O., *The Poor of Eighteenth-Century France* (Oxford: Clarendon Press, 1974).

Humphries, J., 'Enclosures, Common Right, and Women: The Proletarianization of Families in the Late Eighteenth and Early Nineteenth Centuries', *Journal of Economic History*, 50:1 (1990), pp. 17–42.

Jackson, J. H., *Migration and Urbanization in the Ruhr Valley, 1821–1914* (Atlantic Highlands, NJ: Humanities Press, 1997).

Jackson, J. J., and L. P. Moch, 'Migration and the Social History of Europe', in D. Hoerder and L. P. Moch (eds), *European Migrants: Global and Local Perspectives* (Boston, MA: Northeastern University Press, 1996), pp. 52–69.

Jacquemyns, G., *Histoire de la crise économique de Flandres, 1845–1850* (Bruxelles, 1929).

Jaspers, L., and C. Stevens, *Arbeid en tewerkstelling in Oost-Vlaanderen op het einde van het ancien régime* (Gent, 1985).

Jennes, M., 'De Franse scheepswerven Danet & Co te Antwerpen (1802–1807)', in Lombaerde (ed.), *Antwerpen tijdens*, pp. 33–40.

Jerome, H., *Migration and Business Cycles* (New York: National Bureau of Economic Research, 1926).

Jeuninckx, K., 'De havenbeweging in de Franse en Hollandse periode', in *Bouwstoffen voor de geschiedenis*, pp. 94–123.

Jones, G. S., *Outcast London: A Study in the Relationship between Classes in Victorian Society* (Oxford Eng.: Clarendon Press, 1971).

Kappelhof, A., 'Toenemende spanningen', in Van Uytven (ed.), *De geschiedenis van Brabant*, pp. 529–37.

Kittell, A. H., 'The Revolutionary Period of the Industrial Revolution: Industrial Innovation and Population Displacement in Belgium, 1830–1880', *Journal of Social History*, 1:2 (1967), pp. 119–48.

Klep, P. M. M., *Bevolking en arbeid in transformatie: Een onderzoek in Brabant, 1700–1900* (Nijmegen: SUN, 1981).

—, 'Urban Decline in Brabant: The Traditionalization of Investments and Labour (1374–1806)', in Van der Wee (ed.), *The Rise and Decline*, pp. 261–86.

Knotter, A., *Economische transformatie en stedelijke arbeidsmarkt: Amsterdam in de tweede helft van de negentiende eeuw* (Zwolle: Waanders, 1991).

—, 'A New Theory of Merchant Capitalism?', *Review*, 20:2 (1997), pp. 193–210.

—, 'Problems of the "Family Economy": Peasant Economy, Domestic Production and Labour Markets in Pre-Industrial Europe', in Prak (ed.), *Early Modern Capitalism*, pp. 135–60.

—, 'Poverty and the Family Income Cycle: Casual Laborers in Amsterdam in the First Half of the 20th Century', *History of the Family*, 9:2 (2004), pp. 221–37.

Knotter, A., and J. L. van Zanden, 'Immigratie en arbeidsmarkt te Amsterdam in de 17e eeuw', *Tijdschrift voor sociale geschiedenis*, 13:4 (1987), pp. 403–31.

Kok, J. (ed.), *Levensloop en levenslot: Arbeidsstrategieën van gezinnen in de negentiende en twintigste eeuw* (Groningen: Nederlands Agronomisch Historisch Instituut, 1999).

—, 'Migratie als gezinsstrategie in midden-Nederland', in Kok (ed.), *Levensloop en levenslot*, pp. 89–156.

—, 'Comment on Pooley and Turnbull', *Annales de Démographie Historique*, 2 (2002), pp. 113–18.

—, 'The Challenge of Strategy: A Comment', *International Review of Social History*, 47 (2002), pp. 465–85.

—, 'Choices and Constraints in the Migration of Families: The Central Netherlands, 1850–1940', *History of the Family*, 9:2 (2004), pp. 137–58.

Kok, J., and H. Delger, 'Success or Selection? The Effect of Migration on Occupational Mobility in a Dutch Province, 1840–1950', *Histoire et Mesure*, 13 (1998), pp. 289–322.

Kok, J., K. Mandemakers and H. Wals, 'City Nomads: Changing Residence as a Coping Strategy, Amsterdam 1890–1940', *Social Science History*, 29:1 (2005), pp. 15–43.

Kooij, P., 'Migrants in Dutch Cities at the End of the Nineteenth Century', in Menjot and Pinol (eds), *Les immigrants et la ville*, pp. 193–206.

Kruithof, J., 'De demografische ontwikkeling in de 19de eeuw', in *Bouwstoffen voor de geschiedenis*, pp. 508–43.

Kuijpers, E., *Migrantenstad: Immigratie en sociale verhoudingen in 17e-eeuws Amsterdam* (Hilversum: Verloren, 2005).

Kussmaul, A., *Servants in Husbandry in Early Modern England* (Cambridge and New York: Cambridge University Press, 1981).

Lambert, K., 'Industrialisatie in een plattelandsgemeente: Effecten op bevolking en arbeid te Sleidinge, 1820–1914', *Revue Belge d'Histoire Contemporaine* (1984), pp. 381–419.

Langewiesche, D., and F. Lenger, 'Internal Migration: Persistence and Mobility', in K. J. Bade (ed.), *Population, Labour and Migration in 19th- and 20th-Century Germany* (Leamington Spa: Berg, 1987), pp. 87–100.

Laureys, M., 'Bijdrage tot de sociale geschiedenis van het Leuvens ambachtelijke milieu: Het ambacht van de timmerlieden, de houtbrekers en de molenmakers' (Licentiaat dissertation, Katholieke Universiteit Leuven, 1980).

Leblicq, Y., and M. De Metsenaere, 'De groei', in J. Stengers and A. André (eds), *Brussel: Groei van een hoofdstad* (Antwerpen: Mercatorfonds, 1979), pp. 167–77.

Leboutte, R., *Reconversions de la main d'ouvre et transition démographique. Les bassins industriels en aval de Liège, 17e–19e siècles* (Paris: Les Belles Lettres, 1988).

—, 'Le rôle des migrations dans la formation des bassins industriels en Europe, 1800–1914', in Eiras Roel and Rey Castelao (eds), *Les migrations internes*, pp. 443–82.

Leboutte, R., and R. Obotela, 'Les registres de population en Belgique: Genèse d'une technique administrative et d'une source de démographie historique', *Handelingen van de Koninklijke Commissie voor Geschiedenis*, 154:3–4 (1988), pp. 285–305.

Lebrun, P., M. Bruwier, J. Dhondt and G. Hansotte, *Essai sur la révolution industrielle en Belgique, 1770–1847* (Bruxelles: Palais des Académies, 1979).

Lee, R., 'The Socio-Economic and Demographic Characteristics of Port Cities: A Typology for Comparative Analysis?', *Urban History*, 25:2 (1998), pp. 147–72.

—, 'Urban Labor Markets, In-Migration, and Demographic Growth: Bremen, 1815–1914', *Journal of Interdisciplinary History*, 30:3 (1999), pp. 437–74.

Lee, R., and R. Lawton, 'Port Development and the Demographic Dynamics of European Urbanization', in R. Lawton and R. Lee (eds), *Population and Society in Western European Port Cities, ca. 1650–1939* (Liverpool: Liverpool University Press, 2002), pp. 1–36.

Leenders, K. A. H. W., 'Naar de climax van het gesloten landschap', in van den Eerenbeemt (ed.), *Geschiedenis van Noord-Brabant*, pp. 142–51.

Lesger, C., *Handel in Amsterdam ten tijde van de Opstand: Kooplieden, commerciële expansie en verandering in de ruimtelijke economie van de Nederlanden, ca. 1550–ca. 1630* (Hilversum: Verloren, 2001).

—, 'Informatiestromen en de herkomstgebieden van migranten in de Nederlanden in de Vroegmoderne Tijd', *Tijdschrift voor Sociale en Economische Geschiedenis*, 3:1 (2006), pp. 3–23.

Lesger, C., and L. Noordegraaf (eds), *Entrepeneurs and Entrepreneurship in Early Modern Times: Merchants and Industrialists within the Orbit of the Dutch Staple Market* (Den Haag: Stichting Hollandse Historische Reeks, 1995).

Lesger, C., L. Lucassen and M. Schrover, 'Is There Life Outside the Migrant Network? German Immigrants in 19th Century Netherlands and the Need for a More Balanced Migration Typology', *Annales de Démographie Historique*, 104:2 (2002), pp. 29–50.

Lesthaeghe, R. J., *The Decline of Belgian Fertility, 1800–1970* (Princeton, NJ: Princeton University Press, 1977).

—, R. Lesthaeghe, *Onderzoeksmethoden in mens- en maatschappijwetenschappen: Een inleiding, vol. 2* (Brussel: VUB, 1994).

Levine, D. (ed.), *Proletarianization and Family History* (Orlando, FL: Academia Press, 1984).

Lis, C., 'Woontoestanden en gangsaneringen te Antwerpen in het midden van de negentiende eeuw', *Belgisch Tijdschrift voor Nieuwste geschiedenis*, 1:1 (1969), pp. 93–131.

—, 'Verarmingsprocessen te Antwerpen, 1750–1850' (PhD dissertation, Vrije Universiteit Brussel, 1975).

—, 'Sociale politiek in Antwerpen, 1779: Het controleren van de relatieve overbevolking en het reguleren van de arbeidsmarkt', *Tijdschrift voor Sociale Geschiedenis*, 2 (1976), pp. 146–66.

—, *Social Change and the Labouring Poor: Antwerp, 1770–1860* (New Haven, CT: Yale University Press, 1986).

Lis, C., and H. Soly, 'Policing the Early Modern Proletariat, 1450–1850', in Levine (ed.), *Proletarianization and Family History*, pp. 163–228.

—, *Een groot bedrijf in een kleine stad: De firma de Heyder en Co. te Lier, 1757–1834* (Lier: Liers Genootschap voor Geschiedenis, 1987).

—, 'Neighbourhood Social Change in West European Cities', *International Review of Social History*, 38 (1993), pp. 1–30.

—, 'Different Paths of Development: Capitalism in the Northern and Southern Netherlands during the Late Middle Ages and the Early Modern Period', *Review*, 20:2 (1997), pp. 211–42.

Lis, C., H. Soly and D. Van Damme, *Op vrije voeten? Sociale politiek in West-Europa (1450–1914)* (Leuven: Kritak, 1985).

Lombaerde, P., 'De militaire werken van Louis-Charles Boistard en Simon Bernard te Antwerpen tijdens het Eerste Keizerrijk', *Belgisch Tijdschrift voor Militaire Geschiedenis*, 25 (1984), pp. 285–328.

— (ed.), *Antwerpen tijdens het Franse keizerrijk, 1804–1814. Marine-arsenaal, metropool en vestingstad* (Antwerpen: Simon Stevinstichting, 1989).

—, 'De bouwgeschiedenis van het scheepsarsenaal te Antwerpen', in Lombaerde (ed.), *Antwerpen tijdens*, pp. 41–56.

Long, J., 'Rural–Urban Migration and Socioeconomic Mobility in Victorian Britain', *Journal of Economic History*, 65:1 (2005), pp. 1–35.

Lottin, A., and H. Soly, 'Aspects de l'histoire des villes des Pays-Bas méridionaux et de la Principauté de Liège (milieu du 17e siècle à la veille de la Révolution Française)', in J.-P. Poussou (ed.), *Etudes sur les villes en Europe Occidentale (milieu du 17e siècle à la veille de la Révolution Française)* (Paris, 1981), pp. 213–306.

Lourens, P., and J. Lucassen, *Arbeitswanderung und berufliche Spezialisierung: Die lippischen Ziegler in 18. und 19. Jahrhundert* (Osnabrück: Vandenhoeck & Ruprecht, 1999).

Lucassen, J., *Naar de kusten van de Noordzee. Trekarbeid in Europees perspectief, 1600–1900* (Utrecht, 1984).

—, *Migrant Labour in Europe, 1600–1900: The Drift to the North Sea* (London: Croom Helm, 1987).

Lucassen, J., and L. Lucassen (eds), *Migration, Migration History, History: Old Paradigms and New Perspectives* (Bern: Lang, 1997).

—, 'Migration, Migration History, History: Old Paradigms and New Perspectives', in Lucassen and Lucassen (eds), *Migration*, pp. 9–38.

Lucassen, J., and R. Penninx, *Nieuwkomers: Immigranten en hun nakomelingen in Nederland, 1550–1985* (Amsterdam: Meulenhoff, 1985).

Lucassen, L., 'A Blind Spot – Migratory and Travelling Groups in Western European Historiography', *International Review of Social History*, 38:2 (1993), pp. 209–35.

—, 'The Domination of the National Category: A Review of Some Recent Studies on (Im)migration and Nation Building', *Immigrants and Minorities*, 14:3 (1995), pp. 319–31.

—, 'De selectiviteit van blijvers: Een reconstructie van de sociale positie van Duitse migranten in Rotterdam (1870–1885)', *Tijdschrift voor Sociale en Economische Geschiedenis*, 1:2 (2004), pp. 92–116.

Lucassen, L., and B. de Vries, 'The Rise and Fall of a West-European Textile-Worker Migration System: Leiden, 1586–1700', in G. Gayot and P. Minard (eds), *Les ouvriers qualifiés de l'industrie (16e–20e siècle): Formation, emploi, migrations*, Révue du Nord, Hors série, Collection Histoire n° 15 (Lille: Université Charles-de-Gaulle, 2001), pp. 23–42.

Lucassen, L., and F. Vermeulen, *Immigranten en lokale arbeidsmarkt: Vreemdelingen in Den Haag, Leiden, Deventer en Alkmaar (1920–1940)* (Amsterdam, 1999).

McCray, W. P., 'Creating Networks of Skill: Technology Transfer and the Glass Industry of Venice', *Journal of European Economic History*, 28:2 (1999), pp. 301–33.

McIsaac Cooper, S., 'Service to Servitude? The Decline and Demise of Life-Cycle Service in England', *History of the Family*, 10:4 (2005), pp. 367–86.

Mahaim, E., *Les abonnements d'ouvriers sur les lignes de chemins de fer belges et leurs effets sociaux* (Bruxelles, 1910).

Mendels, F., 'Proto-Industrialization: The First Phase of the Industrialization Process', *Journal of Economic History*, 32:1 (1972), pp. 241–61.

—, *Industrialization and Population Pressure in Eighteenth-Century Flanders* (New York: Arno Press, 1981).

Menjot, D., and J.-L. Pinol (eds), *Les immigrants et la ville: Insertion, intégration, discrimination (XIIe–XXe siècles)* (Paris: Harmattan, 1996).

Mertens, F. H., and K. L. Torfs, *Geschiedenis van Antwerpen, sedert de stichting der stad tot onze tyden, Zevende deel* (Antwerpen: Rederykkamer de Olyftak, 1846).

Mertens, J., 'Burgerlijke stand en bevolkingsregisters', *Vlaamse Stam: Tijdschrift voor Familiegeschiedenis* (1974), pp. 525–39.

Meurkens, P., *Bevolking, economie en cultuur van het Oude Kempenland* (Bergeijk: Stichting Eicha, 1985).

Michielsen, L., 'De handel', in *Antwerpen in de achttiende eeuw*, pp. 94–122.

Moch, L. P., *Paths to the City: Regional Migration in Nineteenth-Century France* (Beverly Hills, CA: Sage Publications, 1983).

—, 'Dividing Time: An Analytical Framework for Migration History Periodization', in J. Lucassen and L. Lucassen (eds), *Migration, Migration History, History: Old Paradigms and New Perspectives* (Bern: Lang, 1997), pp. 41–56.

—, *Moving Europeans: Migration in Western Europe since 1650* (Bloomington and Indianapolis, IN: Indiana University Press, 2003).

Mokyr, J., *Industrialization in the Low Countries, 1795–1850* (New Haven, CT, and London: Yale University Press, 1976).

Mols, R., *Introduction à la démographie historique des villes d'Europe du 14e au 18e siècle*, 3 vols (Louvain: Bibliothèque de l'Université, 1954–6).

Morawska, E., *Insecure Prosperity: Small-Town Jews in Industrial America, 1890–1940* (Princeton, NJ: Princeton University Press, 1996).

Morsa, D., 'Sociale structuren en identiteiten in de Belgische steden in het licht van recente werken', *Tijdschrift van het Gemeentekrediet*, 47:184 (1993), pp. 37–60.

—, 'Les immigrants dans les villes des principautés belges (17e–18e siècles)', in Menjot and Pinol (eds), *Les immigrants et la ville*, pp. 171–91.

—, 'L'urbanisation de la Belgique (1500–1800): Taille, hiérarchie et dynamique des villes', *Revue du Nord*, 79:320–1 (1997), pp. 303–30.

Musschoot, D., *Wij gaan naar Amerika: Vlaamse landverhuizers naar de Nieuwe Wereld 1850–1930* (Tielt: Lannoo, 2002).

Neven, M., 'Retourmigratie in een plattelands samenleving tijdens de Industriële Revolutie: Het land van Herve (België) 1846–1900', *Tijdschrift voor Sociale en Economische Geschiedenis*, 1:1 (2004), pp. 47–75.

Noiriel, G., *Le creuset français: Histoire de l'immigration, XIXe–XXe siècles* (Paris: Seuil, 1988).

Ó Gráda, C., *Black '47 and Beyond: The Great Irish Famine in History, Economy, and Memory* (Princeton, NJ: Princeton University Press, 1999).

Oris, M., 'La transition de la mobilité au 19e siècle: L'expérience de Huy-sur-Meuse (Belgique), entre 1847 et 1900', *Annales de Démographie Historique*, 84:10 (1993), pp. 191–225.

—, 'Fertility and Migration in the Heart of the Industrial Revolution', *History of the Family*, 1:2 (1996), pp. 169–82.

—, 'L'impact d'une dépression économique sur le champ migratoire d'une grande ville industrielle: L'expérience de Seraing entre 1857 et 1900', *Revue du Nord*, 79:320–1 (1997), pp. 531–48.

—, 'The History of Migration as a Chapter in the History of the European Rural Family: An Overview', *History of the Family*, 8:2 (2003), pp. 187–215.

Oris, M., and G. Alter, 'Paths to the City and Roads to Death: Mortality and Migration in East Belgium during the Industrial Revolution', *Belgisch Tijdschrift voor Nieuwste Geschiedenis*, 31:3 (2001), pp. 453–95.

Orrman, E., 'The Condition of the Rural Population in Late Medieval Society (c. 1350–1520)', in K. Helle (ed.), *The Cambridge History of Scandinavia, vol. 1: Prehistory to 1520* (Cambridge: Cambridge University Press, 2003), pp. 581–611.

Pais-Minne, E., 'Weldadigheidsinstellingen en sociale toestanden', in *Antwerpen in de achttiende eeuw*, pp. 156–86.

Paping, R., 'Gezinnen en cohorten: Arbeidsstrategieën in een marktgerichte agrarische economie: de Groningen kleigebieden, 1830–1920', in Kok (ed.), *Levensloop en levenslot*, pp. 17–88.

—, 'Family Strategies concerning Migration and Occupations of Children in a Market-Oriented Agricultural Economy', *History of the Family*, 9:2 (2004), pp. 159–91.

Pasleau, S., 'Structures démographiques d'un faubourg industriel de Liège: Grivegnée en 1856', *Belgisch Tijdschrift voor Nieuwste Geschiedenis*, 16:3–4 (1985), pp. 397–432.

—, 'L'immigration des travailleurs à Seraing durant la seconde moitié du 19e siècle', *Annales de Démographie Historique* (1993), pp. 227–50.

—, 'Les migrations internes en Belgique: Ruptures et continuités du XVIIe au XXe siècle', in Eiras Roel and Rey Castelao (eds), *Les migrations internes*, pp. 179–204.

Patten, J., 'Patterns of Migration and Movement of Labour to Three Pre-Industrial East-Anglian Towns', in Clark and Souden (eds), *Migration and Society*, pp. 77–106.

Pelckmans, G., 'De Duitse kolonie te Antwerpen en haar invloed op de Antwerpse samenleving (19e eeuw – 1914)' (Licentiaat dissertation, Katholieke Universiteit Leuven, 1994).

Pelckmans, G., and J. Van Doorslaer, *De Duitse kolonie 1796–1914* (Kapellen: Pelckmans, 2000).

Perrot, J.-C., *Genèse d'une ville moderne: Caen au XVIIIe siècle* (Paris: Mouton, 1975).

Pfister, U., 'Exit, Voice and Loyalty: Parent–Child Relations in the Proto-Industrial Household Economy', *History of the Family*, 9:4 (2004), pp. 401–23.

Piette, V., *Domestiques et servantes: des vies sous condition* (Bruxelles: Académie Royale de la Belgique, 2000).

Poitrineau, A., 'Aspects de l'émigration temporaire et saisonnière en Auvergne à la fin du XVIIe et au début du XIXe siècle', *Revue d'Histoire Moderne et Contemporaine*, 9 (1962), pp. 5–50.

—, *Remues d'hommes: Essai sur les migrations montagnardes en France aux XVIIe et XVIIIe siècles* (Paris: Aubier Montaigne, 1983).

Pollard, S., 'Labour in Great Britain', in P. Mathias and M. M. Postan (eds), *The Cambridge Economic History of Europe, Vol. VII, Part 1* (Cambridge: Cambridge University Press, 1978), pp. 97–179.

Pooley, C. G., 'Reflections on Migration and Mobility', *Annales de Démographie Historique*, 2 (2002), pp. 125–7.

Pooley, C. G., and J. Turnbull, *Migration and Mobility in Britain since the Eighteenth Century* (London: UCL Press, 1998).

—, 'Migration and Urbanization in North-West England: A Reassesment of the Roles of Towns in the Migration Process', in D. Siddle (ed.), *Migration, Mobility and Modernization* (Liverpool: Liverpool University Press, 2000), pp. 186–214.

Post, J. D., 'Famine, Mortality, and Epidemic Disease in the Process of Modernization', *Economic History Review*, 29:1 (1976), pp. 14–37.

Poulain, M., 'Du registre de population aux statistiques de migration interne en Belgique: Critique des sources et correction des données', *Population et Famille*, 45:3 (1978), pp. 1–45.

Poulain, M., M. Foulon, A. Degioanni and P. Darlu, 'Flemish Immigration in Wallonia and in France: Patronyms as Data', *History of the Family*, 5:2 (2000), pp. 227–41.

Poussou, J.-P., *Bordeaux et le Sud-Ouest au XVIIIe siècle: croissance économique et attraction urbaine* (Paris: Touzot, 1983).

—, 'Mobilité et migrations', in J. Dupâquier (ed.), *Histoire de la population française, Vol. 2: De la Rénaissance à 1789* (Paris: Presses Universitaires de France, 1988), pp. 99–143.

Prak, M. (ed.), *Early Modern Capitalism: Economic and Social Change in Europe, 1400–1800* (London: Routledge, 2001).

Preston, S. H., and E. van de Walle, 'Urban French Mortality in the Nineteenth Century', *Population Studies*, 32:2 (1978), pp. 275–97.

Prims, F., *Antwerpen in 1830* (Antwerpen: Voor God en 't Volk, n.d.).

—, *Geschiedenis van het Antwerpsche turfdragersambacht* (Antwerpen: Veritas, 1923).

—, *Geschiedenis van Antwerpen, Volume IX: Met Oostenrijk en onder de Franschen (1715–1814). Boek 2: De economische orde* (Antwerpen: Standaard, 1947).

—, *Geschiedenis van Antwerpen, Volume X: Nederlandsche en eerste Belgische periode (1814–1914). Boek 2: De economische orde* (Antwerpen: Standaard, 1949).

Radeff, A., 'Des migrations contraintes? Migrants et voyageurs alpins et appenins vers 1800', *Travaux et recherches de l'Université de Marne-la-Vallée*, 7 (2001), pp. 117–42.

Reinhard, M., 'Connaissance de la population de la France pendant la Révolution', in M. Reinhard (ed.), *Contributions à l'histoire démographique de la révolution française, 2me série* (Paris: Commission d'histoire économique et sociale de la Révolution Française, 1965), pp. 7–18.

Roche, D., *Humeurs vagabondes: De la circulation des hommes et de l'utilité des voyages* (Paris: Fayard, 2003).

Rommes, R., *Oost, west, Utrecht best? Driehonderd jaar migratie en migranten in de stad Utrecht (begin 16de–begin 19de eeuw)* (Amsterdam: Stichting Amsterdamse Historische Reeks, 1998).

Ronin, V., *Antwerpen en zijn "Russen". Onderdanen van de tsaar, 1814–1914* (Gent: Stichting Mens & Cultuur, 1993).

Rosental, P.-A., *Les sentiers invisibles: Espace, familles et migrations dans la France du 19e siècle* (Paris: Ecole des Hautes Etudes en Sciences Sociales, 1999).

Saerens, L., *Vreemdelingen in een wereldstad: Een geschiedenis van Antwerpen en zijn Joodse bevolking (1880–1944)* (Tielt: Lannoo, 2000).

Sartorius, F., 'De Fransen in België in de 19de eeuw', in A. Morelli (ed.), *Geschiedenis van het eigen volk. De vreemdeling in België van de prehistorie tot nu* (Leuven: Kritak, 1993), pp. 147–64.

Sassen, S., 'Immigration and Local Labor Markets', in A. Portes (ed.), *The Economic Sociology of Immigration: Essays on Networks, Ethnicity and Entrepreneurship* (New York: Sage, 1995), pp. 87–127.

—, *Guests and Aliens* (New York: The New Press, 1999).

Schepens, L., *Van vlaskutser tot franschman: Bijdrage tot de geschiedenis van de Westvlaamse plattelandsbevolking in de negentiende eeuw* (Brugge, 1973).

—, 'Émigration saisonnière et émigration définitive en Flandre Occidentale au 19e siècle', *Revue du Nord*, 56 (1974), pp. 427–31.

Schlumbohm, J., 'Labour in Proto-Industrialization: Big Questions and Micro-Answers', in Prak (ed.), *Early Modern Capitalism*, pp. 125–34.

Schofield, R., 'Age-Specific Mobility in an Eighteenth-Century Rural English Parish', in Clark and Souden (eds), *Migration and Society*, pp. 253–66.

Schofield, R., D. Reher and A. Bideau (eds), *The Decline of Mortality in Europe* (Oxford: Oxford University Press, 1991).

Scholliers, E., 'Prijzen en lonen te Antwerpen en in het Antwerpse (16e–19e eeuw)', in C. Verlinden (ed.), *Dokumenten voor de geschiedenis van prijzen en lonen in Vlaanderen en Brabant, Deel II* (Brugge: De Tempel, 1965), pp. 641–1056.

Scholliers, P., *Arm en rijk aan tafel: Tweehonderd jaar eetcultuur in België* (Antwerpen: EPO, 1993).

—, *Wages, Manufacturers and Workers in the Nineteenth-Century Factory: The Voortman Cotton Mill in Ghent* (Oxford: Berg, 1996).

Schrover, M., 'The Demographic Consequences of Changing Employment Opportunities: Women in the Dutch Meierij in the Nineteenth Century', *History of the Family*, 2:4 (1997), pp. 451–79.

—, 'Potverkopers, vijlenkappers, winkeliers en stukadoors: Nichevorming onder Duitse migranten in de negentiende-eeuwse stad Utrecht', *Tijdschrift voor Sociale Geschiedenis*, 26:4 (2000), pp. 281–305.

—, *Een kolonie van Duitsers: Groepsvorming onder Duitse immigranten in Utrecht in de negentiende eeuw* (Amsterdam: Aksant, 2002).

Sewell, W. H., *Structure and Mobility: The Men and Women of Marseille, 1820–1870* (Cambridge: Cambridge University Press, 1985).

Sharlin, A., 'Natural Decrease in Early Modern Cities: A Reconsideration', *Past and Present*, 79 (1978), pp. 126–38.

Skeldon, R., *Population Mobility in Developing Countries: A Reinterpretation* (London and New York: Belhaven Press, 1990).

—, *Migration and Development: A Global Perspective* (Harlow: Longman, 1997).

Smekens, F., 'Ambachtswezen en "nieuwe nijverheid"', in *Antwerpen in de achttiende eeuw*, pp. 64–94.

Smits, A., 'Demografische toestanden van de stad Antwerpen in de jaren 1810–1820' (Licentiaat dissertation, Katholieke Universiteit Leuven, 1962).

Snell, K. D. M., *Annals of the Labouring Poor: Social Change and Agrarian England, 1660–1900* (Cambridge: Cambridge University Press, 1985).

Sogner, S., 'Young in Europe around 1700: Norwegian Sailors and Servant-Girls Seeking Employment in Amsterdam', in J.-P. Bardet, F. Lebrun and R. Le Mée (eds), *Mesurer et comprendre: Mélanges offerts à Jacques Dupaquier* (Paris: PUF, 1994), pp. 515–622.

Soly, H., 'Social Aspects of Structural Changes in the Urban Industries of Eighteenth-Century Brabant and Flanders', in Van der Wee (ed.), *The Rise and Decline*, pp. 241–60.

Soly, H., and A. K. L. Thijs (eds), *Minderheden in Westeuropese steden (16de–20ste eeuw)* (Brussel: Belgisch Historisch Instituut te Rome, 1995).

Souden, D., 'Migrants and the Population Structure of Later Seventeenth-Century Provincial Cities and Market Towns', in P. Clark (ed.), *The Transformation of English Provincial Towns, 1600–1800* (London: Hutchinson, 1985), pp. 133–68.

Southall, H. R., 'The Tramping Artisan Revisits: Labour Mobility and Economic Distress in Early Victorian England', *Economic History Review*, 44:2 (1991), pp. 272–96.

Spelkens, E., 'Antwerp as a Port of Emigration, 1843–1913', in *Two Studies on Emigration through Antwerp to the New World* (Brussel, 1976), pp. 51–139.

Spufford, P., 'Population Movement in Seventeenth-Century England', *Local Population Studies*, 4 (1970), pp. 41–50.

Steegen, E., *Kleinhandel en stedelijke ontwikkeling: Het kramersambacht te Maastricht in de vroegmoderne tijd* (Maastricht, 2006).

Steidl, A., *Auf nach Wien! Die Mobilität des mitteleuropäischen Handwerks im 18. und 19. Jahrhundert am Beispiel der Haupt- und Residenzstadt* (Wien: Oldenbourg Wissenschaftsverlag, 2003).

Stengers, J., *Emigration et immigration en Belgique au 19e et 20e siècles* (Bruxelles: Académie royale des sciences d'outre-mer, 1978).

—, 'Les mouvements migratoires en Belgique aux 19e et 20e siècles', in *Les migrations internationales de la fin du 18e siècle à nos jours* (Paris: CNRS, 1980), pp. 284–317.

Suykens, F. (ed.), *Antwerp: A Port for All Seasons* (Deurne: MIM, 1986).

Termote, M. G., 'Statistiques migratoires directes: Le registre de population', in *Migrations intérieures: Méthodes d'observation et d'analyse* (Paris: Centre National de la Recherche Scientifique, 1975), pp. 157–64.

Thijs, A. K. L., *De zijdenijverheid te Antwerpen in de zeventiende eeuw* (Luik: Pro Civitate, 1969).

—, 'De geschiedenis van de suikernijverheid te Antwerpen (16de–19de eeuw): Een terreinverkenning', *Bijdragen tot de Geschiedenis*, 62 (1979), pp. 23–50.

—, 'The River Scheldt Closed for Two Centuries, 1585–1790', in Suykens (ed.), *Antwerp*, pp. 169–278.

—, *Van 'werkwinkel' tot 'fabriek': De textielnijverheid te Antwerpen (einde 15de–begin 19de eeuw)* (Brussel: Gemeentekrediet, 1987).

Tilly, C., 'Migration in Modern European History', in W. H. McNeill and R. S. Adams (eds), *Human Migration. Patterns and Policies* (Bloomington, IN, and London: Indiana University Press, 1978), pp. 48–74.

—, 'Demographic Origins of the European Proletariat', in Levine (ed.), *Proletarianization and Family History*, pp. 1–85.

—, 'Transplanted Networks', in V. Yans-McLaughlin (ed.), *Immigration Reconsidered: History, Sociology and Politics* (London: Oxford University Press, 1990), pp. 79–95.

Van Bavel, J., 'Family Control, Bridal Pregnancy, and Illegitimacy: An Event History Analysis in Louvain, Belgium, 1846–1856', *Social Science History*, 25:3 (2001), pp. 449–79.

Van Damme, D., 'Onderstandswoonst, sedentarisering en stad-platteland-tegenstellingen: Evolutie en betekenis van de wetgeving op de onderstandwoonst in Belgie (einde achttiende tot einde negentiende eeuw)', *Belgisch Tijdschrift voor Nieuwste geschiedenis*, 21:3–4 (1990), pp. 483–534.

van Damme, I., 'Zotte verwaandheid: Over Franse verleiding en Zuid-Nederlands onbehagen, 1650–1750', in R. de Bont and T. Verschaffel (eds), *Het verderf van Parijs* (Leuven: Universitaire Pers Leuven, 2004), pp. 187–204.

Van de Putte, B., 'Homogamy by Geographical Origin: Segregation in Nineteenth-Century Flemish Cities (Gent, Leuven, and Aalst)', *Journal of Family History*, 28:3 (2003), pp. 364–90.

Van de Putte, B., M. Oris, M. Neven and K. Matthijs, 'Migration', in M. van Leeuwen and I. Maas (eds), *Endogamy and Social Class in History* (Amsterdam: Cambridge University Press, 2005), pp. 179–218.

Van den Eeckhout, P., 'Determinanten van het 19de-eeuwse sociaal-economische leven te Brussel: Hun betekenis voor de laagste bevolkingsklassen' (PhD dissertation, Vrije Universiteit Brussel, 1980).

—, 'De rekrutering van de Brusselse armenbevolking in relatie met de afstotingsmechanismen in het gebied van herkomst', *Taal en Sociale Integratie*, 4 (1981), pp. 219–46.

Van den Eeckhout, P., and J. Hannes, 'Sociale verhoudingen en structuren in de Zuidelijke Nederlanden, 1770–1840', in Blok (ed.), *Algemene geschiedenis*, pp. 435–75.

van den Eerenbeemt, H. F. J. M. (ed.), *Geschiedenis van Noord-Brabant, Deel 1: Traditie en modernisering, 1796–1890* (Amsterdam: Boom, 1996).

van der Heijden, M., 'Contradictory Interests: Work, Parents, and Offspring in Early Modern Holland', *History of the Family*, 9:4 (2004), pp. 355–70.

Van der Herten, B., 'La révolution industrielle stimulée par une révolution des communications', in Van der Herten et al. (eds), *La Belgique industrielle*, pp. 41–8.

Van der Herten, B., M. Oris and J. Roegiers (eds), *La Belgique industrielle en 1850: Deux cents images d'un monde nouveau* (Deurne: Crédit Communal, 1995).

Van der Wee, H. (ed.), *The Rise and Decline of Urban Industries in Italy and in the Low Countries (Late Middle Ages–Early Modern Times)* (Leuven: Leuven University Press, 1988).

—, 'Industrial Dynamics and the Process of Urbanization and De-Urbanization in the Low Countries from the Late Middle Ages to the Eighteenth Century. A Synthesis', in Van der Wee (ed.), *The Rise and Decline*, pp. 307–82.

—, 'La "révolution industrielle" en Belgique, 1800–1850: Un survol', in Van der Herten et al. (eds), *La Belgique industrielle*, pp. 29–32.

Van der Wee, H., and K. Veraghtert, 'De economie van 1814 tot 1944', in *Twintig eeuwen Vlaanderen* (Hasselt: Heideland-Orbis, 1978), pp. 130–211.

van der Woude, A., 'Population Developments in the Northern Netherlands (1500–1800) and the Validity of the "Urban Graveyard" Effect', *Annales de Démographie Historique* (1982), pp. 55–75.

van der Woude, A., A. Hayami and J. de Vries, (eds), *Urbanization in History: A Process of Dynamic Interactions* (Oxford: Clarendon Press, 1990).

—, 'Introduction: The Hierarchies, Provisioning, and Demographic Patterns of Cities', in van der Woude et al. (eds), *Urbanization in History*, pp. 3–19.

Van Dijck, M., and W. Peeters, 'Algemene karakterschets van Vlaams-Brabant: Eenheid en verscheidenheid', in J. De Maeyer and P. Heyrman (eds), *Geuren en kleuren: Een sociale en economische geschiedenis van Vlaams-Brabant, 19de en 20ste eeuw* (Leuven: Peeters, 2001), pp. 21–39.

Van Dijk, H., *Rotterdam 1810–1880: Aspecten van een stedelijke samenleving* (Schiedam: Interbook International, 1976).

van Dun, P., '"De Brouwerijen hebben hier van oudts (...) altijdts goede neeringhen gehadt"', in J.-M. Goris (ed.), *Bier, wijn en jenever in de Kempen* (Herentals-Roosendaal: Centrum voor de studie van land en volk van de Kempen, 2002), pp. 69–90.

Van Hout, J., 'De Antwerpse herbergen, 1750–1850' (Licentiaat dissertation, Katholieke Universiteit Leuven, 1981).

Van Houtven, S., 'Een studie naar de buurt en haar conflictregulerende werking: De Antwerpse Seefhoek anno 1879' (Licentiaat dissertation, Vrije Universiteit Brussel, 2005).

Van Isacker, K., *De Antwerpse dokwerker, 1830–1940* (Antwerpen: Nederlandse Boekhandel, 1966).

van Leeuwen, M. H. D., and I. Maas, 'Endogamy and Social Class: An Overview', in M. H. D. van Leeuwen, I. Maas and A. Miles (eds), *Marriage Choices and Class Boundaries: Social Endogamy in History* (Cambridge: Cambridge University Press, 2005), pp. 1–25.

Van Looveren, E., 'De privatisering van de gemene gronden in de provincie Antwerpen: vier case-studies', *Bijdragen tot de Geschiedenis*, 66 (1983), pp. 189–216.

Van Overmeire, D., 'Bevolking, arbeid en strukturele mutaties in het Land van Waas in de 19de eeuw', *Annalen van de Koninklijke Oudheidkundige Kring van het Land van Waas*, 92 (1989), pp. 177–212.

van Poppel, F., and M. Oris, 'Continuities and Disparities in the Pattern of Leaving Home', in F. van Poppel, M. Oris and J. Lee (eds), *The Road to Independence: Leaving Home in Western and Eastern Societies, 16th–20th Centuries* (Bern: Lang, 2004), pp. 1–29.

Van Uytven, R., 'Peiling naar de beroepsstructuur op het Brabantse platteland omstreeks 1755', *Bijdragen tot de Geschiedenis*, 55 (1972), pp. 172–203.

—, 'Brabantse en Antwerpse centrale plaatsen (14de–19de eeuw)', in *Het stedelijk netwerk in België in historisch perspectief (1350–1850): Een statistische en dynamische benadering* (Brussel: Gemeentekrediet, 1992), pp. 29–79.

—, (ed.), *De geschiedenis van Brabant van het hertogdom tot heden* (Zwolle: Waanders, 2004).

van Zanden, J. L., *De industrialisatie van Amsterdam, 1825–1984* (Bergen: Octavo, 1987).

—, *The Rise and Decline of Holland's Economy: Merchant Capitalism and the Labour Market* (Manchester: Manchester University Press, 1993).

—, 'Do we Need a Theory of Merchant Capitalism?', *Review*, 20:2 (1997), pp. 255–67.

Vandenbroeke, C., *Sociale geschiedenis van het Vlaamse volk* (Leuven: Kritak, 1984).

—, 'Migraties tussen Vlaanderen en Noord-Frankrijk in de 19de en 20ste eeuw', *Frans-Nederlands Jaarboek* (1993), pp. 157–68.

Vandenbroeke, C., and W. Vanderpijpen, 'Landbouw en platteland in de Zuidelijke Nederlanden, 1770–1844', in Blok (ed.), *Algemene geschiedenis*, pp. 183–209.

Vanhaute, E., *Heiboeren: Bevolking, arbeid en inkomen in de 19de-eeuwse Kempen* (Brussel: VUBPress, 1992).

—, 'Eigendomsverhoudingen in de Belgische en Vlaamse landbouw tijdens de 18de en de 19de eeuw', *Belgisch Tijdschrift voor Nieuwste geschiedenis*, 24:1–2 (1993), pp. 185–226.

—, 'Processes of Peripheralization in a Core Region: The Campine Area of Antwerp in the "Long Nineteenth Century"', *Review*, 16:1 (1993), pp. 57–81.

—, '"De meest moordende van alle industrieën": De huisnijverheid in België omstreeks 1900', *Tijdschrift voor Sociale Geschiedenis*, 20:4 (1994), pp. 461–83.

Veen, J. H. S. M., 'Spoorwegontwikkeling in het gebied van het voormalige hertogdom Brabant, 1835–1870', *Bijdragen tot de Geschiedenis*, 78:1–4 (1995), pp. 53–66.

Veraghtert, K., 'De havenbeweging te Antwerpen tijdens de negentiende eeuw: Een kwantitatieve benadering', 4 vols (PhD dissertation, KUL, 1977).

—, 'De economie in de Zuidelijke Nederlanden 1790–1970', in Blok (ed.), *Algemene geschiedenis*, pp. 127–39.

—, 'The Antwerp Port, 1790–1814', in J. M. van Winter (ed.), *The Interactions of Amsterdam and Antwerp with the Baltic Region, 1400–1800* (Leiden: Nijhoff, 1983), pp. 193–9.

—, 'From Inland Port to International Port, 1790–1914', in Suykens (ed.), *Antwerp*, pp. 279–422.

—, 'Van ambachtelijke nijverheid naar industriële produktie', in van den Eerenbeemt (ed.), *Geschiedenis van Noord-Brabant*, pp. 223–40.

Verbeemen, J., 'Emigratie uit de Antwerpse Kempen', *Oudheid en Kunst*, 36 (1953), pp. 3–68.

—, 'Mechelen in 1796: Demografische en sociaal-economische studie', *Handelingen van de Koninklijke Kring voor Oudheidkunde, Letteren en Kunst van Mechelen* (1954), pp. 135–79.

—, 'De werking van economische factoren op de stedelijke demografie der XVIIe en der XVIIIe eeuw in de Zuidelijke Nederlanden', *Belgisch Tijdschrift voor Filologie en Geschiedenis*, 34 (1956), pp. 680–700.

—, 'Immigratie te Antwerpen', *Mededelingen van de Geschied- en Oudheidkundige Kring voor Leuven en omgeving Lustrumuitgave: De Brabantse stad* (1959), pp. 81–100.

Verberne, L. G. J., *Noord-Brabant in de negentiende eeuw tot omstreeks 1870: De sociaal-economische structuur* (Nijmegen: De Koepel, 1947).

Vermeiren, L., 'Van gasthuis tot ziekenhuis: De negentiende eeuw (tot 1925)', in *750 jaar St.-Elisabethgasthuis te Antwerpen, 1238–1988* (Brussel: Gemeentekrediet, 1988), pp. 145–226.

Versteegh, P., 'The Ties that Bind: The Role of Family and Ethnic Networks in the Settlements of Polish Migrants in Pennsylvania, 1890–1940', *History of the Family*, 5 (2000), pp. 111–49.

Vervaeck, S., *Gids voor sociale geschiedenis: Bronnen voor de studie van immigratie en emigratie. Hedendaagse tijden, deel 1: Archiefbronnen bewaard in het Algemeen Rijksarchief* (Brussel: ARA, 1996).

Villiers, P., and P. Culerrier, 'Du système des classes à l'inscription maritime: Le recrutement des marins français de Louis XIV à 1952', *Revue Historique des Armées*, 2 (1982), pp. 44–53.

Vliebergh, E., and R. Ulens, *Het Hageland: Zijne plattelandsche bevolking in de 19de eeuw: Bijdrage tot de studie der economische en sociale geschiedenis* (Brussel, 1919).

Vollans, E. C., 'Urban Development in Belgium since 1830', in R. P. Beckinsale and J. M. Houston (eds), *Urbanization and its Problems: Essays in Honour of E. W. Gilbert* (Oxford: Blackwell, 1968), pp. 171–93.

Vrielinck, S., *De territoriale indeling van België (1795–1963): Bestuursgeografisch en statistisch repertorium van de gemeenten en de supracommunale eenheden (administratief en gerechtelijk): Met de officiële uitslagen van de volkstellingen* (Leuven: Universitaire Pers, 2000).

Wegge, S. A., 'Chain Migration and Information Networks: Evidence from Nineteenth-Century Hesse-Cassel', *Journal of Economic History*, 58:4 (1998), pp. 957–87.

White, P. E., 'Internal Migration in the Nineteenth and Twentieth Centuries', in P. E. Ogden and P. E. White (eds), *Migrants in Modern France: Population Mobility in the Later Nineteenth and Twentieth Centuries* (London: Unwyn Hyman, 1989), pp. 13–33.

Whyte, I. D., *Migration and Society in Britain, 1550–1830* (Basingstoke: Macmillan, 2000).

Willekens, E., *Hij leerde zijn volk lezen: Profiel van Hendrik Conscience 1812–1883* (Antwerpen: Stichting Hendrik Conscience, 1982).

Willems, B., 'Krediet, vertrouwen en sociale relaties: Kleine producenten en winkeliers te Antwerpen in de 18de eeuw' (PhD dissertation, Vrije Universiteit Brussel, 2006).

Williamson, J. G., *Coping with City Growth during the British Industrial Revolution* (Cambridge: Cambridge University Press, 1990).

—, 'Coping with City Growth', in R. Floud and D. N. McCloskey (eds), *The Economic History of Britain since 1700, vol. I: 1700–1860*, 2nd edn (Cambridge: Cambridge University Press, 1994), pp. 332–56.

Wilssens, M.-A., *Bevolkingsdruk en boerenverstand: Evolutie van de levensstandaard in het Waasland in de 18de eeuw* (Brussel: Gemeentekrediet, 1992).

Winter, A., 'Vagrancy as an Adaptive Strategy: The Duchy of Brabant, 1767–1776', *International Review of Social History*, 49:2 (2004), pp. 249–78.

—, *Divided Interests, Divided Migrants: The Rationales of Policies Regarding Labour Mobility in Western Europe, c. 1550–1914*, Working Paper 15 (London: Global Economic History Network – London School of Economics, 2005).

—, 'De microcontext van stedelijke groei: Posities en trajecten van immigranten op de Antwerpse arbeidsmarkt in de tweede helft van de achttiende eeuw', *Stadsgeschiedenis*, 1:2 (2006), pp. 122–47.

—, 'Patterns of Migration and Adaptation in the Urban Transition: Newcomers to Antwerp, c. 1760–1860' (PhD dissertation, Vrije Universiteit Brussel, 2007).

—, 'Caught between Law and Practice: Migrants and Settlement Legislation in the Southern Low Countries in a Comparative Perspective, c. 1700–1900', *Rural History*, 19:2 (2008), pp. 137–62.

Wrigley, E. A., 'Brake or Accelerator? Urban Growth and Population Growth before the Industrial Revolution', in van der Woude et al. (eds), *Urbanization in History*, pp. 101–12.

INDEX

Note: Migrants' places of origin or destination are not listed separately, but are grouped together at the level of present-day provinces, regions, countries, continental regions or continents respectively. Place names are listed separately only where they refer to mentions other than migrants' places of origin or destination.

Academy of Fine Arts, 158, 170–1, 265n90, 274n59

Africa, migration to and from, 116, 171

aliens' records *see* migration registration

Americas, migration to and from, 19, 25–8, 55, 106, 116, 134, 164–5, 167, 171, 181

Amsterdam, 12, 23–5, 31, 38, 43, 46, 104–5
see also Netherlands

Antwerp Province, 70, 74, 76, 78
migration to and from, 71–4, 76, 85, 117–18, 131–2, 136, 138, 150, 152–60, 182, 187

Asia, migration to and from, 116, 168

Auvergne, 12, 25, 27
see also France

bakers *see* food industries

bassin démographique see demographic basin

Bauwens, Lieven, 53

beer, production of *see* food industries

Beier, A., 10–11

Belgian Revolution, 58, 61, 105, 116, 129–31, 133–4, 168, 276n84

Boeksteeg, 93, 267n110

Bordeaux, 16, 75
see also France

Brabant Province, 78

migration to and from, 71, 74, 117–18, 132, 136, 138, 142–3, 157–9, 164, 173–6, 183–5

Bras, Hilde, 19, 176

British Isles, 43–5
migration to and from, 38, 49, 113, 116, 135, 165, 169–70

Brussels, 53, 56, 72, 75, 127, 135–6
see also Brabant Province

building industry, 57, 81, 87, 92–3, 102–3, 105, 110–13, 122–8, 130, 134, 137, 144–5, 158, 161–4, 166–7, 171, 174, 176–9, 181, 186, 194, 196, 214, 252n70

burgher books *see* citizenship

butchers *see* food industries

Caen, 48
see also France

Campine region *see* Antwerp Province;
North Brabant Province

capitalism
early modern, 39–41
global, 196
industrial, 48–9

carpenters *see* woodworking

casual labour, 57, 80, 110–13, 122–8, 130–2, 135, 143, 163–4, 169, 171, 176–7, 181, 214

catering, 78, 82–3, 85–6, 90, 93, 96, 124, 134–5, 140, 150–1, 162–3, 170, 173
  see also lodging arrangements
chain migration, 13–15, 23–5, 78, 82, 85, 150–2, 166–7, 172, 178–9, 182–3, 186
Charity Bureau, 134, 143, 156
Charleroi, 53
  see also Walloon regions
children
  abandonment of, 132
  child labour, 57, 69, 79, 81, 96, 106, 111, 168
  migration of, 17, 21, 88, 250n51, 275n72
  registration of, 58, 65, 199, 283n28
citizenship, urban, 7, 11, 70–1, 75, 83–4, 86, 93, 240n116, 246n7, 247n15, 251n57, 252n66, 253nn73–4, 261n38
Clark, Peter, 10–1
clergy, 32, 83, 113
clerks *see* white-collar workers
clothing industry, 23–5, 78, 81, 83, 86, 93, 97, 112, 124–5, 158, 161–2, 165–7, 170, 177–9, 186, 214, 250n51, 252n70, 274n67
Cockerill, William, 53
Cockerill shipyards, 106, 164
Cologne, 105
  see also Germany
Conscience, Pierre, 162–3
construction work *see* building industry
consumer revolution, 82, 251n59
continental blockade, 103
crises, agrarian or industrial, 17, 29–30, 40, 45, 54–5, 59, 62, 67, 104, 129, 133–4, 143–5, 180–2, 186, 193

d'Herbouville, Charles, 102
De Belder, Jos, 66, 86–7, 200, 214
De Schaepdrijver, 135–6
de Vries, Jan, 38–9, 42, 52, 56
demographic basin, 37, 71–2, 118, 136, 152–6, 174, 184, 192
demographic evolution of Antwerp, 58–62, 69–70, 94–6, 197–99
demographic impact of migrants, 36, 42–3, 94–5, 131–3, 139–40, 194
diamond processing *see* luxury trades
dock workers *see* transport, workers

domestic service, 19, 27, 36–7, 57, 75, 81, 83, 85–8, 90–2, 94, 96–8, 113, 122–6, 130–2, 135, 139, 142–3, 152–3, 155, 158, 165, 167–8, 170, 173–4, 176, 179, 187, 264n76
  registration of, 65
Duisburg, 43–4, 48, 141
  see also Germany

Eastern Europe, migration to and from, 27–8, 113, 116
embeddedness of migration patterns, 3, 25, 27, 29–30, 32, 35, 37–40, 47, 86, 127, 153–6, 172, 159, 174–6, 183–7, 191–2
  see also migration, channels
embroidery, 57, 105
employment, irregularity of, 58, 106, 122, 127, 133–5, 137–8, 142, 145–6, 156, 182, 194
  see also labour market, transformation
entertainment sector, 162–3, 168, 170
epidemics, 59, 132

family migration, 17–18, 21, 88–9, 129, 137, 168, 180, 263n18, 266nn100–1, 283n28
  see also life cycle
family strategy, 229n59
famine *see* crises
fertility, 2, 36, 43, 56, 58–60, 98, 128, 131–2, 198–9
fishmongers *see* retail
Flanders, Country of / Provinces of East and West, 54–5, 76, 85, 133
  migration to and from, 55, 71–2, 74–6, 85, 107, 110–11, 117–18, 136–8, 142–3, 157–9, 162, 173, 179–83, 186
food industries, 24, 46, 78, 81, 83–7, 91–3, 96, 122–6, 130, 158, 165, 170–1, 174, 181, 214, 251n58, 253n71, 276n83
France, migration to and from, 25–6, 37, 107, 110–13, 116, 119, 135, 138, 160–3, 165, 181
Fuchs, Jacob, 113

garment trade *see* clothing industry
gender differences
in employment, 11, 18, 27–8, 31–2, 44,
79–83, 88–93, 122–6, 137
see also labour market, segmentation
in migration patterns, 19, 75, 88–91,
110, 112–13, 130, 138–9, 148, 151,
153
see also migration, circuits
in registration practices, 65, 107,
244n139
Germany, migration to and from, 12–14, 25,
44, 107, 110, 112–13, 116, 119, 135,
160–1, 163–7, 169, 173
Ghent, 53, 102, 104, 127
see also Flanders
Gordon, Wendy, 19
Green, Nancy, 25–6
Groenplaats, 163, 165
guilds, 77, 83–4

Hageland *see* Brabant Province
Hannes, Juul, 66, 131, 200–1, 214
hat makers *see* clothing industry
hinterland *see* demographic basin; migration
field; transport, routes
Hochstadt, Steve, 44
hospitals *see* St Elisabeth hospital
household characteristics, influence on
migration, 17–21
housing conditions, 140

illegitimacy, 20, 132
import-processing industries, 69, 105–6, 134
Industrial Revolution, 41
in Belgium, 53–5
industry, abandonment of *see* labour market,
transformation
innkeepers *see* catering
inscription maritime, 111–12, 159, 161,
163–4, 171, 180, 259n25
integration, 66, 99, 185–6, 192
Iron Rhine *see* railways
Italy, migration to and from, 113, 170

Jackson, James Jr, 43–4, 141
Jews, migration of, 27–8, 168, 173

kin, 14, 19, 92–4, 98, 141, 153, 155–6, 159
see also chain migration; migration,
channels
Kloosterstraat, 167
Knotter, Ad, 12, 23–5
Kuijpers, Erika, 23–4

labour market
segmentation, 12, 27, 31, 38, 71, 77–86,
90, 98, 111, 122–8, 144–5, 155, 158,
190–1, 194
transformation, 5, 46–7, 56–8, 101–6,
111, 122–33, 147, 195
lace industry, 52, 57, 69, 79–80, 83, 102,
122–6
leather industry, 23, 78, 81, 83, 123–4, 158,
181
length of stay, 61–2, 65, 87–97, 87–96,
112–13, 128–33, 138, 140–4, 153,
155–60, 164, 167–8, 170, 175–9, 184,
190
Lesger, Clé, 14–15, 24, 32
Leuven, 75
see also Brabant Province
Liège, 53, 104
see also Walloon regions
life cycle, 20, 25, 28, 30, 33, 36, 39, 46–7,
88–97, 101, 129–33, 136–8, 140–5,
148, 153, 157–8, 160, 164–5, 168–70,
193
Limburg Provinces, migration to and from,
71, 74–5, 158, 173, 176–7
linen industry *see* textile industries
Lis, Catharina, 11, 57, 66, 106, 166–7, 214
local opportunity structure *see* labour
market, transformation; migration,
selectivity
local services, 82, 90–3, 122–6, 214
lodging arrangements, 14, 134, 140, 150–2,
159, 161, 164–8, 170, 174, 178
see also catering
Lucassen, Jan, 12–13, 28
luxury trades, 80, 84, 97, 123–4, 158, 165,
168

manoeuvrability, concept of, 7, 22, 26, 28–9, 32–3, 86, 106, 142–3, 145, 147, 156, 183–5, 187, 191, 196, 213

marriage patterns, 20–1, 36, 63, 88, 94–6, 98–9, 131–2, 140, 142, 153, 160–1, 163, 168, 174, 185

Marseille, 44
  see also France

medical school, 158

Meir, 163

merchants *see* trade

metalworking, 81, 110–12, 122–6, 158, 163–4

migration
  channels, 14–16, 23–6, 85–6, 111–13, 127, 149–56, 159, 160–1, 164–7, 169, 171–3, 175–9, 181, 183–5, 191
  circuits, 31–2, 38, 47, 75, 84–6, 89–90, 93–4, 110–13, 125–8, 135–6, 147–88
  explanatory frameworks on, 9–34
  field, 70–6, 106–19, 135–6, 157, 160–82
  information, 6, 9, 15–17, 19, 21–4, 29–33, 37–8, 67, 74, 112, 145, 152–6, 165, 172, 183–4, 187, 190–2
  intensity, 14, 16, 21–2, 72–3, 76, 118, 136–7, 142, 154–6, 174–7, 179–80, 184, 203–5, 208–9
  patterns
    adaptability of, 31–2, 47–50, 147–88, 191–3, *passim*
    as social systems, 3, 29–30, 147–88
    heterogeneity of *see* migration, circuits
    resilience of, 2, 29–33, 36–8, 40, 44, 47, 49–50, 67, 149, 156, 172, 175, 177, 184, 186–8, 190–3
    rates, 60–2, 76, 89, 107–19, 136, 138, 154
  registration, 63–5, 107–19, 150–2, 198–206, 244n140, 259n25
  selectivity, 26–9, 31–3, 40, 44, 98, 129, 133, 181, 186, 193–5
  trajectories, 112–13, 132, 135, 137–44, 149–50, 153, 156, 159–60, 164–5, 168, 170, 180–1, 186, 191–5

military service, 58–9, 61, 65, 107, 112, 159, 161, 164, 168–72, 177, 243n135, 244n140, 259n25

Moch, Leslie, 15

Morawska, Ewa, 27–8

Morsa, Denis, 52

mortality, 2, 36, 39, 42–3, 54, 58–60, 89, 94, 98, 128, 131–2, 198–9, 239n106

Museum of Fine Arts, 158, 170

musicians *see* entertainment sector

Napoleon Bonaparte, 57, 102–3, 171

naties (dock companies), 82, 84–5, 91, 124–8, 155
  see also transport, workers

naval base, Antwerp as, 5, 63, 102–3, 110–13, 112, 128, 171

naval workers, 110–13, 119, 159, 161–4, 167, 244n140, 259n25

Netherlands, migration to and from, 12, 14, 17–18, 40, 72, 75, 77, 96, 110, 112, 116, 135, 138, 160–1, 166–9, 172

Neven, Muriel, 20

North Brabant Province, 73–4, 78
  migration to and from, 72–4, 116–18, 135, 157–8, 160, 173–6, 184–5

occupational profile of migrants, 79–83, 110–19, 122–8, 137
  see also labour market, segmentation; social mobility

office workers *see* white-collar workers

officials *see* white-collar workers

Perrot, Jean-Claude, 48

Pooley, Colin, 43–4

poor
  lists, 143, 259n24
  relief, 5, 18, 39, 62, 64–6, 96, 129, 132, 136, 156, 160, 168–9, 180, 182, 185, 194
  see also settlement examinations

poorterschap see citizenship

population
  growth *see* demographic evolution
  registration, 5, 62–5, 122, 197–8, 197–206
  see also migration, registration

ports
  infrastructure, 102–4, 110–11, 123, 134
  labour market *see* labour market, transformation

port cities, socio-economic and demographic characteristics of, 16, 59, 64, 127–8, 144–5

Poussou, Jean-Pierre, 37

prisoners, registration of, 65, 244n140, 259n25

professions *see* white-collar workers

proletarianization, 11, 35, 40, 46, 54, 58, 101, 128, 154, 175

prostitution, 67, 112, 125, 132, 140, 162, 167–8, 261n38

push and pull, 2, 10–13, 26, 28–9, 31–3, 35, 45, 47, 49, 56, 67, 76, 98, 106, 119, 128–30, 133, 136–7, 142–6, 159–60, 176, 180–2, 189–90, 192–3, 196

railways, 55, 105, 119, 134,155, 157, 167, 175, 181, 271n21

Red Star Line, 106

regime changes, 5, 57, 101, 104, 113, 119
see also Belgian Revolution

residence cards *see* migration, registration

residential clustering, 99, 149–52, 163, 166, 182, 195

retail, 57, 78, 81–7, 90–4, 96, 122–3, 125–6, 130, 132, 134–5, 144, 150, 152–3, 155, 163, 165, 167–8, 170, 173–4, 176, 190, 214

return migration *see* migration, trajectories

Rotterdam, 43, 104
see also Netherlands

rural livelihoods, pressure on, 4–5, 40, 44–6, 50, 54, 56, 58, 76, 101, 106, 128–30, 133–4, 137, 145, 147, 154–5, 175, 180–1, 190
see also crises; proletarianization

sailors, 15, 24–5, 58, 65, 81, 116, 124, 134, 140, 168–9, 171, 197
see also shipping

St Elisabeth hospital, patients of, 5, 59, 65–6, 116, 136, 153, 182, 203, 262nn48–9, 278n107

sawyers *see* woodworking

Scandinavia, migration to and from, 24–5, 113, 116, 171

Scheldt
closure of, 57, 69
freedom of navigation on, 102

seasonal migration *see* length of stay

settlement examinations, 5, 65–7, 136–7, 142–3, 150, 159, 168–9, 180–1, 195, 205–6, 262n48, 275n68, 278nn107, 111

sex ratios
of migrants, 94, 98, 130, 139, 148, 153, 157, 167, 170, 194
of urban population, 94, 98, 139, 194

shipbuilding, 104–6, 110–11, 122, 126, 134, 158–9, 162–3, 176, 179

shipping, 58, 81–2, 103–6, 113, 116, 124, 126, 128, 134, 149, 166, 214
see also sailors; trade; transport

shoemakers *see* leather industry

shopkeepers *see* retail

Sint-Andries, 182

skill, and migration, 18, 37–8, 77–9, 84–5, 96–7, 126–7, 135–6
see also migration, circuits

Snell, Keith, 45

social mobility, of migrants, 2, 44, 47, 86–94, 97, 130–3, 194–5, 213
see also life cycle

social networks *see* chain migration; migration, channels

soldiers, registration of, 65, 112
see also military service

Soly, Hugo, 11

source materials, selection and processing of, 66–7, 199–215

Spain, migration to and from, 27

stepwise migration, 16, 73, 78, 139, 159, 176, 180–3, 187, 193
see also migration, trajectories

stonecutters *see* building industry

structure and agency, 2–4, 21–2, 27, 29, 50, 68, 119, 143
see also manoeuvrability

sugar-refining *see* import-processing industries

Switzerland, migration to and from, 113, 116, 170–1

tailors *see* clothing industry
textile industries, 53–5, 57, 69–70, 74,
    79–81, 83, 85–7, 90–3, 96–8, 101–6,
    111, 122–7, 133–4, 144–5, 154,
    157–8, 175, 180–1, 202, 214
theatre *see* entertainment sector
Tilly, Charles, 46
tobacco processing *see* import-processing
    industries
trade
    development of international, 51, 57,
        103–5, 116, 122, 134, 144
    role of migrants in, 82–3, 86, 112–13,
        116, 123, 149–50, 158, 161–73, 214
trading companies, 104, 113, 134, 164–6,
    170
transport
    routes, 16, 47, 54, 70, 74–6, 82,105,
        116, 119, 134, 143, 160, 173–6, 183,
        187–8, 195
    see also railways
    workers, 57, 81–3, 85–6, 93, 96, 122–8,
        130–1, 134, 137, 144–5, 150, 158,
        174, 190, 194, 262n53
Turnbull, Jean, 43–4
turnover *see* length of stay

urban migration
    in early modern Europe, 36–41, 48
    in Europe's long nineteenth century,
        41–51

urbanization
    in Belgium, 51–6
    in Europe, 1, 35, 41–4

vagrancy, 10, 240n116
van Zanden, Jan Luiten, 23–5, 39–41, 48–9
Verbeemen, J., 71
Verviers, 53
Vienna, 77, 127

wages
    of agricultural workers, 129
    of urban workers, 69–70, 79, 86, 111,
        125–7, 194, 26–7, 158
Walloon regions, 53–4
    migration to and from, 20, 25, 55, 72,
        75, 110–11, 113, 157–8, 165, 173,
        177–9, 183, 186
wealth, distribution of, 69, 86–8, 91, 94
white-collar workers, 18, 37, 83, 91, 113–16,
    119, 122–6, 134, 149, 158, 161–2,
    164–6, 169–72
William I, King of the United Kingdom of
    the Netherlands, 104
Williamson, Jeffrey, 42, 44, 47
Wood, William, 113
woodworking, 78, 81, 83–4, 92, 96, 110,
    122–6, 158–60, 163–4, 167, 169,
    176–7, 181

Zeeland, migration to and from, 19, 176–7

For Product Safety Concerns and Information please contact our EU
representative GPSR@taylorandfrancis.com
Taylor & Francis Verlag GmbH, Kaufingerstraße 24, 80331 München, Germany

www.ingramcontent.com/pod-product-compliance
Ingram Content Group UK Ltd.
Pitfield, Milton Keynes, MK11 3LW, UK
UKHW021621240425
457818UK00018B/673